Montréal &
Québec City

"All you've got to do is decide to go
and the hardest part is over.

So go!"

TONY WHEELER, COFOUNDER – LONELY PLANET

THIS EDITIO

Gregor Clark

Contents

(left) **Québec City p167**
Stroll along historic Old Town streets.

(above) **Parc Jean-Drapeau, Montréal p66** Escape the city bustle at this leafy oasis.

(right) **Grey squirrel**
Often seen in eastern Canada.

Little Italy, Mile End & Outremont p116

Plateau Mont-Royal p101

Quartier Latin & the Village p89

Downtown p71

Old Montréal p46

Parc Jean-Drapeau p66

Welcome to Montréal & Québec City

A captivating blend of old and new, with stone-walled taverns, candlelit drinking dens, wild festivals and a cutting-edge arts scene.

Cuisine Capital

Blessed with one of the most exciting food scenes in North America, Montréal brims with temples dedicated to Kamouraska lamb, Arctic char and, of course, poutine (fries smothered in cheese curds and gravy). You'll find irresistible patisseries, English pubs, 87-year-old Jewish delis and magnificent food markets reminiscent of Paris. There are hipster bars with tiny bowling alleys and innumerable cafes in which to while away a lazy afternoon. And there are late-night eateries where you can linger over wondrous combinations of food and drink that you'll find nowhere else on earth.

Festivals Galore

Toronto may be Canada's economic capital, but Montréal remains the country's cultural juggernaut, with some 250 theater and dance companies, more than 90 festivals and a fascinating medley of neighborhoods where artists, writers and musicians have helped cement the city's reputation as a great arts center. The Festival International de Jazz de Montréal is the headline event, followed by parties dedicated to world cinema, comedy and gay pride. Québec City also dazzles, with its grand Winter Carnival, music-filled summer fests and colorful fireworks over the river.

Cities of Design

Montréal is a slice of old Europe in a pie of contemporary design. A day's wander might take in the photogenic 18th-century facades of Old Montréal before a cycling tour of the lovely Canal de Lachine, or a wander through the glittering shops and restaurants of downtown before ending at the inviting terraced cafes of Plateau Mont-Royal. The architectural sweep of the city takes in a wealth of heritage churches such as the breathtaking Basilique Notre-Dame, as well as 20th-century icons like the Stade Olympique and Habitat 67. Not to be outshone, Québec City is a stunning jewel of old-world design, with cobblestone streets, 17th- and 18th-century stone houses and slender church spires, set on the cliffs above the St Lawrence.

Winter Wonderland

Montréal and Québec City do get some long, cold winters. But the natives have learned to make the best of them, cheering on local hockey legends Les Canadiens de Montréal, tobogganing down snowy slopes, ice skating beside the St Lawrence River and skiing at many fine resorts nearby. If you can't bear the chill, just wander through Montréal's underground city and surface at the nearest pub.

Why I Love Montréal

By Regis St Louis, Author

I'm always struck by the unbridled creativity of this city. You see it in the magnificent inventions being stirred up in restaurant kitchens, in the barroom and on stage, and you even see it walking down the street with incredible urban art lurking in unexpected places. The dual French-English mix adds dynamism to the city as does its unique mash-up of European and North American culture. Most captivating of all are the people themselves. Montréalers embody *joie de vivre*. They eat well, throw great parties and are happy to share their city.

For more about our authors, see p288.

Top: Cathédrale Marie-Reine-du-Monde (p77), Montréal

Montréal's
Top 10

Old Montréal *(p46)*

1 The old city is where Montréal began and where its heart still lies. Stroll the old-world cobblestoned streets and grand plazas, and learn about local history in the museums. The neighborhood also has fine churches, 19th-century (and earlier) buildings juxtaposed with contemporary constructions, excellent shops and boutiques, numerous art galleries and cafes for your inner bohemian, and some of Montréal's finest dining and lodging options. Old Montréal is like traveling in time without leaving the best of modernity behind. BELOW LEFT: HÔTEL DE VILLE (CITY HALL; P51)

◉ *Old Montréal*

Musée des Beaux-Arts de Montréal *(p73)*

2 This ever-expanding gem in the heart of downtown Montréal is one of the best museums in the country. The striking Bourgie Pavilion is in a gorgeous 19th-century church adjacent to the original neoclassical building, while the modern Desmarais Pavilion across the street reflects its engagement with contemporary art. Among the museum's treasures is a beautifully displayed collection of Inuit art, along with some magnificent works by Québecois artists. Temporary exhibitions range from iconic paintings from Moorish Spain to Jean Paul Gaultier retrospectives.

◉ *Downtown*

GREGORY OLSEN / GETTY IMAGES ©

GUYLAIN DOYLE / GETTY IMAGES ©

3

4

Musical Montréal
(p224)

3 Montréalers are justly proud of their passion for cultivating and appreciating good music. What else would you expect from a city that has turned out everything from Leonard Cohen to Arcade Fire? That's part of the reason why thousands gather downtown every summer for the sizzling sounds of the Festival International de Jazz de Montréal, the city's main party. Free outdoor shows, star performers and a wide variety of genres make it one of the best reasons to visit. TOP LEFT: MUSICIANS PERFORMING AT THE FESTIVAL INTERNATIONAL DE JAZZ DE MONTRÉAL (P225)

⭐ *Music & the Arts*

Basilique Notre-Dame *(p48)*

4 The pride of Montréal and one of the most beautiful churches on the continent, the Basilique Notre-Dame is a 19th-century Gothic Revival masterpiece with spectacular craftsmanship. Originally it was a humble building dating from 1683; it was rebuilt in 1829. Everything, from the great bell (12 tons) in the western tower to the 1891 organ with its 7000 pipes and the stained-glass windows depicting the city's history, speaks of the strong faith of the congregations of yesteryear.

◉ *Old Montréal*

Parc du Mont-Royal *(p105)*

5 The lungs of Montréal, Parc du Mont-Royal is the large green space covering much of Mont-Royal, the mountain at the heart of the city. Montréalers grow up spending their winters sledding down its slopes and skating on its ponds. The rest of the year is perfect for looking out over the city from its belvederes, jogging, biking or simply walking its forested paths. An abundance of fauna and flora make it a big draw for nature lovers.

◉ *Plateau Mont-Royal*

Rue St-Denis *(p91)*

6 Few parts of Montréal feel as bohemian and laid-back as Rue St-Denis in the Quartier Latin. On the blocks below Rue Sherbrooke Est, students from the nearby Université du Québec à Montréal (UQAM) sip beer in brasseries, artists hobnob in cafes and everyone else seems to just watch the world go by. No wonder it was at the heart of the student protest movement that erupted in the city in recent years. It's also home to some excellent theaters, cinemas, cafes and restaurants.

⊙ *Quartier Latin & the Village*

Canal de Lachine *(p132)*

7 This old industrial waterway that powered Canada's industrialization has been cleaned, spruced up and made ready to welcome thousands of bikers, joggers and amateur sailors every summer. The best way to enjoy it is to rent a bike and pedal from Old Montréal to the Marché Atwater, where you can browse farm produce, artisanal cheeses and freshly baked goods. The canal's banks are a perfect spot for picnicking with your purchases.

⊙ *Southwest & Outer Montréal*

8

Old Port (p57)

8 There's always something fun happening at Montréal's Old Port, whatever your pleasure. Take in a circus performance at Cirque du Soleil, bring the kids to a science museum, hop on a boat cruise to the Lachine Rapids, pamper yourself in a floating spa or simply park yourself in a cafe along Rue de la Commune and do some serious people-watching. There's even a Plage de l'Horloge, an artificial beach on the riverfront where you can dig your heels in the sand and gaze out over the mighty St Lawrence (but no swimming). LEFT: PLAGE DE L'HORLOGE (P65)

⊙ **Old Montréal**

Marché Jean-Talon *(p118)*

9 Where to begin? This farmers market in Little Italy has hundreds of vendors hawking fresh vegetables, fruit, seafood and baked goods, as well as seemingly endless restaurants and shops selling everything from Québec jams and wine to maple products, goat's cheese, honey, microbrewed beers, crepes, European and Middle Eastern pastries, and artisanal deli meats. Nearby restaurants such as Kitchen Galerie take full advantage, to the delight of foodies.

👁 *Little Italy, Mile End & Outremont*

Parc Jean-Drapeau *(p66)*

10 You might not have a ticket to the Grand Prix du Canada here, but this pair of island parks in the St Lawrence River is a great spot to get a view of the city and plenty of fresh air. The Musée Stewart is a rare, authentic British garrison that tells the history of the city. After walking the forested paths, you can go thrill-seeking at the La Ronde amusement park or, for adults, the Casino de Montréal. Just save enough for the metro ride back. ABOVE: BIOSPHÈRE (P68), DESIGNED BY BUCKMINSTER FULLER

👁 *Parc Jean-Drapeau*

What's New

Île Ste-Hélène

There's much afoot on this island park facing Old Montréal. In preparation for the 50th anniversary of the 1967 Expo, Île Ste-Hélène will get a makeover, with a new riverside promenade and new concert space for its ample summer festival calendar. The Biosphère (p68), inside Fuller's iconic geodesic dome, is also getting a makeover, as is the high-end restaurant on the island, Hélène de Champlain (p69).

New attractions on Île Notre-Dame

Part of Parc Jean-Drapeau, this island (p68) now has wakeboarding on the lake and stand-up paddleboarding (plus yoga). In winter, the beach chalet becomes a *cabane à sucre* (sugar shack).

An ever-expanding collection

One of the city's best museums keeps getting better. Work is underway on yet another wing (its fifth) on the Musée des Beaux-Arts de Montréal. (p73)

Cocktail craze

Montréalers have embraced high-end artfully prepared cocktails, and there are loads of new bars to sample the goods, such as Le Mal Necessaire. (p63)

Microbreweries

A great craft beer is never far from hand, owing to a wealth of new microbreweries and beer bars that have opened. A new favorite is Isle de Garde. (p126)

Expanded Galleries

One of Old Montréal's top museums (the Musée d'Archéologie et d'Histoire Pointe-à-Callière) has a new building next door where it shows temporary exhibitions – often some of the best in town. (p49)

Repurposing the fur district

Several new hot spots have reclaimed buildings of the former fur district. Head to Café Parvis (p80) for delicious lunches, and Furco (p82) next door for drinks after hours.

New Music Festival

Montréal will host yet another electronic-dance-music festival called AIM. It's at Parc Carrillon, around an hour from the city, and you can camp (www.twitter.com/aim_montreal).

Casino de Montréal

The city's casino is looking very stylish indeed following a four-year, $300-million renovation. In addition to bold architecture, it has new restaurants and bars, plus a new lineup of live music. (p69)

Le Vin Papillon

The folks behind Joe Beef have opened this stellar wine and small-plates restaurant, and it should be on the list of any self-respecting foodie who comes to town. (p80)

For more recommendations and reviews, see **lonelyplanet.com/canada/montreal**

Need to Know

For more information, see Survival Guide (p237)

Currency
Canadian dollar ($)

Languages
French and English

Visas
Not required for citizens of Australia, New Zealand, United Kingdom and the United States, among others. See www.cic.gc.ca.

Money
ATMs widespread. Major credit cards widely accepted.

Cell Phones
Buy local prepaid SIM cards for use with international phones.

Time
Eastern Time (GMT/UTC minus five hours, minus four hours March to November).

Tourist Information
Centre Infotouriste (☑877-266-5687, 514-873-2015; www.tourisme-montreal.org; 1255 Rue Peel; ⊘8:30am-7pm; Ⓜ Peel) provides maps, info about attractions and booking services (hotels, car hire, tours).

Daily Costs

Budget: less than $100
➡ Dorm bed: $22–32
➡ Supermarkets, markets, fast-food restaurants: $30
➡ Bixi bike rental, 24 hours: $5
➡ Movie tickets: $12

Midrange: $100–$200
➡ Double room in a B&B: $130–180
➡ Two-course dinner with glass of wine: $60
➡ Theater ticket: $40

Top End: more than $200
➡ Boutique hotel room: $200–350
➡ *Table d'hôte* (fixed-price, multicourse meal) in deluxe restaurant with wine: $80
➡ Canadiens de Montréal hockey ticket: $200

Advance Planning
Two months before Book tickets for hockey games and major festivals such as the Festivale International de Jazz de Montréal, and make reservations for top restaurants.

Three weeks before Scan web listings for festivals and events; book hotels and rental bikes. Be sure to have adequate clothing for winter.

A few days before Check the weather at www.weatheroffice.gc.ca.

Useful Websites

Lonely Planet (www.lonelyplanet.com/montreal) Destination information, hotel bookings, traveler forum and more.

Montreal Gazette (www.montrealgazette.com) Montréal's English-language newspaper covers everything from politics to sports.

The Main MTL (www.themainmtl.com) Insider take on the latest in dining, drinking, music and the arts.

Ville de Montréal (www.ville.montreal.qc.ca) Useful travel info and events calendar from the city's official website.

WHEN TO GO

Despite the high humidity, summer is the best season, followed by spring then fall. Winter can be spectacular if you're up to the cold temperatures.

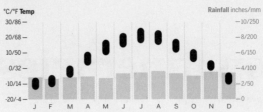

Montréal

Arriving in Montréal

Pierre Elliott Trudeau International Airport Buses and taxis run to downtown Montréal around the clock; buses $10, taxis $40. It takes 45 minutes to an hour to get downtown by bus, and around 30 minutes by taxi.

Gare Centrale Trains pulling in to Montréal arrive at this downtown terminus, within easy reach of many parts of the city by taxi.

Gare d'Autocars de Montréal Most long-distance buses arrive at this station in the Quartier Latin, with handy connections to the Berri-UQAM metro station.

For much more on **arrival**, see p238

Getting Around

➡ **Bus** Buses cover central parts of the island with well-marked routes. They run from 5am to 1am, with separate night services.

➡ **Metro** There are four lines, blue trains and unique rubber wheels. Trains run approximately from 5am to midnight and until 1:30am on Friday and Saturday nights.

➡ **Bicycle** The city's popular Bixi bike-rental system has more than 450 stations, covering central and outlying areas. There is an extensive network of bike paths too.

➡ **Boat** Good for day trips to Parc Jean-Drapeau and cruises on the St Lawrence River.

➡ **Walking** Subway stations are fairly close in the city centre; save a little cash by walking if you only need to go one stop.

For much more on **getting around**, see p239

Sleeping

Finding a place to bunk in Montréal is easy thanks to the many hotels that have opened in the past decade. Summer is peak season, so if you're traveling to see a festival, book well in advance.

Boutique hotels in historic places such as Old Montréal have some of the most sought after rooms, but you can also experience culture at B&Bs housed in heritage buildings in other neighborhoods.

Accommodations range from cheap, no-frills hostels and generic hotels to charming B&Bs, boutique hotels and deluxe suites.

Useful Websites

➡ **Experience Old Montréal** (www.experienceoldmontreal. com) The Antonopoulos Group's collection of hotels, bars and restaurants in the old city.

➡ **Lonely Planet** (lonelyplanet.com/canada/ montreal/hotels) Dozens of author-reviewed hotels, hostels and guesthouses.

➡ **Tourisme Montréal** (www. tourisme-montreal.org) Excellent tourism website.

For much more on **sleeping**, see p154

Top Itineraries

Day One

Old Montréal (p46)

 Take the subway to Place-d'Armes and make a beeline for the stunning **Basilique Notre-Dame**. Explore the cobblestoned streets of the old town, winding your way to the sailors' church, **Chapelle Notre-Dame-de-Bonsecours**. Stroll up **Place Jacques-Cartier** with its many buskers and artists, into the **Château Ramezay** museum.

> ✕ **Lunch** Grab a tasty baguette sandwich at Titanic (p58).

Old Montréal (p46)

Deepen your understanding of the city's history at the excellent **Musée d'Archéologie et d'histoire Pointe-à-Callière** before crossing Pl d'Youville to **Fonderie Darling** for its innovative contemporary-art installations.

> ✕ **Dinner** Garde-Manger (p59) for a fun crowd, and tasty cocktails and dishes.

Old Montréal (p46)

 If you're not dining in style, grab a quick pizza at **Bevo** before catching a show at **Cirque du Soleil** in the Old Port. You might also consider watching the sky turn various colors at sunset while downing an old-fashioned on the rooftop patio at **Terrasse Nelligan**. Party the night away at scenester magnet **Velvet** or **Philémon**, which will rock you until 3am.

Day Two

Downtown (p71)

 Start your tour of downtown Montréal at **Musée des Beaux-Arts de Montréal** for its excellent collection of Old Masters and contemporary art. Architecture aficionados will dig the contemporary Desmarais pavilion as well as the **Claire & Marc Bourgie Pavilion** in an 1890s church. Next stroll down **Rue Sherbrooke Ouest**, home to tiny shops and heritage mansions, toward **McGill University**.

> ✕ **Lunch** Vegetarian-friendly Lola Rosa (p79) has great food and ambience.

Canal de Lachine (p132)

Hop on the metro to Lionel-Groulx and walk down to **Marché Atwater** for a look at the farmers' produce, croissants and cheese. If you have the energy, rent a Bixi bike from a nearby station and pedal the **Canal de Lachine**. If not, consider a cruise on the canal.

> ✕ **Dinner** For incredible Québecois fare, try Joe Beef (p81) if you can get in.

Downtown (p71)

 Upstairs has nightly jazz performances, or better yet the jazz festival will be rocking the blocks around **Place des Arts** if your timing is right. Otherwise grab a postdinner glass at the **Dominion Square Tavern** or hear some beats at underground **Bleury Bar à Vinyle**.

Day Three

Little Italy, Mile End & Outremont (p116)

 Make for Little Italy to explore the mouthwatering **Marché Jean-Talon**. Stroll down to the local church, the **Église Madonna della Difesa**, and be sure to spot Mussolini on the ceiling. Browse the old-world shops along Blvd St-Laurent before hopping a bus (or Bixi) to Mile End.

 Lunch Enjoy market-fresh fare at the charming little Arts Cafe (p118).

Little Italy, Mile End & Outremont (p116)

Ramble along **St-Viateur** and **Bernard**, visiting **Drawn & Quarterly** for its whimsical book selections, hipster curiosities at **Monastiraki** and artfully recycled objects at **Galerie CO**. Before dinner, grab a taxi to **Parc du Mont-Royal** for a panoramic view of the city from **Kondiaronk lookout**.

Dinner Inventive Vietnamese fusion and drinks at Hà (p110).

Plateau Mont-Royal (p101)

Head down to **Casa del Popolo** and see what the hipster kids are cheering for on stage. Afterward, take a late-night bar crawl down Blvd St-Laurent. Stop in **Big in Japan** for elegance and high-end libations, **Majestique** for oysters and cocktails, and **Apt 200** for a loft-like house-party vibe.

Day Four

Parc Jean-Drapeau (p66)

 A river runs through it, dividing Parc Jean-Drapeau into two isles. Begin at **Île Ste-Hélène** with a tour of remarkable buildings from yesteryear. Learn about the environment and our impact on it at the **Biosphère**, housed in Buckminster Fuller's geodesic dome built for Expo '67. Not far away, the **Musée Stewart** is the site of an authentic British garrison.

 Lunch Snacks along the forested paths.

Parc Jean-Drapeau (p66)

Wander the island's walking paths, taking in the outdoor sculptures before kicking up your heels at **Piknic Électronik**, a summertime electronica dance fest. If it's not on, try for some thrills on the world's tallest wooden roller coaster at **La Ronde**. You can grab panoramic but decidedly slower views of the city from 45m up on the Ferris wheel.

Dinner High-end fare at a new restaurant in the Casino de Montréal (p69).

Parc Jean-Drapeau (p66)

The island is a perfect spot to watch the sky explode with fireworks during **L'International des Feux Loto Québec**. If not, the **Casino de Montréal** has everything you need for a good time; just bring luck. Or take a long walk or quick taxi ride to **Habitat '67**, the block-city left over from Expo '67. The winking lights of the Old Port will be beckoning you back across the water.

If You Like...

Historic Buildings

Basilique Notre-Dame Dating from the 19th century, this Gothic Revival masterpiece simply dazzles. (p48)

Château Ramezay A well-preserved 18th-century governors' home. (p50)

Hôtel de Ville Rebuilt in 1926, the city's gorgeous city hall displays local art by the legislative chamber. (p51)

Bank of Montreal Canada's oldest bank has a stunning marble interior and vaulted ceiling. (p49)

Vieux Séminaire de St-Sulpice The clock on this 1680s seminary was a present from Louis XIV. (p49)

Cathédrale Marie-Reine-du-Monde This 19th-century landmark was a symbol of Catholic power in Protestant Montréal. (p77)

Live Music

Place des Arts There's always something going on amid the plaza's high-tech concert halls. (p83)

L'Astral This jazz venue in a century-old building is a favorite for the jazz festival. (p83)

Casa del Popolo From folk guitarists to spoken-word poets, Casa does artsy like nowhere else. (p113)

Rue St-Paul (p46), Old Montréal

DAVID MADISON / GETTY IMAGES ©

Metropolis From raves to David Bowie, this former cinema has seen it all and keeps delivering. (p84)

Dièse Onze A charming basement jazz den with brassy beats and decent snacks. (p113)

Cafe Culture

Le Cagibi Café Bohemian spot for coffee or vegetarian fare by day, drinks and arts events by night. (p120)

Caffè Italia This very unpretentious coffee shop in Little Italy really feels like the old country. (p123)

Pikolo Espresso Bar The signature drink in this stylish space is the Pikolo *ristretto,* which goes down smooth. (p80)

Olive + Gourmando With such yummy sandwiches, this bakery-cafe in the heart of Old Montréal is easy to love. (p58)

Flocon Espresso Tiny joint where coffee nerds high-five over some of the city's best espressos. (p109)

Café Olimpico A fun, buzzing crowd with great people-watching potential in Mile End. (p120)

Carré St-Louis Montréal's prettiest little square has a tiny cafe with outdoor tables. (p103)

Quaint Backstreets

Mile End Explore streets that are home to bagel bakeries, funky cafes and bars, and hipster hangouts in this multiethnic district. (p45)

Plateau Mont-Royal From Ave du Mont-Royal to Carré St-Louis, the Plateau is the city's bohemian quarter, with artsy cafes, plentiful parks and unusual boutiques. (p45)

Westmount The national historic site is awash in Victorian homes, leafy parks and its heritage city hall. (p76)

Old Montréal Head down shop- and restaurant-lined Rue St-Paul, then lose yourself in the quiet backstreets. (p54)

Museums

Musée des Beaux-Arts de Montréal A showcase of old masters and contemporary artists. (p73)

Musée d'Art Contemporain A weighty collection of artworks from Québecois legends. (p74)

Musée Stewart This old British garrison displays relics from Canada's past. (p68)

Château Ramezay A home of French governors and one of the finest examples from the ancient regime. (p50)

Musée d'Archéologie et d'Histoire Pointe-à-Callière An excellent history museum built on the spot where European settlers put up their first camp. (p49)

Fur Trade at Lachine National Historic Site This 1803 stone depot in Lachine tells the story of the fur trade in Canada. (p132)

Green Spaces

Parc du Mont-Royal The city's main mountain, with wintertime skating and sledding, and biking and jogging in summer. (p101)

Parc La Fontaine A leafy park with a chalet restaurant overlooking a lake (and outdoor rink in winter). (p103)

Parc des Rapides Watch the rushing rapids from a picturesque spot on the St Lawrence River. (p132)

> **For more top Montréal spots, see the following:**
>
> ⇒ Eating (p28)
> ⇒ Drinking & Nightlife (p32)
> ⇒ Entertainment (p36)
> ⇒ Shopping (p40)

Canal de Lachine This once industrial canal has been transformed into a 14km-long cycling and pedestrian pathway. (p132)

Jardin Botanique Stop to smell the flowers in these lush 75-hectare gardens. (p133)

Plage des Îles This lovely if artificial beach makes a great destination on a hot day. (p70)

City Cycling

Canal de Lachine Follow the peaceful waterway from Old Montréal out to the Lac St-Louis. (p132)

Boulevard de Maisonneuve Much of this one-way street cutting through downtown has its own bike lanes. (p45)

Parc Jean-Drapeau These two park islands have winding trails for cycling and walking. (p66)

Parc du Mont-Royal It's a slog to pedal up here, but the wooded trails make it well worth the effort. (p101)

Bixi You'll get places fast by hopping around the city on these bike shares. (p240)

Pampering

Bota Bota A delightful spa perched on the water near Old Montréal. (p65)

Strøm Nordic Spa This beautiful Scandinavian-style spa sits on an island a few kilometres from downtown. (p141)

Studio Bliss Get active in a yoga class, then treat yourself to a massage. (p115)

Aveda Montréal Lifestyle Salon Spa & Academy Offers a full range of treatments, including an indulgent Rejuvenating Experience. (p115)

Ovarium Experience weightlessness in the relaxing salt-filled flotation baths. (p128)

Art

Musée d'Art Contemporain Québec's finest contemporary artworks, in a sleek downtown museum. (p74)

Fonderie Darling Cutting-edge installations in a hidden corner of Old Montréal. (p50)

PHI Center Arts center with evocative exhibitions, plus frequent film screenings. (p50)

Galerie Simon Blais This prestigious gallery in Mile End features some of Québec's finest contemporary art. (p128)

DHC Art Features mind-bending contemporary works. (p64)

Aquatic Adventures

Saute-Moutons Go for a high-speed cruise on the waterfront on these thrilling jet boats. (p65)

Stand-Up Paddleboards Get a workout paddling around the lake on Île Notre-Dame. (p70)

Parc de La Rivière-des-Mille-Îles Take a self-guided canoe trip among 10 islands near Laval. (p141)

Rafting Montréal Head off on a white-water paddle down the Lachine Rapids. (p142)

H2O Adventures Rents kayaks and pedal boats for a leisurely glide on the peaceful Canal de Lachine. (p142)

Panoramic Views

Terrasse Place d'Armes Come summertime, this rooftop bar is the best place for a sundowner. (p62)

Kondiaronk lookout Magical views over the city from atop Mont-Royal. (p105)

Île Ste-Hélène Fantastic city and waterfront views from an island just one metro stop from Old Montréal. (p68)

Olympic Stadium Spectacular views from the inclined tower (and from the cable-car ride going up). (p135)

Chapelle Notre-Dame-de-Bonsecours This 18th-century sailors' chapel commands splendid harbor views. (p50)

Oratoire St-Joseph You'll earn those memorable views after climbing the 300 steps (though some prefer the lift). (p131)

Unusual Sights

Place Jean-Paul-Riopelle Time your visit to see the ring of fire on this striking fountain and sculpture. (p55)

Gare Windsor Look for ghosts of the past in this hauntingly empty former railway concourse. (p77)

Illuminated Crowd This sidewalk sculpture offers a rather dark view of humanity. (p75)

Gibeau Orange Julep The great orange ball atop this fast-food joint has become a city landmark. (p137)

Underground City (p75) Lose yourself among the interconnected malls, metro links and passageways. (p75)

Croix du Mont-Royal Yet another city icon is this tall metal cross that you can hike to in Parc du Mont-Royal. (p105)

Month by Month

January

Montréal kicks off the year with a bang, with New Year's Eve parties at restaurants and clubs throughout the city. Temperatures start to really plummet and ski season begins.

⭐ Fête des Neiges

Montréal's Snow Festival (www.parcjeandrapeau. com) features ice-sculpting contests, dogsled races, snow games and costumed characters such as mascot polar bear Boule de Neige. It is held over four weekends in late January and early February. A great place for sledding, ice-skating, zip-lining, curling and skiing.

⭐ Igloofest

If you love electronic music don't let the -20°C temperatures deter you from this fun outdoor dance party and winter fest (www. igloofest.ca) at the Old Port. It's held over four weekends from mid-January to early February. Dress warm!

February

Amid the deep freeze, snow piles up and Montréalers do their best to beat the blahs by cheering on the Canadiens hockey club. Temperatures can fall below -20°C.

⭐ Montréal en Lumière

Created to help shake off the late-winter doldrums, Montréal en Lumière (www.montrealenlumiere. com) is a kind of wintry Mardi Gras with concerts, exhibitions and fireworks. Place des Arts becomes an illuminated fairground with a Ferris wheel and zip line. Most events happen downtown.

⭐ Nuit Blanche

On a Saturday night in late February, Montréal becomes one giant performance space, with all-night performances, film screenings, art installations and concerts (www. montrealenlumiere.com/ nuit-blanche). Hundreds of venues participate. The biggest challenge is choosing where to go.

April

One sign that winter is over is when the Bixi rental bicycles are deployed and bike lanes are reinstated. Spring is here.

⭐ Blue Metropolis Montréal International Literary Festival

This festival (www. bluemetropolis.org) brings together 200-plus writers from all over the globe for five days of literary events in English, French, Spanish and other languages in late April. There are even events for kids.

May

With the snow gone, rainy, windy weather sets in but doesn't last. A few weeks of mild weather preface rising temperatures, which can soon reach the high 20°Cs.

☆ Piknic Électronik

On Sundays from mid-May to mid-September, you can enjoy outdoor revelry on Parc Jean-Drapeau. House-spinning DJs work the decks on two stages, while young friends gather and dance on the grass (www. piknicelectronik.com).

 Biennale de Montréal

One of Montréal's most creative events (www.bien nalemontreal.org) showcases the best and the brashest of the Canadian art scene, including conferences and seminars on contemporary art. It happens on even-numbered years.

🏃 Tour de l'Île

Also known as the Montréal Bikefest, the Tour de l'Île (www.velo.qc.ca) draws 30,000 cycling enthusiasts for a 50km spin around the island of Montréal and a big party in the city afterward (there's also a 28km route). It's staged in late May or early June, with preregistration required.

June

Amid this hot, festival-packed month, Québecers celebrate their 'national' day, the Fête Nationale du Québec, on June 24. Everyone is out for a drink, some good food and fireworks.

🍷 Montréal Beer Festival

Here's your chance to quaff brews from around the globe (www.festivalmondial biere.qc.ca) over five days in mid-June. It's held inside the Palais des Congrès in downtown.

🏃 Grand Prix du Canada

Formula 1 is going strong in Montréal (www.circuit gillesvilleneuve.ca). It's usually held in early or mid-June on the Circuit Gilles-Villeneuve. Don't forget your earplugs. It brings huge crowds; book accommodation well in advance.

July

The heat is on in July: humidity sets in and Montréalers long for surrounding lakes and distant beaches. Tourists throng the city for the jazz fest and other major festivals.

🎆 L'International des Feux Loto-Québec

Thousands camp out on rooftops and on the Pont Jacques-Cartier for the planet's hottest pyrotechnics display (www.interna tionaldesfeuxloto-quebec. com). The 10 shows last 30 minutes each and are held on Saturday nights and a few Wednesday nights for the entire month of July.

☆ Festival International de Jazz de Montréal

With more than 1000 concerts and nearly two million visitors every year, North America's hippest music fest (www.montreal jazzfest.com) just gets bigger and better, with world music, rock and even pop music sharing the program with jazz legends and upstarts over 10 days from late June to early July. See p225.

☆ Just for Laughs

More than 650 artists perform in over 1000 shows at this comedy festival (www. hahaha.com) which runs for two weeks in mid-July. Past events have featured the Muppets, Kevin Hart, Margaret Cho, Lewis Black, Bob Saget and Bill Hader.

August

Steamy days, heat and thunderstorms mark August, when many Montréalers leave town for seaside resorts. It's high season for travel.

☆ Osheaga Festival Musique et Arts

In early August, Parc Jean-Drapeau is transformed into a giant stage for one of the city's grand rock festivals (www.osheaga.com). More than 100,000 music fans turn up to witness the powerhouse lineup of performers, which in recent years has included heavy hitters such as Jack White, Interpol, Stromae and Vampire Weekend.

☆ Festival du Film de Montréal

One of the most prestigious film events (www.ffm-montreal.org) in Canada, attracting 400,000 visitors to screenings from 70 countries. The stars come

(Top) Street performers, Festival International de Jazz de Montréal (p225)

(Bottom) Montréal en Lumière's Ferris wheel (p21)

out, as well as the directors, producers and writers of the big screen. It's held over 10 days in late August and early September.

🎊 Pride Montréal

Montréal's Gay Pride parade (www.fiertemontreal pride.com) is *the* event on the Village calendar, drawing more than a million people, even in slow years. The streets around Pl Émilie-Gamelin pulse with dancing, art exhibits, concerts and parades. It's held over one week in August.

October

Temperatures begin to fall quickly in October as trees put on a spectacular display of color. It's a perfect time to see the Laurentians and the eastern townships.

☆ Festival du Nouveau Cinéma de Montréal

This festival (www.nouveau cinema.ca) highlights who is up-and-coming in feature films, documentaries, experimental shorts, videos, narrative features and electronic art forms during 10 days in October.

🎊 Black & Blue Festival

One of the biggest events for the gay community (www.bbcm.org), with major dance parties, along with cultural and art shows, all in the second week of October.

With Kids

Montréal has many sights for young visitors. Depending on the season, you can go boating, biking and skating, or get some amusement park or skydiving thrills. On warm days, Parc Mont-Royal and neighborhood parks are great places for picnics and free-spirited outdoor activity.

Circuses

World-renowned Cirque du Soleil (p63) combines dance, theater and circus in powerpacked summertime shows. It will thrill the kids, but is truly for all ages.

For entertaining shows year-round, head to TOHU (p136), a circular theater in the St-Michel district.

Hands-On Activities

Outdoors

At the Old Port (p44) you can hop into a paddleboat, go jet boating on the St Lawrence or tootle along in a minitrain for a grand tour.

Fun with science

Enjoy technological wonders, unusual games and an IMAX cinema at Centre des Sciences de Montréal (p57).

Make a dam and walk on water at hands-on multimedia museum Biosphère (p68) in Parc Jean-Drapeau.

Flying thrills

Children aged four and above can experience the thrill of flying at Skyventure (p141), a unique skydiving simulator.

Kid-Friendly Museums

Kids will love Biodôme (p134), a giant indoor zoo with forest, river and marine habitats; or Jardin Botanique's Insectarium (p133), with 250,000 specimens creeping, crawling or otherwise on display.

Enjoy the Planétarium (p134), with domed theaters and interactive exhibits on outerspace; or take your tots on a virtual mission to Mars in Cosmodôme (p137), an engaging space center.

At Musée Ferroviaire Canadien (p136) there are trains of every kind – stationary, moving, new and old trains that will thrill adults as much as children.

At Musée Stewart (p68) see oversized cannons, military parades and guides in period costumes inside an old British garrison.

Outdoor Fun

Amusement Park

At Québec's largest amusement park, La Ronde (p68), kids will experience chills and thrills galore – plus fireworks on some nights.

Parks & Gardens

Enormous Parc du Mont-Royal (p101) in the heart of the city is especially fun for kids in winter, with tobogganing, skiing, snowshoeing and ice-skating. Or try Parc Nature du Cap-St-Jacques (p137), a verdant park with trails, a beach, a sugar shack and a working farm.

Need to Know

➡ **Babysitting** Get a babysitter through **SOS Sitter** (www.sossitter.ca) or **Denise Miller Babysitting Services** (☎514-365-1704; per hour $20).

➡ **Kid-friendly Restaurants** Try Juliette et Chocolat (p93), Romados (p108) or Espace La Fontaine (p109).

➡ **Specialty Resources** See **Exploring Montréal with Kids** (www.montrealwithkids.com).

Visiting Québec City

With captivatingly picturesque old streets and a cliff-top setting overlooking the St Lawrence River, North America's oldest French-speaking city is a gorgeous, seductive place. An easy excursion from Montréal, Québec City has enough magnetism to keep you occupied for days.

Getting to Québec City

Two superhighways link Québec City with Montréal: Hwy 40 north of the St Lawrence River and Hwy 20 south of the river. Both routes are arrow-straight and easy (if boring) to drive, and each takes just over three hours.

A nicer way to travel between the two cities is by rail; **VIA Rail** (www.viarail.ca) runs four trains daily from Montréal's Gare Centrale to Québec's Gare du Palais (three to 3½ hours, one way/return from $87/173). Frequent and economical bus service (three to 3½ hours, one way/return $59/94) is also offered by **Orléans Express** (www.orleansexpress.com).

When to Go

Summer is the liveliest time to visit, with a jam-packed events calendar and crowds overflowing the Old Town's narrow lanes. Québec's other peak season coincides with Winter Carnival in February. For pleasant weather and smaller crowds, visit in May, September or October.

Québec City Festivals & Events

Winter Carnival (p198) Spanning 17 days in January/February, the world's biggest winter carnival features an ice palace, snow sports, parades, ice sculptures, ice canoe races, music and lots of drinking.

Fête Nationale du Québec (Festival of John the Baptist; www.fetenationale.quebec) Québec City parties hard on June 24. Originally honoring John the Baptist, this holiday has evolved into a celebration of Québec's distinct culture. Major festivities take place on the Plains of Abraham.

Le Grand Rire (www.grandrire.com) This big June/July comedy fest features everything from stand-up shows to street performances.

Festival d'Été (www.infofestival.com) With 300 shows on 10 stages, this 11-day July festival attracts musicians from all over the world. Major acts like the Rolling Stones share the limelight with lesser-known groups from Québec, the Americas, Europe and Africa.

Restaurants in Québec City's Old Town (p171)

Festival d'Opéra de Québec (www.festival operaquebec.com) Opera performances are staged throughout the city during this two-week festival in late July/early August.

Les Grands Feux Loto-Québec (www.les grandsfeux.com) Spectacular fireworks light the skies above the St Lawrence River on Wednesday and Saturday nights during this three-week August festival. Jazz, opera and other musical events are also scheduled.

Fêtes de la Nouvelle-France (www.nouvelle france.qc.ca) This five-day festival in August commemorates Québec's colonial period with historical re-enactments and period costumes.

Fête Arc-en-Ciel (www.arcencielquebec.ca) Québec City's Gay Pride celebrations span five days in September.

Festival International des Musiques Sacrées de Québec (Québec City International Sacred Music Festival) This September festival showcases everything from gospel to Gregorian chants.

Top Sights

In Québec City, just walking down the street is an aesthetic treat. The city's historic core is unlike anyplace else in North America, with hundreds of gorgeous mansard-roofed old stone buildings clustered inside a perfect frame of crenellated town walls. Québec's dramatic cliffside setting enhances its appeal, with picture-postcard views of the St Lawrence River unfolding from the Terrasse Dufferin boardwalk (p171), and scenic stairways connecting the Upper and Lower Towns.

The most memorable sight for first-time visitors is the castlelike Château Frontenac (p170), dominating the Upper Town from its lofty perch. The city also boasts a fine collection of museums, most notably the Musée National des Beaux-Arts du Québec (p182) and the eclectic Musée de la Civilisation (p179). History buffs will love Québec's 19th-century hilltop Citadelle (p169) and two museums offering graphic representations of the battles between France and Britain for control of the city. Just outside the town walls, the vast Battlefields Park (p181) is ideal for cycling, cross-country skiing, snow-shoeing and other outdoor activities.

Québec City for Kids

Youngsters go giddy over the ubiquitous street performers and guides in period costume, the uniformed soldiers beating the retreat at the Citadelle (p169) and the antique cannons sprinkled around Battlefields Park (p181). Walking the Fortifications (p171) or rampaging down the pedestrian-friendly Terrasse Dufferin (p171) helps get the wiggles out, while a slow tour of the Old Town in a *calèche* (horse-drawn carriage) appeals to the whole family.

In winter, children will be mesmerized by the toboggan run on Terrasse Dufferin, the ice palace, ice slides, snow tubing and dog-sledding at Winter Carnival (p198), the whimsically decorated rooms at the Ice Hotel (p207), the outdoor ice-skating rinks at Place d'Youville (p202) and the Plains of Abraham, and the engaging historical dress-ups at the Musée de la Place-Royale (p179). Outside the center, kids also love the polar-bear, walrus and sea-lion shows at the Aquarium du Québec (p184).

Eating

Dozens of *boulangeries* (bakeries) and patisseries, such as Paillard (p184) and Le Croquembouche (p192), dazzle the eyes and taste buds with perfect croissants and abundant, beautiful displays of éclairs, strawberry tarts and *chocolatines* (*pain au chocolat*). For other affordable French-inspired treats, sample the quiches and savory snacks at *traiteurs* (delis) along Ave Cartier or the *crêperies* along Rue St-Jean, or head to the lively Marché du Vieux Port (p199), where purveyors of artisanal cheeses and sausages mingle with farmers selling fresh produce from nearby Île d'Orléans. If it's fine cuisine you're after, prepare to be spoiled at top-of-the-line restaurants such as Panache (p190) and Le Saint-Amour (p188), classy brunch hangouts like Café du Clocher Penché (p193), or trendy bistros like Toast! (p190) and L'Échaudé (p189).

Drinking & Nightlife

From top-notch microbreweries to outdoor stalls selling the potent wintertime elixir known as *caribou*, Québec City is a fine place to drink up some local color. Raise a frosty glass (literally, it's made of ice!) beside the roaring fireplace at the city's incomparable Ice Hotel (p207), quench your midsummer thirst with the eight-beer sampler at La Barberie (p195), get cozy in an ancient stone cellar at L'Oncle Antoine (p194), or sunbathe on the outdoor terraces at Le Sacrilège (p194) and l'Inox (p195). When it's time to move on, dance the night away at a cluster of renovated mansions-turned-discos on Grande-Allée, catch the eclectic mix of shows at Le Cercle (p197) in St-Roch, or check out Le Drague (p194), the lively center of Québec City's gay and lesbian scene.

Entertainment

Entertainment here is a year-round proposition. Grand Théâtre de Québec (p196) and Le Théâtre Capitole (p196) offer venerable settings for drama, classical music and other high culture, while bars around town host everything from Québecois ballads with fiddle and accordion to live rock, alternative music and jazz.

In summer, outdoor music venues pop up like mushrooms, including Kiosque Edwin-Bélanger (p196) on the Plains of Abraham and the 10 stages dedicated to world music performances during Festival d'Été (p25). Summer entertainment also spills onto the streets, with jugglers, acrobats, fire-eaters and street musicians setting up shop on street corners around town.

Shopping

In keeping with the city's historic nature, Québec is an antique-lover's paradise. Rue St-Paul in the Lower Town is crammed with shops offering one-of-a-kind items with a distinctly French-Canadian flavor. Striking an equally retro note, North America's oldest grocery store, JA Moisan Épicier (p200), is another browser's delight. On the cobblestone sidewalks below Château Frontenac, artisans spread out jewelry, leather goods and other handicrafts, while trendy homegrown boutiques abound in the less touristy St-Jean Baptiste, Montcalm and St-Roch neighborhoods. Kids will love the miniature entryway built especially for them at the jam-packed toy emporium Benjo (p201), and fashionistas will swoon over everything from designer shoes to the outrageous glasses frames produced by Québecois designer Anne-Marie Faniel.

Sleeping

Québec City is loaded with atmospheric places to spend the night. Top draws include the river-view rooms in the iconic Château Frontenac (p207) and the plethora of mansions-turned-B&Bs lining the pretty Jardin des Gouverneurs, such as Château Fleur-de-Lys (p206). Other peak sleeping experiences include chilling out in a fur-lined sleeping bag on a bed of ice at the city's famous Ice Hotel (p207); enjoying the homey, high-ceilinged charm and private kitchen facilities at Les Lofts 1048 (p206); bedding down above the century-old Théâtre Capitole (p210); savoring river views and classy in-house restaurants at the Old Lower Town's cluster of boutique hotels, or economizing at two well-located hostels in the Old Upper Town.

Parlez-vous Français?

Québecers, like Montrealérs, grow up studying English, but because the anglophone minority in Québec is so tiny, they rarely use it outside the major tourist areas. Most city residents are fully bilingual, but if you stray into the surrounding countryside, you'll quickly find that French is the province's official language.

Eating

Montréal is one of the great foodie destinations of the north. Here you'll find an outstanding assortment of classic French cuisine, hearty Québecois fare and countless ethnic restaurants from 80-odd nationalities. Today's haute cuisine is as likely to be conjured by talented young Italian, Japanese or British chefs as graduates from the Académie Culinaire du Québec.

Neighborhoods

Montréal has more eating choices per capita than anywhere in North America except for New York City. The dining scene is marked by dazzling variety and quality, and brash chefs who attack their creations with innovation. Life in Montréal revolves around food, and it's as much about satisfying your sensual fantasies as it is about nourishment.

Nearly every neighborhood has culinary stars, which makes for rewarding dining no matter where you wander. Downtown and Plateau Mont-Royal are a diner's nirvana, linked by arteries Blvd St-Laurent and Rue St-Denis. 'The Main,' as locals call Blvd St-Laurent, teems with trendy establishments but shades into the alternative as you move north. Still in the Plateau, Rue Prince-Arthur Est and Ave Duluth Est are popular for their good-time BYOB (bring-your-own-bottle) places. Mile End and Outremont have a wide selection of bistros and ethnic fare, with new places popping up all the time. The key streets here are Ave Laurier, Ave St-Viateur and Rue Bernard. Head to Little Italy for great Italian trattorias along Blvd St-Laurent and Rue Dante. Or find award-winning restaurants hidden down cobblestone streets in atmospheric Old Montréal.

Specialties

Montréalers enjoy an enormous variety of locally produced ingredients and delicacies: raw cheeses, game and maple syrup, to name a few. Outdoor markets carry exotic foodstuffs that weren't available even a decade ago alongside tasty produce from local farms.

Residents argue heatedly over which places serve the best of anything – chewy bagels, espresso, comfort soup, fluffy omelets or creamy cakes. Montréal smoked meat and bagels, of course, have a formidable reputation that stretches across the country and are a constant source of friendly rivalry with New Yorkers. Montréal loyalists insist the secret to the hometown bagel's success is all in the time-tested preparation.

A popular-yet-controversial component of Montréal cuisine is foie gras, a food product made from the fattened livers of ducks or geese. The production of foie gras involves force-feeding the animals via a feeding tube, often in amounts far exceeding what they would eat voluntarily. Animal welfare groups argue that the process is cruel and inhumane, and the production and import of foie gras is banned in several countries around the world.

More than Poutine

Traditional Québecois cuisine is classic comfort food, heavy and centered on meat. The fact that the ingredients are basic is said to be a historical legacy, as French settlers only had access to limited produce. A classic Québecois meal might center on game meat (caribou, duck, wild boar) or the *tourtière,* a meat pie usually made with pork and another meat such as beef or veal along with celery

Poutine (p30)

NEED TO KNOW

Price Range

In our listings we've used the following price codes to represent the average cost of a main meal:

$ under $16
$$ $16 to $30
$$$ over $30

Opening Hours & Meal Times

➡ Restaurants open 11:30am to 2:30pm and 5:30pm to 10pm. Many places close on Monday.

➡ Breakfast cafes open around 8am.

➡ On weekends two dinner sittings are common at 5:30pm to 6pm and 8pm to 8:30pm. Places fill up from 8pm.

Reservations

Reserve on weekends to avoid disappointment. During the week you needn't book unless the place is popular (or formal). Most budget eateries don't take reservations.

Paying

Credit and debit cards widely accepted. Some restaurants accept cash only.

Tipping

A tip of 15% of the pretax bill is customary in restaurants. Your bill will show the total with tax in bold. Some waiters may add a service charge for large parties; in these cases, don't pay a tip unless service was extraordinary.

Websites

➡ **The Main MTL** (www.themainmtl.com)

➡ **Montréal Eater** (www.montreal.eater.com)

➡ **Shut Up & Eat** (www.shutupandeat.ca)

➡ **Eating out in Montréal** (www.eatingoutinmontreal.blogspot.com)

and onions. Another favorite lowbrow staple is poutine (fries smothered in cheese curds and gravy), with inventive versions served across the city.

The city has a fine choice of French food, with bistros and brasseries of all types and price ranges. Many incorporate the best of Québec's produce and market ingredients.

For local recipes and tips on mastering the great dishes of the province, pick up the cookbook *The Art of Living According to Joe Beef* (2011) by Frederic Morin et al.

How Much?

Dining out in Montréal doesn't have to be costly. On average, a multicourse dinner for two (including a glass of wine, taxes and a tip) at a midrange place will cost about $80 to $120. At the city's more famous establishments, expect to pay about twice that for a multicourse meal. At the other end of the scale, you can eat delicious fare at casual spots – vegetarian cafes, Jewish delis and down-market ethnic eateries – for less than $40 for two people.

Keep an eye out for the *table d'hôte,* a fixed-price meal – usually three or four courses – that can be a good way to sample the chef's top dishes of the day. Prices start at around $20. Some restaurants offer a discount menu for late dining (usually starting at 10pm), while others have a policy of *apportez votre vin,* or bring your own wine. There's rarely a corkage fee, so take advantage of this.

Taxes amounting to 15% apply at all restaurants. Most don't include the taxes in their menu prices, but check the fine print.

Food Markets & Groceries

For a slice of old-world Europe, don't miss Montréal's sprawling food markets. You'll find a staggering selection of fruits, vegetables, fresh bakery items, cheeses and more. It's also a chance to interact with the proud farmers, butchers and cheesemakers behind these tasty provisions. The big markets have plenty of stands selling prepared foods

POUTINE!

Broach the topic of poutine with a native Montréaler, and either a look of utter rapture or vomitous disgust will likely cross the face of your interlocutor. One of the world's most humble dishes, poutine was invented in rural Québec sometime in the 1950s. According to legend, a restaurateur experienced an epiphany while waiting on a customer who ordered fries while waiting for his cheese curds. The word poutine itself derives from an Acadian slang term for 'mushy mess' or 'pudding.'

For the uninitiated, poutine at first glance looks like the leftovers from a large dinner party all slopped into one giant pile, scraped onto a plate and plunked down on the table. While recipes and imaginations run wild when it comes to poutine, the basic building block of the Québecois dish is fries smothered in cheese curds and gravy. Varieties include 'all dress' (sautéed mushrooms and bell peppers), 'richie boy' (ground beef), Italian (beef and spaghetti sauce), barbecue or even smoked meat. In the past, going out for poutine had about as much sex appeal as chowing down on boiled hot dogs and tap water; these days, however, even exalted restaurants such as Au Pied de Cochon serve the well-known dish.

➡ **La Banquise** (p107) Serving 25 different types of poutine round the clock, this is the gold standard for classic poutine.

➡ **Au Pied de Cochon** (p111) Changes the simple dish with the addition of foie gras (for information about foie gras, see p28).

➡ **L'Gros Luxe** (p110) Serves a good vegetarian option, as well as filling options topped with bacon, pulled pork or fish and chips.

➡ **Patati Patata** (p108) The house special is Patat-ine, with cheese curds served in an edible crispy potato basket.

(crepes, smoothies, coffees, pastries, sandwiches, pizza slices and more).

The biggest market is Marché Jean-Talon (p118) in Little Italy. Runner-up Marché Atwater (p77), just west of downtown near the Canal de Lachine, is a fine spot for a picnic. If you're wandering around the Village or the Quartier Latin, photogenic Marché St-Jacques (p100) is a slice of Montréal history; a market has stood here since the 1870s.

Blvd St-Laurent in Plateau Mont-Royal, between Ave des Pins and Ave Mont-Royal, is renowned for ethnic food shops. Little Italy has small groceries and deli shops on Blvd St-Laurent, a few blocks south of Rue Jean-Talon. For a journey to the Far East, wander through Chinatown; you'll find tea shops, Asian groceries and loads of eateries.

Eating by Neighborhood

➡ **Old Montréal** The old-world setting, rooftop patios and some of the best restaurants in town are irresistible. Chinatown is next door. (p57)

➡ **Parc Jean-Drapeau** Has very limited eating options. Plan to eat meals elsewhere or bring a picnic with you. (p69)

➡ **Downtown** Loads of great options, from inexpensive ethnic fare to stylish dining rooms, hidden down the backstreets. (p79)

➡ **Quartier Latin & the Village** Best for brasseries and bohemian cafes, as well as great budget eats. (p93)

➡ **Plateau Mont-Royal** Cosmopolitan and hip, with excellent dining options in all price ranges. (p107)

➡ **Little Italy, Mile End & Outremont** One of the best food destinations in the city; has everything from bagels to market-based fine dining. (p118)

➡ **Southwest & Outer Montréal** The city's outer districts are off the beaten path for foodies, but have a few distant gems. (p137)

Lonely Planet's Top Choices

Garde-Manger (p59) Celebrated Old Montréal haunt with a festive vibe.

Joe Beef (p81) Creative meats and seafood, excellent wines and knowledgeable staff.

Au Pied de Cochon (p111) Offers foie-gras poutine.

L'Express (p110) Captivating Parisian-style bistro.

Olive + Gourmando (p58) Delicious baked goods and outstanding lunch fare.

Best by Budget

$

Satay Brothers (p79) Asian street food and fusion in a colorful setting.

L'Gros Luxe (p110) Dine in style (and on a budget) in the Plateau.

Kazu (p79) Ramen noodles and Japanese comfort food.

$$

Foodlab (p80) Creative, ever-changing small plates atop a media and arts center.

Le Serpent (p58) Nicely turned out plates in a minimalist setting.

La Sala Rosa (p110) Spanish cuisine in a festive, culturally minded space.

Café Parvis (p80) Industrial style and delicious salads and pizzas.

$$$

Toqué! (p60) Innovative cuisine and a fantastic tasting menu.

Le Filet (p111) Delectable seafood plates by a celebrated chef.

Impasto (p123) The new darling in town, with fantastic Italian cooking.

Best for Breakfast

Arts Cafe (p118) Market-fresh ingredients and delicious recipes in an artful setting.

L'Avenue (p110) A buzzing spot for Eggs Benedict and thick smoothies.

La Croissanterie Figaro (p120) The best place to linger over coffee and warm croissants.

Best for Small Plates

Le Vin Papillon (p80) Inventive tapas plates and great wines.

Orange Rouge (p61) Creative Asian cooking tucked down a quiet Chinatown lane.

Tapas, 24 (p60) The city's best tapas, from Catalan star Carles Abellán.

Hà (p110) Brilliant Vietnamese dishes take center stage.

Best Vegetarian

Lola Rosa (p79) McGill favorite with lasagna, curries and Tex-Mex.

La Panthère Verte (p118) Casual spot with great salads and sandwiches.

Invitation V (p121) Creative vegan fare in a posh setting.

Best Teahouses

Camellia Sinensis (p100) A tea-lover's paradise with hundreds of varieties.

Cardinal Tea Room (p120) Sip from fine porcelain in an elegant upstairs hideaway.

Best Bakeries

Patrice (p79) Superb pastries and cakes.

Alati-Caserta (p123) Old-school family-owned bakery in Little Italy.

Hof Kelsten (p109) The St-Laurent spot for pastries, sandwiches and soups.

Kouign Amman (p108) Famous for its Breton butter cake.

Best for Atmosphere

Barroco (p59) Stone walls, candles, great cocktails and market-fresh fare.

Bremner (p60) Beautiful plates served in a buzzing subterranean dining den.

Best Cafes

Cafe Aunja (p80) Peaceful art-filled spot in downtown.

Moineau Masqué (p109) Great neighborhood cafe with outdoor seating.

Cafe Névé (p109) Well-loved Plateau cafe with perfect lattes and snacks.

Best of Classic Montréal

Schwartz's (p107) Long-running Jewish deli serving the best smoked meat on earth.

La Banquise (p107) A must for poutine lovers (and the merely curious).

Beauty's (p108) Old-school 1950s-style diner.

St-Viateur Bagel (p121) Fires up some of the city's best bagels.

Gibeau Orange Julep (p137) Make a pilgrimage to the great orange ball.

Le Saint Sulpice (p98), Montréal

🍷 Drinking & Nightlife

Montréalers love a good drink. Maybe it's the European influence: this is a town where it's perfectly acceptable, even expected, to begin cocktail hour after work and continue well into the night. On a sunny Friday afternoon, the cinq-à-sept (traditional 5pm to 7pm happy hour) often becomes cinq-à-last-call.

Nightlife

Montréal nightlife is the stuff of legend; it's a vibrant, exciting and ever-evolving scene on the cutting edge of international trends. That's why touring bands and DJs rave about Montréal audiences. From underground dance clubs to French hip-hop, dub reggae to breakbeat, comedy shows to supper clubs and the still-exciting Anglo indie rock so hyped of late, Montréal after dark holds something for everyone. You just have to know where to look.

Bars

Montréalers treat their bars like a second home, unwinding after work for the legendary *cinq-à-sept* happy hour on Thursdays and Fridays, quaffing wine, beer and cocktails until the wee hours. In late spring and summer this is often done on a rooftop patio as temperatures rise. Come winter, Montréalers are undaunted by snowstorms and long, frigid nights. In fact, that's the best time to find a warm, cozy bar (preferably with a roaring fire) and while the night away among friends and a few creative libations.

COCKTAILS

The cocktail craze has swept through Montréal and many bars have elevated the humble mixed drink to a work of art, blending housemade syrups, high-quality ingredients and top-shelf liquors. Le Lab (p111), in the Plateau, was one of the first bars to lead the mixology madness, with skilled bartenders designing a menu of creative cocktails.

Brewpubs

Locals have always been fond of good beer. But the microbrewery scene has picked up momentum in recent years, with the opening of excellent, creative brewpubs across town. The most famous is Dieu du Ciel (p123) in Mile End, a must-visit for anyone who remotely likes beer. You'll find daring beers among the growing roster of microbreweries – some successful, some not. The settings have evolved too, from sudsy beer halls to brew spots with vintage style, industrial fixtures, reclaimed lumber bars, exposed Edison bulbs and flickering candles.

Drinking & Dining

Wherever you go to drink, food is likely to be a part of the experience. You might come across oysters, fish tacos, gourmet poutine, foie gras (see p28) or even *tartare de cheval* (raw horsemeat), along with the usual assortment of *frites* (fries), *moules* (mussels) and bistro bites.

Likewise, some of Montréal's best restaurants also serve great cocktails, and a party crowd tends to arrive late in the evening at some places, such as Garde-Manger (p59), as the focus shifts from food to drink.

Cafes

Coffee is big here, and most locals start the day with strong, espresso-based drinks at their neighborhood cafes. It's not uncommon for artists, students and self-employed types to spend days hanging out at their favorite cafes, laptops in tow. Many places roast their own beans, and you can buy fair-trade and specialty blends in shops around town.

Clubbing & After-Hours

While established events and club nights have a following, the appeal of one-off con-

NEED TO KNOW

Practicalities

➡ The legal drinking age in the province of Québec is 18.

➡ Buy alcohol from the government-run liquor stores all over town: Societé des Alcools du Québec (SAQ). Opening hours vary, but *dépanneurs* (corner stores) sell wine and beer until 11pm. Some supermarkets sell alcohol.

Opening Hours

➡ Bars open around 5pm and close by 3am.

➡ Clubs typically open around 10pm (some open only Thursday to Saturday).

➡ Pubs, bistros, cafes and other establishments have varied opening hours; check websites.

Tipping

It's common to tip 15% of your bill, or between $1 and $2 for each drink you order.

Costs

You can often find midweek specials; some will waive cover before 11pm. Admission can be as low as $5 or free, but expect to pay $10 to $15 in larger clubs.

Tickets & Guest Lists

Lining up in freezing temperatures can be a real drag, so check club websites for a chance to get on the guest list, to reserve tables, or get advance tickets to events.

Dress Code

Nearly all clubs and bars in the city have a relaxed dress code.

Websites

➡ **Nightlife.ca** (www.nightlife.ca)
➡ **The Main MTL** (www.themainmtl.com)
➡ **MTL Blog** (www.mtlblog.com)

certs and parties (including raves) depends on who's putting it on (and the talent on the bill), rather than the location. Beloved party brands throw events regularly, while indie concert promoters book shows of all musical genres virtually every night. You can catch big names and local up-and-comers before they top the charts.

QUÉBEC'S TOP ARTISANAL BEERS

Dieu du Ciel From its Mile End location in Montréal, this microbrewery cranks out a superb selection of beers. A perennial favorite is the Moralité, an American-style IPA.

Unibroue Fin du Monde (End of the World) is a triple-fermented monster with 9% alcohol that more than lives up to its name; La Maudite (the Damned) is a rich, spicy beer that clocks in a close second at 8%; Blanche de Chambly is a light wheat ale.

McAuslan Brewing Keep an eye out for its apricot wheat ale and especially its St-Ambroise oatmeal stout and St-Ambroise Pale Ale.

L'Alchimiste This Joliette-based brewer (about 60km northeast of Montréal) turns out a stable of different brews but its Bock de Joliette, an amber beer, is the star of the bunch.

Les Trois Mousquetaires Based in Brossard (across the St Lawrence River to the southeast of Montréal), this small brewery's Baltic Porter has won awards overseas for its bold taste.

Charlevoix This microbrewery in Baie St Paul (95km north of Québec City) makes excellent Belgian-style beers as well as a creamy imperial milk stout and an unusual Domus Vobiscum Brut, a so-called 'champagne de bière' made in the traditional champagne fermenting method.

Blvd St-Laurent and Rue St-Denis are the two main club strips, with Rue Ste-Catherine in the Village housing a strip of gay clubs. Fancier clubs have selective door policies and cover charges, but anything goes at most underground spots. Things tend to start late (after midnight) and close at 3am, but Montréal's after-hours scene is very happening, with clubs, plus private warehouse and loft parties; they don't serve alcohol but are made for dancing and all-night club experiences.

Drinking & Nightlife by Neighborhood

→ **Old Montréal** Amid posh lounges and DJ bars is a mix of local scenesters, the fashion crowd and 30s to 40s mob, who have more money to spend. (p61)

→ **Downtown** Rue Crescent is *très* touristy but vibrant bars hide among mainstream options. Along Notre-Dame Ouest at Rue Charlevoix is a satellite downtown eating and drinking scene. (p82)

→ **Quartier Latin & the Village** Frenetic Rue St-Denis packs in students with pubs and patio beer pitchers. Along Rue Ste-Catherine Est, the Village has buzzing bars and gay clubs. (p95)

→ **Plateau Mont-Royal** Along Blvd St-Laurent is a major anglophone bar scene, with drunk 20-somethings (and police to keep order). Bars get more sophisticated along Aves Roy and Mont-Royal. (p111)

→ **Little Italy, Mile End & Outremont** From hipster cafes to whiskey lounges, here you'll find some of the most interesting drinking options. Several cluster around Ave Laurier and Rue Beaubien. (p123)

Lonely Planet's Top Choices

Apt 200 (p111) Great space with ample amusement (pool, arcade games, good drinks, people-watching).

Dieu du Ciel (p123) Fantastic microbrews, all made in house.

Philémon (p61) Rip it up with great club beats and a huge bar in a heritage space.

Le Confessionnal (p62) Sinfully tempting cocktails and a fun crowd in Old Montréal.

Majestique (p112) Great cocktails, excellent bites and a dash of style.

Best Pubs

Dominion Square Tavern (p82) Gorgeous old-world tavern; a fine setting for a drink (or a bite).

Burgundy Lion (p82) Trendy British-style pub near the Marché Atwater.

Sir Winston Churchill (p83) A downtown anchor on bar-lined Rue Crescent.

Best Terraces

Terrasse Nelligan (p62) Great spot for a sundowner with views over Old Montréal.

Terrasse Place d'Armes (p62) An open-air rooftop bar that draws a stylish crowd.

Le Saint Sulpice (p98) The outdoor garden is a great spot on warm days in the Quartier Latin.

Pub Ste-Élisabeth (p83) A downtown favorite for its lush courtyard.

Best Clubs

Stereo (p98) A mecca for lovers of house music.

La Porte Rouge (p112) Upscale partying in the Plateau.

Datcha (p126) Fun and fog-filled dance club in Mile End.

Velvet (p62) Uber-hip club beneath an 18th-century stone cottage.

Luwan (p63) Youthful party-minded club in Chinatown.

Best Gay Bars & Clubs

Club Date Piano-Bar (p98) Sing your heart out in this Village saloon.

Sky Pub & Club (p98) A full night of amusement with dance floors and roof terrace.

Circus (p98) A massive after-hours club with a celebratory crowd.

Unity (p98) A three-story Village favorite.

Best Lounges

Bleury Bar à Vinyle (p82) DJs and the occasional live band in a small downtown den.

Baldwin Barmacie (p126) This apothecary-themed lounge in Mile End is pure eye candy.

Best Brewpubs

Isle de Garde (p126) A Little Italy gem with great beer and a friendly crowd.

Vice Versa (p126) Easy-going beer bar with a good selection of Québecois quaffs.

Les Soeurs Grises (p62) A classy brasserie in Old Montréal.

Benelux (p82) Excellent rotating selection of brews near Place des Arts.

Le Cheval Blanc (p95) Easy-going spot near the Quartier Latin, with an outdoor patio.

Best for Sport

Chez Serge (p126) Festive Mile End bar that's wild for hockey.

Café Olimpico (p120) Italian cafe that shows the big games (like European league football).

Hurley's Irish Pub (p83) A cozy space for watching a game or catching a bit of fiddlin' action on the back stage.

Best Cocktails

Le Lab (p111) Cocktail wizardry in a stylish setting in the Plateau.

Le Mal Necessaire (p63) Tasty libations stirred up in a hidden Chinatown drinking den.

La Distillerie (p111) East Plateau charmer; its huge range of drinks is served in Mason jars.

B1 Bar (p95) Cozy basement space with well-made, unpretentious cocktails.

Big in Japan (p111) Magical sitting for a fancy drink.

SuWu (p112) Easygoing spot with a friendly vibe and good bar food.

Best Wine Bars

Pullman (p82) Extensive wine list and buzzing early-evening gathering spot in downtown.

La Buvette Chez Simone (p123) The best place in town for wine and small plates.

Le Vin Papillon (p80) Much lauded new wine-focused eatery.

The Kinsey Sicks (kinseysicks.com) at Montréal's Just for Laughs Festival (p38)

 # Entertainment

Montréal is Canada's unofficial arts capital, with both French and English theater, dance, classical and jazz music, and all sorts of interesting blends of the above on stage virtually every night of the week. The city's bilingualism makes it creatively unique and encourages creative collaborations and cross-pollinations that light up the performing-arts scene.

Live Rock, Pop, Jazz & Blues

Montréal is a music powerhouse, fostering an incredible variety of talent from cabaret pop stars such as Patrick Watson to Leonard Cohen and jazz legends such as Oscar Peterson. The underground and indie music community has many venues in which to catch rising stars, such as Casa del Popolo, while major acts from elsewhere in Canada and overseas perform at the Bell Centre or occasionally at special venues like the Stade Olympique.

There are dozens of concerts on every week at bars, clubs and concert halls. During summer, major music festivals such as Osheaga showcase big-name bands that bring fans from around the globe. Check local listings for details and try to buy tickets in advance.

Performance Power

While the city is small compared to other artistic capitals (such as New York and London), Montréal boasts some world-class companies renowned on the international circuit: a symphony orchestra, the Orchestre Symphonique de Montréal; an opera, Opéra de Montréal; and a ballet company, Les Grands Ballets Canadiens de Montréal. And don't forget Cirque du Soleil, the magical, Québec-born circus of dance, music and acrobatics that forever changed the art form. Speaking of circuses, Montréal has its own year-round dedicated circus-arts venue. TOHU, in the St-Michel district, hosts an eclectic lineup of shows and circus events, with both homegrown groups and international acts.

Film Hub

The presence of Québec's large French-language film and TV industry, and US productions that shoot here, have made the picturesque city a hotbed of film and TV production. Especially during spring and summer, you're likely to see movie shoots on downtown streets and Hollywood stars nonchalantly roaming around – they may show up in unexpected places.

Cinemas

Montréal has its share of multiplex cinemas, but many also include foreign or independent films in their repertoire. More interesting are the several independent movie houses and repertory theaters. The Cinema Montréal website (www.cinemamontreal.com) is excellent, with reviews and details of discount admissions. The repertory houses offer double bills and midnight movies on weekends. These cinemas are sometimes cheaper than the chains showing first-run films.

Film Festivals

Montréal has so many film festivals that it's hard to keep track. The mainstays are **Montréal World Film Festival** (p90) and **Festival du Nouveau Cinéma de Montréal** (☑514-282-0004; www.nouveaucinema.ca).

Les Rendez-Vous du Cinéma Québecois (www.rvcq.com) In the second half of February, this event showcases the best of Québécois film.

Festival International du Film sur l'Art (www.artfifa.com) A March festival devoted to films and documentaries about art from all over the world.

Vues d'Afrique (www.vuesdafrique.org) Held in late April and early May, this growing festival celebrates films about Africa.

NEED TO KNOW

Tickets

➡ Book tickets well in advance for live performances.

➡ Purchase tickets for concerts, shows and festivals from the venue box office, or call **Admission** (www.admission.com; ☑514-790-1245), **Ticketmaster** (www.ticketmaster.ca; ☑514-790-1111) or **Evenko** (www.evenko.ca).

➡ Beware of buying from touts outside event venues on the night of a performance. Try to check with other attendees whether you're buying a genuine ticket and not a forgery.

➡ General admission to mainstream movie theaters such as Cineplex is around $12 or $13. Some art-house theaters have discounted times and days. Ex-Centris (p113) has lower prices ($10) for tickets on weekdays before 5pm; Cinéma du Parc (p84) has $8 deals on Tuesdays.

➡ Daily newspapers *Montreal Gazette* and French-language *La Presse* are great resources for arts and culture listings, as is the free French weekly *Voir*.

Websites

➡ **Nightlife.ca** (www.nightlife.ca)

➡ **Festival International de Jazz de Montréal** (www.montrealjazzfest.com)

➡ **Cirque du Soleil** (www.cirquedusoleil.com)

➡ **La Scena** (www.scena.org)

➡ **Tourisme Montréal** (www.tourisme-montreal.org/what-to-do/events)

➡ **33mag** (www.33mag.com)

Fantasia Film Fest (www.festivalfantasia.com) This leading genre festival in July and August features works from Asia and appeals to the manga-loving *otaku* (geek) set.

Montréal Stop-Motion Film Festival (www.stopmotionmontreal.com) In late September or early October, fans of stop-motion animation gather to see painstakingly crafted works.

Cinemania (www.festivalcinemania.com) This November festival features films from French-speaking countries, all subtitled in English for non-native speakers.

PERRY MASTROVITO / GETTY IMAGES ©

Crowds at the Festival International de Jazz de Montréal (p225)

Dance

Considered Canada's dance capital, Montréal boasts an avant-garde and extremely vibrant dance scene. These days styles such as ballet, modern, jazz, hip-hop, Latin social dancing and tango exist side by side with cutting-edge contemporary dance that fuses various styles and incorporates theater, music and digital art. Montréal is home to many internationally renowned companies, such as **Les Grands Ballets Canadiens de Montréal** (www.grandsballets.com), **La La La Human Steps** (www.lalalahumansteps.com), **O Vertigo Danse** (www.overtigo.com), **Tangente** (www.tangente.qc.ca), **Les Ballets Jazz De Montréal** (www.bjmdanse.ca) and the popular

theatrical touring dance company **Cirque Eloize** (www.cirque-eloize.com). The fact that Canada's **National Circus School** (www.ecolenationaledecirque.ca) is based here certainly helps feed fresh, unconventional talent into the dance and performing-arts scene.

Comedy

With so many potholes in its roads, long winters and a multiethnic brew, humor comes naturally to Montréal. In July, the city plays host to the world's largest comedy festival – homegrown **Just For Laughs** (www.hahaha.com). The laugh-fest has been going strong for 30 years, attracting top comics such as Lewis Black, Jerry Seinfeld, Dave Chappelle, John Cleese and Jon Stewart, and even exporting itself to Toronto, Chicago and Sydney.

When Just For Laughs isn't on, you can still get knee-slapping laughs at dedicated venues in the city. **Comedy Nest** (www.comedynest.com) specializes in stand-up and open-mic nights. Improv specialty venue **Montréal Improv** (www.montrealimprov.com) has free classes for those who want to be funnier.

Spoken Word

The spoken-word scene is quite popular in Montréal, often linked to the hip-hop community. Some of the most exciting and interesting stuff is being done on university campuses. Since these events tend to move around from bar to bar, it's best to check out the bulletin boards or flyers at McGill or Concordia Universities where new and underground performances are regularly announced. Venues such as Divan Orange also hold spoken-word events, and hip-hop crews and improvisational music collectives such as **Kalmunity** (www.kalmunity.wix.com) organize special spoken-word and improv events. **Throw Collective** (www.throwcollective.com) is a poetry-based collective that holds a monthly poetry slam and other events.

Lonely Planet's Top Choices

Place des Arts (p83) Performing-arts complex, home to everything from jazz to ballet and opera.

Casa del Popolo (p113) One of the best indie-music venues in the city.

Usine C (p99) Former industrial space hosting innovative avant-garde theater and dance.

Théâtre St-Denis (p99) Century-old venue hosting everything from comedy to rock and theater.

Cinémathèque Québécoise (p99) Focused on avant-garde and Québecois features.

Best Classical Music & Opera

Orchestre Symphonique de Montréal (p84) Outstanding repertoire with performances inside the high-tech Maison Symphonique de Montréal on Place des Arts.

Orchestre Métropolitain (p85) A first-rate orchestra that plays in Place des Arts and around the city.

Opéra de Montréal (p85) Good, sometimes spectacular productions; a must for opera fans.

I Musici de Montréal (p85) A 12-member chamber ensemble that plays all over town.

Best for Jazz

Dièse Onze (p113) Atmospheric basement jazz den in the Plateau.

Place des Arts (p83) Free outdoor concerts during Jazzfest.

L'Astral (p83) A larger jazz-focused music space near Place des Arts.

Upstairs (p83) A downtown gem with an outdoor terrace.

House of Jazz (p83) A mainstream downtown jazz club that's been going strong for years.

Best Cinemas

Ex-Centris Cinema (p113) Great indie and world cinema on St-Laurent.

Cinéma du Parc (p84) Cult classics and indie films as well as new releases.

Cinéma Banque Scotia Montréal (p84) High-tech movie screens and IMAX theater.

Cinéma IMAX du Centre des Sciences de Montréal (p63) 3D IMAX films down in the Old Port.

Best Live Rock & Pop Venues

Metropolis (p84) A 2300-seat downtown venue that hosts big-name bands.

Club Soda (p83) An icon of the music scene, featuring bands from around the globe.

Le Divan Orange (p113) A creative venue in the Plateau that hosts a range of indie sounds.

Foufounes Électriques (p87) An edgy St-Catherine venue for punk, metal and rock.

Best Theater & Cabaret

Centaur Theatre (p63) Top English-language performances in a memorable Old Montréal locale.

Monument National (p84) Showcases theater, dance and comedy in a grand 19th-century building.

Théâtre St-Denis (p99) Touring Broadway shows, musicals and other big-production fare.

Cabaret Mado (p99) Uproarious drag shows in the heart of the gay Village.

Théâtre Ste-Catherine (p100) Drama, comedy and a wide variety of cultural fare.

Théâtre Outremont (p127) Restored 1920s concert hall with an excellent lineup of music, dance and film.

Best for Dance

Les Grands Ballets Canadiens de Montréal (p84) Dazzling performances from one of Canada's best dance companies.

Agora de la Danse (p113) Features eclectic and experimental artists and dance troupes.

Circus Arts

TOHU (p136) Great place to see creative groups from around the globe.

Old Port (p63) The summertime venue for Cirque de Soleil.

Shopping

Style is synonymous with Montréal living. The city itself is beautiful and locals live up to the standard it sets. Maybe it's that much-touted European influence, but most Montréalers seem to instinctively lead stylish lives regardless of income level, enjoying aesthetic pleasures such as food, art and, of course, fashion.

Fashion City

Montréal is Canada's unofficial fashion capital and many of the country's most talented and internationally successful designers have roots here. Locally based lines include Frank & Oak, Denis Gagnon, Nadya Toto, Christian Chenail and Travis Taddeo. For more information, check out Québec fashion magazines such as *Clin d'Oeil, Lou Lou* and *Elle Québec*. Better still, visit during Montréal's August **Fashion & Design Festival** (www.festivalmodedesign.com), which showcases new collections.

Something for Everyone

Beyond fashion, Montréal is an ideal shopping city, full of goods you'll want to take home. You'll find the cream of the crop in this shopping paradise – from big international department stores to high-fashion designers, vintage clothing boutiques to weird one-of-a-kind antique shops, used-music stores and booksellers, chic home decor and more. As well, many international megastore chains have shops here, but with a local or European flair.

Sales

Montréal's prices can be high. To save cash, plan your shopping around big sales events. Keep an eye out for sample sales, when designers offload new productions and showroom pieces at rock-bottom prices.

Warehouse sales, featuring big reductions on old stock (with savings of 50% to 90%), are another draw.

When it comes to fashion, bargain hunters shouldn't miss **La Braderie de Mode Québécoise**. Held in April and October, the four-day sale brings big savings on more than 100 brands. It's held in the Marché Bonsecours.

For upcoming sales, check out these sites: MTL Warehouse (www.mtlwarehouse.ca), All Sales (www.allsales.ca) and I Love Sample Sales (www.ilovesamplesales.com).

Shopping by Neighborhood

➡ **Old Montréal** Upscale Rue St-Paul is home to galleries, designer furnishings and clothing shops. Closer to Pl Jacques-Cartier is tourist tat. (p63)

➡ **Downtown** Busy Rue Ste-Catherine has the big names, department stores, and some specialty shops and local fashion boutiques. For antiques head to Rue Notre-Dame Ouest. (p87)

➡ **Plateau Mont-Royal** Hip clothing and home-decor boutiques are located on Blvd St-Laurent and Rue St-Denis. Ave du Mont-Royal has used books and records. (p114)

➡ **Little Italy, Mile End & Outremont** Great for groceries and cooking items. Prices soar on Rue Laurier, Ave Bernard and elegant Westmount Sq. (p127)

GREAT MARKETS OF MONTRÉAL

Montréal is famed for its impressive year-round food markets, where you can sample the great bounty of the north. For more information, visit **Marchés Publics de Montréal** (www.marchespublics-mtl.com).

➡ **Marché Jean-Talon** (p118) The city's largest market has several hundred market stalls selling all manner of produce, plus food counters where you can get juices, crepes, baguette sandwiches and more. Don't miss the Québecois specialty store Le Marché des Saveurs.

➡ **Marché Atwater** (Map p272; 138 Ave Atwater; ⊙7am-6pm Mon-Wed, to 7pm Thu, to 8pm Fri, to 5pm Sat & Sun; ⊘; ⓂAtwater) Located right on the banks of the Canal de Lachine, with scores of vendors outside and high-class delicatessens and specialty food shops inside, in the tiled, vaulted hall under the art-deco clock tower.

➡ **Marché de Maisonneuve** (☎514-937-7754; 4445 Rue Ontario Est; ⊙7am-6pm Mon-Wed, to 8pm Thu-Fri, to 6pm Sat, to 5pm Sun; ⓂPie-IX, then bus 139) About 20 farm stalls, and inside, a dozen vendors of meat, cheese, fresh vegetables, tasty pastries and pastas in a beautiful beaux-arts building (1912–14) girded by pretty gardens.

➡ **Marché St-Jacques** (p100) Traditional food stalls and shops still occupy their 1931 art-deco home in the northern reach of the Village.

Lonely Planet's Top Choices

Le Marché des Saveurs du Québec (p127) A splendor of Québecois goodies: beer, maple syrup, sweets, jams and more.

Frank & Oak (p127) Well-crafted, affordable men's clothing by a Montréal fashion label.

Monastiraki (p127) Avant-garde art zines to eclectic antiques: this hipster retro shrine fascinates.

Galerie CO (p127) Lovely eco-friendly objects for the house.

Drawn & Quarterly (p127) A fine collection of literary works and graphic novels, including its own imprint.

Best Art

Galerie Simon Blais (p128) A prestigious gallery with top-name artists in Mile End.

Galeries d'Art Contemporain du Belgo (p74) An intriguing building with galleries and artist studios.

DHC Art (p64) An Old Montréal spot featuring cutting-edge works by contemporary artists.

Parisian Laundry (p77) A massive space often featuring large-scale installations.

Galerie Le Chariot (p64) Huge collection of Inuit arts and crafts.

Best for Food & Drink

La Tablette de Miss Choco (p114) Chocolates from around the globe.

Camellia Sinensis (p100) Tea lovers shouldn't miss this shop and its adjoining teahouse.

Candy Labs (p87) Flavorful housemade candies almost too pretty to eat.

Best Vintage

Eva B (p87) Step into an alternate universe in this wild vintage emporium.

Friperie St-Laurent (p115) Plateau icon and home to some of the best apparel from the past.

Best Design

Style Labo (p128) Vintage chic and curios from the past.

Espace Pepin (p64) Artful housewares and fashion pieces.

Best Fashion

Rooney (p64) Stylish garments and accessories.

Ibiki (p114) Beautifully made men's and women's wear.

Roots (p88) A great variety of clothing and gear from one of Canada's best-known brands.

Holt Renfrew (p87) A high-end department store with a top selection of well-known brands.

Best for Gifts

Zone Orange (p64) Crafty jewelry, toys, and housewares made by Québecois artisans.

Artpop (p114) Eye-catching T-shirts, bags and frame-worthy prints of Montréal landmarks.

Au Papier Japonais (p127) Gorgeous collection of hand-made paper from Japan.

Best Record Stores

Aux 33 Tours (p114) Extraordinary collection of albums, new and used (plus CDs).

Phonopolis (p128) A music lover's haunt in Mile End.

Explore Montréal & Québec City

MONTRÉAL &
QUÉBEC CITY'S
TOP SIGHTS

Cabane à sucre (maple-sugar shack),
p148

Neighborhoods at a Glance

① Old Montréal p46

On the edge of the St Lawrence River, Old Montréal is the city's birthplace, composed of picturesque squares, grand old-world architecture and a dense concentration of camera-toting tourists. The narrow Rue St-Paul, the old main street, teems with art galleries, shops and eateries, while the broad concourse of the Old Port is lined with green parkland and cafes along Rue de la Commune. Nearby Chinatown is small but packed with cheap, tasty eateries.

② Parc Jean-Drapeau p66

Worlds away from the city bustle, this park stretches across two leafy islands in the midst of the mighty St Lawrence, about half a mile east of the Old Port. The prime

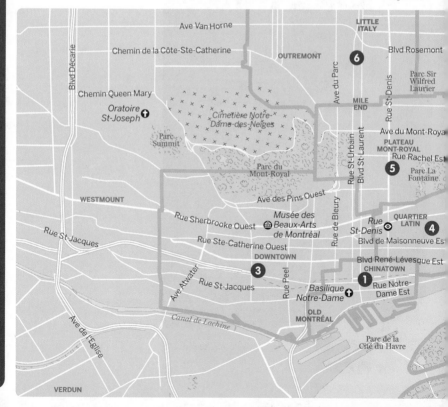

draws are outdoor activities such as cycling and jogging, though you'll also find some noteworthy museums, architectural remnants of the landmark Expo '67, and lake swimming and weekly dance parties in the summer.

❸ Downtown p71

At the feet of its modern skyscrapers and condo developments lie heritage buildings and old-time mansions, top-notch museums and numerous green spaces. The two most common species here are businesspeople, and students from McGill and Concordia Universities. The city's major shopping district is downtown, as is the performing-arts complex, Place des Arts. This is the epicenter of the city's jazz festival in summer.

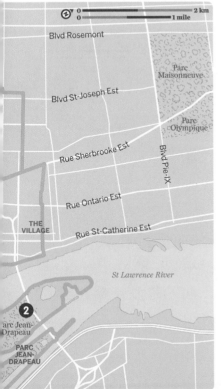

❹ Quartier Latin & the Village p89

The Quartier Latin is a gateway to theaters, lively cafes and low-key bars packed with students from the French-speaking Université du Québec à Montréal. Continue west to reach the Village, a major icon for gay travelers. Shops, restaurants and bars proudly fly the rainbow colors here, and the nightlife and cafe scene rarely slows down.

❺ Plateau Mont-Royal p101

This former immigrant neighborhood houses a wealth of sidewalk cafes, excellent restaurants, bars and boutiques. For many Montréalers and visitors alike, exploring the Plateau is what Montréal is all about. The Plateau is handily located next to Montréal's beloved 'mountain,' Mont-Royal, home to walking and biking trails, a pretty lake and great views over the city.

❻ Little Italy, Mile End & Outremont p116

Just up from the Plateau are Mile End and Outremont, two leafy neighborhoods with upscale boutiques and restaurants; nearby, Little Italy is a slice of the old world, with classic Italian trattorias and espresso bars, neighborhood churches and the sprawling Marché Jean-Talon, the city's best market. These three neighborhoods are also home to some of the best new bars in Montréal.

❼ Southwest & Outer Montréal p129

This grab bag of districts takes in the Canal de Lachine, one of the best biking paths in the city, as well as working-class districts such as Petite-Bourgogne and St-Henri. The highlight, however, is the majestic Oratoire St-Joseph, the iconic hillside church. The eastern part of the city also has some popular attractions, including Olympic Park, home to a planetarium, botanical gardens, a kid-friendly ecosystems museum and an eye-popping stadium.

Old Montréal

OLD MONTRÉAL | OLD PORT | CHINATOWN

Neighborhood Top Five

1 Soaking up the beautiful craftsmanship and soaring architecture of the **Basilique Notre-Dame** (p48), the city's spiritual jewel.

2 Taking in a circus performance, river cruise, or waterfront stroll at the storied **Old Port** (p57).

3 Getting your bearings amid the heritage architecture of **Place d'Armes** (p49) and its monument to Montréal's founder.

4 Journeying back to the Montréal's early foundation on a fascinating subterranean walk inside the **Musée d'Archéologie et d'Histoire Pointe-à-Callière** (p49).

5 Visiting the sailors' chapel in the charming **Chapelle Notre-Dame-de-Bonsecours** (p50), immortalized by Leonard Cohen.

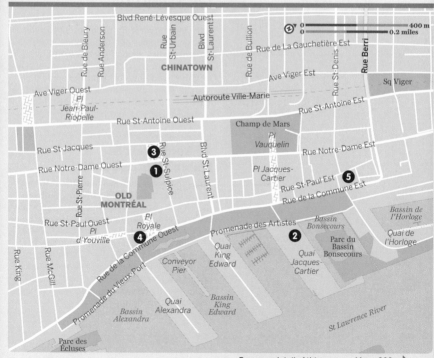

For more detail of this area see Map p268 ➡

Explore Old Montréal

Begin your tour of Vieux-Montréal (Old Montréal) in its heart – historic Place d'Armes. Admire the recently renovated square, with its statue of city founder Paul Chomedey de Maisonneuve, and then head inside the iconic Basilique Notre-Dame. Take your time viewing its finely crafted interior before crossing the square and visiting the Bank of Montreal's 1847 headquarters, with its neoclassical facade and vaulted marble interior.

Next head down Rue St-Sulpice past the basilica to Rue St-Paul Ouest and turn left. It's lined with art galleries, plush boutiques and eateries, but these give way to tacky souvenir shops before you reach Place Jacques-Cartier, a grand square dedicated to the French explorer that's full of artists and buskers. At one end is the photogenic Hôtel de Ville (City Hall) while one block to the north, along Rue St-Paul Est, is the equally pretty Marché Bonsecours with its silver dome. Just past it is the beautiful Chapelle Notre-Dame-de-Bonsecours, a humble sailors' church that is the perfect counterpoint to the basilica.

One block east is Rue de la Commune Est, a breezy waterfront street that gives you access to the Old Port and its museums, the Cirque du Soleil big top and river cruises. Proceed northwest up Blvd St-Laurent for 15 minutes to reach Montréal's small Chinatown. It's an excellent place to grab a cheap but satisfying plate of dumplings.

Local Life

➡**Happy hour** In summer Montréalers love to enjoy *cinq à sept* (happy hour) on rooftop patios in Old Montréal.

➡**Fine dining** Locals flock to the atmospheric stone-walled dining rooms in Old Montréal as well as the cheapie noodle eateries in Chinatown.

➡**Biking** Rent a Bixi (p240) bike and ride from the Old Port to the Canal de Lachine bike path.

Getting There & Away

➡**Metro** To reach Old Montréal or Chinatown, take the metro to Square-Victoria, Place-d'Armes or Champ-de-Mars.

➡**Bus** Bus 14 runs along Rue Notre-Dame in Old Montréal between Rue Berri and Blvd St-Laurent; bus 55 stops on Blvd St-Laurent.

➡**On foot** While it is expansive, the area can be easily explored on foot, and accessed from downtown via streets such as Rue de Bleury.

➡**Biking** The Old Port is an entry point to a bike path that leads to the Canal de Lachine, which connects to the fringes of downtown at Rue Charlevoix.

Lonely Planet's Top Tip

As with many streets in the city, east and west (*est* and *ouest* in French) labels on street signs don't reflect true compass orientations. Remember that 'east–west' streets such as Rue Notre-Dame actually run closer to north–south, and this can be confusing if you like orienteering with maps.

 Best Places to Eat

➡ Olive + Gourmando (p58)
➡ Tapas, 24 (p60)
➡ Orange Rouge (p61)
➡ Barroco (p59)
➡ Garde-Manger (p59)
➡ Toqué! (p60)

For reviews, see p57. ➡

Best Places to Drink

➡ Le Confessionnal (p62)
➡ Le Mal Necessaire (p63)
➡ Philémon (p61)
➡ Terrasse Nelligan (p62)
➡ Les Soeurs Grises (p62)
➡ Terrasse Place d'Armes (p62)

For reviews, see p61. ➡

Best Activities

➡ Ça Roule Montréal (p64)
➡ Bota Bota (p65)
➡ Saute-Moutons (p65)

For reviews, see p64. ➡

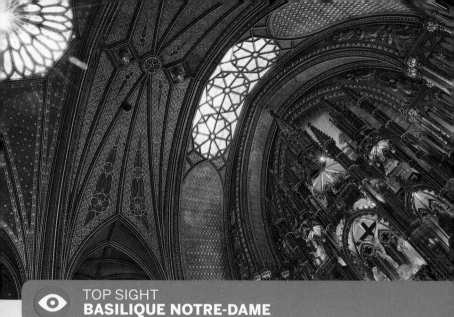

TOP SIGHT
BASILIQUE NOTRE-DAME

This grand dame of Montréal's ecclesiastical treasures is a must-see when exploring the city. The looming Gothic Revival church can hold up to 3200 worshippers and houses a collection of finely crafted artworks, including an elaborately carved altarpiece, vibrant stained-glass windows and an intricate pulpit.

The Sulpicians commissioned James O'Donnell, a New York architect and Irish Protestant, to design what would be the largest church north of Mexico. He converted to Catholicism so he could have his funeral in the basilica, and is buried in the crypt.

Opened in 1829, the basilica has a spectacular interior with a forest of ornate wood pillars and carvings made entirely by hand (and constructed without the aid of a single nail). Gilt stars shine from the ceiling vaults and the altar is backlit in evening-sky blues. The massive 7000-pipe **Casavant organ** provides the powerful anthem at the famous Christmas concerts; the church bell, the Gros Bourdon, is the largest on the continent.

While decoration is fairly minimal on the stone facade, you'll note three prominent statues: the Virgin Mary in the center (patron saint of Montréal), St John the Baptist (representing Québec) to the right, and St Joseph (for Canada) to the left.

The **Chapelle du Sacré Coeur**, located behind the main hall, is nicknamed the Wedding Chapel. The curious mix of styles emerged after a 1978 fire, when the chapel was rebuilt with a brass altar with abstract-modern motifs.

There are periodic choral and orchestral concerts throughout the year, which showcase the church's remarkable acoustics.

DON'T MISS

➡ Casavant organ
➡ Chapelle du Sacré Coeur
➡ A choral concert

PRACTICALITIES

➡ Map p268
➡ www.basiliquenddm.org
➡ 110 Rue Notre-Dame Ouest
➡ adult/child $5/4
➡ ⊙8am-4:30pm Mon-Sat, 12:30-4pm Sun

⦿ SIGHTS

⦿ Old Montréal

BASILIQUE NOTRE-DAME   CHURCH
See p48.

MUSÉE D'ARCHÉOLOGIE ET D'HISTOIRE POINTE-À-CALLIÈRE   MUSEUM
Map p268 (Museum of Archaeology & History; www.pacmuseum.qc.ca; 350 Pl Royale; adult/child $20/7; ⊙10am-5pm Mon-Fri, 11am-5pm Sat & Sun; ⓘ; ⓂPlace-d'Armes) One of Montréal's most fascinating sites, this museum takes visitors on a historical journey through the centuries, beginning with the early days of Montréal. Visitors should start with *Yours Truly, Montréal*, an 18-minute multimedia show that covers the arrival of the Amerindians, the founding of Montréal and other key moments. Afterward, head to the archaeological crypt where you can explore the remains of the city's ancient sewage and river system, and the foundations of its first buildings and public square.

Interactive exhibits allow visitors to hear what life was like in the 17th and 18th centuries from characters on video screens.

Kids will get a kick out of the 'Pirates or Privateers?' exhibit, which explores the world of early-18th-century sailors. Hands-on displays cover the food, navigational gear, tools and weaponry used by the recruits of Captain Iberville. Other attractions include a restored 1915 pumping station. Across the street is the **Mariners' House** (Map p268; 165 Pl D'Youville), which hosts a simulated archaeological dig (great for kids) and temporary exhibitions, including some of Montréal's top gallery shows.

The lookout at the top of the tower (free to visit) provides an excellent view of the Old Port.

PLACE D'ARMES   HISTORIC SITE
Map p268 (ⓂPlace-d'Armes) This open square is framed by some of the finest buildings in Old Montréal, including its oldest bank, first skyscraper and Basilique Notre-Dame. The square's name references the bloody battles that took place here as religious settlers and First Nations tribes clashed over control of what would become Montréal. At its center stands the **Monument Maisonneuve**, dedicated to city founder Paul de Chomedey, *sieur* de Maisonneuve.

The red sandstone building on the north side of the square is the **New York Life Insurance Building**, Montréal's first skyscraper (1888). It's said to be built with the blocks used for ballast on ships bringing goods to Montréal. Next door, the **Aldred Building** is made of limestone and was designed to emulate the Empire State Building. Completed in 1931, it has an opulent, L-shaped, art-deco lobby. On the west side of the square, the **Bank of Montréal** was Canada's first permanent bank.

Near the south side of the square, you'll find horse-drawn carriages waiting to take you for a ride.

BANK OF MONTREAL   HISTORIC BUILDING
Map p268 (119 Rue St-Jacques Ouest; ⊙10am-4pm Mon-Fri; ⓂPlace-d'Armes) **FREE** Modeled after the Pantheon in Rome, the grand colonnaded edifice of Canada's oldest chartered bank, built in 1847, dominates the north side of Pl d'Armes and is still a working bank. The imposing interior has 32 marble columns and a coffered 20m ceiling in Italian Renaissance style over a long row of tellers behind glass partitions. The helmeted marble lady is Patria, representing a minor Roman god of patriotism to honor the war dead.

A snoozy money museum (admission free) inside the bank has a replica of a cashier's window, old banknotes and an account of early banking in Canada.

VIEUX SÉMINAIRE DE ST-SULPICE   RELIGIOUS, SPIRITUAL
Map p268 (116 Rue Notre-Dame Ouest; ⓂPlace-d'Armes) The seminary by the Basilique Notre-Dame and its grounds are closed to the public, but you can see them through the gate. The Catholic order of Sulpicians was given title to the entire Island of Montréal in 1663. The order built the seminary in 1684 and the 3rd-floor apartments of the old seminary have been occupied ever since.

The clock on the facade was a gift from French king Louis XIV in 1701; it is believed to be the oldest working clock in North America. Ancient oaks shade the rear garden laid out in 1715.

RUE ST-JACQUES   STREET
Map p268 (ⓂPlace-d'Armes) Known as the Wall St of Canada into the 1930s, Rue St-Jacques was lined with the head offices of insurance companies and banks that proclaimed Montréal's prosperity for the

best part of a century. In those days it was known as St James St. Some great edifices are veritable temples to capitalism.

The 1902 **Guardian Trust Building** (Map p268; 240 Rue St-Jacques) has helmeted women guarding the entrance while lions and mermaids watch over on the 2nd floor. The Molson beer-brewing dynasty had its own bank, but the **Molson Bank Building** (Map p268; 278-288 Rue St-Jacques) looks more like a royal residence; heads of founder William and his two sons grace the doorway.

The most glamorous of the lot is the **Royal Bank Building** (Map p268; 360 Rue St-Jacques), the city's tallest building (22 stories) when it was built in 1928. Pass under the royal coat of arms into a banking hall that resembles a Florentine palace; the coffered ceilings are of Wedgwood and the walls display insignias of eight provinces, Montréal (St George's Cross) and Halifax (a yellow bird).

CHÂTEAU RAMEZAY   HISTORIC BUILDING
Map p268 (www.chateauramezay.qc.ca; 280 Rue Notre-Dame Est; adult/child $10/5; ⊙9:30am-6pm daily Jun-Sep, 10am-4:30pm Tue-Sun Oct-May; ⓂChamp-de-Mars) A home of French governors in the early 18th century, this mansion is one of the finest examples from the ancient regime. It was built for the 11th governor, Claude de Ramezay, and includes 15 interconnecting rooms with a ballroom of mirrors, as well as mahogany galore. Ramezay went broke trying to maintain it.

American generals used it as a headquarters during the revolution, and Benjamin Franklin held conferences here when attempting (and failing) to convince the Canadians to join the cause. In 1903 turrets were added to give the 'château' its fanciful French look. The building is a repository of Québec history with a collection of 20,000 objects, including valuable Canadian art and furniture. The Governor's Garden (open June to September) in the rear recreates a horticultural garden from the 18th century, including many original varieties of fruit trees and vegetables.

CHAPELLE
NOTRE-DAME-DE-BONSECOURS   CHURCH
Map p268 (☑514-282-8670; 400 Rue St-Paul Est; admission to chapel free, museum adult/student/child $12/9/7; ⊙10am-6pm Tue-Sun May-Sep, 11am-4pm Tue-Sun Oct–mid-Jan; ⓂChamp-de-Mars) Known as the Sailors' Church, this enchanting chapel derives its name from the sailors who left behind votive lamps in the shapes of ships in thanksgiving for safe passage. The restored interior has stained-glass windows and paintings depicting key moments in the life of the Virgin Mary (for whom Montréal – aka Ville-Marie – was originally named). The attached **Musée Marguerite-Bourgeoys** relates the story of Montréal's first teacher and the founder of the Congregation of Notre-Dame order of nuns.

The crypt has artifacts dating back 2000 years and foundations of the original chapel from 1773. The observation tower offers grand views of the Old Port.

FONDERIE DARLING   ARTS CENTER
Map p268 (☑514-392-1554; www.fonderiedarling.org; 745 Rue Ottawa; admission $5, Thu free; ⊙noon-7pm Wed & Fri-Sun, to 10pm Thu; ⓂSquare-Victoria) Tucked away in a little-visited corner of Old Montréal, the Darling Foundry hosts avant-garde, often large-scale exhibitions in its two sizable showrooms. The brick industrial building, which dates back to the early 1900s, once housed a prosperous iron foundry and is today home to the gallery and live-work studios for artists.

In the summertime the foundry hosts occasional Thursday-night street events (with free admission). Check the website for upcoming exhibitions. Also in the foundry is the first-rate restaurant, Le Serpent (p58); its entrance is on Prince St.

PHI CENTER   ARTS CENTER
Map p268 (☑514-225-0525; www.phi-centre.com; 407 Rue St-Pierre; ⊙10am-5pm Mon-Fri, from noon Sat; ⓂSquare-Victoria) One of Old Montréal's most innovative art incubators, the PHI Center stages thought-provoking exhibitions, embracing a wide range of styles and genres. Four or five nights a week, PHI Center screens art films, obscure documentaries, experimental shorts and other works you won't see elsewhere. The center also hosts poetry readings, album launches, foodie events, and much more.

CENTRE D'HISTOIRE
DE MONTRÉAL   MUSEUM
Map p268 (335 Pl d'Youville; adult/child $6/4; ⊙10am-5pm Wed-Sun; ⓂSquare-Victoria) In a handsome old fire hall on Pl d'Youville, the Montréal History Center has 300-plus artifacts that illustrate the city's eventful past while focusing on its social history. You can listen to the tales of long-lost neighbor-

MONTRÉAL'S LITERARY STAR

Émile Nelligan (1879–1941) is one of Québec's literary icons, a star like Oscar Wilde or Lord Byron whose mix of talent and tragedy keeps them in the public consciousness long after their era is over. A poetic genius, Nelligan created most of his famous works by the age of 20 before being committed and spending the rest of his life in mental institutions.

Born in Montréal to an Irish father and a Québecois mother, his bohemian traits were in evidence from the time he was a teenager. He sailed in and out of school to the dismay of his parents and seemed interested in little other than romantic poetry. After submitting two samples of his work, he was accepted by the l'École Littéraire de Montréal (Literary School of Montréal); public readings followed and his poems exploring love and loneliness were regularly published in French-language magazines around Montréal. Nelligan had always marched to a different drum but by 1899 it was apparent his problems were more than just those of a temperamental artist and there was something seriously wrong.

His father had him committed to a mental institution that year. Though he tried briefly to rejoin society in 1925, he was back in care within days. What was wrong with him? Historians who've examined his hospital records believe he may have suffered from schizophrenia.

Though there has been both a movie and play about Nelligan's life, and he was immortalized in a painting by master Québec artist Jean-Paul Lemieux, there is no museum devoted to his work or life. Hunting his ghost around town is the best you'll be able to do. The Château Ramezay is where l'École Littéraire de Montréal used to meet and where Nelligan's poems were first read in public. Nelligan lived in a house on the west side of Carré St-Louis. The square is also the setting for the famous Lemieux painting. Further along, St Patrick's Basilica is where Nelligan was baptized; there's a plaque at the back commemorating this event, along with a plaque devoted to Montréal's other famous Irishman, D'Arcy McGee.

hoods, or travel back in time while watching archival footage from the '40s and '60s.

PLACE JACQUES-CARTIER   SQUARE
Map p268 (MChamp-de-Mars) The liveliest spot in Old Montréal, this gently inclined square hums with performance artists, street musicians and the animated chatter from terrace restaurants linings its borders. A public market was set up here after a château burned down in 1803. At its top end stands the **Colonne Nelson**, a monument erected to Admiral Lord Nelson after his defeat of Napoleon's fleet at Trafalgar.

Nelson's presence is a thorn in the side of many French Québecois, and there have been many attempts to have it removed. Francophones later installed a statue of an obscure French admiral, Jean Vauquelin, in the nearby **Place Vauquelin**, just west of Hôtel de Ville on Rue Notre-Dame.

HÔTEL DE VILLE   HISTORIC BUILDING
Map p268 (City Hall; 275 Rue Notre-Dame Est; ⊗8:30am-5pm; MChamp-de-Mars) FREE
Montréal's handsome City Hall was built between 1872 and 1878, then rebuilt after a fire in 1926. Far from being a humdrum administrative center, it's actually steeped in local lore. Most famously, it's where French leader Charles de Gaulle took to the balcony in 1967 and yelled to the crowds outside 'Vive le Québec libre!' ('Long live a free Québec!'). Those four words fueled the fires of Québecois separatism and strained relations with Ottawa for years.

Peer into the Great Hall of Honor for some scenes of rural Québec and busts of Jacques Viger, the first French-speaking mayor (1833–36), and Peter McGill, the first English-speaking mayor (1840–42).

MARCHÉ BONSECOURS   MARKET
Map p268 (Bonsecours Market; www.marchebonsecours.qc.ca; 350 Rue St-Paul Est; ⊗10am-9pm late Jun-Aug. to 6pm Sep-Mar; MChamp-de-Mars) This sprawling neoclassical building houses shops selling arts and crafts, leather goods and garments, and several cafes. The upstairs hall hosts periodic fashion shows and art auctions, and a number of restaurants front the facade on Rue St-Paul.

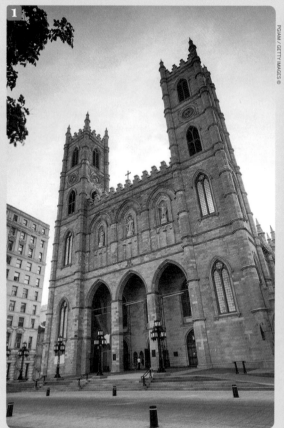

PERRY MASTROVITO / GETTY IMAGES ©

1. Basilique Notre-Dame (p48)
A Montréal must-see, this Gothic Revival church has a spectacular interior.

2. Hôtel de Ville (p51)
Montréal's handsome City Hall is both an administrative center and an icon of the separatist movement.

3. Fall in Montréal
Colorful trees and Marché Bonsecours (p51) are reflected in the St Lawrence river.

4. Chapelle Notre-Dame-de-Bonsecours (p50)
The 'Lady of the Harbor' statue stands atop this enchanting chapel, which is also known as the Sailors' Church.

MLENNY / GETTY IMAGES ©

THE GREY NUNS

Born in Varennes, Québec, in 1701, Marguerite d'Youville was initially known as the wife of a bootlegger, François d'Youville, who had a bad reputation for selling liquor to indigenous people on the black market. When he died of illness at age 30, Marguerite decided to dedicate her life to help the poor in an age where there was no social welfare. Fired by a religious devotion, her work drew other women to her cause. In those days, drunks were described as being *grisé par l'alcool* (grey from alcohol) and memories of François' profiteering earned the sisters the derisive nickname Les Soeurs Grises (the Grey Nuns). Undaunted, they founded a religious order in 1737 and 10 years later were granted a charter to run the General Hospital of Montréal, caring for orphans, prostitutes, the elderly and the poor. Marguerite, who died at the hospital in 1771, retained the name Grey Nuns to remind the sisters of their humble beginnings. She was canonized in 1990, becoming Canada's first homegrown saint.

Opened in 1847, the building has played a wide-ranging role in the city's history. It's been everything from a farmers market to a concert theater, and even served briefly as Montréal's city hall (1852–78).

It's also where the government of United Canada retreated, in order to continue the legislative session after the parliament buildings nearby were burned down by an angry Anglo mob in 1849.

LIEU HISTORIQUE DE SIR GEORGE-ÉTIENNE-CARTIER   MUSEUM

Map p268 (☑514-283-2282; www.parkscanada. gc.ca/cartier; 458 Rue Notre-Dame Est; adult/child $4/2; ☺10am-5pm Wed-Sun late Jun–early Sep, 10am-5pm Fri-Sun early Sep–late Dec & early May–late Jun; Ⓜ Champ-de-Mars) The Sir George-Étienne Cartier National Historic Site consists of two historic houses owned by the Cartier family. Exhibitions in the first detail the life of Sir George-Étienne Cartier, one of the founders of the Canadian Confederation, and illustrate the changes that society saw in his lifetime. The other house is a faithful reconstruction of his home during the Victorian era. Staff in period costume run guided tours throughout the day and hold dramatic presentations on etiquette and a servant's life.

In season, the program includes a Victorian Christmas.

COURS LE ROYER   SQUARE

Map p268 (Ⓜ Place-d'Armes) Montréal's first hospital was founded on this narrow lane by Jeanne Mance in 1644. Later a huge commercial complex was built here, leaving several beautiful 19th-century warehouses behind. The buildings caught the eyes of developers in the 1970s and were convert-

ed into apartments and offices. Today the buildings line this quiet pedestrian mall pocked with lush greenery.

MUSÉE DES SOEURS-GRISES   MUSEUM

Map p268 (☑514-842-9411; www.sgm.qc.ca; 138 Rue St-Pierre; ☺appointment only 9:30-11:30am & 1:30-4pm Wed-Sun; Ⓜ Square-Victoria) FREE Dedicated to St Marguerite d'Youville, founder of the community of the Sisters of Charity, better known as the Grey Nuns, this museum has a small but wonderfully presented set of exhibits. Tours of the museum in French and English are available by appointment only.

RUE ST-PAUL   STREET

Map p268 (Ⓜ Place-d'Armes) This narrow cobblestone street, the oldest in Montréal, was once a dirt road packed tight by horses laden with goods bound for the Old Port. Today it's a shopping street with galleries, boutiques and restaurants, touristy in spots but undeniably picturesque and enjoyable to wander.

PLACE ROYALE   SQUARE

Map p268 (Ⓜ Place-d'Armes) This little square in the west of Old Montréal marks the spot where the first fort, Ville-Marie, was erected. Defense was a key consideration due to lengthy fighting with the Iroquois Indians. In the 17th and 18th centuries this was a marketplace; it's now the paved forecourt of the 1836 **Old Customs House** (Vieille Douane; Map p268; Pl Royale) and linked to the Musée d'Archéologie et d'Histoire Pointe-à-Callière (p49) by an underground passage.

The neoclassical building looks much the same today as when it was built, but now serves as the museum's gift shop.

RUE DE L'HÔPITAL & AROUND
NEIGHBORHOOD

Map p268 (MPlace-d'Armes) Named for a hospice set up by nuns in the 17th century, the Rue de l'Hôpital and adjoining streets are full of architectural quirks and highlights. On the corner of Rue St-François-Xavier, the **Canadian Pacific Telegraph Chambers** was the 19th-century equivalent of a national internet provider. It houses condominiums today but the wild-eyed keystone over the entrance remains. The **Lewis Building** was built as the head office of the Cunard Shipping Lines.

One mischievous character on the facade is holding a bag full of loot; a more scholarly colleague is taking notes. The Centaur Theatre performs English-language plays in the old Montréal Stock Exchange building. Opened in 1903, the huge columns recall imperial Rome while the interior has sumptuous marble and wood paneling.

COURTHOUSES
NOTABLE BUILDINGS

Map p268 (MPlace-d'Armes) Along the north side of Rue Notre-Dame Est near Place Jacques-Cartier stand three courthouses. The most fetching is the neoclassical **Vieux Palais de Justice**, Montréal's old justice palace and oldest courthouse (1856) that's now an annex of the Hôtel de Ville. It's a popular backdrop for wedding photos.

The **Édifice Ernest Cormier** from the 1920s was used for criminal trials before being turned into a conservatory and later a court of appeal. The ugly stepsister is the oversized **Palais de Justice**, built in 1971 when concrete and smoked glass were all the rage.

PLACE JEAN-PAUL-RIOPELLE
SQUARE

Map p268 (cnr Ave Viger Ouest & Rue de Bleury; ⊘ring of fire every hour 6:30-10:30pm mid-May–mid-Oct; MPlace-d'Armes) The big draw of this square by the Palais Des Congrès is the **fountain** that releases a ring of fire (and an ethereal mist) at certain times of year. The fountain and sculpture by Jean-Paul Riopelle (1923–2002), called *La Joute* (The Joust), was inaugurated here in 2003. During the day this area is filled with nearby office workers having lunch, but summer nights are a big draw – that's when the pyrotechnics take place.

SQUARE VICTORIA
SQUARE

Map p276 (MSquare-Victoria) In the 19th century this was a Victorian garden in a swanky district of Second Empire homes and offices. Today Square Victoria is a triangle of manicured greenery and water jets in the midst of modern skyscrapers. The only vestige of the period is a statue of Queen Victoria (1872). The art-nouveau entrance railing to the metro station was a gift from the city of Paris for Expo '67.

PALAIS DES CONGRÈS
NOTABLE BUILDING

Map p268 (☑514-871-8122; www.congresmtl. com; 201 Ave Viger Ouest; MPlace-d'Armes) Entering the hall of this convention center with its facade of popsicle-colored panes is akin to strolling through a kaleidoscope. Day brings out the colors, night the transparency. The cutting-edge Palais integrates

---

A CAPITAL EXPERIMENT

Montréal would have a very different place in history but for a boozy rabble and a few newspaper articles. When the city became the capital of the United Provinces of Canada in 1844, the government moved into a two-story limestone building on the elongated Place d'Youville, which at the time was a public market. It was here that Canada's first prime minister, John A Macdonald, made his inaugural speech to a joint French–English parliament.

Montréal's tenure as capital came to an abrupt end in 1849. Egged on by inflammatory editorials in the *Gazette*, an anglophone mob set fire to the assembly and the building burned to a crisp. The crowd was protesting a law that would require the Crown to compensate French Canadians for damages inflicted by the British army in the rebellion of 1837. As a consequence Montréal lost its status as capital, and the seat of government shifted back and forth between Québec City and Toronto until 1858, when Queen Victoria declared Ottawa the new capital.

Nothing was saved from the flames except a legislative mace and a portrait of Queen Victoria; the latter now hangs in the federal parliament building in Ottawa. The location of the first Canadian parliament (the east end of the square) is today a parking lot.

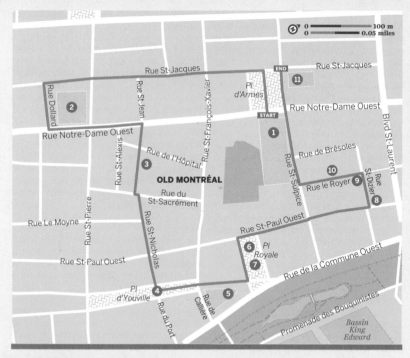

Neighborhood Walk
Art & Architecture in Old Montréal

START BASILIQUE NOTRE-DAME
END PL D'ARMES
LENGTH 2KM, TWO HOURS

On the southeast of Pl d'Armes plaza is the city's most celebrated cathedral, magnificent **1 Basilique Notre-Dame** (p48). Inside is a spectacularly carved pulpit and richly hued stained-glass windows relating key events from the city's founding.

Head along Rue St-Jacques, once known as Canada's Wall Street. Stop at the grand **2 Royal Bank Building** (p50; Montréal's tallest edifice in 1928), to see its palatial interior.

Loop onto Rue Notre-Dame and down Rue St-Jean. On the corner of Rue de l'Hôpital, the **3 Lewis Building** has dragons and mischievous gargoyles on the facade. It was built for Cunard Shipping Lines, a steamship company founded in 1840.

A few blocks further is **4 Place d'Youville**, one of Old Montréal's prettiest squares. Some of the first Europeans settled here in 1642. An obelisk commemorates the city's founding. Nearby is fascinating **5 Musée d'Archéologie et d'Histoire Pointe-à-Callière** (p49). Inside see the city's ancient foundations, or go to the top floor for views over the Old Port.

Across the road is the 1836 **6 Old Customs House** (p54). It's in front of **7 Place Royale** (p54), the early settlement's marketplace in the 17th and 18th centuries.

Walk down Rue St-Paul to see the 2006 bronze sculpture **8 Les Chuchoteuses** (the Whisperers), tucked in a corner near Rue St-Dizier. This was one of many projects to revitalize the old quarter.

Head up St-Dizier and turn left onto lovely **9 Cours Le Royer** (p54), a tranquil pedestrian mall with fountains. On the north-side passageway is a **10 stained-glass window of Jérôme Le Royer**, one of Montréal's founders.

Turn right on St-Sulpice and return to Pl d'Armes. Note the **11 New York Life Insurance Building** (p49), Montréal's first skyscraper (1888), eight stories tall.

several historic buildings: a 1908 fire station, the art-deco Tramways building from 1928 and a Victorian-era office complex. Immediately east of the Palais lies a landscaped garden with stone pathways linking 31 heaps of earth, each topped off with Montréal's official tree, the crab apple.

⊙ Old Port

QUAI ALEXANDRA & AROUND   PIER
Map p268 (Ⓜ Place-d'Armes) This easternmost pier in the port is home to the Iberville Passenger Terminal, the dock for cruise ships that ply the St Lawrence River as far as the Magdalen Islands out in the Gulf of St Lawrence. Nearby, the **Parc des Écluses** (Park of Locks) holds exhibitions of landscape architecture, shows and concerts. A bicycle path starts here and runs southeast along the pretty Canal de Lachine.

The abandoned 17-story-tall concrete silo on the south side of the locks is the last big relic of Montréal's heyday as a grain port.

QUAI JACQUES-CARTIER & AROUND   PIER
Map p268 (Ⓜ Champ-de-Mars) This pier is the anchor of the Old Port area, home to restaurants, an open-air stage and a handicraft center. Every year the port stages a number of temporary exhibits, shows and events. Montréal's world-renowned Cirque du Soleil performs under its eye-catching big top here in warmer months. Tours of the port area depart from the pier, and a ferry can take you to Parc Jean-Drapeau.

The ferry can also stop at Parc de la Cité-du-Havre, where there's a restaurant and picnic tables, as well as the nearby Habitat 67 building.

PARC DU BASSIN BONSECOURS   PARK
Map p268 (Ⓜ Champ-de-Mars) Perched over the river, this grassy expanse is enclosed by a waterway and crisscrossed with footbridges. In summer you can rent paddleboats or remote-control model sailboats; in winter the ice-skaters take over at the Patinoire (p65). There's a well-placed bistro with outdoor seating in the summer.

CENTRE DES SCIENCES
DE MONTRÉAL   MUSEUM
Map p268 (Montréal Science Centre; www.montrealsciencecentre.com; King Edward Pier; adult/teen/child $15/13/9, with IMAX 3D movie $23/20/14; ⊘9am-4pm Mon-Fri, 10am-5pm Sat

& Sun; Ⓜ Place-d'Armes) This sleek, glass-covered science center houses virtual and interactive games, technology exhibits and an 'immersion theater' that puts a video game on giant screens. Note that there is a huge range of different admission prices depending on which combinations of films and/or exhibits you want to take in. The center also has an IMAX cinema that shows vivid nature and science films.

RUE DE LA COMMUNE   STREET
Map p268 (Ⓜ Champ-de-Mars) Set back from the waterfront, 'the Common' is a showcase of the rejuvenation that has swept Old Montréal. Compare it with old photos and you'll see the warehouses and factory buildings haven't changed much on the outside, but the tenants are upmarket hotels, restaurants and converted condos. Though the street has lost its raw, industrial feel, the original stone walls can still be viewed inside many buildings.

SAILORS' MEMORIAL
CLOCK TOWER   MONUMENT
Map p268 (Quai de l'Horloge; ⊘10am-7pm mid-Mar–Dec; Ⓜ Champ-de-Mars) At the eastern edge of the historic port stands the striking white Tour de l'Horloge. This notable clock commemorates all of the sailors and shipmen who died in the world wars. Visitors can climb the 192 steps for a view over Old Montréal and the river.

✕ EATING

Vieux-Montréal has experienced a culinary renaissance in recent years, with a number of acclaimed restaurants winning over discerning diners and food critics alike. Here you'll find top-notch Québecois and fusion fare, among some of the city's most atmospheric dining rooms (it's hard to beat the 18th-century backdrop). That said, Old Montréal still has plenty of touristy restaurants (mostly along Place Jacques-Cartier) where quantity not quality is the name of the game. The touristy-local divide is roughly Blvd St-Laurent, with the better restaurants lying to the west of this iconic street.

Billowy steam and scrumptious odors waft out of kitchens and into the streets of Montréal's tiny but lively Chinatown.

You'll find Cantonese, Vietnamese and even Mongolian eateries along Blvd St-Laurent and the pedestrian Rue de la Gauchetière.

✕ Old Montréal

TITANIC
SANDWICHES $

Map p268 (445 Rue St-Pierre; sandwiches around $10; ⊗8am-4pm Mon-Fri; ⏴🖉; Ⓜ Square-Victoria) The sandwiches here have office workers scurrying to these cramped basement quarters from all over Old Montréal on their lunch breaks. The varieties are endless and can include grilled veggies with feta, smoked salmon with sweet roasted peppers or roast beef with horseradish. Excellent salads, soup, quiche and antipasto misto are popular takeouts that round out the mix.

SOUPESOUP
CAFE $

Map p268 (www.soupesoup.com; 649 Rue Wellington; soups $4-7; ⊗7am-8pm Mon-Fri, 11am-4pm Sat & Sun; Ⓜ Square-Victoria) The brainchild of chef, writer and all-around soup-lover Caroline Dumas, this warm cafeteria-like eatery housed in a former factory offers more than 200 varieties of soup, as well as sandwiches and salads. It's one of eight locations in the city.

CAFÉ DIFFÉRANCE
CAFE $

Map p268 (www.cafedifferance.ca; 449 Ave Viger Ouest; pastries $2-3; ⊗7:15am-5pm Mon-Fri, 9am-4pm Sat, 10am-4pm Sun; ⏴; Ⓜ Square-Victoria) Hipster baristas whip up delightfully smooth lattes at this bright little espresso bar on the edge of Old Montréal to a mostly hurried professional crowd. Big windows, tall ceilings and great pastries make Café Différance a fine pitstop before venturing in or out of the old city.

CAFÉ SANTÉ VERITAS
CAFE $

Map p268 (www.cafesanteveritas.com; 480 Blvd St-Laurent; mains $7-13; ⊗7am-7pm Mon-Fri, 10am-6pm Sat & Sun; ⏴; Ⓜ Place-d'Armes) Serving coffee brewed from beans from Vancouver's 49th Parallel Roasters, this bright little cafe and snack spot whips up excellent java. The health-oriented kitchen menu features low-fat, low-carb choices such as Cajun chicken salad, as well as veggie sandwiches and mouthwatering breakfast crepes.

★OLIVE + GOURMANDO
CAFE $$

Map p268 (www.oliveetgourmando.com; 351 Rue St-Paul Ouest; mains $10-17; ⊗8am-5pm Tue-Sat; 🖉; Ⓜ Square-Victoria) Named after the owners' two cats, this bakery-cafe is legendary in town for its hot panini, plump salads and flaky baked goods. Excellent choices include the melted goat's-cheese panini with carmelized onions, decadent mac 'n' cheese, and 'the Cubain' (a ham, roast pork and Gruyère sandwich).

You'll also find decent morning choices (poached eggs, granola, housemade ricotta and toast) and fresh loaves for takeout (including olive and rosemary bread). Try to avoid the lunch rush (11:30am to 1:30pm).

LE SERPENT
ITALIAN $$

Map p268 (☎514-316-4666; www.leserpent.ca; 257 Rue Prince; mains $16-32; ⊗11:30am-2pm Tue-Fri & 6-11pm Mon-Sat; Ⓜ Square-Victoria) Industrial style dominates at this renovated factory next to the Fonderie Darling art space, which draws a creative tech-industry crowd. The menu features a creative mix of risottos and pastas (such as bucatini with pork confit) and a handful of well-executed seafood and meat dishes (veal filet with ricotta tortellini), plus a changing daily special.

DA EMMA
ITALIAN $$

Map p268 (☎514-392-1568; 777 Rue de la Commune Ouest; mains $21-42; ⊗noon-2pm Mon-Fri, 6-10:30pm Mon-Sat; Ⓜ Square-Victoria) The old stone walls and beamed ceiling of this atmospheric place – a former women's prison – today provide the backdrop to delicious Italian cooking. Osso buco, fresh grilled fish, agnolotti with stuffed veal and satisfying homemade pasta with mushrooms are the top picks from the changing menu. Reservations are recommended.

LE CARTET
CAFE $$

Map p268 (www.lecartet.com; 106 Rue McGill; mains $11-20; ⊗7am-7pm Mon-Fri, 9am-4pm Sat & Sun; ⏴; Ⓜ Square-Victoria) A great anytime place, Le Cartet has a spacious interior where you can stop in for crepes or eggs in the morning, sandwiches or salads for lunch, and coffee and desserts at other times. There's also a small shop that sells artisanal chocolates, Québec jams and cheeses, and delicious brioche.

You can also get your meal to go and head to the waterfront.

RESTAURANT HOLDER BISTRO $$
Map p268 (☑514-849-0333; www.restaurant holder.com; 407 Rue McGill; mains $18-28; ⊘11:30am-11pm Mon-Fri, 10am-3pm & 5:30-10pm Sat & Sun; MSquare-Victoria) High ceilings, a warm color scheme and beautifully turned-out dishes are just part of the appeal of this classic bistro on busy Rue McGill. It's a buzzing place (sometimes quite noisy), where the crowd – good-looking media and corporate types – dines on lobster ravioli, grilled hangar steak, pan-seared tilapia and other bistro classics.

BORIS BISTRO BISTRO $$
Map p268 (☑514-848-9575; www.borisbistro.com; 465 Rue McGill; mains $19-29; ⊘noon-11pm Jun-Aug, 11:30am-2pm Mon-Fri, 6-10pm Tue-Sat Sep-May; MSquare-Victoria) You'll be elbowing your way through everyone from Armani-clad executives to disheveled artists to get a table at this popular bistro – book ahead. Once settled, you can feast on a mouthwatering assortment of dishes, including artfully presented salads, a much-touted duck risotto with oyster mushrooms or favorites such as roasted sea bass on asparagus risotto.

BEVO ITALIAN $$
Map p268 (☑514-861-5039; 410 Rue St-Vincent; pizzas $13-21; ⊘4-11pm Sun-Wed, to 2am Thu-Sat; MPlace-d'Armes) In a smartly renovated 1850s stone building, this pizzeria delivers reliably tasty pies from its wood-fired oven including pizzas topped with all manner of prosciutto and pepperoni. Porcini risotto, veal poutine and roasted pork loin round out the menu, while the interior old-world stone and brick contrast with a stylish bar.

The scene spills out onto Rue St-Vincent in the summer for alfresco dining.

STASH CAFÉ POLISH $$
Map p268 (☑514-845-6611; www.stashcafe.com; 200 Rue St-Paul Ouest; mains $12-19; ⊘noon-10pm; MPlace-d'Armes) Hearty Polish cuisine is served up with good humor in a dining room with seats made of church pews and daringly low red lights illuminating the tables. Staff range from gregarious to stand-offish, but the food is consistent, with quality fare such as pierogi (dumplings stuffed with meat or cheese, with sour cream) and potato pancakes with apple sauce.

GANDHI INDIAN $$
Map p268 (www.restaurantgandhi.com; 230 Rue St-Paul Ouest; mains $14-25; ⊘noon-2pm Mon-Fri, 5:30-10:30pm daily; MSquare-Victoria) Gandhi has a core of loyal fans who come here for classics like tandoori chicken as well as the extensive curry menu with adventurous fare such as *malaya*, a curry of pineapple, lychees and cream. The vegetable samosas are finely spiced, and faves such as lamb tikka and butter chicken also go down nicely. Reservations are recommended.

BOCATA INTERNATIONAL $$$
Map p268 (☑514-507-8727; www.bocata.ca; 310 Rue St-Paul; mains $19-34; ⊘5-10:30pm; MSquare-Victoria) Like its sibling restaurant Barroco next door, Bocata has abundant old-world charm with stone walls and low ceilings – and a dash of new-world verve with its groovy music selection. The menu is wide-ranging, but the seafood is the highlight, with whole lobster, roasted black cod and squid-ink risotto among the favorites. It has a great wine selection.

★**BARROCO** INTERNATIONAL $$$
Map p268 (☑514-544-5800; www.barroco.ca; 312 Rue St-Paul Ouest; mains $22-39; ⊘6-10:30pm; MSquare-Victoria) Small, cozy Barroco has stone walls, flickering candles and beautifully presented plates of roast duck, braised short ribs and grilled fish. The selection is small, but you can't go wrong here, particularly if you opt for the outstanding seafood and chorizo paella.

Don't miss the exceptional cocktail menu, cleverly pasted into a hard-back volume. Fun staff and a jazzy soundtrack add to the buzzing atmosphere.

GARDE-MANGER INTERNATIONAL $$$
Map p268 (☑514-678-5044; www.crownsalts.com/gardemanger; 409 Rue St-François-Xavier;

A RIDE IN THE CALÈCHE

Horse-drawn carriages are one of the most popular and romantic ways to see downtown. Calèche drivers pony up in front of Pl d'Armes and next to Pl Jacques-Cartier by the Old Port. You can even sometimes score sleigh rides through Parc du Mont-Royal once the winter weather arrives. Drivers have a fair bit of knowledge about the old quarters and will happily rattle off some history along the way. A half-hour ride is $48, one hour is $80.

mains $34-40; ⏰5:30pm-midnight Tue-Sun; Ⓜ Place-d'Armes) The buzz surrounding Garde-Manger has barely let up since its opening back in 2006. This small, candlelit restaurant attracts a mix of local scenesters and haute-cuisine-loving out-of-towners who come for lobster risotto, short ribs, Cornish hen stuffed with foie gras (see p28) and other changing chalkboard specials. The stage is set with stone walls, great cocktails and a decidedly not-stuffy vibe.

It's loud and festive, so not the place for an intimate dinner. Reservations essential.

TAPAS, 24 SPANISH $$$
Map p268 (420 Notre-Dame Ouest; tapas $6-20, mains $25-30; ⏰11:30am-11pm Mon-Fri, 5-11pm Sat; Ⓜ Square-Victoria) Celebrated Catalan chef Carles Abellan brings a bit of Barcelona magic to the new world with this outstanding addition to Old Montréal – his first foray outside of Spain. Mouth-watering dishes include razor clams, garlic shrimp, Galician-style octopus and Iberian ham, as well as heartier plates of *fideua* (Catalan-style paella). Prix-fixe lunch ($15) and dinner ($39) menus are a great way to sample the goods.

BREMNER INTERNATIONAL $$$
Map p268 (☑514-544-0446; www.lebremner. ca; 361 Rue St-Paul; mains $32-40; ⏰6-11pm Mon-Sat; Ⓜ Champ-de-Mars) Celebrated chef Chuck Hughes (the mastermind behind Garde-Manger) has wowed his fans with this subterranean, low-lit haunt across from the Marché Bonsecours. The menu changes regularly and features fried quail, crab and kimchi toast, succulent grilled sea bream and roast pork chop with clams.

The vibe: laid-back servers, hip hop playing overhead and a preparty crowd sipping first-rate cocktails (try the Negronis). The entrance is unmarked; look for number 361 above the stairs. Reservations are essential.

L'ORIGNAL QUÉBECOIS $$$
Map p268 (☑514-303-0479; www.restaurant lorignal.com; 479 Rue St-Alexis; mains $25-38; ⏰6pm-midnight Mon-Wed, to 3am Thu-Sat; Ⓜ Place-d'Armes) This cozy chalet-style restaurant specializes in exquisitely prepared game meat and fresh seafood. Start with oysters or venison-heart tartare before moving on to braised wild boar or crusted cod with caviar. The service is excellent and the cedar-filled dining room is a great spot to linger over a memorable meal.

Its modest bar makes a great spot for a drink, but the official policy is that customers have to be dining as well.

LE LOCAL FRENCH $$$
Map p268 (☑514-397-7737; www.resto-lelocal. com; 740 Rue William; mains $25-32; ⏰11:30am-10pm Mon-Fri, from 5:30pm Sat & Sun; Ⓜ Square-Victoria) On the western edge of Old Montréal, Le Local serves delectable fare in an architecturally stunning dining room. Well-dressed 20- and 30-somethings feast on inventive dishes with market-fresh ingredients to the backdrop of unobtrusive electronica. There's an outdoor terrace and an extensive wine list (and an award-winning sommelier). Reservations recommended.

TOQUÉ! FRENCH $$$
Map p268 (☑514-499-2084; www.restaurant-toque.com; 900 Pl Jean-Paul-Riopelle; mains $42-52; ⏰11:30am-1:45pm Tue-Fri, 5:30-10pm Tue-Sat; Ⓜ Square-Victoria) Chef Normand Laprise has earned rave reviews for his innovative recipes based on products sourced from local farms. The bright, wide-open dining room has a glass-enclosed wine cave with suspended bottles looming. The seven-course *menu dégustation* ($120) is the pinnacle of dining in Montréal – allow three hours for the feast.

LE CLUB CHASSE ET PÊCHE FRENCH $$$
Map p268 (☑514-861-1112; www.leclubchasseet peche.com; 423 Rue St-Claude; mains $36-40; ⏰6-10:30pm Tue-Sat year-round, noon-2:30pm Tue-Sat early Jun–Sep; Ⓜ Champ-de-Mars) One of the pillars of Old Montréal's grand dining scene, this elegant restaurant serves fantastic new-wave French fare, including roast suckling pork and sautéed scallops with fennel and citron confit. Given the prices, it's a favorite among execs and Montréalers celebrating a special occasion.

In the summer, eat lunch alfresco in the Château Ramezay garden over the road.

GIBBY'S STEAK $$$
Map p268 (☑514-282-1837; www.gibbys.com; 298 Pl d'Youville; mains $35-54; ⏰5:30-11pm; Ⓜ Square-Victoria) A purveyor of the good old-fashioned steak, Gibby's serves excellent grilled meats and seafood, including a respected rack of lamb. A mix of corporate types clink glasses inside the elegant stone building dating back to the 1700s. There's an open courtyard in the back.

✕ Chinatown

MAI XIANG YUAN   CHINESE $
Map p268 (1084 Blvd St-Laurent; mains $6-10; ⊙11am-9pm Mon-Sun; MPlace-d'Armes) You'd be hard-pressed to find better dumplings in Montréal than the perfect little bits of heaven, pan-fried or steamed, served in this humble hole-in-the-wall. Each plate comes with 15 dumplings and fillings include everything from lamb and onion to pork and leek, as well as tomato and egg for vegetarians.

NOODLE FACTORY   CHINESE $
Map p268 (www.restonoodlefactory.com; 1018 Rue St-Urbain; mains $8-12; ⊙11am-10pm; MPlace-d'Armes) Noodle fanatics roll up to this bustling hole-in-the-wall for chef Lin Kwong Cheung's famed homemade noodles. You can watch him in the open kitchen kneading the dough into fine strips before devouring it yourself. Cash only.

PHO BANG NEW YORK   VIETNAMESE $
Map p268 (📞514-954-2032; 1001 Blvd St-Laurent; mains $10-16; ⊙10am-9:30pm; MPlace-d'Armes) Near the gateway to Chinatown, Pho Bang New York has decor and service geared more toward Westerners who want to have their *pho* (noodle soups) in swisher digs. The food is good and regularly turns up on people's 'top' lists, but it lacks the manic energy that makes the other Vietnamese places on this drag so atmospheric.

BEIJING   CHINESE $
Map p268 (📞514-861-2003; www.restaurantbeijing.net; 92 Rue de la Gauchetière Ouest; mains $10-17; ⊙11:30am-3am; MPlace-d'Armes) Every Montréaler has a favorite Chinatown restaurant, a familiar place where a warm welcome awaits when turning up in the neighborhood. The unassuming and always-buzzing Beijing tops many lists, with a reputation built on tasty, fresh Cantonese and Szechuan dishes, friendly service and late-night hours.

HOANG OANH   VIETNAMESE $
Map p268 (📞514-954-0053; 1071 Blvd St-Laurent; sandwiches around $4; ⊙9am-6:30pm; MPlace-d'Armes) The Vietnamese baguette sandwiches here are the very best in Chinatown. There's an endless choice of fillings but the grilled chicken or the tofu varieties topped with mayonnaise, veggies and coriander are pretty much unbeatable.

★ORANGE ROUGE   ASIAN $$
Map p268 (📞514-861-1116; www.orangerouge.ca; 106 de la Gauchetière Ouest; small plates $7-17; ⊙11:30am-2:30pm Tue-Fri, 5:30-10:30pm Tue-Sat; MPlace-d'Armes) Hidden down a narrow lane, Orange Rouge has a quaint, low-lit interior that's rather nondescript save for the bright open kitchen at one end and a neon-lit crab sculpture on the wall. Grab a seat at the dark lacquered bar or on one of the banquettes for a feast of Asian fusion. Recent hits include chrysanthemum salad, shrimp and cabbage *okonomiyaki* (Japanese pancake) and fried rice with softshell crab. With great cocktails, a speakeasy-like interior and eclectic dishes, there's nowhere else like it in Chinatown.

LA MAISON KAM FUNG   CHINESE $$
Map p268 (📞514-878-2888; www.restaurantchinatownkimfung.com; 1111 Rue St-Urbain; mains $9-16; ⊙7am-3pm & 4:30-10pm; MPlace-d'Armes) This is generally considered the best place in town for dim sum, and is especially popular for Saturday and Sunday brunch. Waiters circle the tables with carts of dim sum ($3 to $7 each) – you pick and choose from tender dumplings, spare ribs, mushrooms, spicy shrimp and much more.

The entrance is hidden in the rear of a shopping passage up an escalator. Reservations recommended.

LITTLE SHEEP HOT POT   MONGOLIAN $$
Map p268 (50 Rue de la Gauchetiere; all-you-can-eat lunch/dinner $14/20; ⊙11am-10pm; MPlace-d'Armes) For something different, head upstairs to this clean, well-lit dining room, where you can feast on juicy morsels of lamb, shitake mushrooms, noodles, watercress and tofu. You pick your ingredients, which are brought raw to your tableside for you to cook up in the simmering hot pot.

🍷 DRINKING & NIGHTLIFE

🍸 Old Montréal

★PHILÉMON   CLUB
Map p268 (www.philemonbar.com; 111 Rue St-Paul Ouest; ⊙5pm-3am Mon-Sat, from 6pm Sun; MPlace-d'Armes) A major stop for local scenesters rotating between watering holes

in the old city, Philémon was carved out of stone, brick and wood with large windows looking out over Rue St-Paul. Twenty-somethings fill the space around a huge central bar sipping basic cocktails and nibbling on light fare (oysters, charcuterie plates, smoked-meat sandwiches), while a DJ spins house and hip-hop.

★ TERRASSE NELLIGAN   BAR

Map p268 (www.terrassenelligan.com; 106 Rue St-Pau Ouest; ⊙11:30am-11:30pm summer; Ⓜ Place-d'Armes) Above heritage Hôtel Nelligan, this delightful patio is the perfect spot to down a mojito while the sun sinks. There's a full menu for lunch and dinner, and splendid views over the St Lawrence River and the Old Port. It's less of a scene than Terrasse Place d'Armes but equally enjoyable.

VELVET   CLUB

Map p268 (www.velvetspeakeasy.ca; 426 Rue St-Gabriel; ⊙10pm-3am Thu-Sat; Ⓜ Champ-de-Mars) Who knew that an inn dating from 1754 could be so hip? Beneath restaurant Auberge St-Gabriel, walk through a long, candlelit stone passageway to this grooving grotto of electronic beats done up like a speakeasy of yore. Fashionistas and scenesters flock here, and there's often a long lineup outside. The other downside: there's usually a lot more guys than gals here.

LE CONFESSIONNAL   BAR

Map p268 (www.confessionnal.ca; 431 Rue McGill; ⊙5pm-3am Tue-Fri, from 8pm Sat; Ⓜ Square-Victoria) Playing heavily on churchy themes, Le Confessionnal is a tempting spot to rack up a few sins. It has low red lighting, a glowing alabaster-like bar and low-hanging

---

LOCAL KNOWLEDGE

PROMENADE DU VIEUX-PORT

In warm weather the Promenade du Vieux-Port is a favorite recreation spot for both joggers and in-line skaters, while cyclists can take in the view from the city bike path that runs parallel to it. There is also plenty of green space for those seeking a little relaxation or for phenomenal views of the L'International des Feux Loto-Québec. In winter, skating at the outdoor rink, with the St Lawrence River shimmering nearby, may well warm your soul, but it will leave the rest of you quite chilly.

---

chandeliers, with old-school R&B playing overhead. Signature cocktails loosely reference the seven deadly sins (try 'Le Lazy Boy' with tequila, agave, citron frais and Hoegarden), and there are DJs on weekends.

LES SOEURS GRISES   PUB

Map p268 (www.bblsg.com; 32 Rue McGill; ⊙11:30am-11pm Sun-Thu to 3am Fri & Sat; Ⓜ Square-Victoria) Named after the famous Montréal religious order of nuns founded by St Marguerite d'Youville, this swanky bistro-brasserie is equal parts microbrewery and smokehouse, serving a winning combination of brews and bites. Grab some smoked baby-back ribs, candied pheasant thighs or smoked trout and wash it down with excellent house beers.

Try the Camélia – a white beer with a hint of floral and green-tea finish. Its location near the Old Port bike path makes it a good spot to unwind after cycling the Canal de Lachine.

TERRASSE PLACE D'ARMES   BAR

Map p268 (☑514-904-1201; www.terrasseplacedarmes.com; 8th fl, 710 Côte de la Pl d'Armes; ⊙11am-3am summer; Ⓜ Place-d'Armes) The rooftop terrace above the boutique Hôtel Place-d'Armes is a requisite stop on the nightlife circuit if you're around during the summer. Nicely mixed cocktails, eclectic cuisine and a fantastic view over Pl d'Armes and the Basilique Notre-Dame never fail to bring in the beautiful crowd.

TAVERNE GASPAR   PUB

Map p268 (www.tavernegaspar.com; 89 Rue de la Commune Est; ⊙5pm-midnight; Ⓜ Champ-de-Mars) Facing the Old Port, this cozy watering hole in the Auberge du Vieux Port has delicious faux-retro decor, a long zinc bar, and a menu with lobster sliders, oysters, fish and chips, and a delish mac 'n' cheese. The house brew is the Gaspar lager, and other local beers include St-Ambroise suds.

L'ASSOMMOIR   PUB

Map p268 (www.assommoir.ca; 211 Rue Notre-Dame Ouest; ⊙5pm-2am Sun-Wed, 3pm-3am Thu-Sat; Ⓜ Place-d'Armes) Like its sister pub in Mile-End, L'Assommoir is home to a beautiful long bar that makes a great place to start the night with a house cocktail such as the GHB (gin, chartreuse, kiwi, maple syrup and a bit of apple and pear juice) and a few snacks (fried calamari or mixed ceviche).

CLUB PEOPL
CLUB

Map p268 (www.clubpeopl.com; 390 Notre-Dame Ouest; ⊙10pm-3am Wed-Sat; MSquare-Victoria) With its edgy, art-covered walls and chic lighting, this basement venue reels in 20- and 30-somethings with its electro-house, live jazz, and many sofas in the relaxing lounge. Enter on Rue Ste-Hélène.

WUNDERBAR
LOUNGE

Map p268 (☑514-395-3100; www.wunderbar montreal.com; 901 Sq Victoria; ⊙4pm-3am Mon-Sat, 5pm-1am Sun; MSquare-Victoria) This modern room in the W Hotel is among the city's safest bets for a soiree on the town. Weekly DJ nights attract a well-dressed, dance-loving crowd.

PUB ST-PAUL
PUB

Map p268 (☑514-874-0485; www.pubstpaul.com; 124 Rue St-Paul Est; ⊙11:30am-3am; MChamp-de-Mars) In the heart of Old Montréal's most touristy drag is this rock pub, a hit among students, jocks and passersby. A lunch and dinner menu of upscale pub fare is served, live bands rock out weekend nights, and drink specials complete the Top 40 formula.

FLYJIN
COCKTAIL BAR

Map p268 (☑514-564-8881; www.flyjin.ca; 417 Rue St-Pierre; ⊙7pm-3am Mon-Sat; MSquare-Victoria) Flyjin walks a fine line between speakeasy and high-end Asian brasserie, serving up tender sashimi, tuna tataki and green papaya salad to a party-minded crowd who are equally interested in the finely crafted cocktails (such as sake mojitos and cachaça-dragon fruit combos). It has a barely marked entrance leading to the subterranean but beautifully designed space.

🍸 Chinatown

LE MAL NECESSAIRE
COCKTAIL BAR

Map p268 (www.lemalnecessaire.com; 1106 Blvd St-Laurent; ⊙4:30pm-2am Tue-Fri, from 6pm Sat & Sun; MSt-Laurent) For some of the tastiest cocktails in Montréal, look for the neon-lit green pineapple and descend the stairs to this vaguely Tiki-inspired bar hidden along pedestrian-filled St Laurent. Fruity elixirs are tops here – especially the Abacaxi mai tai, served in a pineapple. You can also order pork dumplings, General Tao chicken and other simple dishes off the menu – it comes from the no-nonsense Chinese restaurant upstairs (available until 11pm).

LUWAN
CLUB

Map p268 (1050 Clark St; ⊙9pm-3am Thu-Sat; MPlace-d'Armes) Hidden down a quiet lane, Luwan draws a young, cocktail-swilling crowd who come for chatter early in the night (on banquettes with views over the lane) and dancing to hard-driving DJs as the night progresses. It's a fairly open minimalist space, but the staff is friendly and laidback, and the crowd is out for a good time.

⭐ ENTERTAINMENT

CIRQUE DU SOLEIL
THEATER

Map p268 (www.cirquedusoleil.com; Quai Jacques-Cartier; MChamp-de-Mars) Globally famous Cirque du Soleil, one of the city's most famous exports, puts on a new production of acrobats and music in this marvelous tent complex roughly once every two years in summer. These shows rarely disappoint; don't pass up a chance to see it on home turf.

CINÉMA IMAX DU CENTRE DES SCIENCES DE MONTRÉAL
CINEMA

Map p268 (☑514-496-4724; www.montreal sciencecentre.com; Quai King-Edward; MPlace-d'Armes) Located in the Centre des Sciences de Montréal, this theater brings specially produced adventure, nature and historical films to oversized screens. Watch faraway galaxies, dinosaurs or marine life come tumbling into your lap with the aid of 3D glasses and translation headsets. Great for kids.

CENTAUR THEATRE
THEATER

Map p268 (☑514-288-3161; www.centaurtheatre.com; 453 Rue St-François-Xavier; MPlace-d'Armes) Montréal's chief English-language theater presents everything from Shakespearean classics to works by experimental Canadian playwrights. It occupies Montréal's former stock exchange (1903), a striking building with classical columns.

SHOPPING

MARCHÉ BONSECOURS
SHOPPING MALL

Map p268 (www.marchebonsecours.qc.ca; 350 Rue St-Paul Est; ⊙generally 10am-6pm, to 9pm late Jun–early Sep; MChamp-de-Mars) This majestic old building has housed the Canadian parliament, city hall and, now, a collection of cute boutiques selling Québec-made wares and goodies such as fashion, accessories, jewelry and crafts. Restaurants and terraces are also on-site, and the *marché* is often used for trade shows and art events.

ZONE ORANGE   CRAFTS

Map p268 (410 Rue St-Pierre; ⊙11am-6pm Wed-Sat; ⓂSquare-Victoria) This small colorful boutique just off Rue St-Paul has unique works by different artists and artisans, whose custom-designed ceramics, jewelry, toys and housewares line the shelves. There are animal-print pillows, whimsically embroidered mobiles and illustrations of iconic Montréal sights, among other unusual finds.

ESPACE PEPIN   HOMEWARES

Map p268 (378 Rue St-Paul Ouest; ⊙10am-6pm Mon-Sat, 11am-5pm Sun; ⓂSquare-Victoria) Boasting a vintage chic aesthetic, Espace Pepin is a fun place to browse for gift ideas. You'll find items such as wood-branch pepper and spice mills, elegant glassware, lambswool blankets and colorful baskets of handwoven hemp. A few doors down (at 370 Rue St-Paul Ouest) is Pepin's fashion store, with high-end clothing and accessories.

U&I   FASHION

Map p268 (☑514-508-7704; www.boutiqueuandi. com; 215 St-Paul Ouest; ⊙10am-6pm Sat-Mon, from 11am Tue-Fri; ⓂSquare-Victoria) Specializing in outerware, this eye-catching boutique features beautifully made men's and women's garments – as well as footwear, fragrance and handbags. High-quality brands from Canada are well-represented including Canada Goose, Montréal-based Soia Kyo and Krane Design (out of Toronto).

DHC ART   GALLERY

Map p268 (http://dhc-art.org; 451 Rue St-Jean; ⊙noon-7pm Wed-Fri, 11am-6pm Sat & Sun; ⓂPlace-d'Armes) Opened in 2007, this excellent contemporary art gallery features mind-bending works by artists such as Valerie Belin, Ryoji Ikeda and Marc Quinn.

MY CUP OF TEA   FOOD & DRINK

Map p268 (www.mcot.ca; 1063 Blvd St-Laurent; ⊙11am-7pm; ⓂPlace-d'Armes) This stylish Chinatown tea shop has more than 50 tea varieties in loose and teabag form, including its popular blooming tea, which opens up from a ball once immersed. It also has a range of attractive glassware and tea containers.

GALERIE LE CHARIOT   ART

Map p268 (446 Pl Jacques-Cartier; ⊙10am-6pm; ⓂChamp-de-Mars) This arts emporium claims to have the largest Inuit collection in Canada. Choose from First Nations art carved mainly from soapstone, as well as fur hats, mountain-goat rugs and fleecy moccasins.

GALERIE ST-DIZIER   GALLERY

Map p268 (☑514-845-8411; www.saintdizier. com; 24 Rue St-Paul Ouest; ⊙11am-6pm Tue-Sun; ⓂChamp-de-Mars) This spacious old gallery has always been at the forefront of the avant-garde scene in Montréal. Works are split between local and heavyweight artists known abroad, including Besner, St-Pierre and Tetro. Its forte is naive and modernist art and sculpture.

ROONEY   FASHION

Map p268 (☑514-543-6234; www.rooneyshop. com; 395 Rue Notre-Dame Ouest; ⊙11:30am-6pm Mon-Wed, to 8pm Thu & Fri, noon-5pm Sat & Sun; ⓂSquare-Victoria) Rooney is an inviting shop with lots of stylish streetwear and accessories, with plenty of ideas to help gents score a new look. You'll find Rag & Bone button-downs, nicely cut Levis Vintage denim jackets and jeans, classic Chuck Taylors, soft Mismo wallets, classy Filson duffels and a table of art-minded fashion mags.

BOUTIQUE ANNE DE SHALLA   FASHION

Map p268 (www.annedeshalla.com; 350 Rue St-Paul Est, Maré Bonsecours; ⊙10am-6pm; ⓂChamp-de-Mars) French fashion diva Anne de Shalla studied fashion in Paris and came to Montréal in the 1970s. She now selects from up to 30 Québec designers every year for her exclusive shop collection – stretchy leathers, semisheer dresses, blouses and wrap-around casuals. It's inside the Marché Bonsecours.

🏃 SPORTS & ACTIVITIES

ÇA ROULE MONTRÉAL   BICYCLE RENTAL

Map p268 (www.caroulemontreal.com; 27 Rue de la Commune Est, Old Port; bikes per hr/day from $8/30, in-line skates 1st/additional hr $9/4; ⊙9am-8pm Apr-Oct, 10am-6pm Mar & Nov-Dec; ⓂPlace-d'Armes) Near the Old Port, Ça Roule Montréal has a wide selection of bicycles, in-line skates, spare parts and a good repair shop. Each rental includes a lock, helmet, patch kit and cycling map. You can rent children's bikes, tandems and bike trailers too. Tours are also available.

Prices listed are for weekday rentals; weekend rentals cost slightly more.

BOTA BOTA   SPA

(☑514-284-0333; www.botabota.ca; 358 Rue de la Commune Ouest; admission $35-70; ☺10am-10pm Mon-Thu, from 9am Fri-Sun; Ⓜ Square-Victoria) Bota Bota, a unique floating spa, is actually a 1950s ferry that's been retooled as an oasis on the water. It's permanently docked by the Old Port and offers a range of treatments on its five beautifully redesigned decks. The Water Circuit admission gives you access to saunas, hot tubs and the outdoor terraces.

Treatments run the gamut from manicures and pedicures to facials, wraps and full-body massages (one hour $95). There's also a restaurant on-site, serving healthy seasonal cuisine (open 11am to 8pm) and periodic yoga and pilates classes (currently Monday and Thursday nights). Admission varies depending on day and time (it's cheapest on weekdays before 11am or after 6pm).

SAUTE-MOUTONS   BOAT TOUR

(☑514-284-9607; www.jetboatingmontreal.com; 47 Rue de la Commune Ouest, Old Port; jet boat tour per adult/teen/child $67/57/47, speedboat $26/21/19; ☺10am-6pm May-Oct; Ⓜ Champs-de-Mars) Thrill-seekers will certainly get their money's worth on these fast, wet and bouncy boat tours to the Lachine Rapids. The aluminum jet boats take you through foaming white water, from Quai de l'Horloge, on hour-long tours. There are also speedboats that take 20-minute jaunts around the Parc des Îles from the Jacques Cartier pier. Reservations are a must.

PLAGE DE L'HORLOGE   BEACH

Map p268 (www.vieuxportdemontreal.com/plage-de-lhorloge.html; Old Port; ☺10:30am-7:30pm daily mid-Jun–early Sep, Sat & Sun only to late Sep; Ⓜ Champ-de-Mars) **FREE** Montréal opened this 'urban beach' along the Quai de l'Horloge in 2012, trucking in sand, Adirondack chairs, parasols and a bar. There's no swimming here, but it's a fine spot to take in views of the river and to catch some rays.

PATINOIRE DU BASSIN
BONSECOURS   SKATING

Map p268 (Parc du Bassin Bonsecours, Old Port; adult/child $7/4, skate rentals $9; ☺10am-9pm Mon-Wed, to 10pm Thu-Sat Dec–early Mar; ▣14, Ⓜ Champ-de-Mars) This is one of Montréal's most popular outdoor-skating rinks, located on the shore of the St Lawrence River next to the Pavilion du Bassin Bonsecours. DJs add to the festivities. At Christmas time there's a big nativity scene.

AML CRUISES   BOAT TOUR

Map p268 (☑514-842-9300, 866-856-6668; www.croisieresaml.com; adult/child $30/17; ☺11:30am & 2pm May–mid-Oct; Ⓜ Place-d'Armes) These 1½-hour river tours in a glassed-in sightseeing boat take in the Old Port and Île Ste-Hélène. Other options include brunch cruises and night cruises with a band, dancing and a multicourse dinner. Early and late cruises are in high season only.

LE BATEAU MOUCHE   BOAT TOUR

Map p268 (☑514-849-9952; www.bateaumouche.ca; 1hr tours adult/child $25/13; ☺11am, 2:30pm & 4pm May-Oct; Ⓜ Champ-de-Mars) This comfortable, climate-controlled sightseeing boat with a glass roof offers narrated cruises of the Old Port and Parc Jean-Drapeau. Brunch cruises are also available. Phone ahead for reservations and make sure you board the vessel 15 minutes before departure.

LE PETIT NAVIRE   BOAT TOUR

Map p268 (☑514-602-1000; www.lepetitnavire.ca; Quai Jacques-Cartier; 45min tour per adult/child $20/9, 2hr tour $26/19; ☺mid-May–mid-Oct; Ⓜ Champ-de-Mars) Aside from rowing a boat yourself, this outfit offers the most eco-friendly boat tours in Montréal. The silent, electric-powered Le Petit Navire takes passengers on 45-minute tours departing hourly around the Old Port area. Equally intriguing are the 1½-hour cruises up the Canal de Lachine (departing Fridays, Saturdays and Sundays at 11:30am from Quai Jacques-Cartier and 2pm from Marché Atwater).

LUNA YOGA   YOGA

Map p268 (☑514-845-1881; www.lunayoga.com; Ste 200, 231 Rue St-Paul Ouest; 1½hr class $18; Ⓜ Square-Victoria) Conveniently located in Old Montréal, this yoga center offers a small selection of daily Vinyasa classes. Go online or pop in to find out its latest schedule.

Parc Jean-Drapeau

ÎLE STE-HÉLÈNE | ÎLE NOTRE-DAME

Neighborhood Top Five

1 Taking a breather from the hustle of the city by soaking up some sunshine and fresh air on verdant **Île Ste-Hélène** (p68).

2 Riding the world's tallest wooden roller coaster at **La Ronde** (p68). Or getting eye-popping views of the city from the Ferris wheel.

3 Grabbing a picnic and joining music lovers on the grass, during the laid-back summer fest of **Piknic Électronik** (p68).

4 Fighting the good fight, 18th-century style, with military parades at **Musée Stewart** (p68), housed in a British garrison.

5 Getting active, by taking a **Stand-Up Paddleboard Yoga class** (p70), kayaking off the Plage des Îles or wakeboarding.

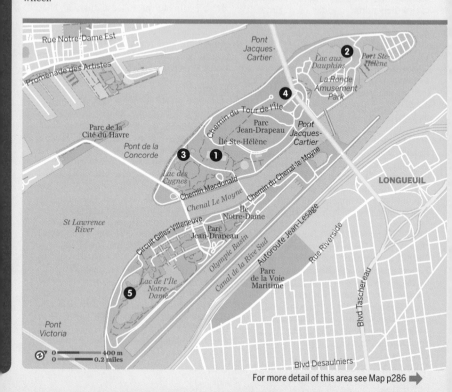

For more detail of this area see Map p286 ➡

Explore Parc Jean-Drapeau

In the middle of the mighty St Lawrence, this alluring green space spreads across Île Ste-Hélène and Île Notre-Dame. Together, the two islands offer a fine choice of recreational activities, along with some worthwhile museums. The park is also home to a casino, a Formula 1 racetrack, an old-fashioned amusement park and summer festivals (see www.parcjeandrapeau.com).

You can easily spend the better part of a day exploring Parc Jean-Drapeau. From Jean-Drapeau station on the yellow line, walk north to the Biosphère (built for Expo '67) and take in its unique superstructure and environment-themed exhibits. Continue along Chemin du Tour de l'Île, which winds its way around the center of Île Ste-Hélène, toward Musée Stewart, where you might be able to catch retro military maneuvers in action. Take in the historical pageantry and exhibits before continuing north along the chemin to the amusement park La Ronde. While you're walking through the island, note the numerous outdoor sculptures, the most famous of which is Alexander Calder's *L'Homme,* as well as other buildings that are leftovers from Expo '67; the western side of the island offers great views of the city.

If you're looking for thrills of another kind, hop on bus 167 to the Casino de Montréal on Île Notre-Dame and try your luck at roulette, slots and other games of chance.

Local Life

➡**Festivals** Parc Jean-Drapeau comes into its own during excellent festivals and events such as the Osheaga Festival Musique et Arts (p68).

➡**Beach bumming** The St Lawrence River doesn't make for good swimming, but there's the decent Plage des Îles (p70) artificial beach on Île Notre-Dame (p68).

➡**Formula 1** The main event that brings most Montréalers to Parc Jean-Drapeau is the Grand Prix du Canada (p70).

Getting There & Away

➡**Metro** Jean-Drapeau on the yellow line brings you to the heart of the park.

➡**Bus** No 767 travels from Jean-Drapeau station to La Ronde when it's open. In the summer, it also stops at the Plage des Îles. Bus 777 travels from Jean-Drapeau station to the Casino de Montréal.

➡**Ferry** In summer, catch a ferry (www.navettes maritimes.com; one-way adult $7.50, child free) to the park from the Jacques-Cartier Pier at the Old Port.

➡**Bicycle** The best way to get around the park is by bike – access is via the busy Pont Jacques-Cartier or the circuitous but more peaceful route via Cité du Havre.

Lonely Planet's Top Tip

Parc Jean-Drapeau has a few snack bars and vending machines, but almost no eating options in terms of restaurants. If you're visiting in early spring, late fall, or winter, you should consider packing a lunch or snacks. At a pinch, try the restaurants at the Casino de Montréal (p69).

Best Places for Fun

➡ La Ronde (p68)
➡ Casino de Montréal (p69)
➡ Grand Prix du Canada (p70)
➡ Plage des Îles (p70)

For reviews, see p68.

Best Events

➡ L'International des Feux Loto Québec (p68)
➡ Fête des Neiges (p68)
➡ Grand Prix du Canada (p70)
➡ Osheaga Festival Musique et Arts (p68)
➡ Piknic Électronik (p68)

For reviews, see p68.

Best Outdoor Activities

➡ Stand-up Paddleboards (p70)
➡ Wakeboarding (p70)
➡ Swimming (p70)
➡ Kayaking (p70)

For reviews, see p70.

◉ SIGHTS

◉ Île Ste-Hélène

There are walkways meandering around this island, past gardens and among the old pavilions from the Expo '67. The western part of the island was transformed into an open-air stage for shows, concerts and after-hour parties. A large metal sculpture, **L'Homme** (Humankind; Map p286), was created by American artist Alexander Calder for Expo '67.

It's also here, near the sculpture, that the fantastic **Piknic Électronik** (Map p286; www.piknicelectronik.com; Pl de l'Homme; admission $12; ⊙2-9pm Sun late May–Oct) takes place. DJs spin techno and electronic music while you dance or lounge on the grass. Going strong since 2006, **Osheaga Festival Musique et Arts** (www.osheaga.com; Pl de l'Homme; ⊙early Aug) is the island's major music festival, showcasing local alternative bands as well as big-name international acts. Other major music festivals include **Heavy Montréal** (www.heavymontreal.com), bringing together metal and hard-rock lovers in early August, and **Île Soniq** (www.ilesoniq.com), an electronic-music fest held in mid-August.

Mainly on weekends from late June to early August, the **L'International des Feux Loto Québec** (www.internationaldesfeuxloto-quebec.com/en; ⊙mid-Jun–late Aug) fireworks show at the La Ronde amusement park lights up the skies with pyrotechnics from around the world.

Held over four weekends from mid January to early February, you can join the wintery action at the **Fête des Neiges** (www.parcjeandrapeau.com; ⊙late Jan–early Feb). This family-friendly event features ice sculpting, horse-drawn sleigh rides, dog sledding, ice skating, tubing, zip lines, plus shows and concerts.

In preparation for the 50th anniversary of the Expo, which will take place in 2017, Île Ste-Hélène will get a makeover, with a new riverside promenade and a new amphitheater for shows in summer and winter. The Place des Nations, where cultural events and ceremonies took place during Expo '67, will be given new life with a $12.5 million restoration – though exactly what it will look like or what purpose it will serve still remains under debate. Lastly, there will be new promenades between the metro, the Calder sculpture and Place des Nations.

BIOSPHÈRE   SCIENCE CENTER

Map p286 (www.biosphere.ec.gc.ca; adult/child $12/free; ⊙10am-5pm daily Jun-Sep, Wed-Sun Oct-May; Ⓜ Jean-Drapeau) Housed in Buckminster Fuller's striking geodesic dome built for the American pavilion at Expo '67, this nature center has its own geothermal energy system and fun interactive displays involving hand-pumps and water spouts. Exhibits focus on urban ecosystems and emerging ecotechnologies; there's a model house outside built using sustainable design principles. The upstairs gallery about Fuller, and the exterior belvederes, offer spectacular river views.

At research time, major renovations were underway on the building, although the museum will remain open throughout the work.

LA RONDE   AMUSEMENT PARK

Map p286 (www.laronde.com; adult/child $62/47; ⊙hours vary) Québec's largest amusement park, La Ronde has a battery of impressive rides, including Le Monstre, the world's highest double wooden roller coaster; and Le Vampire, a corkscrew roller coaster with gut-wrenching turns. For a more peaceful experience, there's a Ferris wheel and a gentle minirail that offers views of the river and city.

MUSÉE STEWART   MUSEUM

Map p286 (www.stewart-museum.org; adult/child $10/free; ⊙11am-5pm Wed-Sun) Inside the old Arsenal British garrison (where troops were stationed in the 19th century), this beautifully renovated museum displays relics from Canada's past in its permanent exhibition, History and Memory. In summer, there are military parades outside by actors in 18th-century uniforms; check the website for details. It's a 15-minute walk from Jean-Drapeau metro station.

◉ Île Notre-Dame

This isle (Map p286) emerged in 10 months from the riverbed, atop millions of tons of earth and rock excavated from the new metro created in 1967. The planners were creative with the use of water, carving out canals and pretty garden walkways amid the parklands that stretch across the isle. The **Circuit Gilles-Villeneuve** continues to host the uberpopular Grand Prix du Canada in summer, while the more recent Casino de Montréal draws punters year-round.

THE LAST GOOD YEAR

For Montréalers who are old enough, there are few events in the history of the city that evoke such an emotional response as the 1967 International and Universal Exposition, fondly known as Expo '67. For six months of that year, what is now Parc Jean-Drapeau hosted 62 nations from around the world and drew 50 million visitors (more than double Canada's population), including VIPs such as Queen Elizabeth II, Lyndon Johnson and Charles de Gaulle. In no small part thanks to the efforts of Mayor Jean Drapeau, Expo '67 became one of the most successful world fairs ever held. It also coincided with the centenary of Canadian confederation, and the country – and Montréal itself – seemed on top of the world (one of the fair's many legacies was the Expos, Montréal's pro baseball team from 1969 to 2004).

However, in the decades that followed the Expo, the sovereigntist political movement, an exodus of Anglophones and economic stagnation precipitated for many a period of decline for the city. And thus there is a deep longing for Expo and its glories.

HABITAT 67   NOTABLE BUILDING
(www.habitat67.com; Ave Pierre-Dupuy) The artificial peninsula **Cité-du-Havre** was created to protect the port from vicious currents and ice. Here, in 1967, architect Moshe Safdie designed a set of futuristic cube-like condominiums for Expo '67 when he was just 23 years old. This narrow spit of land connects Île Ste-Hélène with Old Montréal via the Pont de la Concorde.

EATING

LA CABANE CHEZ JEAN   QUÉBECOIS $$
Map p286 (☑438-382-3335; Plage des Îles; prix-fixe adult/child $30/20; ☑7pm Fri & Sat, 1pm Sat & Sun) The chalet overlooking Plage des Îles hosts its *cabane à sucre* (sugar shack) during maple season. With a flickering fire in the corner and views across the frozen lake, the warmly lit chalet does a fine stand-in for the countryside if you can't get out of town. It's a weekend-only event from mid-March to mid-April. Reserve ahead.

At long communal tables, diners feast on maple-syrup-tinged dishes such as sausages, beer-braised ham, baked beans, potatoes seared in duck fat and maple-sugar pie.

LE PAVILLON 67   BUFFET $$$
Map p286 (www.casinosduquebec.com/montreal; 5th fl, 1 Ave du Casino, Île Notre-Dame; buffet $27-36, Sun brunch $25; ☑4:30-10pm Wed-Sun, 10am-2pm Sun; Ⓜ Jean-Drapeau, then bus 167) Located in the Casino de Montréal, Le Pavillon 67 spreads an excellent buffet. On weekends, you'll find lobster, crab legs, poached salmon, roast lamb, grilled shrimp and many other appealing dishes. The options are more limited on weekdays.

On Sundays, there's also a decadent jazz brunch with live music. Note that the casino does not admit children under 18.

There are several other eating and drinking spots in the casino: Ajia serves Asian fusion and is open hours similar to Le Pavillon 67; L'Instant has sandwiches and other deli fare, and is open 24 hours; there's also sleek modern Bar Le Poker, open from 11am to 3am (with food served until 2am).

HÉLÈNE DE CHAMPLAIN   FRENCH $$$
Map p286 (☑514-395-2424; 200 Chemin du Tour de l'Île, Île Ste-Hélène; Ⓜ Jean-Drapeau) Named after Hélène Boullé, wife of explorer Samuel de Champlain, this illustrious eatery served as a pavilion of honor during Expo '67. The city of Montréal has spent more than $16 million updating the stone homestead dating from 1930. It offers a varied menu of seafood and meats. It is closed indefinitely for renovations, though will likely reopen by 2017.

ENTERTAINMENT

CASINO DE MONTRÉAL   CASINO
Map p286 (www.casinosduquebec.com/montreal; 1 Ave du Casino; ☑24hr; ☎; Ⓜ Jean-Drapeau, then bus 777) Based in the former French pavilion from Expo '67, the Montréal Casino opened in 1993 and was so popular (and earned so much money) that expansion occurred almost instantly. It remains Canada's biggest casino, and has quite a sleek design, following a four-year, $300-million makeover completed in 2013. It has more than 3000 slot machines and 120 gaming tables.

Grab a drink at the Poker Bar in the middle of the casino, or try one of the other enticing new eating and drinking options.

RETURN OF THE MONTRÉAL MELON

In its heyday it was truly the Queen of Melons. A single specimen might easily have reached 9kg and its spicy flavor earned it the nickname 'Nutmeg Melon.' The market gardeners of western Montréal did a booming business in the fruit.

After WWII small agricultural plots in Montréal vanished as the city expanded, and industrial farms had little interest in growing a melon with ultrasensitive rind. By the 1950s the melon was gone – but not forever. In 1996 an enterprising Montréal journalist tracked down Montréal melon seeds held in a US Department of Agriculture collection in Iowa. The first new crop was harvested a year later in a new collective garden in Notre-Dame-de-Grâce, the heart of the old melon-growing district. To sample this blast from the past, visit local markets such as Marché Atwater (p77) or Marché Jean-Talon (p118) after the harvest every September.

Regular weekend concerts take place here (jazz, folk, blues). Arched footbridges link the casino to the **Jardin des Floralies**, a rose garden that is wonderful for a stroll.

SPORTS & ACTIVITIES

PLAGE DES ÎLES   BEACH

Map p286 (Île Notre-Dame; adult/child $9/4.50; ⏰10am-7pm daily mid-Jun–late-Aug, noon-7pm Sat-Mon late Aug–early Sep; Ⓜ Jean-Drapeau, then bus 767) On warm summer days this artificial sandy beach can accommodate up to 5000 sunning and splashing souls. It's safe, clean and ideal for kids; picnic facilities and snack bars serving beer are on-site. There are also paddleboats, canoes and kayaks for rent.

COMPLEXE AQUATIQUE   WATER SPORTS

Map p286 (www.parcjeandrapeau.com; Île Ste-Hélène; adult/child $7/3.50; ⏰10am-8pm daily early Jun–late Aug, noon-7pm daily late Aug–early Sep, noon-7pm Sat & Sun late May–early Jun; Ⓜ Jean-Drapeau) This pool complex was rebuilt when Montréal scored the 2005 World Aquatic Championships. The magnificent 55m by 44m warm-up pool is open for recreational swimming. There's also a bay-like portion of the pool with a shallow, gently sloping bottom that's great for kids and families.

OLYMPIC BASIN   WATER SPORTS

Map p286 (www.parcjeandrapeau.com; 1 Circuit Gilles-Villeneuve, Île Notre-Dame; ⏰6am-9pm late Apr–Oct; Ⓜ Jean-Drapeau, then bus 767) Competitive rowers and kayakers, along with other amateur athletes, train at this 2.2km-long former rowing basin built for the 1976 Olympic Games. You can take in many competitive boating events here such as the **Canadian Masters Championships** and the

Montréal International Dragon Boat Race Festival (☎514-866-7001; www.22dragons. com), held in late July.

STAND-UP PADDLEBOARDS   ADVENTURE SPORTS

Map p286 (www.ksf.ca; Pavillon des Activités Nautiques; 1/2hr hire $15/25, yoga class $30; ⏰mid-Jun–Aug; Ⓜ Jean-Drapeau, then bus 767) On Île Notre-Dame, you can hire stand-up paddleboards for a bit of exercise out on the lake. Kayak Sans Frontières (KSF) offers an intro class if you've never done it. There's also SUP Yoga, where an instructor leads a small group class out on the water (you balance on your board while doing the poses).

TTS MONTRÉAL   ADVENTURE SPORTS

Map p286 (☎514-567-2567; www.ttsmontreal. com; Pavillon des Activités Nautiques; per session incl equipment $18; ⏰Jun–mid-Sep; Ⓜ Jean-Drapeau, then bus 767) Near the beach on Île Notre-Dame, TTS can set you up with a wakeboard and all the gear you'll need (including a helmet) for an action-packed glide across the water. You hold onto a waterskiing-style grip, which is attached by long cord to a cable that pulls you across the lake. Ramps and other obstacles allow you to get some air on your eight-minute ride.

GRAND PRIX DU CANADA   CAR RACING

(www.circuitgillesvilleneuve.ca; Circuit Gilles-Villeneuve, Île Notre-Dame; tickets $46-575; ⏰Jun; Ⓜ Jean-Drapeau) Canada's only Grand Prix race has been held on Île Notre-Dame since 1978, though it went on hiatus in 2009 due to a dispute between the city and Formula 1 supremo Bernie Ecclestone. It remains one of the most popular motorsport events in the world, selling out and packing Montréal's hotels in early June. Be sure to reserve your tickets early.

Downtown

Neighborhood Top Five

❶ Spending a few hours exploring a treasure trove of traditional and contemporary art at the **Musée des Beaux-Arts de Montréal** (p73).

❷ Getting your festival freak on with thousands of others when the jazz festival hits town at **Place des Arts** (p74).

❸ Enjoying quiet time inside one of downtown's beautiful historic churches, such as the **Cathédrale Marie-Reine-du-Monde** (p77).

❹ Browsing the eye-catching boutiques and heritage buildings along **Rue Sherbrooke Ouest** (p76).

❺ Learning all about cutting-edge building designers at the excellent **Centre Canadien d'Architecture** (p79).

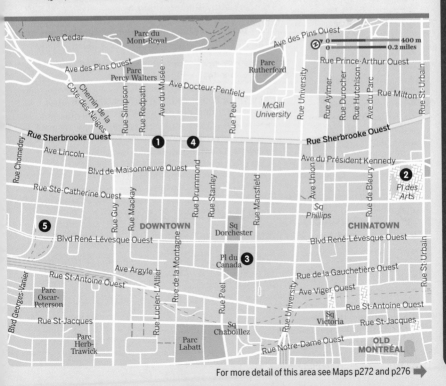

For more detail of this area see Maps p272 and p276 ➡

Lonely Planet's Top Tip

While there's much to see during the day, downtown is also a major nighttime draw for the performing arts. It's worth planning an evening around a performance happening in one of the top theaters. If hockey or Canadian football is more your speed, catch a game at the Bell Centre (p88) or Molson Stadium (p88).

 ### Best Places to Eat

➡ Joe Beef (p81)

➡ Jatoba (p81)

➡ Foodlab (p80)

➡ Café Parvis (p80)

➡ Satay Brothers (p79)

➡ Imadake (p79)

For reviews, see p79.

Best Places to Drink

➡ Bleury Bar à Vinyle (p82)

➡ Pub Ste-Élisabeth (p83)

➡ Dominion Square Tavern (p82)

➡ Burgundy Lion (p82)

➡ Benelux (p82)

➡ Le Vin Papillon (p80)

For reviews, see p82. ➡

Best Entertainment

➡ Place des Arts (p83)

➡ Foufounes Electriques (p87)

➡ Upstairs (p83)

➡ Monument National (p84)

➡ Les Grands Ballets Canadiens de Montréal (p84)

For reviews, see p83.

Explore Downtown

Downtown Montréal's wide boulevards, glass skyscrapers and shopping galleries give the area a decidedly North American flavor, while numerous green spaces, eye-catching heritage buildings and 19th-century churches add a more European character to the bustling city streets. You can explore the area easily in the better part of a day with a pause for lunch.

Begin your tour at the Musée des Beaux-Arts de Montréal, spending the morning taking in its vast collection of Old Masters and modern Canadian art, before grabbing a snack or lunch at nearby spots like the cafe in Cafe Aunja. Make your way along Rue Sherbrooke Ouest, passing the heritage houses and tiny businesses en route, before reaching McGill University, a bustling haven of green with its own museums.

From the university, you can climb toward Parc du Mont-Royal if you really want to stretch your legs, or turn down Ave McGill College to reach Rue Ste-Catherine Ouest, downtown's main shopping drag. To the west, there's Rue Crescent and Rue Bishop, the traditional anglophone centers of nightlife with an array of bars and restaurants. More shopping centers and the festival-oriented Quartier des Spectacles – including Place des Arts, the performing-arts complex and hub of the jazz festival – are within a short walk to the east along Rue Ste-Catherine Ouest. From Place des Arts, it's easy to walk to Chinatown, and even Old Montréal, for dinner.

Local Life

➡**Pedaling** Rent a Bixi bike and pedal up and down Blvd de Maisonneuve to the leafy suburb of Westmount.

➡**Hiking** Hoof it up hills such as Rue Peel to reach one of the entrances to Parc du Mont-Royal.

➡**Drinks, Theater** Have a drink and a bite at Foodlab, then catch a play or a dance performance across the street at the Monument National (p84).

Getting There & Away

➡**Metro** Peel and McGill are both central and convenient.

➡**Bus** Bus 15 runs on Rue Ste-Catherine and Blvd de Maisonneuve, bus 24 on Rue Sherbrooke and bus 150 on Blvd René-Lévesque.

➡**Bike** Bixi bikes have numerous stations in the area. If you're cycling, head to Blvd de Maisonneuve, which has separate protected bike lanes.

TOP SIGHT
MUSÉE DES BEAUX-ARTS DE MONTRÉAL

Montréal's Museum of Fine Arts is an accessible and beautifully updated oasis of art housed in architecturally striking buildings. This is Canada's oldest museum and the city's largest, with works from Old Masters to contemporary artists.

The collection is currently housed in four pavilions. The beaux-arts, marble-covered **Michal & Renata Hornstein Pavilion** at 1379 Rue Sherbrooke Ouest presents World Cultures – everything from ancient African to modern Japanese art.

Behind this building is the **Liliane & David M Stewart Pavilion**, where you'll find an eye-catching decorative arts collection. Glass, ceramics, textiles, furniture and industrial design pieces from around the globe have been assembled.

Across Museum Ave, the **Claire & Marc Bourgie Pavilion** is situated in a renovated 1894 church and displays some magnificent works of Canadian and Québecois art. Head to the top floor to delve into Inuit art and its cultural legacy. The church's Bourgie Concert Hall features gorgeous Tiffany stained-glass windows and live shows.

The modern Moshe Safdie–designed annex across Sherbrooke is the **Jean-Noël Desmarais Pavilion**, home to the Old and Modern Masters, with paintings from the Middle Ages stretching through the Renaissance and classical eras up to contemporary works. It can be reached via an underground passage from the Hornstein Pavilion.

On the horizon is a fifth pavilion, which will feature international works as well as an education center. It's scheduled to open in late 2016.

DON'T MISS

➡ Pablo Picasso's *Embrace*
➡ Jean-Paul Riopelle's *Austria*
➡ Bourgie pavilion

PRACTICALITIES

➡ Museum of Fine Arts
➡ Map p272
➡ www.mbam.qc.ca
➡ 1380 Rue Sherbrooke Ouest
➡ permanent collection adult/under 31 $12/ free, special exhibitions $20/12
➡ ⊙10am-5pm Sat & Sun, 11am-5pm Tue-Fri, to 9pm Wed (special exhibition only)
➡ Ⓜ Guy-Concordia

◉ SIGHTS

MUSÉE DES BEAUX-ARTS
DE MONTRÉAL
MUSEUM

See p73.

CHURCH OF ST JAMES
THE APOSTLE
CHURCH

Map p272 (☑514-849-7577; www.stjamesthe
apostle.ca; 1439 Rue Ste-Catherine Ouest; ◷8am-
5pm Wed & Sun; ⓂGuy-Concordia) Built in 1864
on a sports field for the British military, this
Anglican church used to be called St Crick-
ets in the Fields for the matches that took
place here. The stained glass in the east tran-
sept, the Regimental Window, was donated
in memory of the WWI fallen. The Writers'
Chapel honors Canadian poets and authors
such as John Glassco and AJM Smith.

LE CHÂTEAU
HISTORIC BUILDING

Map p272 (1321 Rue Sherbrooke Ouest; ⓂGuy-
Concordia) This fortress-like apartment complex from 1926 was designed by the famed
Montréal architects George Ross and Robert
MacDonald. The style would do Errol Flynn
proud: Scottish and French Renaissance
with stone battlements, demons and pavilion
roofs. Fossilized shells are visible in the limestone blocks. Famed local author Mordecai
Richler resided here for more than 20 years.

MUSÉE D'ART CONTEMPORAIN
MUSEUM

Map p276 (www.macm.org; 185 Rue Ste-Catherine
Ouest; adult/child $14/5, 5-9pm Wed admission
half price; ◷11am-6pm Tue, to 9pm Wed-Fri, 10am-
6pm Sat & Sun; ⓂPlace-des-Arts) This showcase
of modern Canadian and international art
has eight galleries divided between past
greats (since 1939) and exciting current developments. A weighty collection of 7600 permanent works includes Québecois legends
Jean-Paul Riopelle, Paul-Émile Borduas and
Geneviève Cadieux; there's also temporary
exhibitions of the latest trends in current
art from Canadian and international artists.
Forms range from traditional to new media,
from painting, sculpture and prints to installation art, photography and video.

PLACE DES ARTS
ARTS CENTER

Map p276 (☑box office 514-842-2112; www.
placedesarts.com; 175 Rue Ste-Catherine Ouest;
ⓂPlace-des-Arts) Montréal's performing-arts
center is the nexus for artistic and cultural
events. Several renowned musical companies call the Place des Arts home, including
the Opéra de Montréal and the Montréal

Symphony Orchestra, based in the acousti-
cally brilliant 2100-seat **Maison Symphonique**. It's also center stage for the Festival
International de Jazz de Montréal.

A key part of the **Quartier des Spectacles**, the complex embraces an outdoor plaza with fountains and an ornamental pool
and is attached to the **Complexe Desjardins** shopping center via an underground
tunnel. The six halls also include the
3000-seat **Salle Wilfrid-Pelletier**, where
Les Grands Ballets Canadiens de Montréal
(p84) and the Opéra de Montréal (p85)
perform. The 1500-seat **Théâtre Maisonneuve** hosts variety shows, dance performances and circus arts; while the smaller
Cinquième Salle hosts cabaret, experimental theater and small concerts.

GALERIES D'ART
CONTEMPORAIN DU BELGO
ARTS CENTER

Map p276 (www.thebelgoreport.com; 372 Rue Ste-
Catherine Ouest; ◷hours vary; ⓂPlace-des-Arts)
More than a decade ago the Belgo building
was a rundown haven for struggling artists.
It has since earned a reputation as one of
Montréal's most intriguing exhibition spaces with some 30 galleries and artist studios,
along with dance, yoga and photography
studios. Check the website for ongoing exhibitions and upcoming openings.

MAISON DU FESTIVAL
RIO TINTO ALCAN
MUSEUM

Map p276 (305 Rue St-Catherine Ouest;
◷11:30am-6pm Tue-Sat, to 5pm Sun; ⓂPlace-
des-Arts) A key concert venue during the
Jazz Festival, this multistory building hosts
concerts year-round in the Salle l'Astral. It
also has a small gallery with listening stations and memorabilia from some of the
greats who've played at the fest. Check out
Dave Brubeck's spectacles, Leonard Cohen's
hat, Pat Metheny's guitar and Ella Fitzger-
ald's wig. A big video screen shows highlights from past concerts.

MUSÉE MCCORD
MUSEUM

Map p276 (McCord Museum of Canadian History; www.mccord-museum.qc.ca; 690 Rue Sherbrooke Ouest; adult/student/child $14/8/free,
special exhibitions extra $5, admission free after
5pm Wed; ◷10am-6pm Tue, Thu & Fri, to 9pm
Wed, to 5pm Sat & Sun; ⓂMcGill) With hardly
an inch to spare in its cramped but welcoming galleries, the McCord Museum of Canadian History houses thousands of artifacts
and documents illustrating Canada's social,

THE UNDERGROUND CITY

Brilliant marketing that conjures up images of subterranean skyscrapers and roads has made the underground city one of the first things visitors seek out in Montréal.

The underground city doesn't actually have any of these things. What it does have is a network of some 2600 shops, 200 restaurants and 40-odd cinemas, theaters and exhibition halls, all hidden neatly beneath the surface in more than 30km of tunnels and underground spaces. For most travelers, it's a major letdown, because no matter what tourism officials call it, it is basically just a kind of colossal network of interlocking shopping malls. Where it does get interesting, however, is for residents living in downtown Montréal, as it gives them a reprieve from winter – hundreds of thousands use it every day of the year.

The 60-odd distinct complexes that make up this network are linked by brightly lit, well-ventilated corridors; fountains play to maintain humidity and the temperature hovers around 20°C. Add the metro and you have a self-contained world, shielded from the subarctic temperatures. If you move to Montréal and pick the right apartment building, it could literally be the middle of winter and you would be able to go to work, do your grocery shopping, go see a movie and take in a performance at Place des Arts and never need more than a T-shirt.

cultural and archaeological history from the 18th century to the present day.

MUSÉE REDPATH   MUSEUM

Map p276 (859 Rue Sherbrooke Ouest; ⊙9am-5pm Mon-Fri, 11am-5pm Sun; MMcGill) FREE
A Victorian spirit of discovery pervades this old natural-history museum, though you won't find anything more gruesome than stuffed animals from the Laurentians hinterland. The Redpath Museum houses a large variety of specimens, including a dinosaur skeleton and seashells donated from around the world. A highlight is the 3rd-floor World Cultures Exhibits, which includes Egyptian mummies, shrunken heads and artifacts from ancient Mediterranean, African and East Asian communities.

CATHÉDRALE CHRIST CHURCH   CATHEDRAL

Map p276 (635 Rue Ste-Catherine Ouest; ⊙7am-6pm; MMcGill) Montréal's first Anglican bishop had this cathedral built (modeled on a church in Salisbury, England) and it was completed in 1859. The church was the talk of the town in the late 1980s when it allowed a shopping center, the **Promenades de la Cathédrale**, to be built underneath it. Spectacular photos show the house of worship resting on concrete stilts while construction went on underneath.

The interior is sober apart from the pretty stained-glass windows made by William Morris' studios in London. In the rear cloister garden stands a memorial statue to Raoul Wallenberg, the Swedish diplomat who saved 100,000 Jews from the concentration camps in WWII.

MCGILL UNIVERSITY   UNIVERSITY

Map p276 (www.mcgill.ca; 845 Rue Sherbrooke Ouest; MMcGill) Founded in 1828 by James McGill, a rich Scottish fur trader, McGill University is one of Canada's most prestigious learning institutions, with 39,000 students. The university's medical and engineering faculties have a fine reputation and many campus buildings are showcases of Victorian architecture. The campus, at the foot of Mont-Royal, is rather nice for a stroll and also incorporates the Musée Redpath.

ST JAMES UNITED CHURCH   CHURCH

Map p276 (☎514-288-9245; 463 Rue Ste-Catherine Ouest; ⊙11am-4pm Tue & Thu, from 10am Fri & Sat, 9am-2pm Sun; MMcGill) The excellent acoustics at St James United are coveted for organ and choir concerts as well as performances at the international jazz festival. The church was originally opened in 1889.

ILLUMINATED CROWD   MONUMENT

Map p276 (1981 Ave McGill College; MMcGill) Constructed of polyester resin, Raymond Mason's sculpture of 65 people is one of Montréal's most photographed pieces of public art. The work shows a rather dark side of humanity. A crowd of onlookers stands pressed tightly together. The first row merely looks off into the distance, while behind them, the mood gradually degenerates as figures show a range of emotions – melancholy, fear, lust, hatred and terror.

WANDERING IN WESTMOUNT

Though short on traditional sights, the leafy, upper-class neighborhood of Westmount makes for a good afternoon stroll. Here you'll find a mix of sleepy backstreets set with Victorian mansions and manicured parks (parts of the city were named a national historic site in 2012), while the main boulevard, Rue Sherbrooke Ouest, has high-end boutiques, cafes and bistros. Wander about and grab a bite while you're there.

The town's highlight is **Westmount Park & Library** (☑514-989-5300; 4575 Rue Sherbrooke Ouest; ⊙10am-9pm Mon-Fri, to 5pm Sat & Sun; Ⓜ Atwater). The lovely Westmount Park encompasses pathways, streams and concealed nooks that recall the whimsical nature of English public gardens. The Westmount Public Library, built in 1899, stands stolid, with its Romanesque brickwork, leaded glass and delightful bas-reliefs dedicated to wisdom. The attached **Westmount Conservatory** is a gorgeous 1927 greenhouse where time stands still among the orchids.

Walking northwest from Westmount Park, you'll pass increasingly large and expensive homes as you climb to **Summit Woods** and **Summit Lookout**, a 57-acre forest and bird sanctuary atop the hill of Westmount with a belvedere commanding views of the St Lawrence River. Following Summit Circle road and Chemin Belvedere, you can soon walk to Parc du Mont-Royal and Cimetière Notre-Dame-des-Neiges.

Back down along Rue Sherbrooke Ouest, the faux medieval towers of **Westmount City Hall** (☑514-989-5200; 4333 Côte St-Antoine; ⊙8:30am-4:30pm Mon-Fri; Ⓜ Vendôme then bus 104) come as a surprise after the skyscrapers of downtown. This Tudor gatehouse in rough-hewn stone looks like something from an English period drama. A lawn-bowling green lies in the rear.

For some window-shopping, stroll along the boutique-lined **Avenue Greene** to the northeast of Westmount City Hall. **Westmount Square** (Map p272; cnr Ave Greene & Blvd de Maisonneuve Ouest; Ⓜ Atwater) is a chic 1966 mall by architect Ludwig Mies van der Rohe. For a bite to eat, stop in **Chez Nick** (Map p272; ☑514-935-0946; www.cheznick.ca; 1377 Ave Greene; mains $10-16; ⊙7am-8pm Mon-Fri, to 6pm Sat, 8am-6pm Sun; Ⓜ Atwater), a classic diner that's been going strong since 1920.

A fine vantage point is on the 'Secret Bench,' an evocative sculpture by Lea Vivot on the other side of Rue McGill.

PLACE VILLE-MARIE
NOTABLE BUILDING

Map p276 (www.placevillemarie.com; 1 Pl Ville-Marie; Ⓜ McGill) Known for its rotating rooftop beacon that illuminates downtown at night, the 42-story Place Ville-Marie tower marked the beginning of Montréal's Underground City five decades ago. Its cruciform shape was chosen to commemorate Maisonneuve's planting of a great cross on Mont-Royal in 1642. Today it houses some 75 shops and restaurants, plus 10,000 occupants.

RUE SHERBROOKE OUEST
STREET

Map p276 (Ⓜ Peel) Until the 1930s the downtown stretch of Rue Sherbrooke Ouest was home to the **Golden Square Mile**, one of the richest residential neighborhoods in Canada. You'll see a few glorious old homes along this drag, including the **Reid Wilson House**, the **Louis-Joseph Forget House** and the **Mount Royal Club**. There are good

interpretation panels outside them explaining their history. The route is also home to visit-worthy churches, some first-rate museums and strings of energetic students en route to McGill University.

SQUARE DORCHESTER
SQUARE

Map p276 (Ⓜ Peel) This leafy expanse in the heart of downtown was known until 1988 as Dominion Sq, a reminder of Canada's founding in 1867. A Catholic cemetery was here until 1870 and bodies still lie beneath the grass. Events of all kinds have taken place here over the years – fashion shows, political rallies and royal visits.

The square still exudes the might of the British Empire, with statues of Boer War booster Lord Strathcona, Queen Victoria and poet Robert Burns, plus Wilfrid Laurier, Canada's first francophone prime minister, who faces off a statue of John A Macdonald, the first anglophone prime minister, in Place du Canada across Blvd René-Lévesque Ouest. The city's main tourist office lies on the square's northwest side.

RUE STE-CATHERINE OUEST
STREET

Map p276 (MPeel, McGill, Place-des-Arts) Lively Rue Ste-Catherine Ouest is one endless orgy of shops, restaurants, bars and cafes on the hyperactive stretch between Rue Crescent and Rue St-Urbain. Shopping malls, department stores and multiplex cinemas are sprinkled along the way.

MAISON ALCAN
HISTORIC BUILDING

Map p276 (1188 Rue Sherbrooke Ouest; MPeel) This mélange of four carefully restored 19th- and 20th-century buildings integrates the old Berkeley Hotel and four houses, including the Atholstan House, a Québec historic monument. To the rear is an intriguing atrium with a pretty garden. Also on the property stands the **Emmanuel Congregation Church**, which belongs to the Salvation Army. The property was the symbolic headquarters of the Alcan aluminum concern (now part of Rio Tinto Alcan), before its sale in 2013 to Cirque de Soleil. According to rumor, the site may eventually be turned into a hotel and entertainment hall.

CATHÉDRALE
MARIE-REINE-DU-MONDE
CHURCH

Map p276 (514-866-1661; 1085 Rue de la Cathédrale; 7:30am-6:15pm; MBonaventure) FREE The Cathedral of Mary Queen of the World is a smaller but still magnificent version of St Peter's Basilica in Rome. The architects scaled it down to a quarter of its size, mindful of the structural risks of Montréal's severe winters. This landmark was built from 1870 to 1894 as a symbol of Catholic power in the heart of Protestant Montréal.

The 13 statues of saints over the entrance are sculpted in wood and covered with copper; at night they are brilliantly illuminated. The neobaroque altar canopy, a replica of Bernini's masterpiece in St Peter's, is fashioned of gold leaf and copper with swirled roof supports.

GARE WINDSOR
HISTORIC BUILDING

Map p272 (514-395-5164; 1160 de la Gauchetière Ouest; MBonaventure) The massive Victorian building hugging the slope west of the Marriott Château Champlain is the old Windsor Station, opened in 1889 as the headquarters of the Canadian Pacific Railway. The Romanesque structure inspired a château style for train stations across the country; its architect, Bruce Price, would later build the remarkable Château Frontenac in Québec City.

Take a stroll through the restored Salle des pas perdus, a 25,000-sq-ft concourse, where millions of travelers once set off on train trips. Today, it's hauntingly vacant.

PLACE DU CANADA
PARK

Map p276 (Rue Peel; MBonaventure) This park immediately southeast of Sq Dorchester is best known for its monument of John A Macdonald, Canada's first prime minister, who addressed the maiden session of parliament in Montréal. The two cannons around the base were captured in the Crimean War; if you look closely you'll see the dual-headed eagle of Czar Nicholas I. The statue was decapitated by vandals in 1992 and the head vanished for two years.

MARCHÉ ATWATER
MARKET

Map p272 (138 Ave Atwater; 7am-6pm Mon-Wed, to 7pm Thu, to 8pm Fri, to 5pm Sat & Sun; MAtwater) Just off the Canal de Lachine, this fantastic market has a mouthwatering assortment of fresh produce from local farms, excellent wines, crusty breads, fine cheeses and other delectable fare. The market's specialty shops operate year-round, while outdoor stalls open from March to October. The excellent Première Moisson is a popular cafe and bakery. It's all housed in a 1933 brick hall, topped with a clock tower. The grassy banks overlooking the Canal de Lachine make a great picnic spot.

PARISIAN LAUNDRY
GALLERY

Map p272 (514-989-1056; www.parisianlaundry. com; 3550 Rue St-Antoine Ouest; noon-5pm Tue-Sat; MLionel-Groulx) A former industrial laundry turned monster (15,000-sq-ft) gallery, this space is worth a trip for the old building itself. Recent exhibitions have included works by New York conceptual artist Adam Pendleton and Québec sculptor Valérie Blass. Be sure to check out exhibits upstairs and in the basement.

ST PATRICK'S BASILICA
CHURCH

Map p276 (514-866-7379; www.stpatricksmtl. ca; 454 Blvd René-Lévesque Ouest; 9am-6pm; MSquare-Victoria) Built for Montréal's booming Irish population in 1847, the interior of St Patrick's Basilica contains huge columns from single pine trunks, an ornate baptismal font and nectar-colored stained-glass windows. The pope raised its status to basilica in 1989, in recognition of its importance to English-speaking Catholics in Montréal. It's a sterling example of French-Gothic style and is classified a national monument.

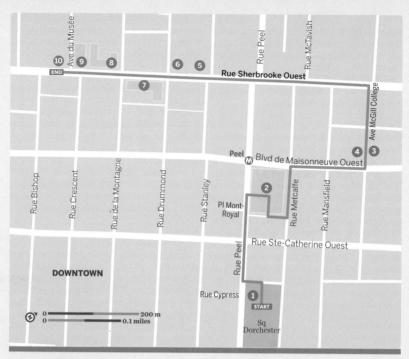

Neighborhood Walk
Downtown

START SQ DORCHESTER
END MUSÉE DES BEAUX-ARTS
LENGTH 2.5KM, TWO HOURS

Start at ① **Square Dorchester** (p76). The statue to the northeast is of Lord Strathcona, a philanthropist who sponsored Canada's efforts in the South African Boer War. Wander south for a statue of Sir Wilfrid Laurier (1841–1919), one of Canada's most respected prime ministers.

Walk northwest to the upscale shopping complex ② **Les Cours Mont-Royal** (p87). The central atrium has bird sculptures with human heads and a chandelier from a Monte Carlo casino. Cut through the building and continue up Rue Metcalf. Turn right on Blvd de Maisonneuve Ouest and left on Ave McGill College. About 20m up the block on the right is the ③ **Illuminated Crowd** (p75) sculpture. Designed by Raymond Mason, it illuminates the darker side of human nature. Head across Ave McGill College to the ④ **Secret Bench**, a sensual work

with a seated couple that provides a fine counterpoint to the unruly mob.

Continue on and turn left at Rue Sherbrooke Ouest, Montréal's most prestigious residential street in the early 20th century. It features glorious old homes, including the ⑤ **Mount Royal Club**, once an exclusive men-only club that now opens its doors to all.

Nearby, impressive ⑥ **Reid Wilson House** is a mansion with its original carriage house in back. Continue along Sherbrooke; you'll soon reach the ⑦ **Ritz-Carlton** (p161), which has a lavish afternoon tea in the Palm Court.

Further along Sherbrooke is the fortress-like apartment complex ⑧ **Le Château** (p74), with vestiges of shell fossils in the limestone. Next door is a stone church with Tiffany stained-glass windows. It now houses the ⑨ **Salle Bourgie** concert hall, part of the Musée des Beaux-Arts de Montréal. End your tour with a look at the neoclassical facade of the museum's ⑩ **Michal & Renata Hornstein Pavilion**. Each ionic column took six men three months to cut and shape with pneumatic hammers.

The Irish-Canadian patriot D'Arcy McGee was buried here after his assassination in 1868; his pew (number 240) is marked with a small Canadian flag.

CENTRE CANADIEN D'ARCHITECTURE
MUSEUM

Map p272 (CCA; www.cca.qc.ca; 1920 Rue Baile; adult/child $10/free, 5.30-9pm Thu admission free; ⏰11am-6pm Wed & Fri, to 9pm Thu, to 5pm Sat & Sun; MGeorgest-Vanier) A must for architecture fans, this center is equal parts museum and research institute. The building incorporates the **Shaughnessy House**, a 19th-century gray limestone treasure. Highlights in this section include the conservatory and an ornate sitting room with intricate woodwork and a massive stone fireplace. The exhibition galleries focus on remarkable architectural works of both local and international scope.

The CCA's sculpture garden is located on a grassy lot overlooking south Montréal. There's also a busy, well-stocked bookstore.

MONTRÉAL CANADIENS HALL OF FAME
MUSEUM

Map p272 (☎514-925-7777; www.hall.canadiens.com; 1909 Ave des Canadiens-de-Montréal; adult/child $11/8; ⏰10am-6pm Tue-Sat, noon-5pm Sun; MLucien-L'Allier) Hockey fans can pay their respects to one of the greatest teams in hockey history at this small hall-of-fame museum inside the Bell Centre. The hall contains jerseys, game sticks, photos, memorabilia and info on the sport dating back to the early 1900s. If you want a peek in the locker rooms, you can add a guided tour of the arena for an extra $6 (not available on game days).

If you have tickets to a hockey game, tickets to the hall of fame are $6 on the same day.

 EATING

★SATAY BROTHERS
ASIAN $

(www.sataybrothers.com; 3721 Notre-Dame Ouest; mains $8-15; ⏰11am-11pm Wed-Sun; MLionel-Groulx) Amid red walls, hanging lamps and mismatched thrift-store furnishings, this lively and colorful spot serves some of the best 'street food' in Montréal. Crowds flock here to gorge on delicious chicken-satay sandwiches, tangy green papaya salad, braised pork (or tofu) buns, and *laksa lemak,* a rich and spicy coconut soup. It has great cocktails too.

The Winnicki brothers quickly gained a cult following after opening a food stall in Atwater market, which is still open in the summer.

LOLA ROSA
VEGETARIAN $

Map p276 (☎514-287-9337; www.lola-rosa.ca; 545 Rue Milton; mains $10-13; ⏰noon-9:30pm; ⚡; MMcGill) At this charming vegetarian cafe, even skeptical carnivores are won over by plates of creamy rich lasagna, sweet-potato and coconut-milk curry, and nachos piled high with black beans, mozzarella, avocado and sour cream.

Fresh juices, decent coffee and decadent desserts (try the chocolate cake with raspberry coulis) complete the picture. Lola Rosa also hosts a popular weekend brunch. There's a second location in the Plateau.

IMADAKE
JAPANESE $

Map p272 (☎514-931-8833; www.imadake.ca; 4006 Rue Ste-Catherine Ouest; mains $6-15; ⏰noon-2:30pm Mon-Fri, 5-10:30pm nightly; MAtwater) On the fringes of the Concordia Chinatown, Imadake is the closest thing to an authentic *izakaya* (Japanese pub-eatery) in the city. Staff scream *irrashaimase!* (welcome!) when you walk in, and there's an excellent assortment of *izakaya* standbys such as *tsukune* (chicken meatballs), *takoyaki* (octopus croquettes) and *okonomiyaki* (Japanese pancake with seafood or pork). The ramen noodles are excellent.

KAZU
JAPANESE $

Map p272 (1862 Rue Ste-Catherine Ouest; mains $10-17; ⏰noon-3pm Sun, Mon & Wed-Fri, 5:30-9:30pm Wed-Mon; MGuy-Concordia) Kazuo Akutsu's frenetic hole-in-the-wall in the Concordia Chinatown draws long lines of people waiting for *gyoza* (dumplings), ramen noodle soup and awesome creations such as the 48-hour pork.

THALI
INDIAN $

Map p272 (www.thalimontreal.com; 1409 Rue St-Marc; mains $5-10; ⏰11:30am-10pm Mon-Fri, 1-11pm Sat, 4-10pm Sun; MGuy-Concordia) A popular budget gem in the Concordia Chinatown, Thali offers quick plates of delish Indian fare, with three-course specials for $8 to $10. The naan bread, butter chicken and lamb kebab are particularly delectable.

PATRICE
BAKERY $

Map p272 (2360 Rue Notre Dame Ouest; pastries $3-5; ⏰10:30am-6:30pm Mon-Fri, 9:30am-6:30pm

Sat, 9:30am-5pm Sun; Ⓜ Lionel-Groulx) The modern, Scandinavian-like design of this patisserie makes a fine backdrop to the heavenly creations on offer. Perennial favorites: the Kouign Amman (a Breton-style butter cake), *choux a la creme* (a mix of chocolate, caramel and banana cream enclosed in pastries), and the chocolate-coffee St Henri cake. At lunch, there's soup, salads and sandwiches.

CAFE AUNJA
CAFE $

Map p272 (www.aunja.com; 1448 Rue Sherbrooke Ouest; snacks $4-10; ⊙10am-10pm; Ⓜ Guy-Concordia) Despite the location along busy Sherbrooke, Cafe Aunja feels like a peaceful oasis from the downtown bustle. Changing artwork adorns the brick walls of this Persian teahouse, and there's a regular lineup of readings and live music. A mix of book- and laptop-absorbed people and quietly chatting friends gather over creamy lattes and steaming pots of tea. Sandwiches, salads and soups round out the menu.

BOUSTAN
LEBANESE $

Map p272 (2020 Rue Crescent; mains $5-10; ⊙11am-4am Mon-Sat, from 5pm Sun; Ⓜ Guy-Concordia) This friendly little Lebanese joint scores high in popularity on the city's *shwarma* circuit because of its delicious toasted pita sandwiches. Its late hours make it a favorite with pub crawlers in need of sustenance between bars.

PIKOLO ESPRESSO BAR
CAFE $

Map p276 (www.pikoloespresso.com; 3418b Ave du Parc; ⊙7:45am-6pm Mon-Fri, 9am-6pm Sat & Sun; 🐱; Ⓜ Place-des-Arts) Plateau hipsters roll up to this friendly split-level joint nestled in a heritage building at the bottom of Ave du Parc for its yummy baked goods and the signature drink, the Pikolo. Its *ristretto* shot of espresso goes down very smoothly.

MYRIADE
CAFE $

Map p272 (1432 Rue Mackay; ⊙7:30am-8pm Mon-Fri, 9am-7pm Sat & Sun; Ⓜ Guy-Concordia) A few steps from Concordia, Myriade is a small student favorite for its perfectly pulled espressos and well-balanced lattes (with beans from 49th Parallel and Phil & Sebastien). There is no wi-fi, so it draws more conversationalists than MacBook users. The drawback: there's not a lot of seating.

★ CAFÉ PARVIS
BISTRO $$

Map p276 (☏514-764-3589; www.cafeparvis. com; 433 Rue Mayor; small plates $6-8; ⊙7am-

11pm Mon-Fri, 11am-11pm Sat, 11am-3pm Sun; 🍴; Ⓜ Place-des-Arts) Hidden on a quiet lane, Cafe Parvis is set with oversized windows, hanging plants and vintage fixtures. Once part of the fur district, this cleverly repurposed room serves up delicious pizzas in inventive combinations (such as smoked salmon, fennel and mascarpone; or roasted vegetables with Gruyère). These are matched by equally creative salads (such as beets, pears and goat's cheese). Dishes are small; you'll want to order a few.

★ LE VIN PAPILLON
INTERNATIONAL $$

Map p272 (www.vinpapillon.com; 2519 Rue Notre-Dame Ouest; small plates $7-17; ⊙3pm-midnight Tue-Sat; 🍴; Ⓜ Lionel-Groulx) The folks behind Joe Beef continue the hit parade with this delightful wine bar and small-plate eatery next door to Liverpool House (another Joe Beef success). Creative, mouthwatering veggie dishes take top billing with favorites such as tomato and chickpea salad, sauteed chanterelles, or smoked eggplant caviar, along with roasted cauliflower with chicken skin, guinea-fowl confit, and charcuterie and cheese platters. No bookings – arrive early!

FOODLAB
INTERNATIONAL $$

Map p276 (☏514-844-2033; www.sat.qc.ca/fr/foodlab; 3rd fl, 1201 Blvd St-Laurent; mains $15-25; ⊙5-11pm Tue-Fri; Ⓜ St-Laurent) On the upper floor of SAT, Foodlab is a creative culinary space, where the small menu changes every two weeks, and ranges across the globe. It's a casual but handsomely designed space, where patrons sip creative cocktails and watch fast-moving chefs in the open kitchen. There's outdoor seating in the summer and a yurt set up in the winter.

LE BALSAM INN
ITALIAN $$

Map p276 (☏514-507-9207; www.lebalsaminn. com; 1237 Rue Metcalfe; small plates $12-18; ⊙11:30am-midnight Tue-Fri, from 4:30pm Sat & Sun; Ⓜ Peel) This charming addition to the downtown dining scene serves up delectable plates of Italian fare, with standouts such as citrus-drizzled calamari, osso buco with polenta, and pasta with pancetta and parmesan. It's also a great spot for an evening (or afternoon) libation with a good wine selection and well-executed cocktails.

FURUSATO
JAPANESE $$

Map p276 (☏514-849-3438; 2137 Rue de Bleury; mains $16-34; ⊙noon-2pm Tue-Fri, 6-9:30pm

Tue-Sat; MPlace-des-Arts) This humble eatery presents some of the most authentic Japanese in town. Ultrafresh sushi, decent sake, shrimp and vegetable tempura, sukiyaki and grilled horse mackerel *(hokke)* are some of the stars of the menu, along with black-sesame ice cream for dessert. Reservations recommended.

LE TAJ   INDIAN $$

Map p276 (☏514-845-9015; www.restaurant letaj.com; 2077 Rue Stanley; mains $18-23; ☺11:30am-2:30pm Sun-Fri, 5-10:30pm daily; ☝; MPeel) Le Taj throws down the gauntlet for some excellent Indian dishes. The time to go is at lunch, when downtowners line up for a succulent buffet ($16) featuring a bounty of rich flavors from the East – tandoori chicken, vegetable korma, palaak paneer and tender lamb, along with steaming piles of naan bread, custard-like desserts and many other temptations.

BISTRO ISAKAYA   JAPANESE $$

Map p276 (☏514-845-8226; www.bistroisakaya. com; 3469 Ave du Parc; mains $19-26; ☺11:30am-2pm Tue-Fri, 6-10pm Tue-Sat, 5:30-9pm Sun; MPlace-des-Arts, then bus 80 or 129) This authentic, unpretentious Japanese restaurant has fairly simple decor but the fish is incredibly fresh. The owner, Shige Minagawa, is known for handpicking his seafood and preparing it in classic Japanese fashion.

PHAYATHAI   THAI $$

Map p272 (☏514-933-9949; 1235 Rue Guy; mains $15-20; ☺11:30am-2:30pm Tue-Fri, 5-10pm Tue-Sun; ☝; MGuy-Concordia) Just off the beaten track, this elegant little restaurant serves some of the best Thai cuisine in town. Fresh-tasting curries, crispy boneless duck and seafood plates are among the many delicacies from the East.

MANGO BAY   CARIBBEAN $$

Map p272 (☏514-875-7082; www.mangobay. ca; 1202 Rue Bishop; mains $13-20; ☺noon-10pm Mon-Fri, 3pm-midnight Sat, 5-10pm Sun; MGuy-Concordia) Situated in a converted Victorian house with pretty stained-glass windows, Mango Bay serves up authentic chicken jerky or stew, curried goat or island chicken fajitas with a terrific side order of plantain. Watch out for the incendiary hot sauces, and be sure to save room for a slice of the signature mango cheesecake or rum cake.

REUBEN'S   DELI $$

Map p276 (☏514-866-1029; 1116 Rue Ste-Catherine Ouest; mains $10-21; ☺6:30am-midnight Mon-Fri, 8am-midnight Sat & Sun; MPeel) A classic, long-running deli, Reuben's has squishy booths and a long counter, where patrons line up for towering smoked-meat sandwiches served with big-cut fries. Burgers, smoked pork chops and other old-school favorites round out the menu. Try to avoid the busy lunch rush.

JOE BEEF   QUÉBECOIS $$$

Map p272 (☏514-935-6504; www.joebeef.ca; 2491 Rue Notre-Dame Ouest; mains $29-50; ☺6pm-late Tue-Sat; MLionel-Groulx) In the heart of the Little Burgundy neighborhood, Joe Beef is the current darling of food critics for its unfussy, market-fresh fare. The rustic, country-kitsch setting is a great spot to linger over fresh oysters, braised rabbit, roasted scallops with smoked onions and a changing selection of hearty Québecois dishes – all served with good humor and a welcome lack of pretension. In summer, some of the best seats are in the backyard garden. Reserve weeks in advance.

JATOBA   ASIAN $$$

Map p276 (☏514-871-1184; www.jatobamontreal. com; 1184 Pl Phillips; mains $24-39; ☺11:30am-2:30pm & 5pm-1am Mon-Fri, 5pm-3am Sat; ☝; MMcGill) Celebrated chef Antonio Park is behind the menu at this artfully designed space just off Pl Phillips. Park, who was born to Korean parents but grew up in South America and went to cooking school in Japan, brilliantly melds flavors from around the globe. Yellowfin sashimi with Asian pear and jalapeño, king oyster mushrooms in a sweet miso gratin, and beef tataki with truffle peaches and puffed quinoa are among the outstanding dishes.

FERREIRA CAFÉ   PORTUGUESE $$$

Map p276 (☏514-848-0988; www.ferreiracafe. com; 1446 Rue Peel; mains $26-45; ☺noon-3pm Mon-Fri, 5:30-11pm Mon-Wed, 5:30pm-midnight Thu-Sat, 5:30-10pm Sun; MPeel) This warm and inviting restaurant serves some of Montréal's best Portuguese fare. The *cataplana* (a bouillabaisse-style seafood stew) is magnificent, tender morsels of grilled fish come to the table cooked to perfection, while meat-lovers can feast on rack of lamb or spice-rubbed Angus rib-eye steak. Late diners can enjoy three-course, $24 meals from 10pm to close.

🍷 DRINKING & NIGHTLIFE

BENELUX
MICROBREWERY

Map p276 (www.brasseriebenelux.com; 245 Rue Sherbrooke Ouest; ⊘2pm-3am Sat-Wed, from 11am Thu & Fri; 🛜; ⓂPlace-des-Arts) Benelux deserves high praise for its beautifully crafted microbrews, with a dozen or so offerings on hand (including one cask ale). Options rotate regularly, though long-time favorites are always on hand, such as Sabotage IPA and the blond Lux. Knowledgeable bartenders are happy to guide you in the right direction. You can match those drafts with panini or Benelux's famed 'EuroDog' juicy veal or pork hot dog, garnished with sauerkraut and served on baguette.

BIIRU
BAR

Map p276 (⌨514-903-1555; 1433 Rue City Councillors; ⊘11:30am-2pm Tue-Fri, 5:30-10pm Tue-Thu, 5.30-11pm Fri & Sat; ⓂMcGill) Despite the name, this colorfully designed *izakaya* doesn't serve much *biiru* (beer). What it does have: creative cocktails, tasty snacks and a festive environment that draws the after-work crowd. You can nibble on *gyoza* (dumplings), duck magret salad or mushroom *okonomiyaki* (Japanese pancake), while admiring the Hokusai-inspired mural and engaging in the discreet art of people-watching.

FURCO
COCKTAIL BAR

Map p276 (⌨514-764-3588; www.barfurco.com; 425 Rue Mayor; ⊘4pm-3am; ⓂPlace-des-Arts) In a previous life, this stylish but industrial hideaway was a fur factory, and its raw concrete pillars, copper bar and modular light fixtures form the backdrop to a buzzing scene just a short stroll from Place-des-Arts. You'll find well-crafted cocktails and upmarket snacks (come for $1 oysters on Sundays and Mondays). Heartier fare includes seared cod or pork and mushroom dumplings. Come early to beat the crowds.

BLEURY BAR À VINYLE
BAR

Map p276 (www.vinylebleury.ca; 2109 Rue de Bleury; ⊘7pm-3am Tue, from 8pm Wed-Thu, 9pm-3am Fri & Sat; ⓂPlace-des-Arts) It's in a bit of a nightlife desert, but this cozy lounge-like space is well worth the trip if you're into music. A blend of DJs and live bands mix things up, with a packed calendar of soul, funk, new-wave disco, world beats and house music. Bleury Bar draws a young, friendly crowd and the cocktails are first-rate.

There's a small cover charge (most nights around $4 to $7), though Tuesdays are free.

★DOMINION SQUARE TAVERN
TAVERN

Map p276 (www.dominiontavern.com; 1245 Rue Metcalfe; ⊘11:30am-midnight Mon-Fri, 4:30pm-midnight Sat & Sun; ⓂPeel) Once a down-and-out watering hole dating from the 1920s, this beautifully renovated tavern recalls a classic French bistro but with a long bar, English pub–style. Executive chef Éric Dupuis puts his own spin on pub grub, with mussels cooked with bacon, and smoked trout salad with curry dressing.

PULLMAN
BAR

Map p276 (⌨514-288-7779; www.pullman-mtl.com; 3424 Ave du Parc; ⊘4:30pm-midnight; ⓂPlace-des-Arts) This beautifully designed wine bar is a favorite haunt of the 30-something set. It's primarily a restaurant, but the downstairs bar of this two-level space gets jammed (or *jammé*, as they say in Franglais) after work and becomes quite a pickup spot, so be prepared to engage in some flirting. Knowledgeable staff can help you choose from the sprawling wine list.

★BURGUNDY LION
PUB

Map p272 (⌨514-934-0888; www.burgundylion.com; 2496 Rue de Notre-Dame Ouest; ⊘11:30am-3am Mon-Fri, 9am-3am Sat & Sun; ⓂLionel-Groulx) This trendy take on the English pub features British pub fare, beers and whiskies galore, and an attitude-free vibe where everyone (and their parents) feels welcome to drink, eat and be merry. Things get the good kind of crazy late-night weekends. Tip your cap to Queen Elizabeth, whose portrait adorns the bathroom door.

MCKIBBIN'S
PUB

Map p272 (⌨514-288-1580; www.mckibbinsirishpub.com; 1426 Rue Bishop; ⊘11:30am-3am; ⓂGuy-Concordia) With its garage-sale furniture, McKibbin's cultivates a familiar, down-at-heel pub atmosphere. Its live entertainment varies from Celtic and pop to punk music. The office crowd pops in at lunchtime for burgers, chicken wings and salads.

NYKS
PUB

Map p276 (⌨514-866-1787; www.nyks.ca; 1250 Rue de Bleury; ⊘11am-3am Mon-Fri, 4pm-3am Sat; ⓂPlace-des-Arts) Its artsy-chic vibe makes this warm bistro the preferred lunch and after-work spot of Plateau cool kids who happen to work in downtown offices. Daily happy hours and pub finger-foods are a joy to downtowners seeking an authentic experience. Sometimes it even has live jazz.

UPSTAIRS
JAZZ BAR

Map p272 (☎514-931-6808; www.upstairsjazz. com; 1254 Rue Mackay; ☉11:30am-1am Mon-Fri, 5:30pm-2am Sat, 6:30pm-1am Sun; ⓜGuy-Concordia) This slick bar hosts quality jazz and blues acts nightly, featuring both local and touring talent. The walled terrace behind the bar is enchanting at sunset, and the dinner menu features inventive salads and meals such as the Cajun bacon burger.

BRUTOPIA
BREWERY

Map p272 (www.brutopia.net; 1219 Rue Crescent; ☉2pm-3am Sat-Thu, noon-3am Fri; ⓜGuy-Concordia) This fantastic brewpub has eight varieties of suds on tap, including honey beer, nut brown and the more challenging raspberry blonde. The brick walls and wood paneling are conducive to chats among the relaxed student crowd. Live blues bands play nightly (from 10pm). It really picks up after the night classes from nearby Concordia get out.

HURLEY'S IRISH PUB
PUB

Map p272 (☎514-861-4111; www.hurleysirishpub. com; 1125 Rue Crescent; ☉11am-3am; ⓜGuy-Concordia) This cozy place on bar-lined Rue Crescent features live rock and fiddling Celtic folk on the rear stage and beer-soaked football and soccer matches on big-screen TVs. Classic pub grub – Irish lamb stew, fish 'n' chips and burgers – is also served.

LE VIEUX DUBLIN PUB & RESTAURANT
PUB

Map p276 (☎514-861-4448; www.dublinpub.ca; 636 Rue Cathcart; ☉11am-3am Mon-Sat, 4pm-3am Sun; ⓜMcGill) The city's oldest Irish pub has the expected great selection of brews (from $7 to $9 per pint) and live Celtic or pop music nightly. Curries rub shoulders with burgers on the menu. It has 50 single malts.

PUB STE-ÉLISABETH
PUB

Map p276 (www.ste-elisabeth.com; 1412 Rue Ste-Élisabeth; ☉4pm-3am; ⓜBerri-UQAM) Tucked off a side street, this handsome little pub is frequented by many for its heavenly vine-covered courtyard and drinks menu with a great selection of beers, whiskies and ports. It has a respectable lineup of beers on tap, including imports and microbrewery fare such as Boréale Noire and Cidre Mystique.

SIR WINSTON CHURCHILL PUB
PUB

Map p272 (www.winniesbar.com; 1455 Rue Crescent; ☉11:30am-3am; ⓜGuy-Concordia) This Rue Crescent staple is the go-to spot of the block. Winnie's cavernous, split-level pub draws a steady crowd of tourists and students and an older Anglo crowd. Among multiple bars, pool tables and pulsating music, meals are served all day and happy-hour drink specials abound.

CLUB SODA
LIVE MUSIC

Map p276 (☎514-286-1010; www.clubsoda. ca; 1225 Blvd St-Laurent; adult/student $5/3; ☉9pm-3am; ⓜSt-Laurent) This venerable club hosts some of the city's most eclectic bands. Up-and-coming indie-rock, punk, metal, country and hip-hop groups have all taken the stage, as have well-known stars like Bebel Gilberto and Rufus Wainwright. There are also tribute nights (to Pink Floyd, the Doors, Italian metal bands), evenings of comedy, and the odd Muay Thai match.

Check the website to see what's on.

HOUSE OF JAZZ
JAZZ CLUB

Map p276 (☎514-842-8656; www.houseof jazz.ca; 2060 Rue Aylmer; ☉4-11:30pm Mon, 11:30am-1:30am Tue-Fri, 5pm-1:30am Sat & Sun; ⓜMcGill) Formerly known as Biddle's, this mainstream-but-excellent jazz club and restaurant changed names when owner-bassist Charlie Biddle passed away in 2003. Today, Southern-style cuisine and live jazz are on the menu daily. Prepare to wait if you haven't reserved. Cover is $5 to $12.

Concerts happen at 7:30pm from Sunday to Thursday and at 6:30pm and 9:30pm on Friday and Saturday.

☆ ENTERTAINMENT

PLACE DES ARTS
PERFORMING ARTS

Map p276 (☎box office 514-842-2112; www.place desarts.com; 175 Rue Ste-Catherine Ouest; ⓜPlace-des-Arts) Montréal's premier music venue, the storied Place des Arts is at the heart of the growing Quartier des Spectacles.

L'ASTRAL
MUSIC VENUE

Map p276 (www.sallelastral.com; 305 Rue Ste-Catherine St Ouest; ⓜPlace-des-Arts) Recent renovations to the century-old Blumenthal Building have added another venue to Montréal's jazz fest as part of the Quartier des Spectacles. With more than 300 seats and standing room for 600, L'Astral nestles in the Maison du Festival Rio Tinto Alcan, which also houses Le Balmoral, a jazz club and bistro with a patio on the ground floor.

MONUMENT NATIONAL   PERFORMING ARTS

Map p276 (☑514-871-2224; www.monument national.com; 1182 Blvd St-Laurent; MSt-Laurent) Québec's oldest theater still in use, the grand Monument National opened in 1893, and has been showing a wide range of cultural fare ever since. Shows here run the gamut from Molière to Sam Shepard, with acting, directing and technical production performed by graduating students of the National Theatre School.

True to the city's bilingual roots, the theater stages works in both French and English. There are two halls, one with 800 seats, the other with 150. The smaller theater stages about three original works a year by student playwrights. Comedy and modern dance are also part of the repertoire.

LES GRANDS BALLETS CANADIENS DE MONTRÉAL   DANCE

Map p276 (☑514-842-2112; www.grandsballets. qc.ca; Pl des Arts; MPlace-des-Arts) You can be assured of a treat if you see Québec's leading ballet troupe. As well as staging six shows per season (October through May) annually in Montréal at various venues, the dancers head off on several international tours per year. Its classical and modern programs are both innovative and accessible.

Recent hits include adaptations of *The Little Prince* and *Anna Karenina* as well as more traditional fare such as *Don Quixote*. Check the website for details.

ORCHESTRE SYMPHONIQUE DE MONTRÉAL   CLASSICAL MUSIC

Map p276 (OSM; ☑514-842-9951; www.osm.ca/ en; 1600 Rue St-Urbain, Maison Symphonique, Pl des Arts; MPlace-des-Arts) This internationally renowned orchestra plays to packed audiences in its Place des Arts base, the **Maison Symphonique de Montréal**, a venue with spectacular acoustics that was inaugurated in 2011. The OSM's Christmas performance of *The Nutcracker* is legendary.

Rock-star conductor Kent Nagano, a Californian with a leonine mane and stellar credentials, took over as music director in 2006 and has proven very popular. Check for free concerts at the Basilique Notre-Dame, the Olympic Stadium and in municipal parks in the Montréal area.

CINÉMA DU PARC   CINEMA

Map p276 (☑514-281-1900; www.cinemaduparc. com; 3575 Ave du Parc; MPlace-des-Arts, then bus 80) In the lower level of the Galeries du Parc complex, Montréal's English-language repertory cinema is a favorite of Plateau cinephiles. It shows cult classics as well as cool new releases and lots of foreign films. Despite the shabby decor, its charm and authenticity add to the cinematic experience.

CINÉMA BANQUE SCOTIA MONTRÉAL   CINEMA

Map p276 (www.cineplex.com; 977 Rue Ste-Catherine Ouest; MPeel) This entertainment monstrosity features crowds darting through junk-food kiosks amid a riot of flashing lights and booming sounds to get to the IMAX megascreens. One step up from IMAX, is the D-Box cinema, where movie-goers can feel vibrations in their seats, which sync to the action and audio on screen. Hollywood blockbusters are the general fare at this multilevel cinema.

METROPOLIS   LIVE MUSIC

Map p276 (☑514-844-3500; www.montreal metropolis.ca; 59 Rue Ste-Catherine Est; MSt-Laurent) Housed in a former art-deco cinema, this beautiful old space (capacity 2300) has featured everyone from indie rockers Interpol to blues legend Buddy Guy to local favorite Jean Leloup. It's sometimes used as a party or rave venue with DJs and dancing. Buy tickets at the **box office** (1413 Rue St-Dominique) around the corner.

POLLACK CONCERT HALL   CONCERT VENUE

Map p276 (www.mcgill.ca/music; 555 Rue Sherbrooke Ouest; MMcGill) McGill University's main music hall features concerts and recitals from its students and faculty, notably the McGill Chamber Orchestra. It's in the stately 19th-century building behind the statue of Queen Victoria.

SAT   ARTS CENTER

Map p276 (☑514-844-2033; www.sat.qc.ca; 1195 Blvd St-Laurent; MSt-Laurent) Officially called La Société des Arts Technologiques, this slick warehouse and new-media space hosts a range of thought-provoking fare. The 360-degree Satosphere shows cutting-edge audiovisual works, while the Espace Sat stages technology-driven exhibitions and the odd theater troupe and performing artist. Also on-site (on the 3rd floor, next to the Satosphere) is Foodlab (p80), a creative eating and drinking venue.

MONTRÉAL BY BIXI

Montréal is one of the most bike-friendly cities in North America, with hundreds of kilometers of bicycle paths across the city. In 2009 the city unveiled Bixi (p240), an extensive network of bike-renting stations around town, with bikes available from mid-April through October. For short jaunts, it's great value (a 24-hour/72-hour subscription fee is $5/12; bikes are free for the first 45 minutes and $1.75 for the next 15 minutes). If you're just going to use it once for a quick jaunt, opt for the one-way trip which, at $2.75, costs less than a bus fare. The network includes more than 5000 bikes scattered around 400 stations. Bixi has since inspired bike-rental systems in other cities, including London and New York City.

Checking out a bike from a stand is easy. Just insert a credit card and follow the instructions. The majority of Bixi stands display a network map showing other docking stations across the city. Once you dock the bike, you must wait two minutes before checking out another one. Just reinsert your credit card and go. (Bixi tallies up the charges at the end of a 24-hour period. As long as you always return a bike within 45 minutes, you'll only be charged the one-time fare.) Although the bikes are fine for short hops, the pricing structure discourages longer trips (it costs $1.75 for 45- to 60-minutes of usage, $3.50 for the next 30 minutes and $7 for every 30 minutes thereafter). If you're planning a long day's outing, it's better to rent from a bike shop.

Throughout the year, SAT holds the occasional party night. DJs and performance artists push the envelope with banks of multimedia installations, while an arty, electro-loving fan base dance and carouse.

I MUSICI DE MONTRÉAL   CLASSICAL MUSIC
Map p276 (☑514-982-6038; www.imusici.com; 279 Rue Sherbrooke Est; MSt-Laurent) Under the leadership of Jean-Marie Zeitouni, this 12-member chamber ensemble has won many awards for its baroque and contemporary performances. Over the past 20 years I Musici has recorded more than 30 CDs and toured the world. They play in a variety of venues, including the Chapelle Historique du Bon-Pasteur.

OPÉRA DE MONTRÉAL   OPERA
Map p276 (☑514-985-2258; www.operade montreal.com; Pl des Arts; MPlace-des-Arts) Holds lavish stage productions in the Salle Wilfrid-Pelletier that feature big names from Québec and around the world. The repertoire includes four or five operas each year, with a focus on classics such as *Madame Butterfly, The Barber of Seville* and *Turandot*, as well as contemporary works – such as the Pulitzer Prize–winning *Silent Night,* which premiered in 2011.

Translations (French and English) are run on a video screen above the stage. Tickets cost around $49 to $121 during the week and slightly more on Saturday.

ORCHESTRE MÉTROPOLITAIN   CLASSICAL MUSIC
Map p276 (☑514-842-2112; www.orchestre metropolitain.com; 1600 Rue St-Urbain; MPlace-des-Arts) This hip 60-member orchestra is comprised of young professional musicians from all over Québec, and led by conductor Yannick Nézet-Séguin. The orchestra's mission is to democratize classical music, so aside from playing inside the swish Maison Symphonique at Place des Arts, you may see the orchestra playing Mahler or Haydn in churches or colleges in the city's poorest neighborhoods for reduced admission.

Ticket prices start at $33 ($29 for those age 34 and under, and just $12 for youths).

SALSATHÈQUE   DANCE
Map p276 (☑514-875-0016; www.salsatheque. ca; 1220 Rue Peel; ☺10pm-3am Thu-Sat; MPeel) This bright, busy, dressy place presents large live salsa bands pumping out tropical rhythms. The Latin community (and their admirers) come out in droves to tear up the dance floor. When you need a break, you can refuel with a margarita while watching the 25-to-50s crowd gyrate into exhaustion.

SHARX   BILLIARDS
Map p272 (☑514-934-3105; www.sharx.ca; 1606 Rue Ste-Catherine Ouest; ☺11am-3am; MGuy-Concordia) This underground cavern has no fewer than 25 billiard tables amid a vaguely club-like setting, with loud pumping music, low lighting and an industrial design. The

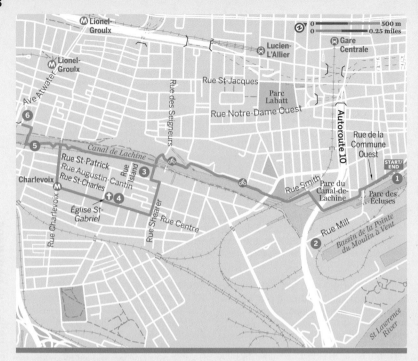

Cycling Tour
Cycling the Canal de Lachine

START CANAL LOCKS
END CANAL LOCKS
LENGTH 7KM; TWO HOURS

The prettiest cycle path in Montréal stretches along the Canal de Lachine. On warm days you'll see sunbathers on the grass, families at picnic tables, and cyclists and in-line skaters gliding along.

Start at the ❶ **Canal locks** at the southwestern end of the Old Port. This area has an industrial feel thanks to the abandoned grain silo southeast of the locks.

Pedaling southwest along Rue de la Commune Ouest, you'll pass under Autoroute 10. Continue along the downtown side of the canal, lined with strips of greenery. The enormous neon sign ❷ **Farine Five Roses** crowns a former flour mill.

The path switches sides at the bridge at Rue des Seigneurs, where you come to a ❸ **former silk mill** that ran its operations on hydraulic power from the canal. The red-brick factory has been reborn as lofts.

Continue south on Rue Shearer and turn right on Rue Centre. You'll come to Romanesque ❹ **Église St-Charles** on your right. Push your bike over to French-style Église St-Gabriel, taking in the charm of this little-visited neighborhood.

Cycle to Rue Charlevoix, turn right and you'll soon be on the bike path again. Turn left, and you'll come to ❺ **H2O Adventures** (p142), a kayak-rental outfit. If you're interested in getting out on the water, this is the place to do it.

Continue on the bike path and turn right at the pedestrian bridge to head to ❻ **Marché Atwater**, one of the city's best markets. Assemble a picnic here to enjoy by the water, followed by an easy pedal back to the port. If you want to explore further, head west. Another 10km along the path will take you to a sculpture garden at the edge of scenic Lac St-Louis – a favorite spot at sunset. To head back, simply follow the canal path back to the Canal Locks.

10-lane bowling alley is bathed in fluorescent light with glowing balls and pins. It draws a younger crowd – though not too young; it's age 18 and up. There's also a golf simulator.

FOUFOUNES ÉLECTRIQUES   LIVE MUSIC

Map p276 (www.foufouneselectriques.com; 87 Rue Ste-Catherine Est; ⊙4pm-3am; MSt-Laurent) A one-time bastion of the alternafreak, this cavernous quintessential punk venue still stages some wild music nights (rockabilly, ska, metal), plus the odd one-off (a night of pro-wrestling or an indoor skateboarding contest). On weekends the student-grunge crowd plays pool and quaffs brews with electro kids and punk stragglers. DJ nights range from free to $8. Concerts cost $10 to $25.

 # SHOPPING

HENRI HENRI   FASHION

Map p276 (www.henrihenri.ca; 189 Rue Ste-Catherine Est; ⊙10am-6pm Mon-Fri, to 5pm Sat & Sun; MSt-Laurent) Going strong since 1932, this classy millinery sells an impressive assortment of hats, including top global brands such as Stetson, Akubra and Kangol, as well as the Henri Henri house brand. You'll also find gloves, scarves, suspenders and other gentlemanly attire.

Curious footnote: between 1950 and 1970, Henri Henri used to award a free hat to a hockey player who scored three goals or more in a match at the Montréal forum – hence the origin of the term 'hat trick.'

CANDY LABS   FOOD

Map p272 (www.candylabs.ca; 2305 Rue Guy; ⊙11am-7pm Sun-Wed, to 9pm Thu & Fri; MGuy-Concordia) Head to this bright little shop for jewel-like hard candy. You can watch the candy makers in action since these artful sweets are made onsite, and then packaged in pretty glass jars that make great gifts. There are some 40 flavors available, and the friendly staff are happy to let you sample a wide assortment.

SALVATION ARMY   CLOTHING

Map p272 (1620 Rue Notre Dame Ouest; ⊙9am-9pm Mon-Fri, to 5pm Sat; MLucien l'Allier) This sprawling secondhand store has seemingly endless racks of clothes, plus 99¢ books (French and English), records, sports gear (including skis and snowboards) and more.

HOLT RENFREW   DEPARTMENT STORE

Map p272 (☎514-842-5111; www.holtrenfrew.com; 1300 Rue Sherbrooke Ouest; ⊙10am-6pm Mon-Wed & Sat, to 9pm Thu & Fri, 11am-6pm Sun; MPeel) This Montréal institution is a godsend for label-conscious, cashed-up professionals and upscale shoppers. From fragrances to cosmetics, jewelry and men's and women's fashion, Holt's is the go-to spot for prestigious brands such as Gucci and Prada. Services include personal shoppers and concierges, and the excellent Holts Café.

LES COURS MONT-ROYAL   MALL

Map p276 (www.lcmr.ca; 1455 Rue Peel; ⊙10am-6pm Mon-Wed, to 9pm Thu & Fri, to 5pm Sat, noon-5pm Sun; MPeel) This elegant shopping mall is a reincarnation of the Mount Royal Hotel (1922), at the time the largest hotel in the British Empire. The 1000-room hotel was converted into a snazzy mix of condos and fashion boutiques in 1988. You'll find designer names like Ursula B, DKNY and Desigual among the boutiques here.

Under the skylight you'll see birdman sculptures by Inuit artist David Pioukuni. The spectacular chandelier is from Monte Carlo's old casino. The atrium food court is a notch above most mall eateries, with sushi, Thai, Tex-Mex and other options.

HUDSON BAY CO   DEPARTMENT STORE

Map p276 (☎514-281-4422; www.thebay.com; 585 Rue Ste-Catherine Ouest; ⊙10am-7pm Sun-Wed, to 9pm Thu & Fri, 9am-7pm Sat; MMcGill) La Baie, as it's called in French, found fame three centuries ago for its striped wool blankets used to measure fur skins. The unique blankets are still available, in wool and fleece, on the ground floor. Take the escalators to reach the clothing boutiques, where you can find all the top labels (Theory, Moschino, Ralph Lauren, Stella McCartney, John Varvatos).

EVA B   VINTAGE

Map p276 (www.eva-b.ca; 2015 Blvd St-Laurent; ⊙11am-9pm Mon-Sat, noon-7pm Sun; MSt-Laurent) Stepping into this graffiti-smeared space is like entering a theater's backstage with a riot of fur coats, bowling shirts, cowboy boots, leather jackets, wigs, suede handbags, dresses, patterned sweaters and denim of all shapes and sizes. There's lots of junk, but prices are low, and you can unearth a few treasures if you have the time.

There's also a cafe (with coffee, baked goods, samosas and salads).

LES ANTIQUITÉS
GRAND CENTRAL ANTIQUES

Map p272 (☑514-935-1467; www.grandcentral inc.ca; 2448 Rue Notre-Dame Ouest; ☻9:30am-5:30pm Mon-Fri, 11am-5pm Sat; ⓂLionel-Groulx) The most elegant store on Rue Notre-Dame's Antique Row is a pleasure to visit for its English and continental furniture, lighting and decorative objects from the 18th and 19th centuries. Get buzzed in to see the Louis XIV chairs, full dining-room suites and chandeliers in Dutch cathedral or French Empire style, with price tags in the thousands.

ROOTS FASHION

Map p276 (☑514-845-7995; www.canada.roots. com; 1035 Rue Ste-Catherine Ouest; ☻10am-9pm Mon-Fri, 9am-8pm Sat, 10am-6pm Sun; ⓂPeel) One of Canada's best known home-grown brands, Roots started off as a humble shoemaker in the '70s. Now its range includes Roots for kids, Roots athletics, leather and home accessories. Tastes are accessible and geared to teens and 20-somethings; they are fashionable and at times even innovative.

PLACE MONTRÉAL TRUST MALL

Map p276 (www.placemontrealtrust.com; 1500 Ave McGill College; ☻10am-6pm Mon-Wed, to 9pm Thu & Fri, to 5pm Sat, 11am-5pm Sun; ⓂMcGill) One of downtown's most successful malls, with enough rays from the skylights to keep shoppers on their day clock. Major retailers here include La Senza lingerie, Indigo books, Winners and Zara. It has a tremendous water fountain with a spout 30m high, and during the holidays a Christmas tree illuminates the five-story space.

🏃 SPORTS & ACTIVITIES

MONTRÉAL CANADIENS HOCKEY

Map p272 (☑514-932-2582; www.canadiens.com; 1200 Rue de la Gauchetière Ouest, Bell Centre; tickets $54-277; ⓂBonaventure) The Canadiens of the National Hockey League have won the Stanley Cup 24 times. Although the team has struggled in recent years, Montréalers have a soft spot for the 'Habs' and matches at the **Bell Centre** (Map p272; ☑877-668-8269, 514-790-2525; www.centrebell. ca; 1909 Ave des Canadiens-de-Montréal) sell out routinely. Scalpers hang around the entrance on game days, and you might snag a half-price ticket after the puck drops.

Bring your binoculars for the rafter seats. The center also hosts big-name concerts, boxing matches and Disney on Ice.

MONTRÉAL ALOUETTES FOOTBALL

Map p276 (☑514-871-2255; www.montreal alouettes.com; Ave des Pins Ouest, Molson Stadium; tickets from $29; ⓂMcGill) The Montréal Alouettes, a star franchise of the Canadian Football League, folded several times before going on to win the league's Grey Cup trophy in 2002, 2009 and 2010. Rules are a bit different from American football: the field is bigger and there are only three downs. Games are held at McGill University's Molson Stadium and sometimes at the Stade Olympique. Purchase advance tickets online or at Molson Stadium. On game day, there are free shuttles from Square-Victoria and McGill metro stations.

MY BICYCLETTE BICYCLE RENTAL

(☑514-317-6306; www.mybicyclette.com; 2985 Rue St-Patrick; bicycle per hr/day from $10/30; ☻9am-6pm Sun-Fri, to 7pm Sat mid-Apr–Oct; ⓂCharlevoix) Located along the Canal de Lachine (just across the bridge from the Atwater market), this place rents bikes and other gear during the warmer months. It also sponsors city bike tours, and the repair shop next door is a good place to go if your bike conks out on the Lachine Canal path.

ATRIUM SKATING

Map p276 (☑514-395-0555; www.le1000.com; 1000 Rue de la Gauchetière Ouest; adult/child $7.50/5, skate rentals $7; ☻11:30am-6pm Mon, to 9pm Tue-Fri, 12:30-9pm Sat & Sun; ⓂBonaventure) Enjoy year-round indoor ice skating at this excellent glass-domed rink near Gare Centrale. On weekends, kids and their families have a special session from 11am to 12:30pm. Special events change regularly – such as the summertime 'Bermudas Madness,' a cheesy good time of skating in shorts and T-shirts while DJs spin summer-inflected beats. Call for operating hours as the schedule changes frequently.

ASHTANGA YOGA STUDIO YOGA

Map p276 (☑514-875-9642; www.ashtangamon treal.com; ste 118, 372 Rue Ste-Catherine Ouest; 1½ hr class $17; ⓂPlace-des-Arts) Ashtanga is an intense, aerobic form of the exercise. This professional center has big studios, friendly staff and offers 30-plus classes for all age groups and skill levels. Multiclass discount cards available (five classes $75). It's inside the gallery-filled Belgo building.

Quartier Latin & the Village

Neighborhood Top Five

1 Sipping *un café*, beer or whiskey and soaking up the bohemian atmosphere on colorful **Rue St-Denis** (p91).

2 Letting it all hang out while partying until dawn at one of the many bars and clubs in the **Village** (p95).

3 Admiring the neo-Gothic interior of **Église St-Pierre Apôtre** (p92) and its moving chapel dedicated to AIDS victims.

4 Stepping back in time to the 1920s at the **Éco-musée du Fier Monde** (p92), for a glimpse of life in working-class Montréal.

5 Catching a cutting-edge show at **Usine C** (p99), followed by drinks and tapas at **Le C** (p95).

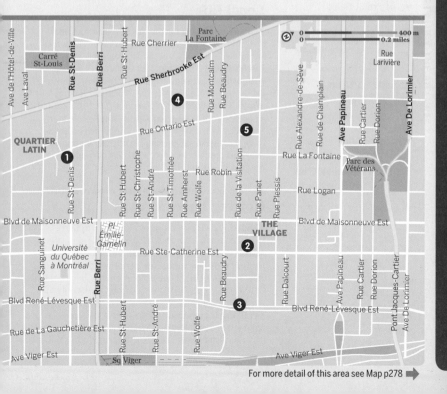

For more detail of this area see Map p278 ➡

Best Places to Eat

→ Ma'Tine (p95)

→ Le Grain de Sel (p93)

→ Kitchenette (p93)

→ Au Petit Extra (p93)

→ O'Thym (p93)

For reviews, see p93. →

Best Places to Drink

→ Le Cheval Blanc (p95)

→ B1 Bar (p95)

→ L'Île Noire (p95)

→ Le Saint Sulpice (p98)

→ Le Saint-Bock (p98)

For reviews, see p95. →

Best Entertainment

→ Usine C (p99)

→ Théâtre St-Denis (p99)

→ Cabaret Mado (p99)

For reviews, see p99. →

Best Places to Shop

→ Camellia Sinensis (p100)

→ Zéphyr (p100)

→ Archambault (p100)

For reviews, see p100. →

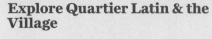

Explore Quartier Latin & the Village

The boisterous district of Quartier Latin and the Village is fairly compact and easy to explore in an afternoon with the option to kick back and party into the night. Start at Rue Sherbrooke and Rue St-Denis and explore the latter to Rue Ste-Catherine. Be sure to pause for a beverage or snack as you go.

St-Denis picks up at night when local watering holes, restaurants and clubs attract students and other bons vivants who come together over beer and *bouffe* (food). It's best to do a bit of roaming and absorb the free-spirited energy of the quarter. If you want to take a breather during the day, try Carré St-Louis, north of Rue Sherbrooke and off Rue St-Denis, or Place Émilie-Gamelin along Rue Ste-Catherine.

One of the hottest gay meccas in North America, the Village is quiet during the day, but starts to pick up around 9pm. Packed with eclectic eateries, shops and nightspots, Rue Ste-Catherine is the main thoroughfare here, so it's easy to navigate. August is the most frenetic time as international visitors gather to celebrate Divers/Cité, the massive annual Gay Pride parade.

Local Life

→**Eating out** Even starving artists need fuel. Rue St-Denis has some casual-eating brasseries such as Le Saint-Bock (p98), but the best options, such as Kitchenette (p93), are further afield.

→**Nightlife** Start your evening with a drink on Rue St-Denis, then mosey over to the Village for a floorshow in drag at Cabaret Mado (p99) and let the night unfold.

→**Festivals** The **Montréal World Film Festival** (☏514-848-3883; www.ffm-montreal.org) and **Montréal Pride** (www.fiertemontrealpride.com) make this neighborhood nearly as festive as Downtown on Montréal's celebration circuit.

Getting There & Away

→**Metro** The orange and green lines run to Berri-UQAM; the green line continues to Beaudry and Papineau.

→**Bus** Bus 24 runs along Rue Sherbrooke, the 30 along Rue St-Denis and Rue Berri, and the 15 along Rue Ste-Catherine. The Station Centrale bus terminal (www.stationcentrale.com) is a hub for intercity and international coach services.

→**Walking** It's relatively easy to reach the Quartier Latin from either Downtown or Plateau Mont-Royal, and you can also stroll along Rue Ste-Catherine to the Village.

TOP SIGHT
RUE ST-DENIS

One of the few streets to cross the entire island of Montréal, Rue St-Denis coalesces in four blocks below Rue Sherbrooke – a carnivalesque collection of restaurants, brasseries, cafes and arts venues. It captures the heart of francophone Montréal, just as St-Laurent was once the preferred hangout of Anglos. This is where you'll find students from nearby Université du Québec à Montréal (UQAM) grabbing a pint after protesting tuition hikes, or big-name US comics doing stand up at Théâtre St-Denis. It's a heady mix best enjoyed with a drink in summer.

The terraced cafes and restaurants of the Quartier Latin are great spots to watch the world go by, over coffee, croissants or even a bowl of borscht. Popular with students at UQAM, which number in the tens of thousands, the Quartier Latin is unrivaled when it comes to budget dining, inexpensive bistro fare and meals in a hurry. There are also abundant bars nearby, making for an easy transition from dinner to nighttime amusement.

In the 19th century the neighborhood was an exclusive residential area for wealthy Francophones. Although many original buildings burned in the great fire of 1852, there are a number of Victorian and art-nouveau gems hidden on the tree-lined streets. Today, the quarter is a hotbed of activity, especially during summer festivals, when energy spills from the streets 24 hours a day.

Rue St-Denis is also an entry of sorts to the Village, one of the largest gay communities in North America. Packed with eclectic eateries, shops and outrageous nightspots, Rue Ste-Catherine is the Village's main thoroughfare, and it closes to traffic periodically in the summer.

DON'T MISS

➡ People-watching with a drink

➡ Just for Laughs comedy festival

➡ Divers/Cité Gay Pride parade

PRACTICALITIES

➡ Map p278

➡ Ⓜ Berri-UQAM

● SIGHTS

RUE ST-DENIS   STREET
See p91.

**BIBLIOTHÈQUE ET ARCHIVES
NATIONALE DU QUÉBEC**   LIBRARY
Map p278 (www.banq.qc.ca; 475 Blvd de Maisonneuve Est; ⊙10am-10pm Tue-Thu, to 6pm
Fri-Sun; ⓂBerri-UQAM) Opened in 2005, this
stunning building houses both the library
and national archives of Québec. The library itself is 33,000 sq meters, connected
to the metro and underground city. Everything published in Québec (books, brochures, sound recordings, posters) since
1968 has been deposited here. Aside from
books, the library has changing exhibitions,
performances (poetry, jazz) and workshops.

ÉGLISE ST-PIERRE-APÔTRE   CHURCH
Map p278 (☏514-524-3791; 1201 Rue de la Visitation; ⊙10:30am-4pm Mon-Fri, noon-5pm Sat,
9:30am-4pm Sun; ⓂBeaudry) The Church of
St Peter the Apostle belonged to the monastery of the Oblate fathers who settled in
Montréal in the mid-19th century. Located

in the Village, this neoclassical church has
a number of fine decorations – flying but-
tresses, stained glass, statues in Italian
marble – but nowadays the house of worship is more renowned for its gay-friendly
Sunday services.

It also houses the Chapel of Hope, the
first chapel in the world consecrated in
1997 to the memory of victims of AIDS.

ÉCOMUSÉE DU FIER MONDE   MUSEUM
Map p278 (☏514-528-8444; www.ecomusee.
qc.ca; 2050 Rue Amherst; adult/child $8/6;
⊙11am-8pm Wed, 9:30am-4pm Thu & Fri,
10:30am-5pm Sat & Sun; ⓂBerri-UQAM) This
striking ex-bathhouse explores the history of Centre-Sud, an industrial district
in Montréal until the 1950s and now part
of the Village. The museum's permanent
exhibition, *Triumphs and Tragedies of a
Working-Class Neighborhood,* puts faces
on the industrial era through a series of
photos and multimedia displays.

The 1927 building is the former Bain
Généreux, an art-deco public bathhouse
modeled on one in Paris. Frequent modern-
art exhibitions are also held here.

THE METRO MUSEUM OF ART

Primarily a mover of the masses, the Montréal metro was also conceived as an enormous art gallery, although not all stations have been decorated. Here are a few highlights from the central zone; many more await your discovery.

Berri-UQAM

A set of murals by artist Robert La Palme representing science, culture and recreation
hangs above the main staircase leading to the yellow line. These works were moved
here from the *Man and His World* pavilion of Expo '67 at the request of mayor Jean
Drapeau, a buddy of La Palme.

Champ-de-Mars

The station kiosk boasts a set of antique stained-glass windows by Marcelle Ferron,
an artist of the Refus global movement. The abstract forms splash light down into the
shallow platform, drenching passengers in color as their trains roll through.

Peel

Circles, circles everywhere: in bright single colors on advertising panels, in the marble
of one entrance, above the main staircases, as tiles on the floor – even the bulkhead
vents are circular. They're the work of Jean-Paul Mousseau of the Québecois art
movement Les Automatistes.

Place-des-Arts

The station's east wall has a backlit stained-glass mural entitled *Les Arts Lyriques,*
by Québecois artist and Oscar-winning filmmaker Frédéric Back. It depicts the evolu-
tion of Montréal's music from the first trumpet fanfare played on the island in 1535 to
modern composers and conductors.

CHAPELLE
NOTRE-DAME-DE-LOURDES CHURCH

Map p278 (☑514-845-8278; www.cndlm.org;
430 Rue Ste-Catherine Est; ⊘11am-6pm Mon-Fri,
10:30am-6:30pm Sat, 9am-6:30pm Sun; ⓂBerri-
UQAM) Now hidden among the university
buildings, this Romanesque gem was built
by the Sulpicians in 1876 to cement their
influence in Montréal. The chapel was designed by Rue St-Denis resident and artist
Napoléon Bourassa. His frescoes, which are
dotted about the interior, are regarded as
his crowning glory.

RUE STE-CATHERINE EST STREET

Map p278 (ⓂBeaudry) Montréal's embrace
of the gay community is tightest along the
eastern end of Rue Ste-Catherine, a one-
time bed of vice and shabby tenements.
This strip of restaurants and clubs has been
made so presentable that middle-class families mingle with drag queens on the pave-
ments, all part of the neighborhood scenery.

UNIVERSITÉ DU
QUÉBEC À MONTRÉAL UNIVERSITY

Map p278 (☑514-987-3000; www.uqam.ca;
405 Rue Ste-Catherine Est; ⓂBerri-UQAM) The
modern, rather drab buildings of Montréal's French-language university blend into
the cityscape and are linked to the underground city and the Berri-UQAM metro
station. The most striking aspect here is the
old Gothic steeple of the **Église St-Jacques**,
which has been integrated into the university's facade.

🍴 EATING

JULIETTE ET CHOCOLAT CAFE $

Map p278 (☑514-287-3555; 1615 Rue St-Denis;
mains $8-15; ⊘11am-11pm; ⓂBerri-UQAM)
When the urge to devour something chocolaty arrives, make straight for Juliette et
Chocolat, a bustling little cafe where chocolate is served in every shape and form –
drizzled over crepes, blended into creamy
milkshakes and coffees, or straight up in a
blood-sugar-boosting chocolate 'shot.' The
setting is charming but small and busy.
For less hustle and bustle, visit the Laurier
location (p120).

1000 GRAMMES CAFE $

Map p278 (www.1000grammes.com; 1495 Rue
Ste-Catherine Est; mains $10-13; ⊘9am-10pm

Mon-Thu, to midnight Fri, 10:30am-midnight Sat,
10:30am-10pm Sun; ⓂPapineau) Known for
its decadent desserts such as *tarte aux
pacanes* (pecan pie) and ginormous salads
and sandwiches, this cafe is a fun, daytime
hangout for a mostly gay crowd. Grab a
table beside the huge windows, sip your
coffee and watch life go by. Staff are very
friendly and helpful.

KITCHENETTE AMERICAN $$

Map p278 (☑514-527-1016; www.kitchenetteres
taurant.ca; 1353 Blvd René Lévesque Est; mains
$17-30; ⊘11am-2pm & 5-11pm Tue-Fri, 5-11pm Sat
& Sun; ⓂBeaudry) Whether it's corn chowder
with smoked oysters or beer-braised short
ribs with mashed potatoes, Kitchenette
likes experimenting with southern comfort
food while keeping it simple and delicious.
Fridays are given over to mountainous fish
'n' chips. Be sure to reserve a spot in this
airy, elegant space.

O'THYM FRENCH $$

Map p278 (☑514-525-3443; www.othym.
com; 1112 Blvd de Maisonneuve Est; mains $25-
31; ⊘11:30am-2:30pm Tue-Fri, 6-10pm nightly;
ⓂBeaudry) O'Thym buzzes with foodies who
flock here from all over town. It features an
elegant but understated dining room (exposed brick walls, floodlit windows, oversized mirrors), and beautifully presented
plates of fresh seafood and grilled game.
Bring your own wine. The multicourse
lunch ($17 to $20) is a great way to dine well
without breaking the bank.

AU PETIT EXTRA FRENCH $$

Map p278 (☑514-527-5552; www.aupetitextra.
com; 1690 Rue Ontario Est; mains $22-31;
⊘11:30am-2:30pm Mon-Fri, 5:30-9:30pm nightly;
ⓂPapineau) This sweet little place serves
traditional bistro fare to a garrulous local
crowd. The blackboard menu changes frequently but features simple, flavorful dishes
(*steak frites,* foie gras (see p28), duck confit,
fish soup), and staff can expertly pair wines
with food. Reservations are advised.

LE GRAIN DE SEL BISTRO $$

Map p278 (☑514-522-5105; www.restolegrain
desel.ca; 2375 Rue Ste-Catherine Est; mains $22-
30; ⊘11:30am-2pm Tue-Fri, 6-10pm Thu-Sat;
ⓂPapineau, then bus 34) This tiny, friendly
bistro just beyond the eastern edge of the
Village exudes old-world ambience with a
small bar and open kitchen. The menu offers bistro fare and other delights such as

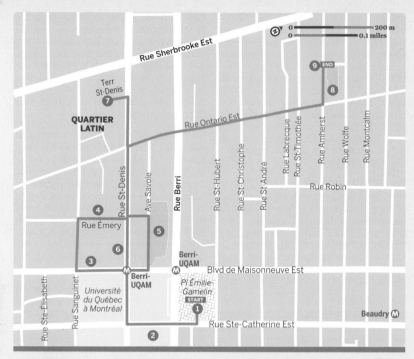

Neighborhood Walk
Bohemian Life in the Quartier Latin

START PL ÉMILIE-GAMELIN
END ÉCOMUSÉE DU FIER MONDE
LENGTH 2.5KM; ONE TO TWO HOURS

Begin your walk in the somewhat unkempt **1 Place Émilie-Gamelin**, site of spontaneous concerts, wacky metal sculptures, outdoor chess matches and punks with beleaguered pets.

Head southwest along Rue Ste-Catherine. Peek inside **2 Chapelle Notre-Dame-de-Lourdes** (p93), commissioned in 1876. This Romanesque gem has imaginative frescoes by Napoléon Bourassa.

Head up to Blvd de Maisonneuve and continue to the **3 Cinémathèque Québécoise** (p99). Look at the cinema exhibits on the 1st floor and check out the latest screenings – you can catch rare films here that you won't find elsewhere.

Loop around the block and head along tiny Rue Emery. Stop for a pick-me-up in **4 Camellia Sinensis** (p100), one of Montréal's best-loved teahouses. You can buy countless loose-leaf teas next door.

Cross Rue St-Denis and continue down the narrow lane. You'll reach the **5 Bibliothèque et Archives Nationale du Québec** (p92), a massive library housing an astounding collection of all things Québecois. Go into the main hall and downstairs to the gallery, which often hosts fascinating (and free) exhibitions.

Return to Rue St-Denis and turn right. You'll soon pass two of the neighborhood's cultural mainstays. **6 Théâtre St-Denis** (p99) is the city's second-largest theater. Continue up the street, noting the terrace cafes, lively pubs and quirky shops. The little side street, **7 Terrasse St-Denis**, was a meeting place of Montréal's bohemian set at the turn of the 20th century.

Walk back down and turn left on Rue Ontario Est, then left onto Rue Amherst. On your right is the grand art-deco **8 Marché St-Jacques** (p100), a tranquil market with great snack options. Up the street is the **9 Écomusée du Fier Monde** (p92), a small museum about working-class life in the neighborhood prior to the 1960s. It's in a former bathhouse built in 1927.

escargot, organic pork shoulder, fish and chips, and wild-mushroom ravioli. The waiters will marry the right wines with your meal. Reservations are advised.

MA'TINE
FRENCH $$

Map p278 (☎514-439-9969; 1310 Maisonneuve Est; mains $11-20; ☺7am-5pm Wed-Fri, 9am-3pm Sat & Sun; MBeaudry) A lovely addition to the Village, Ma'Tine has a bright, vintage-inspired setting where regulars pop by for a light meal from the ever-changing menu. The chefs prepare inventive but flavorful combinations such as endive, bearnaise sauce, smoked pork and a quail egg (that's one dish) or a trout croissant with goat's cheese and a fried egg.

In warm weather, grab a table on the spacious terrace – this is also where the restaurant grows its fresh herbs.

LE C
SPANISH $$

Map p278 (☎514-521-6002; www.restolec.com; 1901 Rue de la Visitation; small plates $6-18, paella $40-48; ☺4pm-midnight Tue-Thu, to 3am Fri & Sat; MBeaudry) On the lower level of the creative performing center Usine C, you'll find this low-lit Spanish-style tavern serving up excellent tapas, paella for two and first-rate cocktails and wine. Treat yourself to *gambas al ajillo* (shrimp with garlic), *sepia amb pessoals* (cuttlefish with chickpeas) and *albonidgas* (meatballs) along with a glass of tempranillo before catching a show next door.

SALOON
BISTRO $$

Map p278 (☎514-522-1333; www.lesaloon.ca; 1333 Rue Ste-Catherine Est; mains $15-27; ☺11:30am-2pm & 5-10pm Mon-Wed, 11:30am-11pm Thu-Fri, 10am-11pm Sat & Sun; MBeaudry) With nearly 20 years under its belt, this gay bar-bistro has earned a spot in Village hearts for its chilled atmosphere, live DJs, patio seating, cocktails and wide-ranging menu, including some good vegetarian options. A stylish pre-club pit stop.

🍷⚓ DRINKING & NIGHTLIFE

LE CHEVAL BLANC
MICROBREWERY

Map p278 (809 Rue Ontario Est; ☺3pm-3am; MSherbrooke) An icon of Montréal's brewery scene, Le Cheval Blanc has about 10 drafts on hand, all brewed in house, as well as some Belgian options by the bottle. It's a lively, easygoing place with a friendly all-ages crowd, smiling bartenders and an outdoor patio in the summer.

Our favorites: the raspberry-tinged framboise, the easy-drinking blanche (a wheat beer) and the Ch'fal Dublin, an Irish-style red ale.

B1 BAR
COCKTAIL BAR

Map p278 (www.barb1.com; 2021 Rue St-Denis; ☺5pm-3am Tue-Sun; MSherbrooke) Head downstairs to this subterranean drinking den for tasty cocktails and a bubbly crowd, which skews on the young side most nights. It's an atmospheric space with stone walls and low ceilings, served with a touch of quirkiness – some nights there's body painting, on others the gents can get a haircut and cocktail (a deal at $30).

DJs also spin from time to time.

RANDOLPH PUB
BAR

Map p278 (www.randolph.ca; 2041 Rue St-Denis; ☺4pm-1am Mon-Fri, from noon Sat & Sun; MBerri-UQAM) For something completely different, head to Randolph Pub. You pay a $5 cover, which gives you all-night access to the pub's vast selection of board games (over 1500 in its library). Then you can spend the evening playing games, drinking microbrews and noshing on nachos, sandwiches and salads. Avoid going on weekends, when the lines are long.

No reservations, and it's age 18 and up.

LOUP GAROU
BAR

Map p278 (1738 Rue St-Denis; ☺6pm-3am Mon-Sat; MSherbrooke) In the heart of bar-lined St-Denis, Loup Garou has a warm chalet-like vibe (exposed brick, wood paneling) with framed images of werewolves (*loup-garous*) everywhere. It's a casual spot with decent cocktails, a DJ and a young crowd. Language nerds shouldn't miss the Friday night Mundo Lingo events, where you can converse in your language(s) of choice with people from across the globe.

L'ÎLE NOIRE
PUB

Map p278 (www.ilenoire.com; 1649 Rue St-Denis; ☺3pm-3am; MBerri-UQAM) Roll into this slice of the Scottish Highlands in the heart of the Quartier Latin and sip from their selection of more than 140 scotches and whiskeys, as well as 15 varieties of beer on tap and several dozen wine choices.

BUENA VISTA IMAGES / GETTY IMAGES ©

1. Gay Montréal
Packed with clubs and restaurants, Rue St Catherine Est (p93) is the heart of the city's gay scene.

2. Art of the City
A Cabaret Mado (p99) sculpture brightens up the walls in the Village.

3. Row Houses
A colorful residential street in Montréal's Quartier Latin (p89).

4. Quartier Latin (p89)
This lively area is a gateway to vibrant cafes and laid-back bars.

The vibe here is decidedly less bohemian than other watering holes on Rue St-Denis, perfect if you want to take a breather from the surrounding carnival.

SKY PUB & CLUB   GAY
Map p278 (✏514-529-6969; 1474 Rue Ste-Catherine Est; ⊙noon-3am Tue-Sun; ⓜBeaudry) This is one of those popular Village complexes designed to suck you in for an entire Saturday night of partying. If you're a gorgeous guy or looking for one, start the evening in the 1st-floor pick-up pub before heading up to the dance floors (disco and energized house/hip-hop). The legendary roof terrace is a perfect place to catch L'International des Feux Loto-Québec (the fireworks competition) in summer.

LE SAINT SULPICE   PUB
Map p278 (www.lesaintsulpice.ca; 1680 Rue St-Denis; ⊙3pm-3am; ⓜBerri-UQAM) This student evergreen is spread over four levels in an old Victorian stone house – a cafe, several terraces, a disco and a sprawling back garden for drinks 'n' chats. The music changes with the DJ's mood, from hip-hop and ambient to mainstream rock and jazz.

LE SAINT-BOCK   PUB
Map p278 (www.lesaintbock.com; 1749 Rue St-Denis; ⊙11:30am-3am; ⓜBerri-UQAM) This convivial, low-lit brasserie has a decent selection of beers on tap and menu offerings that sometimes rise above conventional pub fare. It's a good spot to watch hockey on the screens before getting down to some serious drinking elsewhere.

CIRCUS   CLUB
Map p278 (www.circushd.com; 917 Rue Ste-Catherine Est; ⊙2am-8am Thu-Sun; ⓜBerri-UQAM) Sometimes featuring circus performers and dancers, this hot spot is more glamorous than you might expect from an after-hours joint; in fact, it ranks as the biggest of its kind in Canada. More than 200 visiting DJs a year appear behind the decks, to the dancing delight of glostick-brandishing ravers and clubbers who are not ready to call it a night.

Get there early to avoid the long line; alcohol is served before 3am.

LE MAGELLAN BAR   BAR
Map p278 (✏514-845-0909; www.pelerin magellan.com; 330 Rue Ontario Est; ⊙11am-9pm Mon, to 10pm Tue, Wed & Sat, to midnight Thu & Fri; ⓜBerri-UQAM) This is a good spot to enjoy an evening of eclectic offerings, from jazz to chansons. The interior is sprinkled with maritime doodads (there's an interesting gallery of antique maps upstairs), the front terrace is great for people-watching, while the back terrace is perfectly verdant in summer. It's joined to Le Pélerin restaurant.

STUD   GAY
Map p278 (✏514-598-8243; www.studbar.com; 1812 Rue Ste-Catherine Est; ⊙5pm-3am; ⓜPapineau) This Village meat market attracts older, heavier men, and its dark, down-at-the-heels design might bring to mind New York gay bars of the 1970s. The upside is that it's not pretentious at all, there's cheap beer and no cover charge, and the upstairs disco can be lots of fun.

CLUB DATE PIANO-BAR   PUB, GAY
Map p278 (1218 Rue Ste-Catherine Est; ⊙8am-3am; ⓜBeaudry) This gay tavern knew exactly what it was doing when it karaokefied the spot. A mixed crowd cheers on aspiring vocalists from all walks of life, from the hilariously awful to the downright star-worthy. Cheap drinks and a weird saloon vibe guarantee you a night to remember – or forget.

STEREO   CLUB
Map p278 (✏514-658-2646; www.stereonight club.net; 858 Rue Ste-Catherine Est; ⊙2am-11am Fri & Sat; ⓜBerri-UQAM) Montréal's giant of underground house music has opened and closed for various reasons throughout the years. Featuring a sound system so amazing that regulars gush about out-of-body experiences, Stereo is open for business once again, attracting anyone – gay, straight, students and drag queens – looking to lose sleep in style.

UNITY   GAY
Map p278 (www.clubunitymontreal.com; 1171 Rue Ste-Catherine Est; ⊙10pm-3am Thu-Sun; ⓜBeaudry) This three-floor Village favorite features not only a club and pub but a VIP lounge, pool tables and rooftop terrace. Saturdays are the best nights, while Fridays are given over to a mostly 20-something crowd.

APOLLON   GAY
Map p278 (www.apollonmtl.com; 1450 Rue Ste-Catherine Est; ⊙10pm-3am Tue & Thu-Sun;

MIXED MEMORIES

On every car in Montréal, you'll notice the motto 'Je me souviens' (I remember). Officially adopted as part of Québec's coat of arms in 1939, it has been the subject of intense debate as to its meaning. Some say it represents Québec's French heritage before the British victory on the Plains of Abraham in 1760. Others believe it has to do with perceived constitutional injustices that Québec has suffered in the 20th century. Actually, Québec bureaucrat Eugene Taché had it carved in the province's coat of arms on the Parliament building in Ottawa in 1883. Though he did not explain its meaning, it appears to originate in a poem he wrote, part of which runs as follows: *'Je me souviens que né sous le lys, je fleuris sous la rose.'* (I remember that I was born under the *fleur de lys*, but I blossomed under the rose.) It would suggest that Québec should remember that it was born from France (the lily) but matured under the institutions inherited from Britain (the rose). The motto's cryptic meaning is far from universally agreed upon, however. Montréal's aggressive drivers are usually too busy honking at each other to discuss it.

Berri-UQAM) Opened in the beautiful Station Postale C, a heritage post office built in 1912 that later hosted Village standby KOX, Apollon has an open-concept setup where you can look down on the gyrating bodies from balconies above. Saturday nights draw an older crowd, while Friday nights see a mix of mainstream pop music.

⭐ ENTERTAINMENT

USINE C
PERFORMING ARTS

Map p278 (🖉514-521-4493; www.usine-c. com; 1345 Ave Lalonde; MBeaudry) This former jam factory in the Village is home to the award-winning Carbone 14 theatrical dance troupe that performs here regularly. Its two flexible halls (450 and 150 seats) can be rejigged to accommodate circuses or concerts, but you're more likely to find interesting international drama collaborations.

To bump into its talented performers, head for the cozy tavern restaurant, Le C (p95), downstairs.

THÉÂTRE ST-DENIS
PERFORMING ARTS

Map p278 (🖉514-849-4211; www.theatrestdenis.com; 1594 Rue St-Denis; ⊙box office noon-6pm Mon-Sat; MBerri-UQAM) This Montréal landmark and historic movie house hosts touring Broadway productions, rock concerts and various theatrical and musical performances. Its two halls (933 and 2218 seats) are equipped with the latest sound and lighting gizmos and figure prominently in the Just for Laughs festival.

CINÉMATHÈQUE QUÉBÉCOISE
CINEMA

Map p278 (🖉514-842-9763; www.cinematheque.qc.ca; 335 Blvd de Maisonneuve Est; adult/student $10/9; ⊙10am-9pm Mon-Fri, 4-9pm Sat & Sun; MBerri-UQAM) This is a university-flavored venue noted for showing Canadian, Québecois and international avant-garde films. In the lobby there's a permanent exhibition on the history of filmmaking as well as a TV and new-media section.

CABARET MADO
CABARET

Map p278 (www.mado.qc.ca; 1115 Rue Ste-Catherine Est; tickets $5-15; ⊙4pm-3am Tue-Sun; MBeaudry) Mado is a flamboyant celebrity who has been featured in *Fugues,* the gay entertainment mag. Her cabaret is a local institution, with drag shows featuring an assortment of hilariously sarcastic performers in eye-popping costumes. Shows take place Tuesday, Thursday and weekend nights; check the website for details.

BISTRO À JOJO
BLUES

Map p278 (🖉514-843-5015; www.bistroajojo. com; 1627 Rue St-Denis; ⊙noon-3am; MBerri-UQAM) This brash venue in the Quartier Latin has been going strong since 1975. It's the nightly place for down 'n' dirty French- and English-language blues and rock groups. Sit close enough to see the band members sweat.

LE NATIONAL
LIVE MUSIC

Map p278 (🖉514-845-2014; www.latulipe.ca; 1220 Rue Ste-Catherine Est; MBeaudry) This 750-capacity concert venue situated in the Village was one of the first professional

French theaters in Montréal. In tandem with sister venue La Tulipe on Ave Papineau, it hosts a variety of acts from hardcore bands to pop shows. Check the website for listings.

THÉÂTRE STE-CATHERINE PERFORMING ARTS

Map p278 (514-284-3939; www.theatresainte catherine.com; 264 Rue Ste-Catherine Est; MBerri-UQAM) From film to theater, stand-up comedy to music concerts, this venue presents a variety of shows: Oscar Wilde one night, burlesque dance the next. Its Sunday Night Improv (sketch and comedy) performances are quite popular with the city's theatrical community; the Montreal Sketch Comedy Festival is in late May.

CINÉMA QUARTIER LATIN CINEMA

Map p278 (www.cineplex.com; 350 Rue Emery; 11:30am-10:15pm; MBerri-UQAM) This large cinema plays French films and French versions of some Hollywood movies, as well as live broadcasts of performances from the Metropolitan Opera in New York several times a month (check www.cineplex.com/opera for the schedule). It's also a host theater for the Montréal World Film Festival (p90).

 # SHOPPING

MARCHÉ ST-JACQUES MARKET

Map p278 (2035 Rue Amherst; 9am-7pm Mon-Fri, to 6pm Sat, to 5pm Sun; MBeaudry) A market has stood here since 1879, making it one of the oldest public *marchés* in Canada. The current building dates from 1931 and boasts a lovely art-deco design. While the offerings are limited (especially compared to Marché Jean-Talon and the Atwater market), this is still a fine place to pick up a picnic or a quick bite while exploring the Village.

You'll find bakery items, cheeses, smoked fish, sandwiches, pastas and pizza (at Rouge Tomate) and espresso drinks, along with shiny fruits and vegetables. There's also a popular creperie (Crêpanita) in front of the market, near Rue Ontario.

★CAMELLIA SINENSIS FOOD & DRINK

Map p278 (www.camellia-sinensis.com; 351 Rue Emery; 10am-6pm Mon-Wed, Sat & Sun, to 9pm Thu-Fri; MBerri-UQAM) Right in front of the Cinéma Quartier Latin, this welcoming tea shop has more than 200 varieties of tea from China, Japan, India and elsewhere in Asia, plus quality teapots, tea accessories, books, and workshops such as pairing tea with chocolate. You can taste exotic teas and carefully selected desserts in the salon next door, which features brews from recent staff travels.

AUX QUATRE POINTS CARDINAUX MAPS

Map p278 (www.aqpc.com; 551 Rue Ontario Est; 10am-6pm Mon-Wed, to 9pm Thu & Fri, to 5pm Sat; MBerri-UQAM) The globe-trotting folks at AQPC pack a range of goods for the seasoned traveler including atlases, globes, maps, aerial photographs, and travel guides in English and French, including a good selection of Lonely Planet books.

ZÉPHYR ART

Map p278 (514-529-9199; 2112 Rue Amherst; 10am-5pm Mon-Sat; MSherbrooke) One of several interesting shops along this stretch of Amherst, Daniel Roberge's bright gallery focuses on contemporary art from Québec, and Canadian artists such as Michel Roy and Danièle DeBlois.

BOUTIQUE SPOUTNIK ANTIQUES

Map p278 (www.boutiquespoutnik.com; 2120 Rue Amherst; 12-5pm Tue-Wed, Sat & Sun, 12-6pm Thu-Fri; MSherbrooke) Spoutnik has enough shiny retro stuff for your home, such as vintage wooden desks and globular lighting fixtures, that you'd swear you're back in the shagadelic '60s.

ARCHAMBAULT BOOKS, MUSIC

Map p278 (514-849-6202; www.archambault. ca; 500 Rue Ste-Catherine Est; 9:30am-9pm Mon-Fri, 9am-5pm Sat, 10am-5pm Sun; MBerri-UQAM) Behind the art-deco portals you'll find Montréal's oldest and largest book and record shop, an emporium that boasts CDs and books, plus assorted musical supplies such as pianos and sheet music.

PRIAPE SEX & FETISH

Map p278 (514-521-8451; www.priape.com; 1311 Rue Ste-Catherine Est; 11am-8pm Mon-Wed, to 10pm Thu-Sat, noon-7pm Sun; MBeaudry) Montréal's biggest gay sex store is well plugged into mainstream erotic wares (DVDs, mags and books), and also has high-quality clothing with a titillating edge – shrink-wrapped jeans, but also a vast choice of black leather gear in the basement.

Plateau Mont-Royal

PARC DU MONT-ROYAL AREA

Neighborhood Top Five

❶ Enjoying the fresh air, sweeping vistas and feathered friends of **Parc du Mont-Royal**, the beloved heart of Montréal.

❷ Join locals at the sun-drenched cafe **Moineau Masqué** (p109), then wander the Plateau's leafy backstreets.

❸ Exploring the old-world groceries that rub shoulders with stylish drinking dens along **Boulevard St-Laurent** (p103).

❹ Trolling the quirky shops, from old records to single-origin chocolate, along bohemian **Avenue du Mont-Royal** (p103).

❺ Chilling out in summer and ice-skating in winter in the broad expanse of local favorite **Parc La Fontaine** (p103).

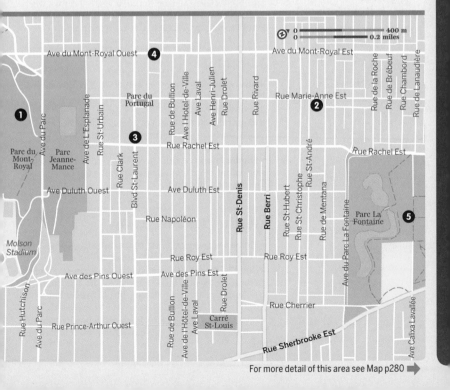

For more detail of this area see Map p280 ➡

Best Places to Eat

➡ L'Gros Luxe (p110)

➡ L'Express (p110)

➡ Hà (p110)

➡ Le Filet (p111)

➡ Au Pied de Cochon (p111)

➡ Schwartz's (p107)

For reviews, see p107. ➡

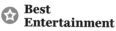 **Best Places to Drink**

➡ Le Lab (p111)

➡ La Distillerie (p111)

➡ Apt 200 (p111)

➡ Majestique (p112)

➡ SuWu (p112)

➡ Big in Japan (p111)

For reviews, see p111. ➡

⭐ **Best Entertainment**

➡ Casa del Popolo (p113)

➡ Dièse Onze (p113)

➡ Agora de la Danse (p113)

➡ La Tulipe (p113)

For reviews, see p113. ➡

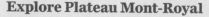

Explore Plateau Mont-Royal

This is a large area, but a good chunk can be explored in a day. Begin at leafy Carré St-Louis, where old-slate Victorian mansions and duplexes house bohemian souls and B&Bs. Originally a working-class neighborhood, in the 1960s and '70s the Plateau became the place where writers, singers and all manner of artists lived.

Make your way along Rue Prince-Arthur Ouest to Blvd St-Laurent, the legendary divide between anglophone and francophone Montréal once known as 'the Main.' Today the Main is a mix of hip cafes and nightspots, old-world delis and grocery stores, and funky hipster shops. The stretch to Ave Duluth, known for its BYOB restos, attracts hordes of 20-somethings on weekend nights. For lunch or a relaxing coffee, take a break at Café Santropol (p108), an old standby on Rue St-Urbain.

Continuing northwest up Blvd St-Laurent, you'll enter Montréal's Portuguese community, passing Parc du Portugal. Another block to the northwest lies Ave du Mont-Royal. It's worth turning right here and wandering down several blocks, lined with eclectic boutiques, record shops and bookstores.

When you're in the mood for fresh air, hop on bus 11 on the northwest side of Ave du Mont-Royal and ride up to 'the Mountain,' the Parc du Mont-Royal. Hop off at the parking lot near Maison Smith, a visitors center where you can have a drink and learn about the park's history before spending the rest of the day exploring it.

Local Life

➡**Bar-hopping** Coasting up and down Blvd St-Laurent is the quintessential bar-hopping experience for younger Montréalers.

➡**Mountainsides** It doesn't get much more Montréal than picnicking, sunbathing and tobogganing (in winter) on the Mountain.

➡**Foodie faves** You can't go wrong with a bagel, some smoked meat and poutine (see p30) in your quest to be an authentic Montréaler.

Getting There & Away

➡**Metro** Metro access is via the orange line, at the stations of Sherbrooke, Mont-Royal and Laurier.

➡**Bus** The 55 runs along Blvd St-Laurent; bus 30 coasts along Rue St-Denis; bus 80 travels Ave du Parc; bus 11 climbs up to Parc du Mont-Royal from Ave du Mont-Royal.

➡**Bike** You can rent a Bixi bike to reach much of Plateau Mont-Royal; pedaling up the mountain itself is a tough slog.

⊙ SIGHTS

BOULEVARD ST-LAURENT   STREET
Map p280 (Ⓜ St-Laurent then bus 55) A dividing line between the city's east and west, Blvd St-Laurent (previously 'the Main') has always been a focus of action, a gathering place for people of many languages and backgrounds. In 1996 it was declared a national historic site for its role as ground zero for so many Canadian immigrants and future Montréalers. The label 'the Main' has stuck in the local lingo since the 19th century. Today it's a gateway into the Plateau and a fascinating street to explore.

For a food- and culture-focused tour of the Main, from Chinatown to Little Italy, contact Fitz & Follwell (p115).

PARC LA FONTAINE   PARK
Map p280 (cnr Rue Sherbrooke Est & Ave du Parc La Fontaine; Ⓜ Sherbrooke) At 34 hectares, this great verdant municipal park is the city's third largest, after Parc du Mont-Royal and Parc Maisonneuve. In the warmer months weary urbanites flock to leafy La Fontaine to enjoy the walking and bicycle paths, the attractive ponds and the general air of relaxation that pervades the park. There's also a chalet where you can grab a bite or a drink, Espace La Fontaine (p109).

The view down the steep banks from Ave du Parc La Fontaine is impressive, especially if the fountains are in play. You can rent paddleboats in summer and go ice-skating in winter. The open-air Théâtre de Verdure draws a laid-back crowd on evenings in July.

ÉGLISE ST-JEAN-BAPTISTE   CHURCH
Map p280 (www.lestjeanbaptiste.com; 309 Rue Rachel Est; ⊙ 4-6pm Mon-Thu, 4:30-6:30pm Sat, 9:30-11am & 4:30-6:30pm Sun; Ⓜ Mont-Royal) Dedicated to St John the Baptist, the patron saint of French Canadians, this church was the hub of working-class Catholic families in the late 19th and early 20th centuries. The altar is white imported marble, the chancel canopy is pink marble and there are two Casavant organs. The acoustics are splendid and the church plays host to classical-music concerts throughout the year.

AVENUE DU MONT-ROYAL   STREET
Map p280 (Ⓜ Mont-Royal) Old-fashioned five-and-dime stores rub shoulders with a wide array of trendy cafes and fashion boutiques on Ave du Mont-Royal. The nightlife here has surged to the point that it rivals Blvd St-Laurent, with bars and nightclubs ranging from the sedate to uproarious. Intimate shops, secondhand stores and ultramodern boutiques offer eye-catching apparel.

CARRÉ ST-LOUIS   SQUARE
Map p280 (cnr Rue St-Denis & Rue Prince-Arthur; Ⓜ Sherbrooke) This lovely green space with a three-tiered fountain is flanked by beautiful rows of Second Empire homes. In the 19th century a reservoir here was filled, and a neighborhood emerged for well-to-do French families. Artists and poets gathered in the area back then, and creative types like filmmakers and fashion designers now occupy houses in the streets nearby. The cafe, which opens in summer, is a good spot for a pick-me-up, with occasional musicians creating the soundtrack for the square.

Carré St-Louis feeds west into **Rue Prince-Arthur**, a former slice of 1960s hippie culture that has refashioned itself as a popular restaurant strip.

PARC DU PORTUGAL   PARK
Map p280 (cnr Blvd St-Laurent & Rue Marie-Anne; Ⓜ St-Laurent then bus 55) This quaint little park is dedicated to Portuguese immigrants and their community, founded in

---

❶ MOUNTAIN GUIDE

There's much to experience on Mont-Royal, but it's wise to have a plan before you go. For a walking tour, see p106.

Getting there Along Ave du Mont-Royal (including in front of the metro station), catch bus 80, which stops at Belvédère Camillien-Houde, Chalet du-Mont-Royal and Lac des Castors.

On foot The main entry points are Rue Drummond and Peel in downtown and Rue Rachel in the Plateau.

Eating Maison Smith (p105) is the best place to go for a casual lunch or snack stop. For something more up-scale, head to Le Pavilion overlooking Lac des Castors.

Activities Head to Lac des Castors (p105) for winter sports and summer boating.

Information There are park info centers at Chalet du Mont-Royal (p105) and Maison Smith (p105). You'll also find loads of info online (including a map). Visit www.lemontroyal.qc.ca.

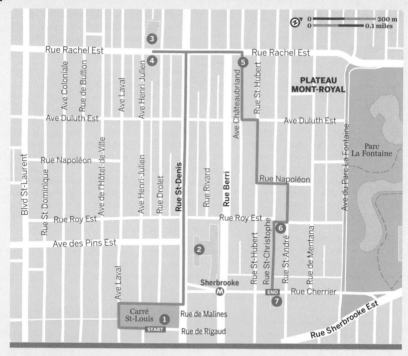

Neighborhood Walk
Strolling the Plateau

START CARRÉ ST-LOUIS
END RUE CHERRIER
LENGTH 3KM; ONE TO TWO HOURS

Start at the ❶ **Carré St-Louis** (p103), a pleasant, green, shady oasis with a splashing fountain. It's surrounded by beautiful old houses built for wealthy French residents in the 19th century.

Walk around the park (stopping for a coffee at the summertime cafe near Ave Laval), then walk up Rue St-Denis. On your right you'll pass the majestic buildings of the former ❷ **Institut des Sourdes-Muettes** (now known as the Institut Raymond-Dewar) – note the little silver cupola.

Continue up Rue St-Denis and turn left onto Rue Rachel. You'll see the baroque ❸ **Église St-Jean-Baptiste** (p103), its enormous interior decorated with gilded wood and pink marble. The acoustics are excellent, making it popular for concerts.

Exiting the church, look right to see the winged angel on the imposing Sir George-Étienne Cartier monument, way down the end of the street at the leafy base of Mont-Royal. Directly opposite the church stands ❹ **Les Cours Rachel**, once a boarding school but now converted into condos.

Walk northeast along Rue Rachel Est and turn right onto ❺ **Avenue Châteaubriand**. A rundown street in the 1970s, today this narrow lane has been spruced up with blue, green and turquoise paint and potted plants hanging outside the windows. Here you'll spot another of this town's signature objects: the external staircase.

Zigzag down to Rue Roy and Rue St-André. You'll find ❻ **Place Roy**, a tiny leafy square with an art installation by sculptor Michel Goulet. Draw your own conclusions about the meaning of the world map juxtaposed with a random arrangement of chairs, some knocked to the ground.

Walk along Rue Roy and turn left down Rue St-Christophe. Continue to Rue Cherrier to see a lovely ❼ **1918 Italian Renaissance building**. It once housed the Palestre Nationale but now belongs to UQAM and Agora de la Danse, a key name in Montréal's contemporary dance scene.

Montréal in 1953. At the rear of the park, next to the little summer pavilion, a plaque commemorates the arrival of Portuguese immigrants in search of a new life. The gates and fountain are covered with colorful glazed tiles.

◎ Parc du Mont-Royal Area

Montréalers are proud of their 'mountain,' so don't call it a hill as Oscar Wilde did when he visited the city in the 1880s. The charming, leafy expanse of Parc du Mont-Royal (Map p272; www.lemontroyal.qc.ca) is charged for a wide range of outdoor activities. The wooded slopes and grassy meadows have stunning views that make it all the more popular for jogging, picnicking, horseback riding, cycling, and throwing Frisbees. Winter brings skating, tobogganing and cross-country skiing. Binoculars are a good idea for the bird feeders that have been set up along some walking trails.

The park was laid out by Frederick Law Olmsted, the architect of New York's Central Park. The idea came from bourgeois residents in the adjacent Golden Square Mile who fretted about vanishing greenery. Note that walking in the park after sunset isn't such a safe idea.

Contrary to what people may try to tell you, this place is *not* an extinct volcano. Rather, Parc du Mont-Royal is a hangover from when magma penetrated the earth's crust millions of years ago. This formed a sort of erosion-proof rock, so while time and the elements were wearing down the ground around it, the 232m-high hunk of rock, which locals affectionately refer to as 'the Mountain,' stood firm.

On the north side of the park there are two enormous cemeteries: Cimetière Mont-Royal is Protestant and nondenominational, while Cimetière Notre-Dame-des-Neiges is Catholic.

For more info on the park visit www.lemontroyal.qc.ca.

BELVÉDÈRE CAMILLIEN-HOUDE   LOOKOUT
(Voie Camillien-Houde; Ⓜ Mont-Royal, then bus 11) This is the most popular lookout on Mont-Royal thanks to its accessibility and large parking lot. Naturally enough, it's a magnet for couples once night falls, making it nearly impossible on summer nights to find a parking space.

You can walk to Chalet du Mont-Royal, about 2km away. To get to this lookout, take the stairs that lead from the parking lot.

CHALET DU MONT-ROYAL   HISTORIC BUILDING
Map p272 (stairs up from Redpath Cres; ⊘8am-8pm; Ⓜ Mont-Royal, then bus 11) Constructed in 1932, this grand old white villa, complete with bay windows, contains canvases that depict scenes of Montréal history. You'll also see carved squirrels in the rafters. Big bands strut their stuff on the huge balcony in summer, reminiscent of the 1930s. Most people, however, flock here for the spectacular views of downtown from the **Kondiaronk lookout** behind the chalet. It's about a 1km uphill walk from the park entrance on Ave de Pins.

Staff at the handy information booth inside can give you tips on exploring the park.

LAC DES CASTORS   LAKE
(🚌11) Created in a former marsh as part of a work-creation project, Beaver Lake is a center of activity year-round. You can rent paddleboats on the lake or, in winter, ice skates, cross-country skis, snow shoes and sleds from **Le Pavillon** (www.pavillonmontroyal.com; 2000 Chemin Remembrance; ⊘10am-6pm Mon-Fri, 9am-6pm Sat & Sun; 🚌11). The slopes above the lake are popular for sledding. Refreshments and sandwiches are sold at a snack bar; there's also a restaurant with more elaborate dishes.

MAISON SMITH   HISTORIC BUILDING
(Voie Camillien-Houd; ⊘9am-5pm; 🚌11) Constructed in 1858 by a merchant who wanted to get away from the pollution and overpopulation of the rest of Montréal, this house contains a small permanent exhibition on the history of the park and its flora and fauna. There's also a visitors center and a cafe, with a pleasant outdoor terrace (open mid-May to mid-October) where you can have grilled sandwiches, soups, desserts, coffees, beer and wine.

A gift shop sells bird-watching paraphernalia, maps of the park and souvenirs.

CROIX DU MONT-ROYAL   MONUMENT
(🚌11) About 550m north of Kondiaronk lookout stands the Mont-Royal Cross, one of Montréal's most familiar landmarks. Made of reinforced steel, the 31m-tall cross was erected in 1924 on the very spot where Maisonneuve placed a wooden cross.

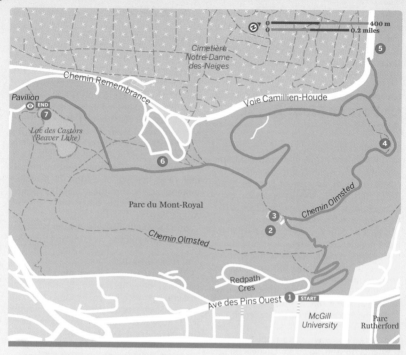

Neighborhood Walk
Montréal's Favorite Mountain

START AVE DES PINS OUEST
END LAC DES CASTORS
LENGTH 6KM; TWO HOURS

Many of Montréal's neighborhoods hug the foot of Parc du Mont-Royal, making everyone feel like they have a bit of green space in their backyard. 'The Mountain,' as Mont-Royal is affectionately known by locals, is cherished for its winding trails, fresh air and terrific views.

The starting point for this walk is on **1 Avenue de Pins Ouest** at the staircase into the park. It's a fairly brisk 10- to 15-minute climb that alternates between steps and inclined trail.

When you reach the large path, turn right and you'll soon see yet more stairs heading up to the **2 Kondiaronk lookout**. The overlook offers stunning views of the downtown area. A few paces from the lookout is the **3 Chalet du Mont-Royal** (p105), which has paintings of some key scenes from local history (and a flickering fire in winter).

From the chalet, walk north along the trail named Chemin Olmsted about 600m to the **4 Croix du Mont-Royal** (p105). This is where city founder Maisonneuve allegedly planted a cross in thanksgiving to the Virgin Mary for saving the city from flood.

Further along you can descend a set of stairs to reach the scenic lookout of **5 Belvédère Camillien-Houde** (p105), one of the most romantic views in the city.

Returning to the path, head south toward **6 Maison Smith** (p105), an 1858 building that houses a permanent exhibition on the history and ongoing conservation of Mont-Royal. A visitors center doles out information on the park; the on-site cafe is a good spot to grab a bite or a cold drink.

Another 500m further south, the artificial pond **7 Lac des Castors** (p105) is a haven of toy-boat captains in summer and ice-skaters in winter. Refreshments are available at the pavilion, and in warm weather the meadows around the pond are full of sunbathers.

According to legend, when floods threatened the fledgling colony in 1643, Maisonneuve prayed to the Virgin Mary to save the town. When the waters receded, out of gratitude Maisonneuve carried a cross up the steep slopes and planted it there.

The white illuminated cross is visible from anywhere downtown.

CIMETIÈRE
NOTRE-DAME-DES-NEIGES   CEMETERY
(☎514-735-1361; www.notredamedesneiges cemetery.ca; 4601 Chemin de la Côte-des-Neiges; ☺8am-5pm, office 8:30am-4:30pm; ⓂCôte-des-Neiges) More than one million people have found their final resting place here since this Catholic cemetery opened in 1854, making it the largest cemetery in Canada and the third largest in North America. It was initially inspired by the Père Lachaise Cemetery in Paris.

The cemetery has several interesting mausoleums. The Pietà Mausoleum contains a full-scale marble replica of Michelangelo's famous sculpture in St Peter's Basilica in Rome. Other mausoleums here emit solemn music, including that of Marguerite Bourgeoys, a nun and teacher who was beatified in 1982 (for more details on her life, visit the **Chapelle Notre-Dame-de-Bonsecours**; p50). Built in 2007, the Esther Blondin Mausoleum houses 6000 crypts and niches, reflecting the increasing popularity of communal memorial spaces.

The catalog of permanent guests includes 20 Montréal mayors, a number of ex-passengers from the *Titanic*, and Calixa Lavallée, the composer of 'O Canada.'

The cemetery office has brochures for self-guided tours around the tombs but there's also a map posted at the entrance.

CIMETIÈRE MONT-ROYAL   CEMETERY
(☎514-279-7358; www.mountroyalcem.com; 1297 Chemin de la Forêt; ☺9am-6pm; ⓂÉdouard-Montpetit) Celebrating its 160th anniversary in 2012, Cimetière Mont-Royal was founded in 1852 for the last journey of Presbyterians, Anglicans, Unitarians, Baptists and non-denominationals. In 1901 it opened Canada's first crematorium. One famous grave is that of Charles Melville Hayes, the president of the Grand Trunk Railway who went down with the Titanic. The cemetery is laid out like a landscape garden and is perfect for the Goth-historically interested; it also hosts history walks, open-air plays and guided tours.

 # EATING

Plateau Mont-Royal has a fantastic variety of bistros, upscale restaurants and bohemian-style cafes. Rue Prince-Arthur Est is a narrow residential street that has been converted into a dining and entertainment enclave. The restaurant segment runs west from leafy Carré St-Louis (just north of Rue Sherbrooke) to a block west of Blvd St-Laurent. Many of the small, inexpensive and mostly ethnic restaurants here aren't licensed to serve alcohol, so bring your own wine.

SCHWARTZ'S   SANDWICHES $
Map p280 (www.schwartzsdeli.com; 3895 Blvd St-Laurent; mains $8-22; ☺8am-12:30am Sun-Thu, to 1:30am Fri, to 2:30am Sat; ⓂSherbrooke) Reuben Schwartz, a Romanian Jew, opened this Montréal icon in 1928, and it's been going strong ever since. Schwartz's meat goes through a 14-day regime of curing and smoking on the premises before landing on your plate after a final three-hour steam. It's widely considered the best smoked meat in Montréal, whether it's brisket, duck, chicken or turkey, all piled high on sourdough rye bread.

You can order it fat, medium (recommended) or lean. Expect the usual long lines. If you don't feel like waiting, head across the street to the Main, which serves a reputable smoked meat sandwich.

LA BANQUISE   QUÉBECOIS $
Map p280 (☎514-525-2415; www.labanquise. com; 994 Rue Rachel Est; mains $7-11; ☺24hr; ⓂMont-Royal) A Montréal legend since 1968, La Banquise is probably the best place in town to sample poutine. More than 30 varieties are available, including a vegan poutine, the boogalou (with pulled pork) and straight-up classic poutine. There's an outdoor terrace, a full breakfast menu and a selection of microbrews, plus the kitchen never closes. Expect big lines on weekends.

SAKA-BA!   JAPANESE $
Map p280 (1279 Ave du Mont-Royal Est; mains $11-15; ☺5-11pm daily, 11:30am-2pm Tue-Fri, 11:30am-3pm Sat & Sun; 🛜🍴; ⓂMont-Royal) On a frosty Montréal evening, steaming bowls of ramen are hard to beat at this fun, whimsical eatery. Take a seat at one of the long red wooden counters (head to the back to watch the chefs in action) and feast on

perfectly cooked noodles with braised pork, bamboo and green onions. There's also a vegetarian version.

Tasty appetizers include octopus salad or pork and cabbage *gyoza* (dumplings).

PATATI PATATA
QUÉBECOIS **$**

Map p280 (📞514-844-0216; 4177 Blvd St-Laurent; mains $7-11; ⏰8am-11pm; MSt-Laurent, then bus 55) This matchbox-sized, bohemian-style eatery is known for its poutine, borscht and miniburgers. It's a Montréal classic with rocking music and young efficient staff, and there's almost always a line snaking out the front. Grab a seat at the window and watch the city stroll past.

OMNIVORE
MEDITERRANEAN **$**

Map p280 (4351 Blvd St-Laurent; mains $6-14; ⏰11am-10pm Mon-Sat; 🌱; MMont-Royal) Amid rustic wood tables and potted plants, the friendly staff at Omnivore whip up delicious sandwiches that are rolled in pita then grilled. There's also hummus, tabouli, baba ghanoush and other Lebanese classics.

SUSHI MOMO
JAPANESE, VEGETARIAN **$**

Map p280 (📞514-825-6363; 8 Ave Duluth; 5-piece rolls $6-8; ⏰11am-2:30pm & 4:30-10pm Tue-Fri, 4-10pm Sat & Sun; 🌱; MSt-Laurent, then bus 55) There are just five tables in this cramped, art-filled sushi joint, but you can always grab a spot along the counter, and join the mostly student crowd for delicious inexpensive rolls. The separate menu for vegetarians is outstanding, with inventive combos such as the Mangue Patate with sweet potato, mango, cucumber, avocado and more. Orders come with steaming spiced bowls of edamame, and you should definitely opt for the miso soup.

BEAUTY'S
DINER **$**

Map p280 (📞514-849-8883; www.beautys.ca; 93 Ave du Mont-Royal Ouest; breakfasts $8-13; ⏰7am-3pm Mon-Fri, to 4pm Sat & Sun; MMont-Royal) This sleek, retro '50s diner serves what some consider Montréal's best breakfast – all day long. Ask for 'the Special' – a toasted bagel with lox, cream cheese, tomato and onion. Lineups on Saturday and Sunday mornings can run up to 40 minutes long, even in winter (arrive before 10am).

JANO
PORTUGUESE **$**

Map p280 (📞514-849-0646; 3883 Blvd St-Laurent; mains $14-16; ⏰5pm-midnight Mon-Wed, 11am-midnight Thu-Sun; 🚌55, MSt-Laurent) The

scent of charcoal-grilled meats and seafood lingers in the air at this welcoming, family-friendly Portuguese restaurant. The menu features straightforward selections of fresh fish, pork and steak, all grilled to choice tenderness. Warm colors and a buzzing atmosphere draw in the crowds, particularly on weekends, when waits can be long.

CAFÉ SANTROPOL
CAFE **$**

Map p280 (www.santropol.com; 3990 Rue St-Urbain; mains $8-12; ⏰11:30am-10pm; 🌱; 🚌55, MSt-Laurent) This bohemian Montréal eatery is known for its towering and creative sandwiches, colorful digs and lush outdoor garden patio. Its creations range from the sweet root (carrots, raisins, coriander, nuts, mayo and fresh apple) to the Santropol (sliced roast beef with blue cheese). Lots of vegetarian options.

ST-VIATEUR BAGEL & CAFÉ
BAGELS **$**

Map p280 (📞514-528-6361; www.stviateurbagel.com; 1127 Ave du Mont-Royal Est; sandwiches $9-12; ⏰6am-10pm; MMont-Royal) A splendid cafe that serves its signature bagels, grilled or *nature,* with soup or salad. There are about a dozen sandwiches but most popular are the traditional smoked lox with cream cheese, and roast beef with Swiss cheese and tomato. You can also find breakfast bagels with eggs and ham.

KOUIGN AMMAN
BAKERY **$**

Map p280 (322 Ave du Mont-Royal Est; pastries $2-3; ⏰7am-6pm; MMont-Royal) The name of this petite bakery – a challenge even for some French speakers – comes from their famous Breton cake (flaky on the outside, rich and tender on the inside), which draws in fans from near and far. The friendly staff also doles out soups, quiches and croissants. The space is tiny with just three tables; most people get their treats to go.

ROMADOS
PORTUGUESE **$**

Map p280 (📞514-849-1803; 115 Rue Rachel Est; mains $6-13; ⏰6:30am-9pm; MMont-Royal) Romados has many admirers for its delicious grilled chicken. Order it with fries and a few *pasteis de nata* (custard tarts). It's an informal place, with just a few tables. If the weather is nice, consider heading to nearby Parc Jeanne-Mance for a picnic.

AU FESTIN DE BABETTE
ICE CREAM **$**

Map p280 (📞514-849-0214; 4085 Rue St-Denis; ice creams $6-7; ⏰10am-7pm; MMont-Royal)

CAFE CULTURE

The Plateau has some of the best cafes in the city. Whether you're after the perfect macchiato or simply a buzzing space to take in the neighborhood, you'll be spoiled for choice. Here are a few favorites:

Moineau Masqué (Map p280; 912 Rue Marie-Anne Est; ☻7:30am-7pm Mon-Fri, from 8:30am Sat, from 9:30am Sun; 🕾; ⓂMont-Royal) Hidden on a peaceful street, the 'Masked Sparrow' whips up tasty, if slightly bitter coffees, which you can enjoy on the outdoor terrace. On cooler days, take a seat at a big communal table or the comfy sofa in the sun-drenched interior. It's a picture-perfect neighborhood cafe.

Flocon Espresso (Map p280; 781 Ave du Mont-Royal Est; coffees $3.50-4.50; ☻7:30am-7pm Mon-Fri, from 9am Sat & Sun; 🕾; ⓂMont-Royal) Coffee nerds flock to this tiny cafe for outstanding espressos, *cortados* (espresso with a dash of milk) and lattes. There are just two communal tables, but a feel-good vibe prevails, with a mix of anglos and francophones chatting or typing away in the cosy space. Go early to get a seat.

Cafe Névé (Map p280; 151 Rue Rachel Est; sandwiches around $8; ☻8am-9pm Mon-Fri, from 9am Sat & Sun; 🕾🖉; ⓂMont-Royal) This much-loved neighborhood haunt serves excellent coffees, and the food selection goes far beyond the typical baked goods found in most cafes. Stop in for eggs Benedict or yogurt, granola and fresh fruit in the morning. For lunch, there are tasty sandwiches (including several vegetarian options) and French onion soup.

Replika (Map p280; 252 Rue Rachel Est; mains $6-9; ☻9am-6pm Mon-Fri, from 10am Sat & Sun; 🕾; ⓂMont-Royal) This spacious coffeehouse has lots of tables for quiet conversation and laptop chatter, plus good coffees, sandwiches, desserts and other snacks. For a jolt, try a Turkish coffee.

Marius (Map p280; 1251 Rue Rachel; mains $8-9; ☻7:30am-7:30pm Mon-Fri, from 9am Sat & Sun; 🕾; ⓂMont-Royal) Along the bike path, this bright and charming cafe and bakery serves up delicious sandwiches, salads and espresso drinks. The summer terrace is beautifully sited across from Parc La Fontaine.

Chez José (Map p280; 173 Ave Duluth Est; ☻9am-6pm Mon-Fri, to 7pm Sat & Sun; ⓂSherbrooke) Jolly owner José often mans the small kitchen of this tiny, colorful cafe set in a mural-covered building. Besides serving some of the 'hood's best and strongest espresso, it's lauded for its breakfasts, seafood soup and Portuguese sausage. A young, bohemian clientele tends to spill onto the sidewalk to chat while eyeing the cast of characters that meanders by.

This charming cafe with sidewalk terrace is famed for its homemade ice cream. The supremely satisfying *crème glacée molle à l'ancienne* is chocolate or vanilla ice cream blended on the spot with fresh raspberries, mango, ginger and other ingredients. In winter, stop in for rich hot chocolate.

ESPACE LA FONTAINE   BISTRO $
Map p280 (📞514-280-2525; www.espacela fontaine.com; Parc La Fontaine; mains $10-16; ☻11am-5pm Wed-Fri, from 10am Sat & Sun; ⓂSherbrooke) In a chalet perched above the water, Espace La Fontaine is a bright and cheery bistro that serves sandwiches, salads and drinks, as well as a good weekend brunch. It has a great outdoor terrace in summer, and in winter, there's ice-skating just below the chalet.

HOF KELSTEN   BAKERY $
Map p280 (4524 Blvd St-Laurent; pastries $2-3, sandwiches $8-9; ☻8am-7pm Wed-Sun; 🖉; ⓂMont-Royal) This sweet bakery has delectable pastries, tasty sandwiches (including an egg-and-cheese breakfast option) and a tempting selection of loaves. At lunchtime, join Montréalers at the long communal table for lox, roast beef or veggie sandwiches – or get it to go and head to nearby Parc Jeanne-Mance.

There's also soup (borscht, matzo ball, latke) and first-rate espresso drinks. You can also come for weekend brunch – challah French toast, schnitzel and eggs – served from 10am to 3pm.

★**L'GROS LUXE**   BISTRO **$$**

Map p280 (www.lgrosluxe.com; 3807 Rue St-André; small plates $5-10; ⊘noon-11:30pm Mon-Fri, from 11am Sat & Sun; ⏸; Ⓜ Sherbrooke) With its big windows, classy vintage decor and inexpensive comfort fare, L'Gros Luxe has obvious appeal. The small dining room is always packed with young Plateau residents who come for pork tacos, veggie burgers, and fish and chips. Plates are small, but nothing costs more than $10, and there's an extensive drinks menu (with much higher prices than the food).

Go early to beat the crowds. There's a second location in Mile End; both locations also draw the weekend brunch crowd.

★**L'EXPRESS**   FRENCH **$$**

Map p280 (⏸514-845-5333; 3927 Rue St-Denis; mains $22-28; ⊘8am-2am Mon-Fri, from 10am Sat & Sun; Ⓜ Sherbrooke) L'Express has all the hallmarks of a Parisian bistro – black-and-white checkered floor, art-deco globe lights, papered tables and mirrored walls. High-end bistro fare completes the picture with excellent dishes such as grilled salmon, bone marrow with sea salt, roast duck with salad and beef tartare. The waiters can advise on the extensive wine list. Reservations are essential.

LES TROIS PETITS BOUCHONS   FRENCH **$$**

Map p280 (⏸514-285-4444; www.lestroispetits bouchons.com; 4669 Rue St-Denis; mains $16-30; ⊘6-11pm Mon-Sat; Ⓜ Mont-Royal) In this delightfully convivial minimalist space, chef Audrey Dufresne's motto is '*terroir* (locally sourced) products are the basis, and our passion does the rest.' Market-based dishes

---

LOCAL KNOWLEDGE

TALKING FOOD

Menus in Montréal are often – but not always – bilingual. Regardless, if you need help with *le français,* don't be shy to ask (the waiters are used to it). Important note: in French, an *entrée* is an appetizer, not a main course – that's *le plat principal.* Another thing to watch out for is recognizing the difference between *pâte,* which means pasta, and pâté, which means that spreadable stuff often made of goose liver (though there are also vegetarian pâtés, such as *pâté aux champignons et tofu* (mushrooms and tofu).

---

such as grilled octopus, veal tartare, Kamouraska lamb and mushroom tartine are some of the gems presented with impeccable service. Reservations are essential.

LA SALA ROSA   SPANISH **$$**

Map p280 (⏸514-844-4227; www.lasalarossa. com; 4848 Blvd St-Laurent; mains $13-17; ⊘5-11pm Tue-Sun; ⏸; Ⓜ Laurier) A festive, local and often Spanish-speaking crowd comes to this little Iberian gem. Sala Rosa is best known for its five tasty varieties of paella (including vegetarian) as well as numerous tapas dishes and a changing lineup of Spanish specials. On Thursday nights (from 8:45pm) there's a live flamenco show and the place gets packed.

HÀ   VIETNAMESE **$$**

Map p280 (⏸514-848-0336; www.restaurantha. com; 243 Ave du Mont-Royal Ouest; mains $12-19; ⊘11:30am-10:30pm Mon-Fri, from 5pm Sat & Sun; Ⓜ Mont-Royal) Inspired by the street foods (and beers) of Vietnam, Chef Hong Hà Nguyen showcases simple but delectable recipes at this neighborhood charmer near the foot of Mont-Royal. The menu is small, with highlights such as grilled beef with watercress salad, lemongrass pork ribs and spicy papaya salad. It's set in a warmly lit dining room (illuminated by sculptural light fixtures), with a lovely terrace in front.

L'AVENUE   BISTRO **$$**

Map p280 (⏸514-523-8780; 922 Ave du Mont-Royal Est; mains $12-20; ⊘8am-4pm Sun-Wed, to 11pm Thu-Sat; Ⓜ Mont-Royal) This self-consciously hip restaurant is a magnet for the young, postparty brunch crowd. More than a dozen different types of omelets, plus all the classics – French toast, waffles, eggs Benedict – arrive nicely prepared. The fresh fruit skewers (served with every plate) are a nice touch. Grooving tunes (nostalgic '80s, ambient electronica) play at all hours.

Artwork and urban murals adorn the walls, and the surreal multimedia-infused washroom is an experience in itself.

PINTXO   SPANISH **$$**

Map p280 (⏸514-844-0222; www.pintxo.ca; 256 Rue Roy Est; mains $24-38, tapas $5-13; ⊘6-11pm Mon-Sat, noon-2pm Wed-Fri, 6-10pm Sun; Ⓜ Sherbrooke) Imaginative plates of tapas rule the day at this petite, artfully decorated Basque restaurant helmed by chef Alonso Ortiz. Start with garlic prawns with roasted red pepper, elk carpaccio or seared scallops with chorizo tapenade before moving onto heartier plates such as duck breast with saffron risotto. It's on a peaceful street in the Plateau and gets packed on weekend nights.

Reservations are necessary.

ROBIN DES BOIS   FUSION $$

Map p280 (☑514-288-1010; www.robindesbois.ca; 4653 Blvd St-Laurent; mains $13-23; ☺11:30am-10pm Mon-Fri, 10am-10pm Sat, 10am-4pm Sun; ⓂSt-Laurent, then bus 55) ✎ Montréal's own Robin Hood, restaurateur Judy Servay donates all profits and tips from this St-Laurent hot spot to local charities. Ever-changing dishes scribbled on the chalkboard could include a succulent braised pork roast, rich French onion soup or a creamy wild-mushroom risotto. Reservations are recommended.

AU PIED DE COCHON   FRENCH $$$

Map p280 (☑514-281-1114; www.aupiededecochon.ca; 536 Ave Duluth Est; mains $27-45; ☺5pm-midnight Wed-Sun; ⓂMont-Royal) One of Montréal's most respected restaurants features extravagant pork, duck and steak dishes, along with its signature foie gras plates (see p28 for details on the production of foie gras). Irreverent, award-winning chef Martin Picard takes simple ingredients and transforms them into works of art.

The famous and surprisingly magnificent *canard en conserve* (duck in a can), for instance, is half a roasted duck magret served with foie gras, cabbage, bacon, venison and spices, sealed and cooked in a can – then opened tableside and dumped over celery root puree on toast. Dishes are rich and portions are large, so bring an appetite. Reservations are essential.

LE FILET   SEAFOOD $$$

Map p280 (☑514-360-6060; www.lefilet.ca; 219 Ave du Mont-Royal Ouest; small plates $14-25; ☺5:45-10:30pm Tue-Fri, from 5pm Sat; ⓂMont-Royal) Le Filet presents masterfully crafted fish and seafood with Japanese touches in a low-lit setting facing Parc Jeanne-Mance. Plates are small and meant for sharing (two people typically order four to five dishes). The grilled octopus with Israeli couscous will make you wish there were more than just eight legs.

The menu is market-based and changes often, but other favorites include the miso-gratin oysters, crab risotto and cavatelli with veal cheeks. Reserve well in advance.

🍷 DRINKING & NIGHTLIFE

LA DISTILLERIE   BAR

(www.pubdistillerie.com; 2047 Ave du Mont-Royal; ☺4pm-3am; ⓂMont-Royal, then bus 97) Although it's a bit of a hike down Ave du Mont-Royal, La Distillerie is worth the trip for its excellent cocktails (served in Mason jars), friendly bartenders and easygoing crowd. The aesthetic is industrial chic, with exposed bulbs, industrial fixtures and a long wooden bar. There's no food, but you can grab pizza from across the street and eat it here.

There are two other branches of La Distillerie in town, including one in the Quartier Latin.

LE LAB   COCKTAIL BAR

Map p280 (☑514-544-1333; www.barlelab.com; 1351 Rue Rachel Est; ☺5pm-3am; ⓂMont-Royal) Home to some of Montréal's best cocktails, Le Lab prides itself on its wildly inventive elixirs and knowledgeable 'labtenders' who can whip up beautiful concoctions to suit your taste. The setting is classy, with a long solid-wood bar, vest- and tie-wearing staff, and old-fashioned decor, but it remains a fun, unpretentious place.

Sometimes there are flames, as the toolkit here includes not only absinthe but also blowtorches and liquid nitrogen. Try the Jerky Lab Jack, a smoky drink made with Jack Daniels, beef jerky and house BBQ bitters that's lit ablaze during preparation.

APT 200   BAR

Map p280 (2nd fl, 3643 Blvd St-Laurent; ☺5pm-3am; ⓂSt-Laurent, then bus 55) Once you've climbed the stairs, you'll arrive at what feels like a private loft party, with groups of friends gathered in the spacious, open-lounge area with high tin ceilings, long couches and big windows overlooking the street. Step to the other side for a seat at the long bar, to shoot a round of pool or play arcade games.

Apt 200 is a fine place for an early-evening libation, to start off the night and see what unfolds. There's no sign, so you'll have to look for the number.

BIG IN JAPAN   COCKTAIL BAR

Map p280 (4175 Blvd St-Laurent; ☺5pm-3am; ⓂSt-Laurent, then bus 55) Completely concealed from the street, Big in Japan always amazes first timers. There you are walking along bustling St-Laurent, you find the unmarked door, walk down a rather unpromising corridor and emerge into a room lit with a thousand candles (or so it seems).

The elegant, but ethereal beauty seems to come through in the cocktails as well, with well-dressed, if standoffish bartenders mixing pricey but painstakingly prepared Manhattans, old fashioneds and dry martinis. It's a great date place.

SUWU   BAR
Map p280 (www.suwumontreal.com; 3581 Blvd St-Laurent; ⊗5pm-3am daily, 11am-3pm Sat & Sun; MSt-Laurent, then bus 55) Don't let the unpronounceable name deter you. SuWu carves up a winning formula of inventive cocktails and delicious eclectic comfort food that makes it a fine go-to spot no matter the time of night. Snack on fish tacos, fried chicken bao or pork shoulder ramen while sipping an East Side (gin, cucumbers, mint) – or rather a West Side (tequila, basil, lime).

There's hip hop playing overhead, gregarious bartenders and a rustically beautiful interior, complete with hanging plants, thick wood-paneled details and artful lighting.

MAJESTIQUE   BAR
Map p280 (☎514-439-1850; www.restobarmajestique.com; 4105 Blvd St-Laurent; ⊗4pm-3am daily, 11am-3pm Sun; MSt-Laurent, then bus 55) The Majestique manages to be both kitschy and classy at the same time, with wood-paneled walls, warm lighting and a buck's head presiding over the tables. The bartenders whip up some beautiful concoctions here, and the food menu is equally creative: try the *bourgots* (snails), the *tartare de cheval* (raw horsemeat); for something simple go for *huîtres* (oysters) or *frites* (fries).

It's a fun and lively place, and more grown-up than most spots along this street.

RESERVOIR   PUB
Map p280 (☎514-849-7779; www.brasseriereservoir.ca; 9 Ave Duluth Est; ⊗3pm-3am; MSt-Laurent, then bus 55) We adore this low-key, friendly brasserie. It's nice but not too pricey and the mixed crowd is artsy but unpretentious. If you appreciate good beer, the owners brew their own on the premises. A small kitchen prepares gourmet lunch, after-work snacks and weekend brunch. In summer, the 2nd-floor terrace overlooks this pedestrian-friendly lane.

BILY KUN   BAR
Map p280 (www.bilykun.com; 354 Ave du Mont-Royal Est; ⊗3pm-3am; MMont-Royal) One of the pioneers of 'tavern chic,' Bily Kun is a favorite hangout for a chilled evening among friends. First-time visitors usually gawk at the ostrich heads that overlook the bar but soon settle into the groove of live jazz (from 6pm to 8pm) and DJs (10pm onwards).

Upstairs, **O Patro Vys** (Map p280; ☎514-845-3855; www.opatrovys.tumblr.com) is a performing-arts hall that features a wide range of bands (folk, French pop, indie rock) as well as electronic installations, poetry slams and other esoteric fare.

ELSE'S   BAR
Map p280 (☎514-286-6689; 156 Rue Roy Est; ⊗noon-3am; MSherbrooke) This is a warm and welcoming neighborhood bar where the vibe is just right for a drink among friends. Settle into one of the worn chairs for an order of fish and chips and a tasty microbrew in front of the ceiling-high windows.

BARFLY   BAR
Map p280 (☎514-284-6665; www.facebook.com/BarflyMtl; 4062 Blvd St-Laurent; ⊗4pm-2:30am; MSt-Laurent, then bus 55) Cheap, gritty, loud, fun and a little bit out of control – just the way we like our dive bars. Live bluegrass and rockabilly bands and bedraggled hipsters hold court alongside aging rockers at this St-Laurent hole-in-the-wall.

PLAN B   BAR
Map p280 (☎514-845-6060; www.barplanb.ca; 327 Ave du Mont-Royal Est; ⊗3pm-3am; MMont-Royal) Warm decor, elegant snacks and a fine cocktail menu make this high-end bar a perfect date and pickup spot. It's also perfect for drinking with friends, and usually not too loud to talk. A sophisticated French-speaking crowd flocks here after work and on weekends.

LA PORTE ROUGE   CLUB
(☎514-264-7399; 1834 Ave du Mont-Royal Est; ⊗10pm-3am Tue, Fri & Sat, from 5pm Thu; MMont-Royal) One of the few dance clubs in the Plateau, La Porte Rouge is a magnet for the fashion-minded, who don't mind paying high prices for cocktails (or opting for bottle service) to be among the beautiful people. The floral wallpaper, house-spinning DJs and nice lighting add to the appeal. To avoid paying sometimes high cover charges, come on Tuesdays.

BIFTECK
BAR

Map p280 (3702 Blvd St-Laurent; ⊘2pm-3am; ☎; Ⓜ St-Laurent, then bus 55) Pool, (free) popcorn and indie rockers hold court alongside students and weirdos at this legendary dive bar that's as much part of the Main's culture as smoked meat and bagels.

BLIZZARTS
BAR

Map p280 (www.blizzarts.ca; 3956a Blvd St-Laurent; ⊘10pm-3am; 🚇55, Ⓜ St-Laurent) Blizz is one of the Plateau's venerable little spots. The tiny dance floor fills up most nights as DJs spin a range of sounds to a small crowd both trendy and friendly. There's no attitude, just the shared desire to have a good time.

Top nights to go: Wednesdays for reggae and dancehall, Fridays for old- and new-school hip-hop, and Saturdays for Mod Club (sexy '60s sounds).

LES FOLIES
CAFE

Map p280 (☎514-528-4343; www.restofolies. ca; 701 Ave du Mont-Royal Est; ⊘9am-midnight Sun-Thu, to 1am Fri & Sat; Ⓜ Mont-Royal) A cross between a bar, cafe and club, the oh-so-chic Folies has a DJ from Tuesday to Saturday nights spinning trendy music and, much more importantly, a sidewalk terrace on Ave du Mont-Royal.

BIÈRES & COMPAGNIE
PUB

Map p280 (☎514-844-0394; www.bieresetcom pagnie.ca; 4350 Rue St-Denis; ⊘noon-midnight; Ⓜ Mont-Royal) This relaxed pub has a great choice of European and local microbrews alongside excellent pub grub such as burgers (bison, caribou or ostrich), beer-breaded onion rings and mussels done several ways.

 ENTERTAINMENT

CASA DEL POPOLO
LIVE MUSIC

Map p280 (www.casadelpopolo.com; 4873 Blvd St-Laurent; admission $5-15; ⊘noon-3am; Ⓜ Laurier) One of Montréal's most charming live venues, the 'House of the People' is also known for its vegetarian sandwiches and salads, its talented DJs and as a venue for art-house films and spoken-word performances. It's associated with the tapas bar La Sala Rosa (p110) and its concert venue La Sala Rossa.

DIÈSE ONZE
LIVE MUSIC

Map p280 (☎514-223-3543; www.dieseonze. com; 4115 Rue St-Denis; admission around $10; ⊘6pm-late; Ⓜ Mont-Royal) This downstairs jazz club has just the right vibe – with an intimate small stage so you can get close to the musicians. There are shows most nights, with an eclectic lineup of artists. You can have a bite while the band plays, with good tapas options as well as a few heartier mains (goat's-cheese burger, mushroom risotto). Call for reservations.

LA TULIPE
LIVE MUSIC

(☎514-526-4000; www.latulipe.ca; 4530 Ave Papineau; Ⓜ Mont-Royal, then bus 97) Best known for its riotously fun '80s dance parties (Saturday nights), La Tulipe also hosts underground indie bands, musical retrospectives and the odd burlesque show. It all takes place in a beautifully restored and intimate theater in the French-speaking east area of the Plateau.

EX-CENTRIS CINEMA
CINEMA

Map p280 (☎514-847-2206; www.cinemaexcentris. com; 3536 Blvd St-Laurent; Ⓜ St-Laurent) A showcase for independent films from around the world, Ex-Centris is geared to provide pure movie enjoyment with excellent seating and high-tech audio. It has three screens and remains a much-loved local art-house cinema.

AGORA DE LA DANSE
DANCE

Map p280 (☎514-525-1500; www.agoradanse. com; 840 Rue Cherrier; ⊘box office noon-5pm; Ⓜ Sherbrooke) One of Montréal's most important names in the contemporary dance world, Agora de la Danse explores modern and experimental forms, staging both homegrown troupes and performers from around the globe. It's set in the striking old Palestre National building. Tickets to most shows cost around $30.

MAINLINE THEATRE
THEATER

Map p280 (☎514-849-3378; www.mainlinethea tre.ca; 3997 Blvd St-Laurent; Ⓜ Mont-Royal) Located on the Main (hence the name), this intimate indie theater presents mostly new plays. It also serves as headquarters for the annual Montréal Fringe theater festival.

LE DIVAN ORANGE
LIVE MUSIC

Map p280 (☎514-840-9090; www.divanorange. org; 4234 Blvd St-Laurent; ⊘5pm-3am; Ⓜ St-Laurent, then bus 50) There's a terrific artistic vibe at this fantastic space, launched as a kind of restaurant-entertainment venue co-op. On any given night there may be a DJ, world-music performer or record launch.

🛍 SHOPPING

AUX 33 TOURS
MUSIC

Map p280 (1373 Ave du Mont-Royal Est; ☉10am-7pm Mon-Wed, to 9pm Thu & Fri, to 6pm Sat & Sun; Ⓜ Mont-Royal, then bus 97) Hands down, Aux 33 Tours is the best record shop in the city. You'll find a staggering selection of new and used vinyl covering every genre, and there's also a decent selection of CDs. The staff is knowledgeable, the bins are well organized and the rare finds are easy to unearth. You'll find loads of albums not sold elsewhere.

IBIKI
FASHION

Map p280 (4357 Blvd St-Laurent; ☉noon-7pm Mon-Wed, to 9pm Thu & Fri, 11am-6pm Sat, noon-5pm Sun; Ⓜ St-Laurent, then bus 55) Sleek and modular Ibiki draws a fashion-forward crowd, who come to ogle a well-curated selection of global designers, clothing and accessories. Check out knits by YMC, dresses by Won Hundred and leather bags by Montreal-based WANT. The art and design magazines up front are a fun browse.

LE 63
CLOTHING

Map p280 (63 Ave du Mont-Royal; ☉11am-6pm Mon-Fri, to 5pm Sat, noon-5pm Sun; Ⓜ Mont-Royal) The vibe is motorcycle chic, with stylish helmets, goggles, leather gloves and other eye-catching gear for sale. The real reason to come, though, is for the vintage selection, with graphic T-shirts, bomber jackets, fur-lined boots and Hawaiian shirts. Check the back room for vintage Playboys and bad priapic pottery. Bonus for furry folks: beard soap (from Brooklyn Grooming).

ARTPOP
CRAFTS

Map p280 (129 Ave du Mont-Royal Est; ☉10am-7pm Mon-Wed & Sat, to 9pm Thu & Fri, 11am-7pm Sun; Ⓜ Mont-Royal) Tiny Artpop is a real find if you're browsing for unique Montréal-themed gift ideas. You'll find graphic T-shirts, bags, pillow covers, iPhone covers and prints with iconic city signage (Farine Five Roses, the big Orange Julep, Habitat 67 or the cross atop Mont-Royal).

LA TABLETTE DE MISS CHOCO
FOOD & DRINK

Map p280 (www.latablette.ca; 838 Ave du Mont-Royal Est; ☉11am-6pm Mon-Wed & Sat, to 8pm Thu-Fri, to 5pm Sun; Ⓜ Mont-Royal) Elevating the humble cacao bean to high art, this elegant shop stocks chocolaty decadence from around the globe, with bars organized by country: Madagascar, Papua New Guinea, Ecuador, Vietnam and dozens of other countries. The on-site cafe serves thick, rich cups of *chocolat intense* as well as milder, tea-like infusions.

There are classes (in French) where you can learn about the chocolate-making process and evening soirees dedicated to pairings with wine and beer.

HADIO
VINTAGE

Map p280 (314 Ave du Mont-Royal Est; ☉10am-6pm; Ⓜ Mont-Royal) A top choice for vintage hunters in the Plateau, Hadio has jammed racks of flannels, crop tops and tank tops, plus cowboy boots, button-downs and lots of new T-shirts with old-school logos and icons (Darth Vader, Michael Jackson, Jaws, Mr T). The prices are great, with many items in the $10 range.

LIBRAIRIE MICHEL FORTIN
BOOKS

Map p280 (📞514-849-5719; www.librairiemichel fortin.com; 3714 Rue St-Denis; ☉9am-6pm Mon-Wed, to 9pm Thu & Fri, to 5pm Sat, 11am-5pm Sun; Ⓜ Sherbrooke) A mecca for every foreign-language student and linguist freak in town. You can find children's books, CDs and DVDs, dual-language readers and novels, covering more than 200 languages.

SCANDALE
FASHION

Map p280 (📞514-842-4707; 3639 Blvd St-Laurent; ☉11am-6pm Mon-Wed, to 9pm Thu & Fri, to 5pm Sat; Ⓜ St-Laurent, then bus 55) Style maven Marie-Josée Gagnon has been running this beautifully designed boutique since 1977, bringing in exotic Parisian imports as well as the creations of the late Georges Lévesque, one of Québec's most talented designers.

DUO
FASHION

Map p280 (📞514-848-0880; www.boutiqueduo. com; 30 Rue Prince-Arthur Ouest; ☉10am-6pm Mon-Wed & Sat, to 9pm Thu & Fri, noon-6pm Sun; Ⓜ Sherbrooke) A shop for the gents, Duo carries stylish apparel by Rag & Bone, Fred Perry and Marc by Marc Jacobs, as well as Canada's own Mackage. You'll also find designer sneakers, fragrances (by Canadian label DSquared) and accessories.

COFFRE AUX TRÉSORS DU CHAINON
VINTAGE

Map p280 (📞514-843-4354; www.lechainon. org; 4375 Blvd St-Laurent; ☉10am-6pm Tue & Wed, to 8pm Thu & Fri, 10am-5pm Sat, noon-5pm

Sun; Ⓜ St-Laurent, then bus 55) This sprawling secondhand store has two floors packed with clothing, shoes, housewares, books and records. Revenue from the store goes directly to the Montréal women's shelter, Le Chaînon.

FRIPERIE ST-LAURENT　　　FASHION, VINTAGE

Map p280 (3976 Blvd St-Laurent; ⏱ 11am-6pm Mon-Wed, to 9pm Thu & Fri, to 5pm Sat, noon-5pm Sun; Ⓜ Sherbrooke) One of the Plateau's best-loved *friperies* (vintage shops) has a small but well-chosen selection of clothing from decades past. Fur-lined bomber jackets, elegant 1950s dresses, cowboy and motorcycle boots are all part of the treasure chest. On recent visits, we spotted kilts and lederhosen.

✦ SPORTS & ACTIVITIES

FITZ & FOLLWELL　　　WALKING, BICYCLE

Map p280 (☎ 514-840-0739; www.fitzandfollwell. co; 115 Ave du Mont-Royal Ouest; tours $75-100, bike hire per 4/8hrs $20/30; ⏱ 10am-7pm Tue-Fri, to 6pm Sat, to 5pm Sun; Ⓜ Place-des-Arts, then bus 80) This recommended outfit offers a range of walking and cycling tours around Montréal. Tours have very much a local flavor, as young, knowledgeable guides take you on day and evening rides, stopping for a park picnic, visiting microbreweries, or exploring the leafy paths of Mont-Royal.

There are also walking tours that explore the history, culture and food of Blvd St-Laurent; fascinating rambles through Old Montréal; and curious walks through the Underground City.

If you prefer to explore on your own, Fitz & Follwell rents bikes – stylish three- or eight-speed Linus models. If you have small children, you can rent Yuba Mundo bikes that carry up to three kids in back, or Babboe City cargo bikes.

LE GRAND CYCLE　　　BICYCLE RENTAL

Map p280 (☎ 514-525-1414; www.legrandcycle. com; 901 Rue Cherrier Est; bicycle per day/24hr from $25/30; ⏱ 9am-7pm Mon-Fri, 10am-5pm Sat; Ⓜ Sherbrooke) Le Grand Cycle is a fine place to get you rolling, with good eight-speed city bikes for rent plus all the extras.

LA MAISON DES CYCLISTES　　　BICYCLE RENTAL

Map p280 (www.velo.qc.ca; 1251 Rue Rachel Est; ⏱ 10:30am-5pm Mon-Fri; Ⓜ Mont-Royal) The nerve center of Québec's biking culture, this three-story house in the Plateau is an essential stop for avid cyclists. There's a shop with cycling books, maps and guides; the Velo Québec association (involved in developing one of the largest bicycling networks in North America); a travel agency for planning biking trips; info on events; and cozy cafe Marius (p109). It's right along the bike path above Parc La Fontaine.

STUDIO BLISS　　　SPA

Map p280 (☎ 514-437-399; www.studiobliss.ca; 3841 Blvd St-Laurent; 1hr yoga class $18, 1hr massage $79; ⏱ 10am-10pm; Ⓜ Sherbrooke) Equal parts spa and yoga studio, Studio Bliss aims to rejuvenate the body by a variety of passive and kinetic means. Vinyasa and Hatha classes are offered daily, and there are two meditation workshops a week. You can also opt for a hot-stone treatment, chocolate wrap, exfoliation and various massages.

AVEDA MONTRÉAL LIFESTYLE SALON SPA & ACADEMY　　　SPA

Map p280 (☎ 514-499-9494; www.avedamontreal-lifestyle.com; 3613 Blvd St-Laurent; ⏱ 10am-8pm Tue & Wed, to 9pm Thu & Fri, 9am-7pm Sat, 10am-5pm Sun; Ⓜ St-Laurent, then bus 55) You'll find friendly staff and a wide range of treatments at this well-liked spa and salon. A favorite is the Rejuvenating Experience ($175), featuring a body wrap, massage, manicure and pedicure. You can also opt for facials, waxing, peels and haircuts.

Little Italy, Mile End & Outremont

MILE END & OUTREMONT | LITTLE ITALY

Neighborhood Top Five

1 Exploring the fresh produce, hawker stalls, and delightful seafood, sandwiches and desserts at the colorful **Marché Jean-Talon** (p118).

2 Snacking on the best bagels in the world – bar none – at **St-Viateur Bagel** (p121).

3 Spoiling yourself with some of Montréal's best dining options at charmers such as **Van Horne** (p122) and **Lawrence** (p122).

4 Trolling quirky neighborhood shops such as **Monastiraki** (p127) for retro junk – or treasures, depending on your taste.

5 Enjoying old-world pleasures by nursing an espresso at **Caffè Italia** (p123) and munching on smoked meat on rye at **Lester's** (p121).

For more detail of this area see Map p284 ➡

Explore Little Italy, Mile End & Outremont

These three neighborhoods are a foodie's nirvana, distilled from a potent mish-mash of Italian, Portuguese, Jewish and Québecois roots. The good thing is there's plenty of walking to be done to burn off those extra calories. Most of the area can be explored in a day, though you might want to return once or twice in the evening for dinner.

Start your day at the flavor cornucopia that is Marché Jean-Talon (p118), grabbing fresh fruit or a crepe for breakfast before diving deeper into Little Italy, taking in the 1930s ceiling fresco of Mussolini at the Église Madonna Della Difesa (p118). Stroll down Blvd St-Laurent, where the green-white-red flag is proudly displayed, pausing for an espresso at Caffè Italia (p123) and some fine contemporary art at galleries near Rue Beaubien.

A bus along the boulevard can bring you back downtown if you're tired out, or drop you near Ave Fairmount. This area is a good spot to explore Mile End, a multi-ethnic neighborhood with great dining along Ave Laurier, fantastic bagels and increasingly trendy hangouts at its epicenter: Rue St-Viateur and Blvd St-Laurent.

Further west, Outremont is largely a residence for wealthy Francophones. Fabulous old mansions lie on leafy streets northwest of Rue Bernard. There is also a significant Hassidic community in Outremont.

Local Life

➡ **Cafe culture** This area has some of Montréal's most charming cafes and teahouses, including Cardinal Tea Room (p120).

➡ **Catch the game** Purchase provisions at Marché Jean-Talon (p118), then head to a park (such as Parc Outremont, p118) for a picnic.

➡ **For the kitchen** Cruise the high-end cooking boutiques such as Les Touilleurs (p128) or try a cooking course at Mezza Luna Cooking School (p128).

Getting There & Away

➡ **Metro** Though not ideally located, Laurier on the orange line gives you access to Ave Laurier, while Jean-Talon (on the orange and blue lines) puts you within easy reach of Marché Jean-Talon. Outremont has its own station on the blue line.

➡ **Bus** Bus 55 runs along Blvd St-Laurent; bus 46 runs on part of Rue Bernard and Ave Laurier; bus 80 runs along Ave du Parc.

➡ **Walking** This is a large area to walk, but strolling along Laurier, Bernard or Saint-Viateur, as well as parts of Blvd St-Laurent, makes for enjoyable exploring.

Lonely Planet's Top Tip

A growing number of bars, restaurants and cafes are popping up along Rue Beaubien, making it a fine place to explore.

 ### Best Places to Eat

➡ Impasto (p123)
➡ Arts Cafe (p118)
➡ Sparrow (p122)
➡ Van Horne (p122)
➡ Kitchen Galerie (p122)

For reviews, see p118.

Best Places to Drink

➡ Isle de Garde (p126)
➡ Dieu du Ciel (p123)
➡ Gainzbar (p126)
➡ Notre Dame des Quilles (p126)
➡ La Buvette Chez Simone (p123)

For reviews, see p123.

Best Places to Shop

➡ Drawn & Quarterly (p127)
➡ Frank & Oak (p127)
➡ Monastiraki (p127)
➡ Galerie CO (p127)

For reviews, see p127.

⊙ SIGHTS

MARCHÉ JEAN-TALON
MARKET

Map p284 (7075 Ave Casgrain; ⊗7am-6pm Mon-Wed & Sat, to 8pm Thu & Fri, to 5pm Sun; MJean-Talon) The pride of Little Italy, this huge covered market is Montréal's most diverse. Many chefs buy ingredients for their menus here or in the specialty-food shops nearby. Three long covered aisles are packed with merchants selling fruit, vegetables, flowers and baked goods. The market is flanked by delis and cafe-restaurants. Even in winter the market is open under big tents.

Snackers can nibble on sandwiches, crepes, tacos, pastries, ice cream, fresh juices and excellent coffee. Be sure to stop by Le Marché des Saveurs du Québec (p127), one of the few large stores in town devoted entirely to Québec specialties such as wine and cider, fresh cheeses, smoked meats, preserves and a huge number of tasteful gifts.

ÉGLISE MADONNA DELLA DIFESA
CHURCH

Map p284 (www.difesa.ca; 6800 Ave Henri-Julien; ⊗7:30-9am Mon-Fri, 7:30am-noon Sun, 2-6pm Tue-Thu, Sat & Sun; MJean-Talon) Our Lady of Protection Church was built in 1919 according to the drawings of Florence-born Guido Nincheri (1885–1973), who spent the next two decades working on the Roman-Byzantine structure. The artist painted the church's remarkable **frescoes**, including one of Mussolini on horseback with a bevy of generals in the background. The work honored the formal recognition by Rome of the pope's sovereignty over Vatican City in 1929 and was unveiled a few years later as Hitler came to power.

During WWII, Nincheri and others who had worked on the building were interned by the Canadian authorities. The fresco can be viewed above the high marble altar.

ÉGLISE ST-VIATEUR D'OUTREMONT
CHURCH

Map p284 (www.saintviateurdoutremont.org; 1175 Ave Laurier Ouest; ⊗4pm-5:30pm Tue & Thu, 4:30-6pm Sat, 10:30am-noon Sun; MLaurier, then bus 51) If you are already on Ave Laurier for the shopping and food, poke your head into this church, opened in 1913. The interior is pure Gothic Revival with ornate paintings, stained glass, hand-crafted cabinets and sculptures by renowned Montréal artists; the impressive ceiling vaults depict the life of St Viateur. It's also home to a magnificent, century-old Casavant organ.

PARC OUTREMONT
PARK

Map p284 (cnr Ave Outremont & Ave St-Viateur; MRosemont) One of Montréal's best-kept secrets, this small leafy green space is a great place for a bit of quiet time. Lovely Victorian homes ring the park, and benches provide a nice vantage point for viewing the small pond with fountain. This is a good spot to go with an ice cream from Le Bilboquet (p120), two blocks northwest.

PARC ST VIATEUR
PARK

Map p284 (cnr Ave l'Épée & Rue Bernard; MOutremont) Just off Ave Bernard a small pedestrian lane leads to this small but handsomely landscaped park. It has a bridge over a narrow circular waterway, which draws ice skaters in winter (bring your own skates).

✗ EATING

✗ Mile End & Outremont

Little Italy is a neighborhood full of old-fashioned trattorias and lively cafes, where the heavenly aroma of freshly brewed espresso hangs in the air. Stylish new eateries, including some of the best in Montréal, have also established a strong presence here.

Mile End and Outremont are duly blessed in the dining department. Strewn with an impressive variety of Parisian-style bistros, high-end ethnic eateries and low-key cafes, these neighborhoods also boast two oven-baked stars of the city's culinary history: the famous Montréal bagel shops.

LA PANTHÈRE VERTE
VEGETARIAN $

Map p284 (☑514-508-5564; www.lapanthere verte.com; 160 Rue St-Viateur Est; mains $6-11; ⊗11am-10pm Mon-Sat, to 9pm Sun; 🖘 ✒; MLaurier) Green in every sense of the word, La Panthère Verte is a casual vegetarian spot, where you can stop for delicious falafel sandwiches, energy-charging juices and smoothies, and fresh salad specials that change daily. Plants, a zippy green paint job and an elegant chandelier help set the scene in the industrial-chic space.

ARTS CAFE
INTERNATIONAL $

Map p284 (☑514-274-0919; www.artscafemon treal.com; 201 Ave Fairmount Ouest; mains $11-16; ⊗9am-7pm Mon-Fri, 10am-4pm Sat & Sun; MLaurier) The Arts Cafe has instant appeal with

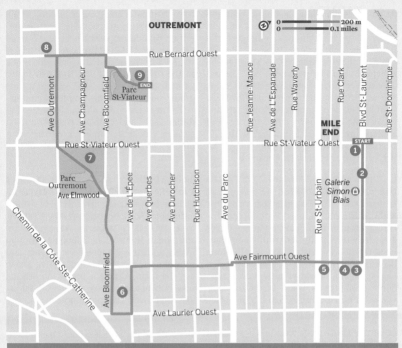

Neighborhood Walk
Exploring Mile End & Outremont

START LE CAGIBI CAFÉ
END PARC ST-VIATEUR
LENGTH 2.5KM; ONE TO TWO HOURS

Multicultural Mile End and Outremont are home to Hassidic Jews, Portuguese, Greeks and Italians, among others. You'll find eclectic cafes, eye-catching boutiques, vegetarian restaurants, lively bars, leafy parks and great bagels.

Start at one of Mile End's great little spots, ❶ **Le Cagibi Café** (p120). Grab a coffee for fuel (return at night for film screenings, live bands, book launches and other eclectic fare).

Turn right along ❷ **Boulevard St-Laurent** (p103) and take in some of the galleries and curio shops, such as the prestigious Galerie Simon Blais.

Continue along Blvd St-Laurent and turn right onto Ave Fairmount. Near the corner is ❸ **Au Papier Japonais** (p127), a sweet little store specializing in handmade paper, art books, origami sets and more.

Made famous in a Mordecai Richler novel, ❹ **Wilensky's Light Lunch** (34 Ave Fairmount Ouest; ⊙9am-4pm Mon-Fri, 10am-4pm Sat) hasn't changed much since opening in 1937. For grilled salami and bologna sandwiches, this is your place.

Continue along Ave Fairmount. Stop for a bagel taste-test at famous ❺ **Fairmount Bagel** (p120), archrival of St-Viateur Bagel.

Continue on Fairmount, turn left on Ave de l'Épee and right on Ave Laurier. The magnificent church on the corner is ❻ **Église St-Viateur d'Outremont** (p118), a neighborhood icon. Exiting the church, turn right up Ave Bloomfield and in two blocks you'll reach ❼ **Parc Outremont** (p118), a beautiful park with a tiny lake and a playground. Lovely Victorian homes surround it.

Exit the park onto Ave Outremont, continuing until Rue Bernard. Go left to ❽ **Le Bilboquet** (p120), one of the best ice-cream shops in Montréal.

Zigzag over to ❾ **Parc St-Viateur**, another peaceful green space in the neighborhood, and enjoy your ice-cream.

its plank floors, white clapboard walls and sculptural knickknacks (a frenzy of light bulbs above the windows, vintage farmhouse relics) that adorn the space. But it's the food that warrants the most attention. Excellent brunch/breakfasts are served all day. Try mouthwatering dishes such as the waffles (served with Guinea-fowl leg, wild berries and pumpkin cream), poutine (made with duck confit, a poached egg and Hollandaise sauce) or kale salad (with wild berries, mascarpone and pork belly). Be prepared for long lines on weekends.

LA CROISSANTERIE FIGARO
CAFE $

Map p284 (✆514-278-6567; www.lacroissant eriefigaro.com; 5200 Rue Hutchison; sandwiches $9-13; ☺7am-1am; Ⓜ Laurier) With its deco fixtures, wrought-iron marble-topped tables and lovely terrace, this charming neighborhood cafe has a Parisian vibe, and has long been a popular meeting spot for well-heeled locals. Stop in for warm, buttery croissants (among Montréal's best), baguette sandwiches or rich desserts. It's also a fine place to nurse a coffee or a cocktail.

JULIETTE ET CHOCOLAT
CAFE $

Map p284 (✆514-510-5651; www.julietteetchoco lat.com; 377 Ave Laurier Ouest; desserts $5-10; ☺11am-11pm Mon-Fri, 10am-11pm Sat & Sun; 🛜; Ⓜ Laurier) Montréal's chocolate lovers unite at this sweet two-level cafe on Laurier. The menu is built around chocolate, from decadent piping-hot crepes to milk shakes, brownies and chocolate 'shots,' not to mention cups of creamy hot chocolate. Black-and-white tile floors, big windows and an inviting ambience seduce lingerers. There are five other locations in town.

LE CAGIBI CAFÉ
VEGETARIAN $

Map p284 (✆514-509-1199; www.lecagibi.ca; 5490 Blvd St-Laurent; mains $8-10; ☺6pm-midnight Mon, from 9am Tue-Fri, from 10:30am Sat & Sun; ✍; Ⓜ Rosemont) Music-lovers and Plateau eccentrics hold court at this plant- and antique-filled vegetarian restaurant by day, bar by night. The menu features tasty burritos, veggie burgers, chili and baked goods. There's a good entertainment lineup by night: DJs, live bands, film screenings, book readings, slide shows and other eclectic fare.

CARDINAL TEA ROOM
BRITISH $

Map p284 (www.thecardinaltea.com; 5326 Blvd St-Laurent; small teapot around $5, snacks $5-10; ☺11am-7pm Thu-Sun; Ⓜ Laurier) Above Spar-

row (Cardinal's food-focused sibling), you'll find a two-story tearoom set with a glittering chandelier, velvet couches, framed artwork and fresh flowers on the tables. It's all very prim and proper, right down to the delicate China and tiny teaspoons. Of course, this is Mile End, so that means groovy bossa nova tunes and hip waitstaff.

The teas are great although on the traditional side, and there are snacks on hand (scones, quiche, cucumber sandwiches). A pianist plays on weekends (from about 1pm or 2pm).

LE BILBOQUET
ICE CREAM $

Map p284 (✆514-276-0414; www.bilboquet.ca; 1311 Rue Bernard Ouest; cones $2.50-6; ☺11am-midnight Jun-Aug, to 8pm mid-Mar–May & Sep-Dec, closed Jan–mid-Mar; Ⓜ Laurier) A legendary institution in Montréal, Le Bilboquet whips up highly addictive homemade ice cream and refreshing sorbets. Long lines often snake out the door. Although there's no seating inside, there are a couple of sidewalk tables, and some lovely little parks nearby.

COMPTOIR 21
FISH & CHIPS $

Map p284 (21 Rue St-Viateur Ouest; mains $8-14; ☺noon-11pm; Ⓜ Laurier) Slide onto a stool around the horseshoe-shaped wooden counter and feast on tender morsels of fish and chips, served on blue-and-white checked paper in pretty wooden baskets. Bonus points for the clever spray bottles of vinegar and the range of sauces (aside from the classic tartare) available. It's a cozy space that draws a good cross-section of Montréal society.

CAFÉ OLIMPICO
CAFE $

Map p284 (✆514-495-0746; 124 Rue St-Viateur; coffees $2-4; ☺7am-midnight; 🛜; Ⓜ Laurier) Its espresso is excellent, yet this rocking, no-frills Italian cafe is all about atmosphere, as young good-looking baristas whip up smooth caffeinated drinks to the jumble of hipsters, tourists and elderly gentlemen who pass through. It's big on sports (especially the Italian football league), so there are TVs inside.

FAIRMOUNT BAGEL
BAKERY $

Map p284 (74 Ave Fairmount Ouest; bagels 90¢; ☺24hr; Ⓜ Laurier) One of Montréal's famed bagel places – people flood in here around the clock to scoop them up the minute they come out of the oven. Bagels are one thing Montréalers don't get too creative with.

THE GREAT BAGEL DEBATE

The Montréal bagel has a long and venerable history. It all started in 1915 when Isadore and Fanny Shlafman, Jews from Ukraine, opened a tiny bakery on Rue Roy in the Plateau. They made the yeast bread rings according to a recipe they'd brought from the bakery where Shlafman's father worked. In 1919 they started the Montréal Bagel Bakery in a wooden shack just off Blvd St-Laurent, a few doors down from Schwartz's deli.

After WWII many Holocaust survivors emigrated to Montréal and the bagel market boomed. Isadore Shlafman decided to build a bakery in the living room of his house at 74 Ave Fairmount, where he opened Fairmount Bagel in 1950. Meanwhile Myer Lewkowicz, a Polish Jew who had survived Auschwitz, went on to establish St-Viateur Bakery in 1957. A legendary rivalry was born and scores of other bagel bakeries sprang up in their wake.

Ask any Montréaler whose bagel is best and passions will flare. Year in and year out tireless critics tour the main bagel bakeries to chat, chew and cogitate. In recent years St-Viateur has edged out Fairmount for the number-one slot. But locals do agree on one thing: they believe that Montréal's bagels are superior to their New York cousins. The Montréal bagel is lighter, sweeter and crustier, and chewy but not dense thanks to an enriched eggy dough that looks almost like batter. The dough hardly rises and the tender rings are formed by hand and boiled in a honey-and-water solution before baking in a wood-burning oven.

They stick to classic sesame or poppy seed varieties, though you can pick up anything from cinnamon to all-dressed here too.

ST-VIATEUR BAGEL
BAKERY **$**

Map p284 (www.stviateurbagel.com; 263 Ave St-Viateur Ouest; bagels 75¢; ⊙24hr; Ⓜ Place-des-Arts, then bus 80) Currently the bagel favorite of Montréal, St-Viateur Bagel was set up in 1957 and has a reputation stretching across Canada and beyond for its perfectly crusty, chewy and slightly sweet creations. The secret to their perfection seems to be boiling in honey water followed by baking in the wood-fired oven. Biting into a warm one straight out of the oven is an absolute delight.

LESTER'S
DINER **$**

Map p284 (☑514-213-1313; www.lestersdeli.com; 1057 Rue Bernard Ouest; mains $7-14; ⊙9am-9pm Mon-Fri, to 8pm Sat; Ⓜ Outremont) With its art-deco-meets-1950s-diner-style decor and period knickknacks adorning the walls, this famed restaurant attracts a fiercely loyal following of locals looking for the perfect smoked-meat sandwich (the old-fashioned is formidable), but there's also smoked salmon, potato salad and *karnatzel* (dried sausage).

LE PETIT ALEP
MIDDLE EASTERN **$**

Map p284 (☑514-270-9361; 191 Rue Jean-Talon Est; mains $6-16; ⊙11am-11pm Tue-Sat; ☑; Ⓜ De Castelnau) The complex flavors of Syrian-Armenian cuisine draw diners from all over Montréal. A big menu includes hummus,

salads and *muhammara* (spread made of walnuts, garlic, breadcrumbs, pomegranate syrup and cumin), plus beef kebabs smothered in tahini, spices and nuts.

Dine in the bright restaurant (the front wall opens up onto the street during nice weather) or, in the evening, the slightly swish dining room next door.

INVITATION V
VEGAN **$$**

Map p284 (☑514-271-8111; 254 Rue Bernard Ouest; mains $14-20; ⊙11:30am-3pm Tue-Sun, 6-10pm Tue-Sat; ☑; ☐160, Ⓜ Beaubien) ⊘ A game-changer in the world of vegan cuisine, Invitation V serves up creative, beautifully presented dishes in an elegant dining room of white brick and light woods. Start with butternut squash and roasted-red-pepper soup and a round of mushroom satay with peanut sauce, before moving onto curry stew with Jasmine rice or a tempeh burger with sweet-potato fries.

The founders profess a strong commitment to sustainability and use organic, locally sourced products where possible. Good brunches too.

TRI EXPRESS
JAPANESE **$$**

(☑514-528-5641; www.triexpressrestaurant.com; 1650 Ave Laurier Est; sushi platters $22; ⊙11am-9pm Tue-Wed, to 10pm Thu-Fri, 4-10pm Sat & Sun; Ⓜ Laurier) Trì Dư prepares superb sushi and sashimi plates, along with inventive salads and soups with a hint of his home country of Vietnam in this hip, vintage-filled eatery

NECTAR OF THE GODS

Québec produces about three quarters of the world's maple syrup, which is perhaps why it enjoys such pride of place, appearing on everything from meat and desserts to foie gras, blended with smoothies and in maple beer. French settlers began producing it regularly in the 1800s after learning from Canadian Aboriginal people how to make it from maple-tree sap. Sap is usually extracted in spring after enzymes convert starch into sugars over the winter. Once the weather warms and the sap starts flowing, Québecers head to *cabanes à sucre* (sugar shacks) out in the countryside. There they sample the first amber riches of the season and do the taffy pull, where steaming maple syrup is poured into the snow and then scooped up on a popsicle stick once it's cooled.

just off the beaten path. You can't go wrong with the Omakase (a mix of sashimi, sushi and maki), a lobster salad (with grapefruit, avocado and mango) and the delicious 'sushi pizza.' The downside: the space is always crowded (tip: call ahead), and there's no alcohol here – you're not allowed to bring your own either. Also cash only (and French only for the menu).

SPARROW   INTERNATIONAL $$
Map p284 (☎514-507-1642; 5322 Blvd St-Laurent; mains $13-18; ⊗6pm-3am daily, 10am-3pm Sat & Sun; ⓜLaurier) In a vintage chic dining room, Mile Enders feast on mussels with white wine and fries, pan-roasted trout, butter chicken and other unfussy but tasty bistro classics. For the price, it's hard to find a better meal in this city. Food aside, Sparrow serves up excellent cocktails, and the festive vibe continues until late into the night.

The Sunday roast and weekend brunch are also quite good (and the only times when reservations are accepted; call ahead).

VAN HORNE   FRENCH $$
Map p284 (☎514-508-0828; www.vanhornerestaurant.com; 1268 Ave Van Horne; mains $21-28; ⊗11:30am-2pm Tue-Fri, 6-10:30pm Tue-Sat; ⓜOutremont) Sophisticated, market-sourced works of art are beautifully presented in this intimate spot that pays tribute to American businessman and gourmet William Van Horne. Chef Jens Ruoff has a limited but rotating menu, featuring delectable choices such as Québec wapiti (elk) with smoked sunchokes, Brussels sprouts and bacon, or skate wing with clams, red cabbage and vermouth emulsion.

Even the desserts are artful: try the deconstructed Snickers bar (peanuts, caramel, chocolate and sea salt).

LAWRENCE   EUROPEAN $$
Map p284 (☎514-503-1070; www.lawrencerestaurant.com; 5201 Blvd St-Laurent; mains brunch $12-16, dinner $26-30; ⊗11:30am-3pm Tue-Fri, 5:30-11pm Tue-Sat, 10am-3pm Sat & Sun; ⓜLaurier) This high-style hipster eatery helmed by British chef Marc Cohen of Sparrow serves up some of the best brunch in Montréal. With high windows looking out over the Main, it's a perfect spot to sink your teeth into smoked trout with scrambled eggs or scones with jam and clotted cream.

In the evening, you can feast on clam and pig-skin stew or stewed octopus with chickpeas. Just don't expect anything too conventional.

PHAYATHAI   THAI $$
Map p284 (☎514-272-3456; www.phayathailaurier.com; 107 Ave Laurier Ouest; mains $10-23; ⊗noon-2:30pm & 5:30-10:30pm; ⓜLaurier) Although the jury is out on who serves the city's best Thai food, this elegant little restaurant is a strong contender. Try the delicious and flavorful seafood soup, tender boneless roasted duck or satisfying pad thai.

KITCHEN GALERIE   FRENCH $$$
Map p284 (☎514-315-8994; www.kitchengalerie.com; 60 Rue Jean-Talon Est; mains $30-50; ⊗6-10pm Tue-Sat; ⓜJean-Talon) Jovial chefs Mathieu Cloutier and Mathieu Bourdages are well situated by the Marché Jean-Talon for their succulently fresh market offerings, which change daily. Expect carnivore-oriented choices such as *bavette saignant* (flank steak) with mashed potatoes, or foie gras (see p28) in various incarnations (the most famous of which is prepared in a dishwasher!). Be sure to call and reserve.

LEMÉAC   FRENCH $$$
Map p284 (☎514-270-0999; www.restaurantlemeac.com; 1045 Ave Laurier Ouest; mains dinner $26-46, brunch $12-18; ⊗11:30am-midnight

Mon-Fri, 10am-midnight Sat & Sun; Ⓜ Laurier) A well-respected name among the well-heeled Laurier crowd, Lémeac has a light and airy setting with huge windows overlooking the street, a lively ambience and beautifully turned-out plates. It's a popular brunch spot on weekends, and at night – the after-10pm multicourse prix-fixe menu is excellent value at $25.

✕ Little Italy

FORTUNE   MEXICAN $
Map p284 (6448 Blvd St-Laurent; tacos around $5; ◷ 11:30am-10pm Tue-Sun; 🖉; Ⓜ Beaubien) For a quick bite when you're strolling St-Laurent, stop in this attractive, breadbox-sized eatery for delicious tacos (fish, pork, chicken or roasted cauliflower). Order at least three if you're hungry.

CAFFÈ ITALIA   CAFE $
Map p284 (🖉 514-495-0059; 6840 Blvd St-Laurent; sandwiches around $8, coffees $2-3; ◷ 6am-11pm; Ⓜ De Castelnau) This old-time Italian cafe has a loyal following. Plain Formica counters and faded Italian soccer posters set the stage for lingering over excellent espresso and unfussy sandwiches. Depending on how things are going (with AC Milan football club), staff can be grumpy or enthusiastically welcoming.

DÉPANNEUR LE PICK UP   DINER $
Map p284 (🖉 514-271-8011; http://depanneur lepickup.com; 7032 Rue Waverly; mains $5-9; ◷ 7am-7pm Mon-Fri, 9am-7pm Sat, 10am-6pm Sun; 🖉; Ⓜ De Castelnau) A hipster favorite, Le Pick Up began as an authentic 1950s *dépanneur* (convenience store) and snack bar before the current owners took it over and added zines (homemade magazines) to the daily necessities on the shelves and '80s synth-pop to the stereo. Nosh on yummy veggie burgers, or grilled haloumi and pulled-pork sandwiches at the grill counter.

ALATI-CASERTA   BAKERY $
Map p284 (🖉 514-271-3013; www.alaticaserta. com; 277 Rue Dante; dessert $3-6; ◷ 10am-5pm Mon, 8am-6pm Tue & Wed, 8am-7pm Thu & Fri, 9am-5pm Sat & Sun; Ⓜ Jean-Talon) For more than four decades, this marvelous family-owned pastry shop in Little Italy has wowed Montréalers with its deliciously decadent cannoli, almond cake, tiramisu and *sfogliatelle* (pastries stuffed with orange and ricotta cheese). Arrive early for the best selection.

PIZZERIA NAPOLETANA   ITALIAN $$
Map p284 (🖉 514-276-8226; www.napoletana.com; 189 Rue Dante; mains $12-18; ◷ 11am-10:30pm Mon-Thu, to 11:30pm Fri & Sat, noon-10:30pm Sun; Ⓜ De Castelnau) Homemade pasta sauces and thick-sauced pizzas (more than 30 different types of each) draw Italian-loving crowds here all year long. The pizza crust – nice and crunchy – is the secret to Napoletana's success. Lines can be long, particularly in summer, so avoid peak hours. Bring your own wine. Cash only.

IMPASTO   ITALIAN $$$
Map p284 (🖉 514-419-4448; www.impastomtl.ca; 48 Rue Dante; mains $28-35; ◷ 11:30am-2pm Thu & Fri, 5-11pm Tue-Sat; Ⓜ De Castelnau) There's much buzz surrounding this polished Italian eatery – in no small part owing to the heavy-hitting foodies behind it: best-selling cookbook author Stefano Faita and celebrated chef Michele Forgione. Both have deep connections to Italian cooking, obvious in brilliant dishes such as braised beef cheeks with Savoy-style potatoes, artic char with cauliflower purée and lentils, and house-made pastas like busiate with lobster. Try to snag a spot facing the open kitchen to watch the masters in action. Reserve ahead.

DRINKING & NIGHTLIFE

🍷 Mile End & Outremont

⭐ LA BUVETTE CHEZ SIMONE   WINE BAR
Map p284 (🖉 514-750-6577; 4869 Ave du Parc; ◷ 4pm-1am; Ⓜ Laurier) An artsy-chic crowd of (mostly) francophone bons vivants and professionals loves this cozy wine bar. The staff know its vino and the extensive list is complemented by a gourmet tapas menu. Weekends, the place is jammed from *cinq-à-sept* (the lively 5pm to 7pm happy hour) into the wee hours.

DIEU DU CIEL   BREWERY
Map p284 (🖉 514-490-9555; www.dieuduciel. com; 29 Ave Laurier Ouest; ◷ 3pm-3am Mon-Fri, 1pm-3am Sat & Sun; Ⓜ Laurier) Packed every night with a young, francophone crowd, this unpretentious bar serves a phenomenal rotating menu of its famous microbrews, running from classic ales to rich stouts such as the imperial coffee stout Péché Mortel.

MEGAPRESS / ALAMY ©

Little Italy eateries (p123)
Head here for a blend of traditional
trattorias and cutting-edge restaurants.

Parc Outremont (p118)
Set amid Victorian-era houses, this small
but lovely park is one of Montréal's best-
kept secrets.

Marché Jean-Talon (p118)
Montréal's most diverse market offers fresh
produce and tempting snacks.

Bagels at St-Viateur Bagel (p121)
St-Viateur Bagel was founded 1957 and is
now – along with its bagels – a Montréal
institution.

CHRIS CHEADLE / GETTY IMAGES ©

CHEZ SERGE SPORTS BAR

Map p284 (📞514-663-4227; 5301 Blvd St-Laurent; ⏱5pm-3am; Ⓜ St-Laurent, then bus 55) How can you go wrong with a bra-adorned moose head on the wall? Hockey games, unbridled kitsch and a mechanical bull reel in neighborhood kids. With cold beer and staff who love dancing (sometimes on the bar), this homey spot gets out of control during hockey and soccer seasons. Reserve ahead (for a table) on game nights.

KABINET COCKTAIL BAR

Map p284 (📞514-274-3555; 92 Rue Laurier Ouest; ⏱8pm-3am Tue-Sat; Ⓜ Laurier) Paying tribute to all things Russian, this stylish little cocktail den draws a slightly more sophisticated crowd than the average Mile End hipster haunt. You can sip well-made drinks such as the Rasputin (bourbon, Lillet blanc, orange liqueur) and nibble on *pelmeni* (dumplings), while taking in czarist regalia adorning the cozy, bunker-like space.

DATCHA CLUB

Map p284 (www.bardatcha.com; 98 Rue Laurier Ouest; ⏱11pm-3am Thu-Sat; Ⓜ Laurier) Datcha is a small night spot with a tiny dance floor that draws a laid-back, groove-loving crowd. Eclectic DJs from around the globe spin here, but the best part of Datcha is the fog machine. Party like it's 1987, while sipping Moscow Mules (vodka, ginger syrup, lime juice) from the adjoining bar Kabinet.

BAR SANS NOM COCKTAIL BAR

Map p284 (5295 Ave du Parc; ⏱5pm-3am; 🚌80, Ⓜ Place-des-Arts) The 'Bar without name' feels like a well-kept secret, owing to its lack of signage and discreet entrance. Once inside, opt for drinks among the potted palms and sleek, well-lit counter tops up front, or the Moroccan-style drinking den in back.

PING PONG CLUB BAR

Map p284 (5788 Blvd St-Laurent; ⏱11am-3am; Ⓜ Rosemont) For a touch of juvenile excitement, join young hipsters at this retro bar for microbrews, comfort food and games. Although there's only one (coveted) ping-pong table, there's also table football and air hockey, and staff can loan board games (Jenga). There's sports on TV, though the feel (with picnic tables, candles and the odd DJ night) is decidedly not a sports bar.

BALDWIN BARMACIE BAR

Map p284 (www.baldwinbarmacie.com; 115 Ave Laurier Ouest; ⏱5pm-3am Tue-Sat; Ⓜ Laurier)

Loud music, live DJs and beautiful 20- and 30-somethings rule this small, apothecary-themed lounge and club. Showy staff mix specialty cocktails while 1960s-inspired design fills your party prescription for flirting. Don't let its quiet residential location fool you, this joint goes off.

🍷 Little Italy

ISLE DE GARDE BAR

(www.isledegarde.com; 1039 Rue Beaubien Est; ⏱3:30pm-1:30am Mon-Wed, 11:30am-3am Thu & Fri, 1pm-3am Sat & Sun; 📶; Ⓜ Beaubien) Beer lovers shouldn't miss this buzzing amber-lit brasserie, which has a dazzling, ever-changing selection of unique microbrews on tap. Friendly bar staff dole out Belgian-style farmhouse ales, American-style IPAs, creamy stouts, and one-of-a-kind brews such as Brasseurs Illimités smoked porter (which tastes like drinking a campfire). There's also kombucha (a fermented tea) for nondrinkers. When hunger strikes, indulge in house fries, mac 'n' cheese, ribs or veggie chili.

GAINZBAR BAR

Map p284 (www.gainzbar.com; 6289 Rue St-Hubert; ⏱3pm-3am; 📶; Ⓜ Beaubien) Set with velvet couches, brassy fixtures and red walls, this low-lit drinking den has a bygone air, with live jazz trios adding to the ambience. It's a fine place for straightforward drinks (no fancy cocktails here) and good conversation.

NOTRE DAME DES QUILLES BAR

Map p284 (www.facebook.com/notredamedes quilles; 32 Rue Beaubien Est; ⏱5pm-3am Mon-Fri, from 4pm Sat & Sun; Ⓜ Beaubien) Does drinking improve your bowling game? That seems to be the question at this hipster outpost near Little Italy, where two free lanes have been set up with pint-sized pins. There's a good mix of Anglophones and Francophones here, and there are fun kitsch-filled nights of karaoke, bingo and spinning DJs.

VICE VERSA BAR

Map p284 (6631 Blvd St-Laurent; ⏱3pm-3am Mon-Wed, from noon Thu-Sun; Ⓜ De Castelnau) Vice Versa is a laid-back spot that draws a loyal neighborhood following who come for the first-rate craft-beer selection. There are more than 30 varieties on tap, with a strong emphasis on local and regional brews. You can match those quaffs with bison burgers, cheese platters, smoked-meat sandwiches and pulled-pork poutine.

⭐ ENTERTAINMENT

THÉÂTRE OUTREMONT THEATER

Map p284 (📞514-495-9944; www.theatreoutre mont.ca; 1248 Rue Bernard Ouest; ⊙box office 2-7pm Mon-Sat, 10am-4pm Sun; Ⓜ Outremont) Built in 1929, this theater was both a repertory cinema and a major concert hall until it was shuttered in the late 1980s. The municipality of Outremont later brought it back to life and the theater was reopened in 2001. Today, the repertoire is wide-ranging with concerts (jazz, folk, flamenco, blues), dance performances (ballet, modern) and family events (marionettes, animated films). Regular Monday film screenings (usually at 4pm and 7:30pm) feature indie cinema from around the globe.

THÉÂTRE RIALTO CONCERT VENUE

Map p284 (📞514-770-7773; www.theatrerialto. ca; 5723 Ave du Parc; Ⓜ Rosemont) This grand 1920s theater was inspired by the Paris Opera house and has recently been restored to its former glory following years of neglect. The repertoire is a bit hit-or-miss, with nights devoted to Elvis and Beatles impersonators, along with swing dancing, burlesque balls and tango shows.

🛍 SHOPPING

DRAWN & QUARTERLY BOOKS

Map p284 (📞514-279-2224; http://211blog. drawnandquarterly.com; 211 Rue Bernard Ouest; ⊙11am-7pm Mon-Wed, to 9pm Thu & Fri, 10am-7pm Sat & Sun; Ⓜ Outremont) The flagship store of this cult independent comic-book and graphic-novel publisher has become something of a local literary haven. Cool book launches take place here, and the quaint little shop sells all sorts of reading matter including children's books, vintage Tintin comics, recent fiction and art books.

GALERIE CO HOMEWARES

Map p284 (www.galerie-co.com; 5235 Blvd St-Laurent; ⊙11am-6pm Tue-Fri, to 5pm Sat, noon-5pm Sun; Ⓜ Laurier) Galerie Co sells all manner of beautiful objects, including cushions adorned with animal prints, artfully simple vases made from recycled glass, wooden watches, eye-catching wallpaper and jewelry made of repurposed cutlery. Galerie CO (from 'eCOlogy, COmmunity and eCOnomy') supports eco-friendly products.

FRANK & OAK CLOTHING

Map p284 (www.frankandoak.com; 160 Rue St-Viateur Est; ⊙10am-7pm Mon-Fri, to 5pm Sat & Sun; Ⓜ Laurier) Although the selection isn't huge, this dapper menswear shop is worth a visit for classic, well-made trousers, sweaters, leather belts and footwear. The prices are great considering it's designed and manufactured in Montréal. There's also a coffee bar and a barber on-site.

MONASTIRAKI VINTAGE

Map p284 (www.monastiraki.blogspot.ca; 5478 Blvd St-Laurent; ⊙noon-6pm Wed, to 8pm Thu & Fri, to 5pm Sat & Sun; Ⓜ Laurier) This unclassifiable store named after a flea-market neighborhood in Athens calls itself a 'hybrid curiosity shop/art space,' but that doesn't do justice to what illustrator Billy Mavreas sells: 1960s comic books, contemporary zines (homemade magazines), silkscreen posters, and myriad antique and collectible knickknacks, as well as recent works mainly by local graphic artists.

LE MARCHÉ DES SAVEURS DU QUÉBEC FOOD & DRINK

Map p284 (📞514-271-3811; www.lemarche dessaveurs.com; 280 Pl du Maré du Nord; ⊙9am-6pm Sat-Wed, to 8pm Thu & Fri; Ⓜ Jean-Talon) Everything here is Québecois, from the food to the handmade soaps to one of the best collections of artisanal local beer, maple products, jams and cheeses in the city. The store was established so local producers could gain wider exposure for their regional products, and it's a joy to browse.

V DE V MAISON HOMEWARES

Map p284 (www.vdevmaison.com; 5042 Blvd St-Laurent; ⊙10am-6pm Mon-Wed, to 9pm Thu & Fri, to 5pm Sat & Sun; Ⓜ Laurier) V de V is packed with striking designs that evoke both a modern and vintage aesthetic, making it a fun place to browse for gift ideas. Among the finds: aromatic candles, deer-head-shaped hooks, gilt-edged drinking glasses, elegant table linens and glass globes with Edison bulbs. You can also have Instagram photos printed on woodblocks for display.

AU PAPIER JAPONAIS ORIGAMI

Map p284 (📞514-276-6863; www.aupapierjapo nais.com; 24 Ave Fairmount Ouest; ⊙10am-6pm Mon-Sat, noon-4pm Sun; Ⓜ Laurier) You might never guess how many guises Japanese paper can come in until you visit this gorgeous little shop, which stocks more than 800 varieties. Origami kits and art books make great gift ideas, as do the elegant tea pots, pottery and Buddha boards (where you can 'paint' ephemeral works with water).

The store is also an arts and crafts hub and offers fun, hands-on workshops.

STYLE LABO   VINTAGE

Map p284 (www.stylelabo-deco.com; 5765 Blvd St-Laurent; ⊗10:30am-6pm Tue-Fri, to 5pm Sat, 11:30am-5pm Sun; ⋈Rosemont) Owners Anne Defay and Romain Castelli mix industrial remnants with quirky antique signage, farmers' furniture and even vintage dentistry equipment in this emporium of tools and gear from yesteryear. They also have accessories ranging from designer clock radios to old flags.

GALERIE SIMON BLAIS   ART

Map p284 (www.galeriesimonblais.com; 5420 Blvd St-Laurent; ⊗10am-6pm Tue, Wed & Fri, to 8pm Thu, to 5pm Sat; ⋈Laurier) One of the most prestigious galleries in Canada, Simon Blais carries works by well known artists such as Lucien Freud, Antoni Tàpies and Jean-Paul Riopelle as well as emerging artists from Montréal and Québec.

LES TOUILLEURS   HOMEWARES

Map p284 (☑514-278-0008; www.lestouilleurs. com; 152 Ave Laurier Ouest; ⊗10am-6pm Mon-Wed, to 9pm Thu & Fri, 11am-5pm Sat & Sun; ⋈Laurier) Beautifully designed Les Touilleurs celebrates Mile End's love affair with good food, presenting gorgeous high-end cookware and cookbooks by local and international chefs. There's a very popular teaching kitchen at the back of the shop, but workshops sell out well in advance. Most courses are held in French but attendees can usually ask questions in English.

QUINCAILLERIE DANTE   HOMEWARES

Map p284 (☑514-271-2057; 6851 Rue St-Dominique; ⊗10am-6pm Mon-Wed, to 9pm Thu & Fri, 9am-5pm Sat, noon-5pm Sun; ⋈De Castelnau) This quirky little Italian-owned hardware and cooking supply store is a household name, selling everything from first-class pots and pans to espresso makers, fishing rods and hunting gear.

PHONOPOLIS   MUSIC

Map p284 (www.phonopolis.ca; 207 Rue Bernard Ouest; ⊗11am-7pm Mon-Sat, to 6pm Sun; ⋈Outremont) Indie rock, jazz, blues, folk and world music – and hybrids thereof – are the raison d'être of this little record shop, which sells (and buys) LPs and CDs.

UN AMOUR DES THÉS   FOOD & DRINK

Map p284 (☑514-279-2999; www.amourdesthes. com; 1224 Rue Bernard Ouest; ⊗10am-6pm Mon-Fri, 9am-5pm Sat, 11am-5pm Sun; ⋈Outremont) More than 260 types of loose tea sit in canisters behind the counter of this charming shop. It stocks classic leaf varieties, as well as flavors you probably didn't know existed. Tea workshops (in French) are also held.

JET-SETTER   TRAVEL GOODS

Map p284 (☑514-271-5058; www.jet-setter.ca; 66 Ave Laurier Ouest; ⊗10am-6pm Mon-Wed, to 9pm Thu & Fri, to 5pm Sat, noon-5pm Sun; ⋈Laurier) An orgy of state-of-the-art luggage and clever travel gadgetry, Jet-Setter has inflatable sacks for wine bottles, pocket-sized T-shirts, 'dry-in-an-instant' underwear, silk sleep sacks, mini-irons and hairdryers, waterproof hats and loads of other items you might find handy when you hit the road.

🏃 SPORTS & ACTIVITIES

OVARIUM   SPA

Map p284 (☑514-271-7515, 877-356-8837; www. ovarium.com; 400 Rue Beaubien Est; floating bath $65, Pulsar $25, Neurospa $40; ⊗8:30am-10pm; ⋈Beaubien) The excellent staff and the Ovarium weightlessness experience have garnered a loyal following at this day spa. Packages are available, such as the half-day 'Essential,' a one-hour flotation bath followed by a one-hour massage ($129). Ovarium's flotation tanks are egg-shaped tubs filled with water and 2000 cups of Epsom salts, making you gravity-free.

Other unusual treatments include the 30-minute 'Pulsar,' where you don a pair of stereo headphones and light-emitting goggles, which create a rhythmic audiovisual program that purportedly leads to a meditative state. Check the website (and Ovarium's Facebook page) for discounts.

MEZZA LUNA
COOKING SCHOOL   COOKING COURSE

Map p284 (☑514-272-5299; www.ecolemezzaluna. ca; 57 Rue Dante; classes from $75; ⋈De Castelnau) Offered in French, English and Italian, Mezza Luna's renowned Italian-cooking classes are held in a small apartment facing a high-end kitchen. They're educational, but not very hands on. The best part is eating the creations at the end. Classes are held several nights a week and on Saturday mornings. Reserve ahead.

Southwest & Outer Montréal

SOUTHWEST MONTRÉAL | CÔTE-DES-NEIGES & NOTRE-DAME-DE-GRÂCE | OLYMPIC PARK & AROUND | OUTER DISTRICTS

Neighborhood Top Five

1 Witnessing the soaring architecture of the **Oratoire St-Joseph** (p131), one of North America's grandest churches.

2 Working off those calories from munching poutine on the **Canal de Lachine** (p132) and its 14km of bike paths.

3 Bringing out your green side at one of the world's largest gardens, the **Jardin Botanique** (p133) and its Insectarium.

4 Chilling out with the penguins and many other fish and fowl at the **Biodôme** (p134), which takes you through four ecosystems.

5 Learning about the history of Canadian railroads at the excellent, kid-friendly **Musée Ferroviaire Canadien** (p136).

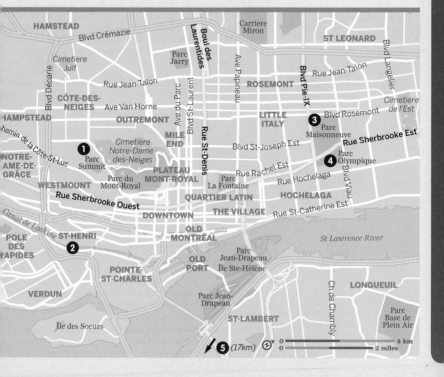

Best Places to Eat

For reviews, see p137. ➡

Best Activities

For reviews, see p141. ➡

Best Panoramic Views

For reviews, see p131. ➡

Explore Southwest & Outer Montréal

Exploring the outlying residential neighborhoods of Montréal allows you to get a deeper experience of life on the island. A good chunk of them lie to the south and west of downtown (remember that Montréal's 'east–west' streets actually run northeast–southwest). Since they're far-flung, it's best to explore them over several days, though it's possible to combine contiguous areas such as Côte-des-Neiges and Notre-Dame-de-Grâce.

A must-experience is the Canal de Lachine (p132), Montréal's best biking course. In downtown or Old Montréal, find your way to a Bixi stand or bike-rental outfit and roll down to the Old Port. From there, get on the bike path that winds along the canal and out to Lachine, where several museums and a breezy riverside park await.

It will take at least an hour, but if you don't want to go that far, stop at the Marché Atwater, walk to Lionel-Groulx metro station and go to Côte-des-Neiges, which lies off the western slope of Parc du Mont-Royal. The magnificent Oratoire St-Joseph and the buzzing campus of the prestigious Université de Montréal are the main draws here. Notre-Dame-de-Grâce (or simply NDG) is a sleepy residential district, livened up by the cafes and restaurants along Ave Monkland.

Also accessible by metro is Olympic Park, nestled in the heart of the blue-collar Hochelaga-Maisonneuve district. The big draw here is the massive Olympic Stadium (p135), built for the 1976 Olympic Games, the kid-friendly Biodôme (p134), a brand new planetarium (p134) and the verdant Jardin Botanique (p133).

Local Life

➡ **Sunning** Rent a bike, scoot along the Canal de Lachine (p132) and pause along its banks to soak up some rays.

➡ **Ahoy there!** Montréal is surrounded by rivers, so why not rent a canoe or kayak and go with the flow?

➡ **Over the hill** For a good workout, hike from downtown over Mont-Royal to Côte-des-Neiges, following the street of the same name.

Getting There & Away

➡ **Metro** Metro access to the area is via Villa-Maria station for NDG, while the Côte-des-Neiges station is for the neighborhood of the same name. To get to the east side of town, take the green metro line to either Pie-IX or Viau.

➡ **Bike** You can rent a Bixi bike to reach NDG, Petite-Bourgogne, St-Henri and Pointe-St-Charles, and to roll along the Canal de Lachine. Bikes are best avoided in hilly Côte-des-Neiges.

TOP SIGHT
ORATOIRE ST-JOSEPH

This stunning church built on the flanks of Mont-Royal commands grand views of the the Côte-des-Neiges area and northwest Montréal. The majestic basilica is a tribute to mid-20th-century design as well as an intimate shrine to Brother André, a local saint said to have healed countless people.

The largest shrine ever built in honor of Jesus' father, this Renaissance-style building was completed in 1960 and commands fine views of the northern slope of Mont-Royal. The oratory dome is visible from anywhere in this part of town.

The oratory is also a tribute to the work of Brother André (1845–1937), the determined monk who first built a little **chapel** here in 1904. Brother André was said to have healing powers – as word spread, a larger shrine was needed, so the church began gathering funds to build one. Rows of discarded crutches and walking sticks in the basement **Votive Chapel** testify to this belief and the shrine is warmed by hundreds of candles. When Brother André died at age 91, a million devotees filed past his coffin over the course of six days. His black granite **tomb** in the Votive Chapel was donated by Québec premier Maurice Duplessis. Brother André was beatified in 1982 and finally canonized in 2010. His **heart** is on display too, in an upstairs museum dedicated to him.

Religious pilgrims might climb the 300 wooden steps to the oratory on their knees, praying at every step; other visitors take the stone stairs or one of the free shuttle buses from the base parking lot.

DON'T MISS

➡ Brother André's room and 1904 chapel
➡ Brother André's tomb and heart
➡ The Votive Chapel
➡ The Grand Organ

PRACTICALITIES

➡ St-Joseph's Oratory
➡ ☏ 514-733-8211
➡ www.saint-joseph.org
➡ 3800 Chemin Queen Mary
➡ ⊙ 6am-9:30pm
➡ Ⓜ Côte-des-Neiges

◉ SIGHTS

◉ Southwest Montréal

CANAL DE LACHINE   CANAL

The Lachine Canal was built in 1825 as a means of bypassing the treacherous Lachine Rapids on the St Lawrence River. It was closed to shipping in 1970, but the area has been transformed into a 14km-long cycling and pedestrian pathway, with picnic areas and green spaces. Since the canal was reopened for navigation in 2002, flotillas of pleasure and sightseeing boats glide along its calm waters. Old warehouses converted into luxury condos line the canal near Atwater market.

It's well worth hiring a bike or in-line skates and heading out along the canal path, but try to avoid summer weekends, when it's particularly crowded. For a canalside spin, you can hire bikes from Ça Roule (p64) in Old Montréal or My Bicyclette (p240) near the Atwater market. Kayaks and boats are also available at nearby H2O Adventures (p142). For a leisurely boat ride where somewhere else does the work, take a ride with Le Petit Navire (p65).

MUSÉE DE LACHINE   MUSEUM

(☎514-634-3471; www.ville.montreal.qc.ca; 1 Chemin du Musée; ⊙noon-5pm Tue-Sun, closed Dec-Mar; ☐110, ⓂAngrignon) FREE It's a great bike ride to this museum, which is practically right on the Canal de Lachine. It is also one of the oldest houses (1669) in the Montréal region, with shooting holes inserted for defense. Back then Lachine was the last frontier for trappers heading west and the final stop for fur shipments. You can see and smell the old fur-storage building from the original trading days.

Adjacent to the museum is a huge waterfront sculpture garden that you can visit anytime from dawn to dusk.

FUR TRADE AT LACHINE NATIONAL HISTORIC SITE   HISTORIC SITE

(www.pc.gc.ca; 1255 Blvd St-Joseph; adult/child $4/2; ⊙10am-5pm late May–early Sep; ☐195, ⓂAngrignon) This 1803 stone depot in Lachine is now an engaging little museum telling the story of the fur trade in Canada. The Hudson Bay Company made Lachine the hub of its fur-trading operations because the rapids made further navigation impossible. Visitors can view the furs and old trappers' gear, and costumed interpreters show how the bales and canoes were schlepped by native trappers.

The site is located about 1km west of the Musée de Lachine.

MAISON ST-GABRIEL   MUSEUM

(☎514-935-8136; www.maisonsaint-gabriel. qc.ca; 2146 Pl Dublin; adult/student/child $10/5/3; ⊙1-5pm Tue-Sun early Jan–mid-Jun & early Sep–mid-Dec, 11am-6pm mid-Jun–early Sep; ☐57 est, ⓂCharlevoix) This magnificent farmhouse in Pointe St-Charles is one of the finest examples of traditional Québec architecture. The house was bought in 1668 by Marguerite Bourgeoys to house a religious order. Young women called the Filles du Roy also stayed here – they were sent from Paris to Montréal to find husbands. The 17th-century roof of the two-story building is of particular interest for its intricate beam work, one of the few of its kind in North America.

The museum has an excellent collection of artifacts going back to the 17th and 18th centuries, with unusual items including sinks made from black stone and a sophisticated water-disposal system.

PARC DES RAPIDES   PARK

(☎514-367-6540; cnr Blvd LaSalle & 7e Ave; ☐58, ⓂDe l'Église) This space on the St Lawrence is the spot to view the Lachine Rapids (and the jet boats that ride them). The park attracts hikers and anglers, and cyclists who pedal the riverside trail. It's also a renowned bird sanctuary – located on a small peninsula, with what's said to be Québec's largest heron colony. The 30-hectare sanctuary is an important site for migratory birds, with some 225 species passing through each year.

Some information displays relate the history of the rapids and of the old hydroelectric plant on the grounds. You can rent kayaks and sign up for classes where you'll learn to surf or kayak the Lachine Rapids – scaredycats need not apply. An adrenaline-rushing experience can be had with Rafting Montréal (p142), a jet-boating and rafting outfit located 2km west of the Parc des Rapides.

MOULIN FLEMING   MUSEUM

(☎514-367-6439; www.ville.montreal.qc.ca; 9675 Blvd LaSalle, LaSalle; ⊙1-5pm Sun mid-May–early Jun, Sat & Sun early Jun–Aug; ☐110, ⓂAngrignon) FREE This restored five-story windmill was built for a Scottish merchant in 1816, and

THE GREAT HEART HEIST

How much is a holy man's heart worth? Fifty-thousand dollars, according to thieves who broke into a locked room in the Oratoire St-Joseph in March 1973. They made off with Brother André's heart sealed in a vial and demanded the sum in a ransom note that scandalized Montréal. The purloined organ was the subject of tabloid articles, musical compositions and even an art exhibition. Church officials reportedly refused the ransom demand, and nothing more was seen of the heart until December 1974 when Montréal lawyer to the underworld, Frank Shoofey, received a mysterious phone call asking him if he wanted to know its whereabouts. Shoofey was directed to an apartment building storage locker that contained a box, and inside was the vial housing Brother André's heart. The thieves were never found, and today the heart is secure in the Oratoire behind a metal grille and a sturdy transparent display case. But some believe the Church actually did pay the ransom to get it back. Was Shoofey, who was shot to death in 1985 in a still-unsolved murder, a go-between? Whatever the case, Montréal's great heart heist has continued to inspire artists long after the saint himself died.

a multimedia exhibit inside covers its two centuries of history. It's a nice diversion if you're out here visiting the other Lachine sites, and a great photo op.

⊙ Côte-des-Neiges & Notre-Dame-de-Grâce

ORATOIRE ST-JOSEPH CHURCH
See p131.

HOLOCAUST MEMORIAL CENTRE MUSEUM
(☑514-345-2605; www.mhmc.ca; 5151 Chemin de la Côte-Ste-Catherine; adult/child $8/5; ☺10am-5pm Mon, Tue & Thu, to 9pm Wed, to 4pm Fri & Sun; ⓂCôte-Ste-Catherine) The Montréal Holocaust Memorial Centre provides a record of Jewish history and culture from pre-WWII Europe, and holds seminars, exhibitions and other events. The museum has many powerful exhibits, and groups of 10 or more can arrange to hear testimonies by Holocaust survivors. The museum is closed on Jewish holidays; see the website to confirm Friday hours between November and March.

AVE DE MONKLAND STREET
(ⓂVilla-Maria) Over the past decade or so Ave de Monkland in Notre-Dame-de-Grâce has been transformed, with coffee bars, restaurants and condominiums springing up like mushrooms after a warm rain. It certainly has a village character as many people walk to the shops from their homes. Access is via the Villa-Maria metro station, from where you can walk down Monkland.

UNIVERSITÉ DE MONTRÉAL UNIVERSITY
(☑514-343-6111; 2900 Blvd Édouard-Montpetit; ⓂUniversité-de-Montréal) This is the second-largest French-language university in the world, after the Sorbonne in Paris. Located on the north side of Mont-Royal, its most recognizable building is an art-deco tower and pale-yellow brick structure. The university was founded in 1878. For more information, see p134.

⊙ Olympic Park & Around

JARDIN BOTANIQUE GARDENS
(www.espacepourlavie.ca/jardin-botanique; 4101 Rue Sherbrooke Est; adult/child $20/10; ☺9am-6pm mid-May–early Sep, to 9pm early Sep–Oct, to 5pm Tue-Sun rest of year; ⓂPie-IX) Montréal's Jardin Botanique is the third-largest botanical garden in the world, after London's Kew Gardens and Berlin's Botanischer Garten. Since its 1931 opening, the 75-hectare garden has grown to include tens of thousands of species in more than 20 thematic gardens, and its wealth of flowering plants is carefully managed to bloom in stages. The rose beds are a sight to behold in summertime. Climate-controlled greenhouses house cacti, banana trees and 1500 species of orchid. Bird-watchers should bring their binoculars.

A popular drawcard is the landscaped **Japanese Garden** with traditional pavilions, tearoom and art gallery; the bonsai 'forest' is the largest outside Asia. The twinning of Montréal with Shanghai gave impetus to plant a **Chinese Garden**. The

HARVARD DE MONTRÉAL

For all the Francophiles among you, the **Université de Montréal** (p133) is kind of like the French-speaking Harvard in Canada, with more than 66,000 students. Maybe because it's on the mountain far from downtown and feels removed from the rest of the city, you'll find an array of cultural events and happenings that remain virtually unknown to those outside the area.

Nearby Chemin de la Côte-des-Neiges is a lively street for strolling, with cafes, bookstores and a green market, the **Marché Côtes-des-Neiges** (cnr Chemin de la Côte-des-Neiges & Rue Jean-Brillant; ⏰7am-6pm Nov-Dec & mid-Mar–early Apr, 24hr early Apr–Oct; MⒸôtes-des-Neiges). A splendid place to while away a few hours is the indie bookstore **Librairie Olivieri** (☎514-739-3639; www.librairieolivieri.com; 5219 Chemin de la Côte-des-Neiges; ⏰9am-9pm Mon-Fri, 10am-6pm Sat & Sun; MUniversité-de-Montréal), which also has an excellent bistro serving poached salmon, *magret de canard* (duck breast) and changing daily specials.

From here you're also within walking distance of the **Oratoire St-Joseph** (p131), a great spot to visit at sunset. Two handy metro stations – Côte-des-Neiges and Université de Montréal – provide easy access to the area.

ornamental penjing trees from Hong Kong are up to 100 years old. A Ming-dynasty garden is the feature around Lac de Rêve (Dream Lake). In the northern part of the Jardin Botanique you'll find the **Frédérick Back Tree Pavilion**, a permanent exhibit on life in the 40-hectare arboretum. Displays include the yellow birch, part of Québec's official emblem. The **First Nations Garden** reveals the bonds between 11 Amerindian and Inuit nations and indigenous plants such as silver birches, maples, Labrador and tea. The Orchidée Gift Shop in the main building has a wonderful selection, including handmade jewelry and crafts, stuffed animals and beautifully illustrated books.

In fall (mid-September to early November) the Chinese garden dons its most exquisite garb for the popular **Magic of Lanterns**, when hundreds of handmade silk lanterns sparkle at dusk. Montréalers are devoted to this event and it can feel like it's standing-room only even though it's held in a huge garden.

Creepy-crawlies get top billing at the bug-shaped **Insectarium**. Most of the 250,000 specimens are mounted but live displays include bees and tarantulas.

The admission ticket includes the gardens, greenhouses and the Insectarium.

BIODÔME
MUSEUM

(www.espacepourlavie.ca; 4777 Ave Pierre de Coubertin; adult/child $20/10; ⏰9am-6pm late Jun–Sep, 9am-5pm Tue-Sun rest of year; ♿; MViau) At this captivating, kid-friendly exhibit you

can amble through a rainforest, explore Antarctic islands, view rolling woodlands, take in aquatic life in the Gulf of St Lawrence, or wander along the raw Atlantic oceanfront – all without ever leaving the building. Be sure to dress in layers for the temperature swings. The five ecosystems house many thousands of animal and plant species; follow the self-guided circuit and you will see everything.

Penguins frolic in the pools a few feet away from groups of goggle-eyed children; the tropical chamber is a cross section of Amazonia with mischievous little monkeys teasing alligators in the murky waters below. The Gulf of St Lawrence has an underwater observatory where you can watch cod feeding alongside lobsters and sea urchins in the tidal pools. The appearance of the Laurentian Forest varies widely with the seasons, with special habitats for lynx, otters and around 350 bats.

The Biodôme is wildly popular, so try to visit during the week, avoiding the middle of the day if possible. Plan two hours to do it justice. You can bring a packed lunch for the picnic tables or dine in the cafeteria. In summer there are educational day camps for kids.

PLANÉTARIUM
LANDMARK

(☎514-868-3000; www.espacepourlavie.ca; 4801 Ave du Pierre-de-Coubertin; adult/child $20/10; ⏰9am-5pm Sun, Tue & Wed, to 8pm Thu-Sat; MViau) Opened in 2013, these futuristic metallic buildings bring a bit of the cosmos to Montréal, courtesy of two high-tech domed theaters and interative exhibits on outer space. The round theaters have slightly different layouts and agendas: the Milky Way Theater is more traditional, with comfy seats and films that give an eye-opening glimpse of what lies beyond earth, while the Chaos theater has bean bags and Adirondack chairs and takes a more philosphical look at the universe.

You can also wander through the permanent exhibition, which has meteorites and fascinating displays that explore the search for life in the universe. Admission includes tickets to two separate shows as well as the permanent exhibition. Allow at least 90 minutes to experience it all. Check the schedule before setting out. Only a handful of shows are in English (there are always English shows at 2:30pm and 3pm, and two to four other screenings on Thursday through Sunday).

The planetarium is next door to the Biodôme, meaning you can explore the wonders on planet earth (or at least planet Canada) before delving into outer space.

OLYMPIC STADIUM   STADIUM

(☎514-252-4141; www.parcolympique.qc.ca; 4141 Ave Pierre-de-Couberti; tower adult/child $23/12; ⏰1-6pm Mon, 9am-6pm Tue-Sun mid-Jun–early Sep, 9am-5pm rest of year; MViau) The Stade Olympique seats 56,000 and remains an architectural marvel, though these days it hosts mostly concerts and trade shows and only rarely hosts sports events. The main attraction is the short (three-minute) ride on the bilevel cable car, which goes up the **Montréal Tower** (Tour de Montréal, also called the Olympic Tower) that lords over the stadium. It's the world's tallest inclined structure (165m at a 45-degree angle). Still, many don't find the overall experience worth the price.

The glassed-in observation deck (with bar and rest area) isn't for the faint of heart but it does afford a bird's-eye view of the city. In the distance you'll see the pointy modern towers of the Olympic Village, where athletes stayed in 1976.

THE BIG OWE

Built for the 1976 Olympic Games, Montréal's Olympic Stadium was plagued with difficulties right from the start. A strike by construction workers meant the inclined tower wasn't finished on time – in fact it took another 11 years to complete. The stadium's affectionate nickname, the 'Big O' (in reference to the huge oval stadium), was redubbed the 'Big Owe' by irate Montréalers.

The 65-ton stadium roof took another two years to complete but never worked properly. Made of Kevlar, the material used in bulletproof vests, the striking orange dome worked like a huge retractable umbrella that opened and closed by the tower cables. It was a sight to behold (if you were so lucky), but winds ripped the Kevlar and mechanical glitches led to its permanent closure. Even when the roof was functioning, there were problems. For instance, the roof could not be moved when winds gusted greater than 40km/h. This resulted in the occasional rain delay during baseball season – an irritating event for fans who were waiting for the roof to simply be closed.

In 1998 the umbrella was folded up for good and replaced with a set model (costing $37 million) that didn't open – though this roof too malfunctioned, collapsing one year later, dumping snow and ice on workers setting up for the Montréal Auto Show (the roof installers were later sued by the stadium). Another unfortunate event over the years was the collapse of a 55-ton support beam in 1991, though luckily no one was injured.

Provincial officials calculated that the total price tag of the stadium (including construction, repairs etc) when it was finally paid off in late 2006 amounted to $1.6 billion (or $1000 per person, if every man, woman and child in the city of Montréal had to pay up).

The irony of the Big O is that now that it's paid off and the roof is no longer broken, no one seems remotely interested in using the stadium. The city's baseball team, the Montréal Expos, played its last game in the stadium in 2004 before it was packed off to Washington, DC and rechristened the Capitals. Today the stadium is often empty save for the odd trade show, big-name concert, soccer match and the occasional visitor who stares up at the empty seats, wondering how such a place could be so cursed.

The **Centre Aquatique** is the Olympic swimming complex, with six pools, diving towers and a 20m-deep scuba pool.

The **Tourist Hall** is a three-story information center with a ticket office, restaurant and souvenir shop, as well as the cable-car boarding station.

CHÂTEAU DUFRESNE   HISTORIC BUILDING

(☎514-259-9201; www.chateaudufresne.qc.ca; 2929 Ave Jeanne-d'Arc; adult/child $14/7, incl Olympic Stadium $28/16; ◎10am-5pm Wed-Sun; MPie-IX) In 1916 brothers Oscar and Marius Dufresne commissioned this beautiful beaux-arts mansion, along the lines of the Versailles Palace in France. The interiors are stunning – tiled marble floors, coffered ceilings in Italian Renaissance style, stained-glass windows – and are open for the public to explore. Italian artist Guido Nincheri was in charge of interior decoration and painted many murals, including one of dainty nymphs in the Petit Salon.

They moved in with their families – Oscar on one side and Marius on the other. Marius' side of the building is furnished in a more masculine style, with a smoking room fitted to look like a Turkish lounge with hookah pipes. The furniture, art and other objects reflect the tastes of Montréal's bourgeoisie of the period, and the building has been declared a national monument.

A new permanent exhibition opened in the Château in late 2014. Dubbed the *Mémoire des objets, Parcours de collectioneurs* (Collectors' hall, items to remember), the collection comprises some 47 artworks and historical items that belonged to famous figures from the past, including Louis XV, Joan of Arc, Marie Antoinette and Napoleon Bonaparte.

◎ Outer Districts

MUSÉE FERROVIAIRE CANADIEN   MUSEUM

(☎450-632-2410; www.exporail.org; 110 Rue St-Pierre/rte 209, St-Constant; adult/child $18/9; ◎generally 10am-5pm) The Canadian Railway Museum contains more than 150 historic vehicles, ranging from locomotives, steam engines, Old Montréal streetcars and passenger cars to snow plows. It's widely acknowledged as one of North America's most outstanding collections. Not particularly well known by Montréalers, this museum gets raves from those who make the trek, especially families, and many claim it's the best museum in the Montréal area.

The aerodynamic steam engine Dominion of Canada broke the world speed record in 1939 by clocking over 200km/h. A special sight is Montréal's famous Golden Chariot, an open-air streetcar with tiers of ornate seats and gilt ironwork. Another good exhibit is the school car, a Canadian invention that served the railway towns of northern Ontario: two cars of each teaching train had a kitchen, living area and classroom with 15 desks.

There always seems to be something special going on here, whether it's the min-

---

MONTRÉAL'S GARBAGE-POWERED CIRCUS CITY

Don't pass up the opportunity to see a show in Montréal's circus mecca. Set in the working-class St-Michel district, **TOHU** (☎514-376-8648; www.tohu.ca; 2345 Rue Jarry Est; guided tour $7; ◎9am-5pm Mon-Fri; Md'Iberville then bus 94) – that comes from the French expression *tohu-bohu*, for hustle and bustle – is an innovative complex with an arena designed only with the circus arts in mind. Aside from the big round theater, the complex includes Cirque du Soleil's international headquarters, artists' residences and the National Circus School. Moreover, it was built on the sight of North America's second-largest waste dump and the whole complex is now powered completely by methane gas from the landfill garbage beneath it.

You can visit the complex on your own (via guided audio tour in French), or on a guided 45-minute tour (in French only) that takes place before shows. TOHU also hosts special exhibitions and outdoor activities (such as petanque tournaments and bike rallies), and you can catch live performances here throughout the year. You can get there by taking the blue metro line to d'Iberville station and then hopping onto bus 94 north (or walking 1km northwest up Rue d'Iberville).

Adjoining the theater is the **TOHU Bistro** (snacks $5-10; ◎8am-2pm Mon-Fri, from 10am Sat) and a small gallery showing changing exhibitions.

iature railway or streetcar rides, weather permitting.

By car, take the Pont Champlain from Montréal to Autoroute 15, then Hwy 132 at the Châteauguay cutoff to route 209. It's a 20-minute drive.

COSMODÔME
MUSEUM

(☏450-978-3600; www.cosmodome.org; 2150 Autoroute des Laurentides; adult/child under 7/ student/family $15/free/$12/40; ☺9am-5pm late Jun–early Sep, 10am-5pm rest of year; 📖61 or 70, Ⓜ Montmorency) You (or your kids) can experience the thrill of space flight in this interactive museum of space and new technologies. Virtual missions include a moon landing and Mars exploration, while exhibits focus on the solar system, satellite communications and space travel, and there are mock-ups of rockets, the space shuttle *Endeavor* and planets.

The center also runs space camps (mostly in French, though some weeks are bilingual) for one to five days for kids aged five to 13 in a sort of mini-NASA training. Older kids (age nine to 15) can take part in three- or six-day camp sessions where they overnight in space-station-like sleeping modules.

MORGAN ARBORETUM
GARDENS

(☏514-398-7811; www.morganarboretum.org; 150 Chemin des Pins, Ste-Anne-de-Bellevue; adult/child $6/3; ☺9am-4pm) This 245-hectare forest reserve holds Montréal's largest grouping of native Canadian trees: fragrant junipers, cedars and yews but also exotic species such as ginkgo, cork and yellowwood. There's a wonderful trail map and the area is perfect for a long hike in the woods, strolling through magnolia blossoms or having a family picnic. Spring and fall offer the best colors.

The grounds of the arboretum serve as an educational facility for McGill's Mac-Donald agricultural school. There are several species of wildlife and reptile, and it's also a stop for 170 species of wintering or migratory birds, making it a thrill for birdwatchers.

In winter, this is a beautiful location for cross-country skiing and snow-shoeing.

Located about 15km west of Montréal on the western tip of the island, the arboretum can be reached most easily from Autoroute 40. Take exit 41 and follow signs for Chemin Ste-Marie; at the stop sign at the top of the hill, turn left onto Chemin des Pins for the registration office.

PARC NATURE DU CAP-ST-JACQUES
PARK

(☏514-280-6871; 20099 Blvd Gouin Ouest, Pierrefonds; beach adult/child $5/4; ☺10am-6pm Jun-Aug, otherwise to 5pm; P; 📖69, Ⓜ Henri-Bourassa) Located about 35km west of the city, Cap-St-Jacques is arguably the most diverse of Montréal's nature parks, with a huge beach, more than 40km of trails for hiking and skiing, a farm and even a summer camp. The maple and mixed deciduous forest in the interior is a great patch for a ramble, and in spring a horse-drawn carriage brings visitors to a sugar shack to watch the maple sap boil.

On the north shore there's the **Eco-Farm**, a working farm with two barns and horses, pigs and chickens, as well as a large greenhouse for viewing. Picnic tables abound and a restaurant serves the farm's produce. The beach is a comfortably wide stretch of fine white sand, and the shallow water is wonderful for splashing with kids, but bear in mind it gets as popular as Cape Cod on summer weekends. You can also rent canoes, kayaks and pedal boats.

By car, take Autoroute 40 west from Montréal to exit 49 (Rue Ste-Marie Ouest), turn north on Rue l'Anse-à-l'Orme and continue on to Blvd Gouin Ouest.

🍴 EATING

MELK
CAFE $

(www.melkbarcafe.com; 5612 Ave Monkland; baked goods around $3; ☺7am-7pm Mon-Fri, from 8am Sat & Sun; Ⓜ Villa-Maria) This tiny neighborhood gem is a requisite pitstop when strolling Ave Monkland. You can enjoy first-rate coffees and heavenly baked goods (buttery scones, flaky donuts) while taking in the tin ceilings and passing people parade.

GIBEAU ORANGE JULEP
FAST FOOD $

(7700 Blvd Décarie; mains $5-11; ☺8am-3am; Ⓜ Namur) Shaped like a giant orange, this vintage snack bar along busy Blvd Decarie is a nostalgic soft spot for generations of Montréalers. While the roller-skating waitresses are long gone, you can still nosh on greasy French fries and hot dogs in your car outside, washing them down with the signature Orange Julep drink created by Hermas Gibeau in the 1920s.

1. Penguin, Biodôme (p134)
There are five ecosystems and thousands of plant and animal species – including penguins – at this wildly popular spot.

2. Jardin Botanique (p133)
The third-largest botanical garden in the world hosts some unusual displays.

3. Waterfall, Jardin Botanique (p133)
One of many sights in the 75-hectare garden.

LOCAL VOICES: DINING À LA QUÉBECOIS

Frédéric Morin, one of the chef-owners of Joe Beef, has garnered much attention for his innovative Québecois fare. He's at the forefront of a movement to bring attention to the great *produits du terroir* (foods sourced from local markets and farms).

What keeps you in Montréal? It's cool to be in such a culturally rich place – growing up, your best friends are Italian and Lebanese, there's a Jewish neighborhood up the street and you're the only Québecois kid on your block. You move between French and English – not just linguistically, but culturally. I like that quote by the prime minister during the independence drive: 'We're all ethnics here; it just depends on your date of arrival.'

What are your favorite dishes? I really love beef – a braised meat in winter, a thick steak in the summer. Sometimes I crave oysters and get the urge for greens. And I love Dover sole.

What's the story behind the garden you've created behind your restaurant? I get some things for the restaurant in there, but most of my greens come from the Atwater market. I do the garden for me. I love working in there. It's my happy place.

What's your take on the restaurant scene here? I love Paris and New York, but it's competitive. Cooks in restaurants here are friends. People rarely come to work pissed off. Maybe it's this laid-back city – the Canal de Lachine, the parks...

SU
TURKISH **$$**

(☎514-362-1818; www.restaurantsu.com; 5145 Rue Wellington; mains $18-26; ◎5-10:30pm Tue-Sat, 10am-3pm Sat & Sun; ⓜVerdun) Chef Fisun Ercan takes her home-style but inventive Turkish cuisine beyond your expectations of kabobs and coffee. She prepares feather-light fried calamari, beef *manti* (dumplings) with garlic yogurt and spiced tomatoes, rich seafood rice (with shrimp, mussels and fish) and delicious *lokum* (Turkish delight). It's worth the trip to Verdun; be sure to reserve.

LA LOUISIANE
CAJUN **$$**

(☎514-369-3073; www.lalouisiane.ca; 5850 Rue Sherbrooke Ouest; mains $16-32; ◎5:30-10:30pm Tue-Sat; ▣105, ⓜVendôme) Montréal meets the Big Easy in this casual Cajun eatery, with amazing results. The menu bears the hearty, delicious flavors of jambalaya, shrimp Creole or chicken *étouffée* (stew-like rice dish), all armed with mysterious peppers and spices. The rich 'voodoo pasta' has spicy Cajun sausage and tomatoes in white wine and cream. Go early, as La Louisiane accepts no reservations.

While you're here, be sure to check out paintings of street scenes by New Orleans native James Michelopoulos.

★TUCK SHOP
QUÉBECOIS **$$$**

(☎514-439-7432; www.tuckshop.ca; 4662 Rue Notre-Dame Ouest; mains $25-34; ◎6-11pm Tue-Sat; ⓜPlace-Saint-Henri) Set in the heart of working-class St-Henri, Tuck Shop could have been plucked from London or New York if it weren't for its distinctly local menu, a delightful blend of market and *terroir* (locally sourced) offerings such as Kamouraska lamb shank, fish of the day with Jerusalem artichoke purée and a Québec cheese plate, all prepared by able chef Theo Lerikos.

The lively atmosphere, warm service and excellent dishes are pitch-perfect, so it's no wonder this place fills up fast. Be sure to reserve.

☆ ENTERTAINMENT

MONTRÉAL IMPACT
SPECTATOR SPORT

(☎514-328-3668; www.impactmontreal.com; Saputo Stadium, 4750 Rue Sherbrooke Est; tickets $25-82; ◎Mar-Oct; ⓜViau) Although Canadians aren't known for doling out the soccer love, the Montréal Impact has played its heart out to earn a local following. Saputo Stadium is a 14,000-seat venue built in 2008 for the club and the second-largest soccer stadium in Canada.

The Impact sometimes plays its opening (March) games at nearby Olympic Stadium, as winter weather poses problems at open-air Saputo.

SEAGAL CENTRE — PERFORMING ARTS

(📞514-739-7944; www.segalcentre.org; 5170 Chemin de la Côte-Ste-Catherine; plays $25–$65; Ⓜ Côte-Ste-Catherine) Montréal's Jewish theater stages dramatic performances in English and Yiddish – although as one of the city's most prominent professional theater venues, plays presented are by no means exclusively Jewish. Recent productions have included *The Apprenticeship of Duddy Kravitz* (based on Mordecai Richler's novel), Tom Stoppard's *Travesties,* and Dora Wasserman's Yiddish masterpiece *The Dybbuk.*

Yiddish plays have supertitles in English and French.

Theater aside, the Seagal Center also has occasional jazz concerts, film screenings and dance performances.

WHEEL CLUB — DANCE

(📞514-489-3322; www.thewheelclub.wordpress. com; 3373 Blvd Cavendish; ⏱8pm-1am; 🚌105, Ⓜ Vendôme) Going strong for more than 50 years, this venerable country-and-western bar is famous for its Hillbilly Night on Mondays, featuring bluegrass, cowboy and fiddle music. House-band Vintage Wine, which plays late '60s and '70s covers, can also get your heels hopping. Otherwise, there are dartboards, a pool table and a full bar. Call ahead for live-music schedules.

🏃 SPORTS & ACTIVITIES

★ STRØM NORDIC SPA — SPA

(📞514-761-2772; www.stromspa.com; 1001 Blvd de la Forêt; ⏱10am-10pm; 🚌168, Ⓜ Square-Victoria) For a get-away-from-it-all experience, it's hard to top this beautifully set-up spa located on the Île des Soeurs, a few kilometers south of downtown. The trim Nordic-style buildings overlook a watery, tree-lined expanse, with grassy lawns and outdoor pools with tiny waterfalls from which to enjoy the pretty scenery.

The 'thermal experience' gives you access to the outdoor Jacuzzis, thermal and Nordic baths, Finnish sauna and eucalyptus steam bath. A range of treatments and packages is available, and there's also a good bistro on hand. Hour-long Swedish massages cost $84 to $89. Prices for the thermal experience vary based on day and time (it's cheapest Monday through Thursday after 6pm).

SKYVENTURE — SKYDIVING

(📞514-524-4000; www.skyventuremontreal. com; 2700 Ave du Cosmodôme, Laval; flight packages from $71; ⏱flights 1-10pm Mon-Thu, 9am-10pm Fri-Sun; 🚌61 or 70, Ⓜ Montmorency) Canada's only skydiving simulator lets you stretch your wings inside a massive vertical wind tunnel that keeps you aloft with gusts of 110mph. You'll get a brief training session with an instructor, a flightsuit, helmet and goggles; kids aged four years and over can try it too.

It's no easy feat maneuvering in the wind tunnel during the one-minute flights, and you may find yourself bumping into the transparent walls in a very ungainly fashion. Helpful instructors fly with you, though, and part of the fun is watching them perform gravity-defying skydiving acrobatics. Be sure to stretch before and after.

PARC DE LA RIVIÈRE-DES-MILLE-ÎLES — WATER SPORTS

(📞450-622-1020; www.parc-mille-iles.qc.ca; 345 Blvd Ste-Rose; kayak/canoe per hr $11/12, per day $37/40; ⏱9am-6pm Sun-Thu, to 8pm Fri & Sat mid-Jun–mid-Aug; Ⓜ Cartier then bus 73) This is one of Montréal's loveliest spots for canoeing and kayaking. This park on the Rivière des Mille-Îles near Laval has 10 islands where you can disembark on self-guided water tours, and about 10km of the river (including calm inner channels) are open for paddling.

You can rent a wide range of watercraft, including 10-seat rabaska ($30 per hour) – canoes like those used by fur trappers.

ACTION 500 — GO-KARTING

(📞514-254-4244; www.action500.com; 5592 Rue Hochelaga; ⏱noon-midnight Mon-Fri, from 9am Sat & Sun; 🚌85, Ⓜ L'Assomption) Canada's largest indoor go-kart center provides plenty of amusement for gearheads. Sharpen your skills in 10-minute races on a large indoor karting track. The racers blaze around the circuit at speeds of up to 46mph. Uniforms and safety helmets are provided; it's $23 to $25 per race.

You can also let off steam in a round of paintball on four terrains strewn with obstacles, bunkers, pyramids and catacombs. The games pit security agents against thieves in a dozen splattering scenarios.

Paintball packages (from $40) include mask, paint gun and 100 paintballs.

H2O ADVENTURES WATER SPORTS

(✆514-842-1306; www.h2oadventures.com; 2985b Rue St-Patrick; pedal boat/kayak/electric boat/voyageur canoe per hr $15/20/50/50; ◷9am-9pm May-Sep; Ⓜ Charlevoix) Located across from the Atwater market on the banks of the Canal de Lachine, H2O rents out kayaks and pedal boats for a gentle glide along the water. There is a variety of courses on offer – white-water, rolling clinic, or introductory two-hour kayaking classes ($50).

RAFTING MONTRÉAL RAFTING

(✆514-767-2230; www.raftingmontreal.com; 8912 Blvd LaSalle; jet boat per adult/child/teen $55/35/45, rafting $46/28/39; ◷9am-6pm May-Sep; ⊞; ☐110, Ⓜ Angrignon) Located near the Lachine Rapids in LaSalle, this outfit offers adrenaline-charged outings on the white waters of the Lachine Rapids. Rafting trips last a little over two hours and are also suitable for kids age six and up. Jet-boat trips offer high-speed 75-minute rides.

For something a bit different, you can try river boarding (not unlike a boogie-board ride along more than 4 miles of rapids) or tandem rafting (where you and a friend brave the white waters in a two-person kayak).

L'ÉCOLE DE VOILE DE LACHINE SAILING

(✆514-634-4326; www.voilelachine.com; 3045 Blvd St-Joseph, Lachine; boat rental per 1hr $25-40, per 3hr $50-100; ◷1-6pm Mon-Fri, 9am-8pm Sat & Sun May-Sep; ☐173, Ⓜ Lionel-Groulx) Located on the edge of Lac St-Louis, the Lachine Sailing School organizes regattas on the St Lawrence River, gives free boat tours in late June and early July and rents light craft (windsurfing boards, small sailboats and catamarans). Qualified instructors give windsurfing and sailing courses in summer. A 20-hour sailing course (one night and one weekend) costs $380.

CENTRE D'ESCALADE HORIZON ROC ROCK CLIMBING

(✆514-899-5000; www.horizonroc.com; 2350 Rue Dickson; admission from $16; ◷5-11pm Mon-Fri, 9am-6pm Sat, 9am-5pm Sun; ☐85, Ⓜ L'Assomption) This enormous 28,000-sq-ft climbing gym features 39ft walls and hundreds of lead and top-rope routes; it's one of the world's largest indoor climbing facilities. You can sign up for lessons, and all the gear (rope, harness, climbing shoes etc) is on hand for hire.

CENTRE AQUATIQUE SWIMMING

(✆514-252-4622; www.parcolympique.qc.ca; 4141 Ave Pierre-de-Courbertin; per adult/child $10/7; ◷6:30am-9pm Mon-Fri, 9am-4pm Sat & Sun; Ⓜ Viau) The competition pools at the Olympic Stadium are great for laps – they're among the fastest in the world thanks to a system that reduces water movement. The six indoor pools include a wading pool for tots, a water slide and a diving basin. Call or check online for the current schedule, which can change owing to events and competitions.

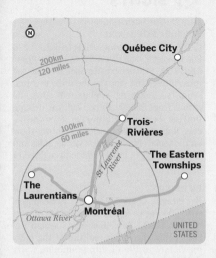

Day Trips from Montréal

Trois-Rivières p144

Midway between Montréal and Québec City, this historic town makes a pleasant stopover, with its attractive riverfront backed by a small cluster of museums and historic buildings.

The Laurentians p146

Montréal's backyard mountain playground, the Laurentians offer countless recreational opportunities, including hiking, downhill and cross-country skiing, and cycling on a 230km converted railway bed.

The Eastern Townships p149

Québec meets New England in this pretty landscape of rolling hills, sparkling lakes, picturesque villages and farms specializing in cider, wine, cheese and maple syrup.

Trois-Rivières

Explore

The pleasant town of Trois-Rivières boasts history dating back to 1634, making it North America's second-oldest city north of Mexico. Although much of the historic center burned down in 1908, a compact cluster of old buildings remains, creating a harmonious ensemble with the town's picturesque tree-lined streets and scenic location along the St Lawrence River's north shore.

The name Trois-Rivières is a bit of a misnomer. Don't bother looking – there aren't three rivers. The name refers to the way the St Maurice River divides as it approaches the St Lawrence.

Cultural highlights include the **Festival International de la Poésie** (International Poetry Festival; www.fiptr.com), a 10-day international poetry festival in October.

The Best...

➡ **Sight** Musée Québécois de Culture Populaire

➡ **Place to Eat** Le Poivre Noir

➡ **Place to Drink** Gambrinus

Top Tip

If you read French, don't miss the interesting interpretive plaques sprinkled around Trois-Rivières' riverfront district, enlivened by vintage photos and engravings tracing four centuries of local history.

Getting There & Away

➡ **Bus** Orléans Express (📞514-395-4000; www.orleansexpress.com) runs six buses daily from Montréal to Trois-Rivières ($36, two hours). Buses arrive at Trois-Rivières' Gare d'Autocars (📞819-374-2944; 275 Rue St-Georges), within a 10-minute walk of the historic riverfront district.

➡ **Car** Autoroute 40

Need to Know

➡ **Area Code** 📞819

➡ **Location** 139km northeast of Montréal

➡ **Tourist Office** (📞819-375-1122; www.tourismetroisrivieres.com; 1457 Rue Notre-Dame; ☺9am-5pm Mon-Fri, 10am-4pm Sat & Sun)

⊙ SIGHTS

MUSÉE QUÉBÉCOIS DE CULTURE POPULAIRE
MUSEUM

(📞819-372-0406; www.culturepop.qc.ca; 200 Rue Laviolette; adult/child $12/7, incl En Prison $19/10.50; ☺10am-5pm Tue-Sun) One of the most interesting stops in the area, this museum has changing exhibits that cover the gamut from folk art to pop culture, delving into the social and cultural life of the Québecois. Recent exhibits include a quirky show on the social significance of garage sales and woodcarvings of birds commonly sighted in the area.

EN PRISON
MUSEUM

(In Prison; 📞819-372-0406; www.enprison.com; 200 Rue Laviolette; adult/child $12/7, incl museum $19/10.50; ☺10am-5pm Tue-Sun) Excons bring the harsh realities of the lock-up vividly to life during 90-minute tours that include a stop at dank underground cells known as 'the pit.' English tours run between 11am and 3:15pm from late June to the end of August, and by reservation the rest of the year. The prison exhibit is connected to adjacent Musée Québécois de Culture Populaire.

URSULINE MUSEUM
MUSEUM

(www.musee-ursulines.qc.ca; 734 Rue des Ursulines; adult/child/student $5/free/4; ☺10am-5pm Tue-Sun May-Nov, 1-5pm Wed-Sun Mar & Apr) Founded by Ursuline nuns in 1639, this museum has a fine collection of textiles, ceramics, books and prints related to Catholicism. Frescoes adorn the adjacent chapel. Nearby, Rue des Ursulines is a pleasant place to stroll, with its picturesque homes (some now operating as B&Bs) and its unseen history, much of which is described on informational plaques throughout the neighborhood.

✕ EATING & DRINKING

RESTAURANT LE GRILL
STEAK $$

(📞819-376-4745; www.restolegrill.com; 350 Rue des Forges; mains $14-37; ☺11:30am-10pm Mon-Fri, 5-11pm Sat & Sun) Locals flock to this trendy steakhouse for filet mignon, but the menu also features gourmet burgers, meal-sized salads, salmon, shrimp, lobster and Le Grill's own jazzed-up version of the Québecois classic poutine: cheesy fries accompanied by peppercorn-cognac sauce

WORTH A DETOUR

A DELIGHTFUL SUMMER RETREAT

If you're continuing east from Trois-Rivières toward Québec City, don't miss **La Domaine Joly de Lotbinière** (📞418-926-2462; www.domainejoly.com; Hwy 132, Rte de Pointe-Platon; adult/child/student $16/1/10; ☺10am-5pm late May–late Sep). This stately museum on a riverside point along the south bank of the St Lawrence River was built for former Québec premier Henri-Gustave Joly de Lotbinière (1849–1908). It's one of the most impressive manors built during the seigneurial period of Québec and has been preserved in its late 19th-century state. The outbuildings and huge cultivated garden are a treat, and the cafe serves lunch and afternoon teas. There's also a farm stand that sells vegetables from mid-June to early September.

or a wine-based *au jus* with rosemary and roasted garlic. The streetside patio puts you right in the middle of all the action.

LE POIVRE NOIR
FUSION $$$

(📞819-378-5772; www.poivrenoir.com; 1300 Rue du Fleuve; mains $22-32; ☺11:30am-2pm Wed-Fri, 5:30-10pm Tue-Sun) At this upmarket place by the riverfront, chef José Pierre Durand's inspired, often daring blend of French, Québecois and international influences creates a memorable dining experience. Appetizers such as asparagus and blood-orange salad, or warm goat's-cheese 'snowballs' with tomatoes and pistachios, are followed by main dishes such as Québecois deer with pine-nut-squash risotto and cranberry chutney. Reservations suggested.

The truly adventurous can finish their meal with pan-fried foie gras (for information on foie gras production, see p28) with dark chocolate and Jack Daniels–infused caramel sauce.

GAMBRINUS
BREWERY

(www.gambrinus.qc.ca; 3160 Blvd des Forges; ☺11am-1am Mon-Fri, 3pm-1am Sat) About 3km north of the riverfront, this decade-old brewery serves more than a dozen varieties of beer, including seasonal cranberry, raspberry and apple ales, an excellent IPA, and an unconventional hemp-and-honey blend called Miel d'Ange.

🛌 SLEEPING

AUBERGE INTERNATIONALE DE TROIS-RIVIÈRES
HOSTEL $

(📞819-378-8010; www.hihostels.ca; 497 Rue Radisson; dm/d $25/55; @☎) This wonderfully clean and friendly youth hostel is set in a two-story brick Georgian home, within easy walking distance of the bus station,

the riverfront and all the city's attractions. Dorms have four to eight beds each, and there are also reasonably priced private rooms. Bicycle rentals are available.

★LE GÎTE LOISELLE
B&B $$

(📞819-375-2121; www.giteloiselle.com; 836 Rue des Ursulines; r $95-135; P✳@☎) Local artwork, magnificent woodwork and tasteful antiques greet you at this Victorian red-brick one block from the river. Basic rooms with private toilets and shared shower put you right in the heart of the historic district. Congenial hosts Lisette and Mario, both avid cyclists and former restaurateurs, serve an ample breakfast to fuel you for the day's adventures.

LE FLEURVIL
B&B $$

(📞819-372-5195; www.fleurvil.qc.ca; 635 Rue des Ursulines; d $99-149; ☎✉) Operated by a gregarious Harley aficionado with a knack for decorating, this homey inn within a stone's throw of the St Lawrence River fronts a lush garden with a maple-shaded pool.

SPORTS & ACTIVITIES

CROISIÈRES AML
BOAT TOUR

(📞866-856-6668; www.croisieresaml.com; adult/child $30/17; ☺mid-Jun–early Sep) For a different perspective on Trois-Rivières, take a 90-minute cruise along the St Lawrence River. Thrice-daily summer-only tours feature historical commentary about the town while traveling from the port to the Laviolette bridge, the Notre-Dame-du-Cap sanctuary, Ile St-Quentin and the confluence of the St Lawrence and St Maurice Rivers. Tours leave from the dock in Parc Portuaire, at the foot of Rue des Forges in the center of the old town.

DAY TRIPS FROM MONTRÉAL TROIS-RIVIÈRES

The Laurentians

Explore

Named for their location along the northern side of the St Lawrence River, the Laurentians (Les Laurentides) are one of Québec's great outdoor playgrounds. In winter, outdoor enthusiasts and nature lovers take to the clear lakes and forest-covered peaks for downhill and cross-country skiing, snowshoeing and snowmobiling. When the weather warms, hikers, cyclists, kayakers and campers come to soak up the natural beauty. People also visit in fall to take in the changing leaves, with hues of ocher, gold and vermilion dramatically coloring the landscape.

While it's possible to come up on a long day trip, some prefer to linger in the region's alpine-style villages, overnighting in cozy chalets, spa retreats and atmospheric B&Bs. Expect higher prices and heavy crowds during high season, which includes the summer months and Christmas holidays.

The Best...

→ **Sight** Parc National du Mont-Tremblant
→ **Place to Eat** La Tablée des Pionniers
→ **Place to Drink** Le Baril Roulant (p148)

Top Tip

Even without your own bicycle, you can cycle Canada's longest rails-to-trails route, the 232km P'tit Train du Nord (p149); Autobus Le Petit Train du Nord will rent you a bike and provide transportation between the start and end points of your choice.

Getting There & Away

→ **Bus** Galland Laurentides (p240) runs buses from Montréal's main bus station to the Laurentians three times daily. Towns serviced include St-Sauveur-des-Monts ($23, 1¾ hours), St-Agathe-des-Monts ($28, 2½ hours) and Mont-Tremblant ($36, three hours).

→ **Car** Autoroute 15 (Autoroute des Laurentides) and provincial Hwy 117

Need to Know

→ **Area Code** ☑450, ☑819
→ **Location** 80km to 150km northwest of Montréal
→ **Tourisme Laurentides** (☑800-561-6673, reservations 450-224-7007; www.laurentides.com; La Porte-du-Nord, Hwy 15, Exit 51; ◎9am-8pm late Jun–early Sep, to 5pm rest of year)

◉ SIGHTS

★**PARC NATIONAL DU MONT-TREMBLANT**   NATIONAL PARK
(☑819-688-2281, reservations 800-665-6527; www.sepaq.com; Chemin du Lac Supérieur; adult/child $7.50/3.25) Opened more than a century ago, this wild, wooded national park covers more than 1500 sq km of gorgeous Laurentian lakes, rivers, hills and woods. You'll find fantastic hiking and mountain-biking trails as well as camping and river routes for canoes. The half-day Méandres de la Diable route from Lac Chat to Mont de la Vache Noire is particularly popular. Reserve a canoe and a place on the shuttle bus by calling the park reservations line well in advance.

MONT-TREMBLANT   VILLAGE
The village of Mont-Tremblant (Secteur Village), some 4km southwest of the Mont-Tremblant ski resort, is spread along the shores of pretty Lac Mercier. You'll find shops, cafes, B&Bs, restaurants and a pretty lakeside section of the P'tit Train du Nord recreation path, perfect for exploring on foot or cross-country skis. In summer, there are cruises out on the water; in winter, the lake adjoining the municipal beach is converted to an ice rink, illuminated for skating until 10pm.

VAL-DAVID   VILLAGE
Tiny Val-David was a major hippie mecca in the '60s, a hangover still apparent today. The village has two artisanal bakeries, jazz music in its cafes on summer weekends and more than its share of arts and crafts people. The Saturday morning **Val-David Farmers Market** (Marché d'Été; ◎9am-1:30pm Sat late May–mid-Oct), directly opposite the village church, is the largest in the Laurentides. The town's tourist office is in a cute

Mont Tremblant

old train station alongside the P'tit Train du Nord recreation trail.

STE-AGATHE-DES-MONTS VILLAGE
This mountain village has a prime location on Lac des Sables. By the beginning of the 1900s, it was a well-known spa town. Later, famous guests included Queen Elizabeth (who took refuge here during WWII) and Jackie Kennedy. **Bateaux Alouette** (☎819-326-3656; www.croisierealouette.com; adult/child $20.75/10.50; ☺Jun-Oct) offers 50-minute cruises on the lake.

ST-SAUVEUR-DES-MONTS VILLAGE
St-Sauveur-des-Monts is a small resort town with four nearby ski hills. Its main drag is often clogged on weekends when day-trippers shuffle through the cafes, restaurants and shops.

MUSÉE D'ART CONTEMPORAIN
DES LAURENTIDES MUSEUM
(☎450-432-7171; www.museelaurentides.ca; 101 Pl du Curé-Labelle, St-Jérôme; admission by donation; ☺noon-5pm Tue-Sun) Less than an hour from Montréal, this contemporary-art museum has small but fine exhibitions of work by regional artists.

EATING & DRINKING

ORANGE & PAMPLEMOUSSE FUSION $$
(☎450-227-4330; www.orangepamplemousse.com; 120 Rue Principale, St-Sauveur-des-Monts; mains $14-32; ☺8am-2:30pm daily, plus 5-9pm Wed-Sun) Tranquil with the soft sounds of a Japanese bamboo water fountain, this restaurant is a great place to devour complex pasta dishes and extraordinary grilled fish. The breakfasts are also divine.

MICROBRASSERIE LA DIABLE PUB FOOD $$
(www.microladiable.com; 117 Chemin Kandahar, Station Tremblant; mains $13-28; ☺11:30am-2am) The hearty sausages, burgers and pastas at this lively tavern fill the belly nicely after a day of tearing down the mountain – although the real highlight is the fine lineup of microbrews: blonde, red and Belgian trappist ales, wheat beer, double-black stout and rotating monthly specials.

★**LA TABLÉE DES PIONNIERS** QUÉBECOIS $$$
(☎855-688-2101; www.latableedespionniers.com; 1357 Rue St-Faustin, St-Faustin-Lac-Carré; multicourse menu $30-50; ☺4:30-9:30pm Thu, 9am-9:30pm Fri-Sun late Feb–mid-May & Sep-Oct) For top-notch traditional Québecois cuisine

LOCAL KNOWLEDGE

SUGAR SHACKS

Québec is the undisputed world champion of maple-sugar production, and there's a long-standing tradition of early-spring visits to *cabanes à sucre* (maple-sugar shacks); English-speaking Québecers refer to such trips as 'sugaring off.' With a roaring fire boiling the sap down into syrup, these cozy places can be found all over the province in March and April, including the Laurentians and the Eastern Townships.

For a list of more than 100 sugar shacks open to the public, see www.bonjourquebec.com. Here are a few shacks within easy driving distance of Montréal to get you started:

Cabane à Sucre Bouvrette (☎450-438-4659; www.bouvrette.ca; 1000 Rue Nobel, St-Jérôme; menus $16-22; �⊙11:30am-8pm Tue-Sun Mar & Apr; ⊞) In business for seven decades, this enormous 'shack' 45-minutes north of Montréal serves a set menu that includes ham, bacon, sausages, *oreilles de crisse* (deep-fried pork jowls), fried potatoes, oven-baked 48-egg omelets, pea soup, baked beans, beet juice and homemade pickles, all slathered in maple syrup. Kids will love the petting zoo, old-fashioned locomotive and horse-drawn sleigh rides. For dessert don't miss the classic *tire d'érable,* maple taffy made by pouring hot, concentrated maple syrup over snow, then rolling the congealed syrup onto wooden sticks.

Cabane à Sucre Au Pied de Cochon (☎450-258-1732; www.cabaneasucreaupieddecochon.com; 11382 Rang de la Fresnière, St-Benoît de Mirabel; adult/child menu $65/20; ⊙5:30-8:30pm Thu & Fri, 11am-8:30pm Sat & Sun mid-Feb–early May) This high-end version of the sugar-shack experience, 45 minutes west of Montréal, is brought to you by renowned Montréal chef Martin Picard. Tables fill up months in advance for his gourmet menu of maple-based delights; book well ahead.

Cabane du Pic-Bois (☎450-263-6060; www.cabanedupicbois.com; 1468 Chemin Gaspé, Brigham; adult/child $29/16; ⊙Fri-Sun Mar & Apr by reservation) The all-you-can-eat spread at this traditional sugar shack includes all the classics – omelets, pork jowls, ham, maple sausage, beans and potatoes – plus cabbage salad dressed with Pic-Bois' famous maple vinegar. It also has a slew of maple desserts: crepes, tarts and *grands-pères au sirop d'érable,* traditional ball-shaped pastries stewed in maple syrup. It's in the Eastern Townships, about an hour east of Montréal.

in rustic country surroundings, don't miss this seasonal roadside eatery between Mont-Tremblant and Ste-Agathe. Multicourse menus, served during maple sugaring and apple-harvest season, feature such delights as split pea, cabbage and bacon soup; smoked-trout soufflés; pulled-pork and mushroom puff-pastry pies; and maple-walnut tarts, accompanied by cider from the family's orchard.

★SEB   MODERN CANADIAN $$$
(☎819-429-6991; www.seblartisanculinaire.com; 444 Rue St-Georges, St-Jovite; mains $29-49, multicourse menu $49-90; ⊙6-11pm Thu-Mon) 🍽 Escape the mediocre and get a little taste of what local culinary artisans can create with seasonal, sustainable local ingredients. A flexible, eager-to-please kitchen, an unforgettable menu and a never-ending wine list enhance the jovial atmosphere. sEb is best described as alpine chalet meets globetrotter (think African masks) meets

Hollywood chic (Michael Douglas is a regular). Reservations essential.

LA PETITE CACHÉE   MEDITERRANEAN $$$
(☎819-425-2654; www.petitecachee.com; 2681 Chemin du Village, Mont-Tremblant; mains $22-45; ⊙5-10pm) In a charming chalet en route to the ski slopes, this place offers tasty choices such as penne with wapiti sausage, poached salmon with rice noodles, or ratatouille pie au gratin with goat's cheese.

★LE BARIL ROULANT   MICROBREWERY
(www.barilroulant.wordpress.com; 2434 Rue de l'Église, Val-David; ⊙3pm-midnight Mon-Thu, noon-1am Fri-Sun) Laid-back and brimming with local color, this artsy microbrewery complements its own creations with a plethora of other brews from the surrounding area. Chill on the outdoor deck in summer, or get cozy on multicolored chairs and couches in the bright interior. Live bands and DJs provide regular entertainment, from jazz to psychedelia to electro-pop.

SPORTS & ACTIVITIES

★P'TIT TRAIN DU NORD   CYCLING, SKIING

(☑450-745-0185; www.laurentides.com/parc lineaire) One of the region's essential experiences, this 232km recreation path follows the old Laurentian train line between Mont-Laurier and Bois-des-Filion. Cyclists hit the path when the weather warms; in winter it's open to cross-country skiers and snowshoers (and also partially to snowmobiles). B&Bs and bike shops abound along the route, and many old train stations house mini-museums, cafes and tourist offices.

MONT-TREMBLANT SKI RESORT   SKIING

(☑514-764-7546, 888-738-1777; www.tremblant. ca; 1000 Chemin des Voyageurs, Mont-Tremblant Village; lift ticket adult/youth/child $82/58/48; ☺8:30am-4pm late Nov–mid-Apr) This ski center has the area's highest peak (968m) and more than 60 runs. Its state-of-the-art summer facilities include golf courses, water sports, cycling and tennis courts. Bikes and skates can be rented at the ski center for the 10km skating/cycling path that runs up to the mountain's edge.

MONT ST-SAUVEUR   SKIING

(☑514-871-0101, 450-227-4671; www.mont saintsauveur.com; 350 Ave St-Denis, St-Sauveur; lift ticket adult/youth/child $54/47/38; ☺9am-10pm Mon-Fri, 8:30am-10pm Sat & Sun) Mont St-Sauveur is one of the area's main ski centers. Hills are a bit tame but there's night skiing, a huge variety of runs and 100% snow coverage in season, thanks to snow blowers built right into the slopes.

🛏 SLEEPING

HI MONT-TREMBLANT HOSTEL   HOSTEL $

(☑866-425-6008, 819-425-6008; www.hos tellingtremblant.com; 2213 Chemin du Village, Mont-Tremblant Village; dm $25-32, d $66-90; @🛜) This attractive hostel right next to Lac Moore (free canoe rentals) has a big kitchen and large party room with bar, pool table and fireplace. The clean and spacious rooms often fill to capacity, especially in the ski season. Look for it along the main road, 1km east of Mont-Tremblant village and 4km west of the slopes.

★LA MAISON DE BAVIÈRE   B&B $$

(☑819-322-3528; www.maisondebaviere.com; 1470 Chemin de la Rivière, Val-David; r $110-160; 🅿@🛜) Fall asleep to the sound of Rivière du Nord outside the window. This inn has hand-painted Bavarian stencils and wooden beams giving it a European ski-chalet feel. Everything is geared toward a day of outdoor pursuits, from its location on the P'tit Train du Nord trail to the energizing full gourmet breakfasts served each morning.

At the end of an activity-filled day, you can relax on the sprawling, pristine grounds overlooking the river. The restaurants and shops of Val-David are a short walk or bike ride away.

AU CLOS ROLLAND   B&B $$

(☑450-229-1939; www.auclosrolland.com; 1200 Rue St-Jean, Ste-Adèle; d incl breakfast $85-125; 🛜) Hidden in an otherwise undistinguished neighborhood, this sprawling 1904 mansion surrounded by vast grassy lawns is an absolute gem. The public spaces downstairs – a library with piano, living room with fireplace and pretty glass-walled breakfast room – are instantly inviting, while the guest rooms, including a couple tucked under the eaves, have cozy beds, wood floors and 'old-house' charm.

The B&B is 300m from the P'tit Train du Nord recreation path, making this a great option for cyclists and cross-country skiers.

The Eastern Townships

···

Explore

Rolling wooded hills, clear blue lakes, quaint villages, covered bridges and round barns set the scene for a delightful ramble through the picturesque Eastern Townships (Cantons de l'Est or l'Estrie in French). Once the homeland of the Abenaki, this region just north of the Vermont and New Hampshire borders became a refuge for Loyalists fleeing the USA after the revolution of 1776; even today it remains one of Québec's most perfectly bilingual regions.

Spring is the season for tapping, boiling and preparing maple syrup. Summer brings fishing and swimming in the numerous lakes; in fall the foliage dazzles with gorgeous colors and fresh-pressed apple cider is served in local pubs. Skiing is a major winter activity, with centers at Mont Orford and Sutton. The district also boasts several up-and-coming vineyards.

The Best...

→ **Sight** Parc de la Gorge de Coaticook

→ **Place to Eat** Auberge Le Coeur d'Or (p152)

→ **Place to Drink** Siboire (p152)

Top Tip

During the busy summer and fall foliage seasons, travel midweek to avoid the crowds and the two-night weekend minimum imposed by many B&Bs.

Getting There & Away

→ **Bus** Transdev Limocar (☑514-842-2281; www.transdev.ca) operates a dozen daily services from Montréal's main bus station to Magog ($37, 1¾ hours) and Sherbrooke ($41, 2½ hours), with less frequent service to Granby ($26, 1¾ hours), Knowlton ($28, 1¾ hours) and Sutton ($28, 2¼ hours).

→ **Car** Autoroutes 10 Est (East) and 55 Sud (South)

Need to Know

→ **Area Code** ☑450, ☑819

→ **Location** 80km to 165km east and southeast of Montréal

→ **Tourist Office** (☑866-472-6292, 450-375-8774; www.easterntownships.org; 100 Rue du Tourisme, Hwy 10, exit 68, St-Alphonse-de-Granby; ☺8:30am-4:30pm)

◉ SIGHTS

PARC DE LA GORGE DE COATICOOK   PARK
(☑888-524-6743, 819-849-2331; www.gorge decoaticook.qc.ca; 400 Rue St-Marc, Coaticook; adult/child $7.50/4.50; ☺year-round; 🖈) Straddling a lovely forested gorge outside the town of Coaticook, this scenic park is famous for having the world's longest pedestrian suspension bridge. Visitors come for hiking, mountain biking and horseback riding in summer, and snow-tubing and snowshoeing in winter. You can also camp or stay in one of the park's cabins. The surrounding area boasts some of the Eastern Townships' prettiest scenery, not to mention some wonderful cheese makers (get the cheese-route brochure from the Coaticook tourist office).

Family-friendly attractions include a minifarm where kids can pet and feed animals and go on pony rides, as well as the

---

CHARTING YOUR COURSE THROUGH THE TOWNSHIPS

There are a number of interesting and well-signposted driving and cycling routes through the Eastern Townships.

The **Chemin des Cantons** (Townships Trail; www.chemindescantons.qc.ca) is a 418km circuit that takes in most of the Townships' prettiest villages and scenery. Coming from Montréal, pick up the route in Granby, Knowlton or Sutton, then simply follow the signs as far as you like.

The **Route des Vins** (Wine Route; www.laroutedesvins.ca) threads its way past 18 wineries on a 120km ramble through the rolling country between Granby and the Vermont border. The route is well signposted from exits 48, 68 and 90 off Hwy 10. Variants of the route focus on gastronomy, outdoor activities and the arts; see the website for details.

Cyclists are invited to become 'Vélomaniacs' (cycling fiends) with the Eastern Townships tourist office's 365km network of **cycling routes** (www.easterntownships. org/cycling). Pick up its excellent printed map describing more than a dozen cycling itineraries.

Further east and off the beaten track, the **Route des Sommets** (Summit Drive; www.routedessommets.com) winds 193km along the high mountain slopes north of the New Hampshire border, passing a series of villages and scenic lookouts between La Patrie and St-Adrien. This is a great option for viewing the spectacular fall colors of the Townships.

recently launched **Foresta Lumina** (www.forestalumina.com; adult/child $16/9; 8:30-10:30pm daily Jul & Aug, Sat & Sun Jun, Sep & early Oct;), a summertime evening event in which forest trails are illuminated with colorful lights, creating magical effects.

PARC NATIONAL
DU MONT-ORFORD   NATIONAL PARK
(819-843-9855; www.sepaq.com/pq/mor; 3321 Chemin du Parc, Orford; adult/child $7.50/3.25; year-round) Just outside the town of Magog, Mont Orford (792m) dominates the lush Parc National du Mont-Orford. In winter, the park is a cross-country and downhill skiing center; summer brings hiking (on 80km of trails), plus swimming, boating and camping on Lac Stukely and Lac Fraser. Canoe, kayak and ski rentals are available.

NORTH HATLEY   VILLAGE
Beautifully sited at the north end of Lac Massawippi, this picturesque village was a popular second home for wealthy US citizens who enjoyed the scenery – and the absence of Prohibition – during the 1920s. Many historic residences have been converted into inns and B&Bs. Popular summer activities include swimming, boating, admiring the lakeshore's natural beauty and browsing the village's galleries, antique and craft shops. In summer, English-language dramas, concerts and comedy acts play at the **Piggery Theatre** (819-842-2431; www.piggery.com; 215 Chemin Simard).

FRELIGHSBURG   VILLAGE
A few miles from the Vermont border, this village makes a pleasant stop along the Eastern Townships Route des Vins (Wine Route). A cluster of stone and wood homes straddles the banks of the brook that runs through town, and the surrounding area is filled with apple orchards. Local eateries specialize in smoked fish and maple products; if you have a sweet tooth, don't miss the famous maple tarts at the old general store-cafe in the center of town.

SUTTON   VILLAGE
One of southern Québec's most attractive villages, Sutton is popular with artsy types and skiers, who come to appreciate the scenic beauty of the surrounding landscape, dominated by the northern Green Mountains. The downtown strip is filled with cafes, restaurants, inns and B&Bs, along with a helpful tourist office. Family-operated **Mont Sutton** (www.montsutton.com; 671 Chemin Maple; day tickets adult/youth/child $60/42/34; 9am-4pm), the ski area 5km east of town, offers 60 downhill runs for all abilities and is especially well known for its glade skiing.

LAC BROME   VILLAGE
South of Autoroute 10, on Hwy 243, is the township of Lac Brome, made up of seven former English Loyalist villages. The main village of **Knowlton** is one of the most interesting and picturesque: its main street is lined with restored Victorian buildings, including many craft and gift shops. A favorite meal in this area is Lac Brome duck, which shows up frequently on the better menus and is celebrated with the town's annual **Canard en Fête** (Brome Lake Duck Festival; www.canardenfete.ca; late Sep).

ABBAYE ST-BENOÎT-DU-LAC   MONASTERY
(819-843-4080; www.st-benoit-du-lac.com; 1 Rue Principale, St-Benoît-du-Lac; church 5am-8:30pm, shop 9-10:45am & 11:45am-5pm Mon-Sat) This peaceful monastery sits on the western shore of Lac Memphrémagog, the largest and best-known lake in the Eastern Townships, where most waterfront properties are privately owned. The monks' chants, cider and finely made cheeses are famous throughout Québec, and people from throughout the province descend on the abbey's shop to buy them along with jams, jellies, sweets and chocolate-covered blueberries.

Visitors can attend services (and join the monks in prayer and Gregorian chanting) at 7:30am, 11am and 5pm. There's a hostel for men here and another for women at a nearby nunnery.

ORFORD ARTS CENTRE   ARTS CENTER
(819-843-3981; www.arts-orford.org; 3165 Chemin du Parc, Orford) Each summer this renowned music academy, dating back to 1951, hosts the **Orford Festival**, a celebration of music and art that features more than 60 concerts by international musicians, performances by guest artists as well as the academy's own advanced students. Between September and May, the center also hosts occasional lunch and dinner concerts featuring jazz and classical artists.

GRANBY ZOO   ZOO
(450-372-9113; www.zoodegranby.com; 525 Rue St-Hubert, Granby; adult/child $20/13;

⊙10am-5pm daily late May–Aug, Sat & Sun only Sep & Oct; 🚹) The town of Granby is known far and wide in Québec as the home of this zoo, with its 1000-plus animals including reptiles, gorillas and kangaroos. One of the most popular spots is at the bottom of the hippopotamus pool, where you can watch hippos lumber from the ground before they swim past viewing windows.

SHERBROOKE   CITY
Sherbrooke is the commercial center of the Townships, with a pleasant central core lying between two rivers. Downtown is a good place to wander, with 11 large outdoor wall murals (pick up a map at the tourist office). Other highlights include the city's small but well-conceived **Musée des Beaux-Arts** (www.mbas.qc.ca; 241 Rue Dufferin; adult/student $10/7; ⊙10am-5pm daily late Jun–Aug, noon-5pm Tue-Sun rest of year), with works by Québecois and Canadian artists, and the 18km Réseau Riverain walking and cycling path along the Magog River, which starts at Blanchard Park, west of downtown.

✕ EATING & DRINKING

LE CAFETIER   CAFE $
(☑450-538-7333; 9 Rue Principale N, Sutton; mains $8-15; ⊙7am-7pm; 🛜) Locals flock to this bustling, cheery cafe in the heart of Sutton for morning coffee, croissants, smoothies, omelets and homemade muesli, but it's just as popular in the afternoon for salads, vegetarian chili, panini and *croque-monsieurs*. Wine and beer, free wi-fi, decks of playing cards and toys for the kids encourage people of all ages to linger.

LES SUCRERIES DE L'ÉRABLE   BAKERY, CAFE $
(☑450-298-5181; www.lessucreriesdelerable. com; 16 Rue Principale, Frelighsburg; mains $9-14; ⊙8:30am-5pm Thu-Mon) Best known for its scrumptious maple pies, this bakery in an attractive old brick-walled general store does double duty as a simple restaurant. Breakfast treats include waffles with blueberries, bananas, crème fraîche and maple sugar, while lunch revolves around salads and sandwiches. Try a bagel topped with local maple-smoked salmon, accompanied by a glass of local cider.

Save room for fresh maple ice cream or maple pie. In summer, it's delightful to sit on the outdoor deck near the river out back.

LE RELAIS   FRENCH $$
(☑450-242-2232; www.aubergeknowlton.ca/ relais; 286 Chemin Knowlton, Lac Brome; lunch $12-21, dinner $14-35; ⊙11am-3pm & 5-10pm Mon-Fri, 8am-10pm Sat; 🛜) Set in a landmark 1849 inn, this place features juicy Lac Brome duck served many ways, such as duck ravioli in mushroom sauce, duck confit in orange sauce and duck livers with blackened butter. The many other options include pork tenderloin with calvados, veal piccata and garlic scampi, along with burgers, salads, soups and pasta. There's terrace seating in summer.

★AUBERGE LE COEUR D'OR   QUÉBECOIS $$$
(☑819-842-4363; www.aubergelecoeurdor.com; 85 Rue School, North Hatley; 4-course meal $40; ⊙6-9pm, closed Mon & Tue Nov-Apr) For a delightful night out, head to this charming farmhouse inn in North Hatley village. The restaurant's four- to five-course dinners make abundant use of local ingredients, including cheeses from Sherbrooke, rabbit from Stanstead, duck from Orford and smoked trout from East Hereford. Save room for profiteroles, chocolate mousse cake, or the Coeur d'Or's trademark trio of crèmes brûlées.

★SIBOIRE   MICROBREWERY
(☑819-565-3636; www.siboire.ca; 80 Rue du Dépôt, Sherbrooke; ⊙7am-3am) Sherbrooke's historic train depot houses this atmospheric microbrewery with nearly a dozen beers on tap, including Siboire's own IPA, wheat beer, oatmeal stout, Irish red ale and seasonal maple scotch ale. High ceilings, old brick walls and a flower-fringed summer terrace create an inviting atmosphere for drinking it all in and enjoying some of the tastiest fish and chips in the Townships.

🛌 SLEEPING

LE BOCAGE   B&B $$
(☑819-835-5653; www.lebocage.qc.ca; 200 Chemin Moe's River, Compton; d $100-125, ste $165-250, all incl breakfast; ⊙Tue-Sun; 🛜💺) From the welcome to the antiques, this Victorian gem of a B&B in the countryside between Coaticook and Sherbrooke is hard to fault. A multicourse meal (three/four/five/ six courses $43/48/55/66) is served nightly and can feature dishes such as guinea fowl stuffed with mushrooms, wild boar,

ICE WINE & ICE CIDER

Ice wine (*vin de glace* in French) was discovered in Germany by accident, when growers found that pressing wine grapes after they froze on the vine left a sweet, highly concentrated juice. Ice wine results when this juice is left on the vine to ferment, creating one of the most coveted dessert wines on the market; it's so expensive because of the amount of grapes that need to be pressed for enough juice to be extracted.

If you're following the Eastern Townships Route des Vins (Wine Route), you'll come across many local varieties. Award-winning ice-wine producer **Chapelle Ste-Agnès** (450-538-0303; www.vindeglace.com; 2565 Chemin Scenic, Sutton; guided visits incl tasting $20-30; guided visits 1:30pm Wed & Sun Jun-Oct, otherwise by arrangement) is one of the very best, just north of the Vermont border near Sutton. Closer to Montréal, in Dunham, **Vignoble l'Orpailleur** (450-295-2763; www.orpailleur.ca; 1086 Rue Bruce, Dunham; 10am-4:30pm) is arguably the province's oldest wine producer. It has a terrific little display on the history of alcohol in Québec, as well as captions in the vineyards explaining the grape varieties and how they grow. Tours of the vineyards are offered, and the on-site restaurant, **Le Tire-Bouchon** (450-295-3335; www.orpailleur.ca; mains $18-25; 11:30am-4pm late Jun–early Oct), serves delicious high-end bistro fare, with seating on a pleasant outdoor terrace.

Another specialty of the frozen north, ice cider (*cidre de glace*) is made from apples which are allowed to stay on the tree after the first frost, then pressed and cold fermented for months. Award-winning **Domaine Pinnacle** (450-298-1226; www.domainepinnacle.com; 150 Chemin Richford, Frelighsburg; 10am-6pm May-Dec, to 5pm Fri-Sun Jan-Apr), the world's largest ice-cider producer, sits among century-old orchards just outside Frelighsburg, 1¼ hours southeast of Montréal. It's open to visitors on weekends in winter and daily the rest of the year.

red-deer medallions or other wild game. Discounts apply for multinight stays and reservations are essential.

AU CHANT DE L'ONDE
B&B $$

(450-776-5676, 450-298-5676; www.auchantdelonde.ca; 6 Rue de l'Église, Frelighsburg; r incl breakfast from $102;) In the heart of pretty Frelighsburg village, this peaceful three-room B&B enjoys a prime location along the banks of the Rivière aux Brochets. Guests have access to a lovely terrace and a spacious backyard within earshot of the river, as well as a library for relaxing, reading or playing board games.

AUBERGE DU
CENTRE D'ARTS ORFORD
INN $$

(819-843-3981; www.arts-orford.org/auberge; 3165 Chemin du Parc; s $78-98, d $98-118) This no-frills lodging offers 89 rooms without TV or telephone, on 90 hectares at the edge of Parc National du Mont-Orford. It's affiliated with the Orford Arts Centre, so rooms are unavailable during the summer music festival. However, come autumn, winter or spring, it's a lovely retreat where you can enjoy trails and mountain scenery right outside your door.

★MANOIR HOVEY
RESORT $$$

(800-661-2421, 819-842-2421; www.manoirhovey.com; 575 Rue Hovey; d $190-530, incl breakfast & 3-course dinner $340-680;) This lovely resort offers handsomely set rooms in a picturesque lakeside setting. You'll find expansive gardens, a heated pool and an ice rink (in winter), and you can arrange numerous outdoor activities – windsurfing, lake cruises and golfing. The award-winning restaurant is among the best in the Eastern Townships, with three-course meals highlighting refined Québecois fare.

Sleeping

Montréal's accommodation scene is blessed with a tremendous variety of rooms and styles. Though rates aren't particularly cheap, they are reasonable by international standards – or even compared with Canadian cities such as Toronto or Vancouver. French- and Victorian-style inns and independent hotels cater to a variety of budgets.

Luxury & Boutique Hotels

Montréal has many choices when it comes to high-end lodging. You'll find top names such as Ritz-Carlton, Sofitel, Fairmont and other luxury brands. But you'll also find plenty of homegrown places such as the Hôtel Le St-James and the Hôtel Nelligan. The big full-service luxury hotels are largely downtown.

For more of the boutique experience, Old Montréal has the best selection. Many of the best are set inside 18th-century buildings and blend original details – stone walls, timber ceilings – with updated interiors (big windows and marble-filled baths). While prices tend to be high at these places, you can find some great deals. This is especially true in low season even if you book at the last minute. Keep an eye out for cut-rate weekend deals and online specials.

Small Hotels & B&Bs

Small, European-style hotels are a Montréal specialty. Located downtown and in the Quartier Latin, they occupy Victorian-era homes that are plain and functional or comfy and charming. Prices are graded by facilities (eg with sink, toilet and/or full bath), but not all places have air-con.

B&Bs are a wonderful alternative. Many of them are set in attractive, 19th-century stone houses close to the Plateau's bar-and-restaurant strips of Blvd St-Laurent and Rue St-Denis, or near Rue Ste-Catherine Est in the Village. The many B&Bs offer heaps of character – the precious commodity that can make all the difference – and their owners are often invaluable sources of travel advice. There are many comfortable but bland chain hotels in town, which may be useful in peak season when the B&Bs and guesthouses are booked solid.

Budget Sleeps

Montréal has an abundance of good budget accommodations. Apart from the usual dorm beds, hostels may offer basic single and double rooms – though these are often booked out weeks in advance. In addition, the universities throw open their residence halls to non-students in summer; prices are competitive.

Planning in advance is key to finding accommodations during big events. The summertime festival season, from late June to the end of August, is the peak period, and conventions can crimp availability in late summer.

Sleeping with Locals

Websites such as www.airbnb.com have hundreds of listings in Montréal. You can stay with Montréalers either by sharing an apartment or having a whole place to yourself. If you don't mind sharing, this is a great way to meet locals and get an insider's take on the city. And if you're after a flashy apartment for your stay in the city, renting local is one of the best ways to go.

Lonely Planet's Top Choices

L Hotel (p156) A lavish hotel that's packed with artwork by Warhol, Stella and other luminaries.

La Maison Pierre du Calvet (p158) The baroque rooms in this centuries-old gem are absolutely over the top.

Hôtel Nelligan (p157) With one of the best rooftop patios in the city, the Nelligan wins with its old-world setting and great staff.

University Bed & Breakfast Apartments (p159) These tidy rooms in the heart of the city are great value.

Best by Budget

$

Auberge St-Paul (p156) Friendly new hostel in a great Old Montréal location.

M Montreal (p162) A great place to meet other travelers, with a first-rate bar.

Le Gîte du Plateau Mont-Royal (p159) Top pick with its rooftop terrace and location near 'the mountain.'

$$

Les Bons Matins (p159) Great value for suites with Jacuzzis and fireplaces.

Hotel Parc Suites (p160) Spacious, attractively designed suites, all with kitchenettes.

Auberge de la Fontaine (p165) Appealing place, particularly the suites with in-room spas and park views.

$$$

Hôtel Le St-James (p157) Refined opulence in a 19th-century building in Old Montréal.

Ritz-Carlton (p161) The Ritz sparkles with elegant decor and world-class service.

Best B&Bs

Le Lit au Carré (p165) Charming three-room inn just a short stroll from one of Montréal's loveliest little parks.

Accueil Chez François (p165) Delicious breakfasts, friendly hosts and good-value rooms.

Alexandre Logan (p162) Rooms at this friendly place are artfully maintained.

Alacoque B&B Revolution (p160) Great value for the attractive rooms and cooked breakfast.

Best Heritage Stays

Auberge Bonaparte (p158) Delve into the past at this inn that would make its namesake proud.

Auberge du Vieux-Port (p158) Original details from the 1880s, plus waterfront views.

Unusual Stays

Héritage Victorien (p162) Period-style rooms are named after the 19th-century family members who resided here.

Hôtel de l'Institut (p165) Great prices and hard-working staff at this training ground for aspiring hoteliers.

A la Carte B&B (p164) Get off the beaten path at this lovely inn in Montréal's east.

Le Petit Hôtel (p157) Rooms come in S, M, L and XL at this boutique stay.

La Citadelle (p160) Feels like a new midrange hotel, but it's actually a student dorm outside summer.

NEED TO KNOW

SLEEPING

Price Range

In our listings the following price codes represent the cost of a double room in high season:

$	less than $75
$$	$75 to $175
$$$	more than $175

Room Rates

➡ In Montréal, the average room rate is around $150, with some seasonal fluctuations (from January to March, rates fall by about 30%).

➡ Prices listed are for high-season travel (June to September) and do not include taxes – another 19% or so.

➡ Hotels charge a premium during the Grand Prix (late May and early June). Check websites for details.

Discounts

We quote rack rates, but prices can vary. Most business and high-end hotels offer discounts, often significant ones, for reservations made in advance – typically on online booking sites or by phone.

Booking Services

Book your hotel well in advance. Good places to browse listings:

➡ **Lonely Planet** (lonelyplanet.com/canada/montreal/hotels) Browse listings and book online.

➡ **BBCanada** (www.bbcanada.com) B&Bs in Montréal and beyond.

➡ **Tourisme Montréal** (☏877-266-5687; www.tourisme-montreal.org) Extensive listings from the city's tourism authority.

Where to Stay

Neighborhood	For	Against
Old Montréal	Ultraconvenient for many sights, old-world charm, access to the Old Port	Crowded with tourists at peak times, few inexpensive rooms, hard to find parking
Downtown	Convenient for public transport and sights throughout the city	Can be congested, with few inexpensive options compared with other districts
Quartier Latin & the Village	Semi-residential area with bohemian charm, restaurants and cafes	Somewhat remote from central sights; has been the center of student protests
Plateau Mont-Royal	Home to the city's most charming B&Bs; atmospheric neighborhood with many parks	Removed from central Downtown and Old Montréal; few key sights

🛏 Old Montréal

Old Montréal has the city's most atmospheric – and highest priced – hotel rooms. Over the past decade or so, many of the area's old buildings have been converted into impeccable boutique hotels with unique ambience and careful, confident service. The proliferation of such distinctive hotels has also inflated the area's B&B and inn rates.

AUBERGE ST-PAUL HOSTEL $

Map p268 (☑438-386-1339; 339 Rue St-Paul Est; dm $20-28, d with shared bath $60-70; P❄🛜; MChamp-de-Mars) In an excellent Old Montréal location, this new hostel has clean-swept rooms with old stone walls, comfortable mattresses and good natural light, with some windows facing onto the picturesque Marché Bonsecours across the road. The welcome is warm and friendly, and all the usual hostel features are here: in-room lockers, kitchen and laundry access, free coffee and tea.

This is a good place to meet other travelers; the hostel arranges pub crawls, music jam sessions, weekend trips out of town and other activities.

AUBERGE ALTERNATIVE HOSTEL $

Map p268 (☑514-282-8069; www.auberge-alternative.qc.ca; 358 Rue St-Pierre; dm incl tax $27-30, r $75-85; @🛜; MSquare-Victoria) This laid-back hostel near the Old Port has a bohemian vibe with an inviting cafe/restaurant where you can mingle with other travelers or enjoy an organic breakfast ($5 extra). Guests bunk in trim, colorfully painted dorms that accommodate anywhere from four to 20 people. There's a laundry and no curfew.

UQAM RESIDENCES APARTMENT $

Map p278 (☑514-987-6669; www.residences-uqam.qc.ca; 303 Blvd René-Lévesque; r from $65; ☉mid-May–mid-Aug; P❄@🛜; MBerri-UQAM) This residence hall at Université de Québec à Montréal (UQAM) offers tidy modern studio apartments with small, fully equipped kitchens in a convenient location not far from the nightlife along Rue St-Denis. It's set in a rather charmless building, and the quarters are simple, but the price is hard to beat. Rooms are available only during the summer.

There's a laundry and a cafe on-site. A second location (at 2100 Rue St-Urbain) near Place des Arts has similar features.

★L HOTEL BOUTIQUE HOTEL $$

Map p268 (☑514-985-0019; www.lhotelmontreal.com; 262 Rue St-Jacques Ouest; d $170-280; P❄🛜; MSquare-Victoria) Inside a grand 1870 building, L Hotel is a major draw for art lovers. Georges Marciano, founder of Guess jeans, opened the hotel in 2010, showering great artworks throughout the rooms and common areas. You might sleep in a room with an original piece by Andy Warhol, Roy Lichtenstein or Frank Stella, or one of scores of other famed artists.

The rooms themselves are uniquely designed (though most tend toward a more refined classical look than a pop-art aesthetic); but all have big windows, high ceilings and luxury finishings.

INTERCONTINENTAL
MONTRÉAL
LUXURY HOTEL **$$**

Map p268 (📞514-987-9900; www.montreal.intercontinental.com; 360 Rue St-Antoine Ouest; d $160-230; 🅿🌼@; MSquare-Victoria) This enormous InterContinental has a unique location between a new high-rise and a restored annex of the 19th-century Nordheimer building. The 357 rooms have a modern, contemporary design done in earthy tones and are fairly spacious. The turret suites are particularly attractive, with superb views to Mont-Royal. There are extensive facilities, including a sauna, 15m lap pool, bar and restaurant.

★HÔTEL NELLIGAN
BOUTIQUE HOTEL **$$$**

Map p268 (📞877-788-2040, 514-788-2040; www.hotelnelligan.com; 106 Rue St-Paul Ouest; d from $220; 🅿🌼@🛜; MPlace-d'Armes) Housed in two restored buildings and named in honor of Québec's famous and tragic poet, Émile Nelligan, this Old Montréal beauty has original details (such as exposed brick or stone) and luxurious fittings (down comforters, high-quality bath products, and Jacuzzis in some rooms). Verses, a plush bar and restaurant, is next door, with a magnificent roof patio, Terrasse Nelligan.

★HÔTEL GAULT
BOUTIQUE HOTEL **$$$**

Map p268 (📞866-904-1616, 514-904-1616; www.hotelgault.com; 449 Rue Ste-Hélène; r from $230; 🅿🌼@🛜; MSquare-Victoria) The Gault delivers beauty and comfort in its 30 spacious rooms. Lovely 19th-century architectural details figure in some rooms, with exposed brick or stone walls, though for the most part it boasts a fashion-forward, contemporary design. Rooms have extremely comfortable beds, ergonomic chairs, high ceilings, huge windows and spotless baths (some with two-person tubs) with heated tile floors.

iPads are available upon request.

LE PETIT HÔTEL
BOUTIQUE HOTEL **$$$**

Map p268 (📞877-530-0360, 514-940-0360; www.petithotelmontreal.com; 168 Rue St-Paul Ouest; r $205-305; 🅿🌼@🛜; MPlace-d'Armes) Set in a 19th-century building, Le Petit Hôtel uses 'small', 'medium', 'large' and 'extra large' to describe its four room classes – identical save for the size. Owned by the same group as the Hôtel Place-d'Armes, its

rooms boast a sleek, contemporary design (polished wood floors, atmospheric lighting and goose-down comforters), while showcasing the old stone walls in some rooms.

You'll also find iPod docking stations, free bike hire and dashes of color – orange – that give a creative zing to the overall look. There's a small spa here and an enticing little cafe, with down-tempo beats, on the ground floor.

AUBERGE BONSECOURS
INN **$$$**

Map p268 (📞514-396-2662; www.aubergebonsecours.com; 353 Rue St-Paul Est; s/d $180-220; 🅿🌼🛜; MChamp-de-Mars) The unusual ambience of these renovated stables lends this secluded hotel particular appeal. All six rooms have exposed brick walls, a cheerful color scheme, designer lighting and floral linen, but each room is cut differently – the front-facing room with pine floors and sloping ceiling is especially popular. All quarters are set around an inner courtyard, remaining blissfully quiet at night.

LE PLACE D'ARMES
HOTEL **$$$**

Map p268 (📞514-842-1887, 888-450-1887; www.hotelplacedarmes.com; 55 Rue St-Jacques; r from $229, ste from $328; 🌼🛜; MPlace-d'Armes) Spread among three regal buildings on the edge of Pl d'Armes, this luxury hotel has stylish rooms, excellent service and a historic location. Rooms have first-class fittings – antique moldings, brick or stone walls, black granite and white marble in the baths, and an entertainment system. Even small quarters feel spacious thanks to views of Mont-Royal or the Basilique Notre-Dame.

There's a full-service spa, fitness center, restaurant and bar, but the crowning touch is the splendid rooftop patio, Terrasse Place d'Armes, which on a summertime night is a magnet for the beautiful crowd.

HÔTEL LE ST-JAMES
BOUTIQUE HOTEL **$$$**

Map p268 (📞514-841-3111; www.hotellestjames.com; 355 Rue St-Jacques; r from $360; 🅿🌼@🛜; MSquare-Victoria) Housed in the former Merchants Bank, the Hôtel Le St-James is a world-class establishment. Lavish guest rooms have beautiful antique furnishings, with oil paintings adorning the walls. There's a candlelit spa, a library and high-tea service. The concierge and staff are particularly kind and helpful, but for dining, you're better off looking elsewhere.

LONGER-TERM RENTALS

The universities offer good deals from May to August, though you should not expect much more than dormitory amenities for the longer-term options.

For a taste of life in the 'real' Montréal, away from the hotel circuit, seek out the clean, trim **Studios du Quartier Latin** (Map p278; ☑514-845-0916; www.studiosquartierlatin. com; 2024 Rue St-Hubert; apt per month $480-980; ✳ 🛜; Ⓜ Berri-UQAM) in the Quartier Latin and the Plateau. All studios generally have fully equipped kitchenette, TV, private telephone and bed linen, plus wireless access.

The modern high-rise **Trylon Apartments** (Map p276; ☑877-843-3971, 514-843-3971; www.trylon.ca; 3463 Rue Ste-Famille; apt per day/week/month from $99/546/1560; Ⓟ ✳ 🛜 🏊; Ⓜ Place-des-Arts) are a plush alternative to top-end hotels at a fraction of the price. The small studios (36 sq meters) and one-bedroom apartments (51 sq meters) have contemporary furnishings with kitchenettes, and guests can enjoy the indoor swimming pool, sauna, exercise room and rooftop terrace. Some rooms have balconies.

AUBERGE DU VIEUX-PORT
BOUTIQUE HOTEL $$$

Map p268 (☑514-876-0081; www.aubergedu vieuxport.com; 97 Rue de la Commune Est; r $200-340; Ⓟ ✳ 🛜; Ⓜ Champ-de-Mars) Set in an 1882 warehouse, this is a stylish boutique hotel with exposed brick or stone walls, wooden beams, wrought-iron beds, high-quality furnishings (including occasional antiques) and big windows overlooking the waterfront. For more space and seclusion (a kitchen, multiple rooms), you can book one of its minimalist **lofts** (www.loftsduvieuxport. com; apt $190-300) in a separate building round the corner.

AUBERGE BONAPARTE
INN $$$

Map p268 (☑514-844-1448; www.bonaparte. com; 447 Rue St-François-Xavier; r $195-255, ste $360; ✳ 🛜; Ⓜ Place-d'Armes) Wrought-iron beds and Louis Philippe furnishings lend a suitably Napoleonic touch to this historic 30-room inn, a former judge's residence built in 1886. The best rooms are warmly decorated and boast high ceilings, dormer windows and bronze lamps. Low-end rooms can seem a little dark and dowdy; and some guests are disappointed with the lack of in-room coffeemakers.

Rooms at the rear overlook a pretty garden with views of the Basilique Notre-Dame. Breakfast is served in the fine Bonaparte Restaurant, which has been done up in Napoleonic Imperial style. There's also a pleasant rooftop terrace.

ÉPIK
BOUTIQUE HOTEL $$$

Map p268 (☑514-842-2634; www.epikmon treal.com; 171 Rue St-Paul Ouest; d/ste from $200/340; Ⓟ ✳ 🛜; Ⓜ Place-d'Armes) Set in a 1723 structure, the Épik is a new boutique hotel with loads of charm. Its 10 beautifully designed rooms have wood-beam ceilings, stone walls and other original details, plus modern flourishes (flat-screen TVs), sleek baths with rain showers, leather armchairs or sofas and elegant bedside lamps.

Enjoy fluffy croissants and fresh-brewed coffee in the morning; in the evening stop in the restaurant for wine and tapas.

LA MAISON PIERRE DU CALVET
HISTORIC INN $$$

Map p268 (☑514-282-1725; www.pierredu calvet.ca; 405 Rue Bonsecours; d $295; Ⓟ ✳ 🛜; Ⓜ Champ-de-Mars) The Pierre du Cavet is the heritage hotel experience par excellence. This historic landmark in Old Montréal was built right into the city defense walls in 1725, and staying here is like stepping back in time: massive stone fireplaces with original carvings, gilded picture frames and four-poster beds surrounded by carefully preserved antiques.

Benjamin Franklin stayed here in 1775 while trying to garner support for the American Revolution. The salon, library, wine cellar and dining rooms all drip the moneyed elegance of the period. There's also a Victorian greenhouse and pretty vine-covered terrace.

HÔTEL ST-PAUL
BOUTIQUE HOTEL $$$

Map p268 (☑514-380-2222; www.hotelstpaul. com; 355 Rue McGill; d $220-300, ste $280-485; Ⓟ ✳ @ 🛜; Ⓜ Square-Victoria) The lobby greets you with a fireplace flickering inside a wall of glowing alabaster – a fine introduction to this beaux-arts hotel on the edge of Old Montréal. Set along dimly lit hallways, the rooms and suites feature high-end mattresses, ambient lighting and large windows, though the design feels a little sparse in the lower-category accommodations.

The St-Paul was gearing for a bottom-to-top renovation in 2016, though it will remain open during the makeover.

🏨 Downtown

The city center is the bastion of the business hotel and large, upper-end chains, but there are some interesting independent hotels, B&Bs and budget establishments scattered throughout the area.

LE GÎTE DU PLATEAU
MONT-ROYAL
HOSTEL $

Map p276 (☑514-284-1276, 877-350-4483; www. hostelmontreal.com; 185 Rue Sherbrooke Est; d $78, dm/d/tr with shared bath from $25/70/65; @🛜; MSherbrooke) This popular youth hostel at the southern end of the Plateau (and the western edge of downtown) has all the expected hostel features (kitchen access, laundry room and lounge), though rooms and facilities are basic. Staff are friendly, and the rooftop terrace and communal lounge are fine places to meet other travelers.

HI MONTRÉAL INTERNATIONAL
YOUTH HOSTEL
HOSTEL $

Map p272 (☑514-843-3317, 866-843-3317; www. hostellingmontreal.com; 1030 Rue Mackay; dm $20-45, r $100; ❄@🛜; MLucien-L'Allier) This large, well-equipped HI hostel has bright, well-maintained dorm rooms (all with air-con) with four to 10 beds, and a handful of private en suite rooms. Rooms are small and, depending on your bunkmates, can feel cramped. Energetic staff organize daily activities and outings (pub crawls, bike tours, day trips), plus there's a lively cafe-bar on the ground floor.

You'll save cash (around $5 per night) with a HI card. There's no curfew and bike hire is available. Reservations are strongly recommended in summer.

HÔTEL Y MONTRÉAL
HOTEL $

Map p272 (☑514-866-9942; www.hotelymontreal. com; 1355 Blvd René-Lévesque Ouest; r $75-130, r with shared bath $55-90; ❄@🛜; MLucien-L'Allier) The YWCA's hotel welcomes both sexes to rooms that are basic but clean – and good value for the city. If you don't mind sharing a bath, opt for the Auberge floor, with clean, quite small private rooms with a sink. Despite the location on busy Blvd René-Lévesque, it's fairly quiet, with rooms on the 6th and 7th floors.

Guests can use the kitchen or laundry facilities, and there's a thrift shop and an unaffiliated cafe on the ground floor. Unfortunately, the Y no longer lives up to its name – there's no fitness center or pool. The money goes to Y programs.

L'ABRI DU VOYAGEUR
HOTEL $

Map p276 (☑514-849-2922, 866-302-2922; www. abri-voyageur.ca; 9 Rue Ste-Catherine Ouest; r with shared bath from $68, studio with bath $135; P❄🛜; MSt-Laurent) It's on a seedy stretch of Rue Ste-Catherine but if you're not turned off by the nearby sex clubs (no pun intended), you can enjoy clean, cozy rooms with exposed brick walls, wood floors and comfortable furnishings. Some rooms are spacious with tiny kitchenettes, while others could use more natural light. Overall, it's good value for money.

★UNIVERSITY BED & BREAKFAST
APARTMENTS
B&B $$

Map p276 (☑866-842-6396, 514-842-6396; www.universitybedandbreakfast.ca; 623 Rue Prince Arthur Ouest; r $115-185; P🛜; MMcGill) Tucked away on a leafy street near McGill University, this handsome three-story townhouse has abundant charm. Accommodations vary in size and style, but have blond-wood floors, wrought-iron beds, classy furnishings and exposed brick. The suites are roomier with modern touches such as flat-screen TVs, kitchenettes and iPod docking stations. Excellent location.

LES BONS MATINS
B&B $$

Map p272 (☑800-588-5280, 514-931-9167; www. bonsmatins.com; 1401 Ave Argyle; r $129, ste $169-189; P❄🛜; MLucien-L'Allier) Charming and seductive with exposed brick walls and vibrantly colored bed sheets and wall hangings, this classy establishment is one of a series of adjoining turn-of-the-century walk-ups. The deluxe room (704) has a private balcony. The deluxe suites are quite stunning, with Jacuzzis and wood-burning fireplaces. Breakfasts are excellent, with omelets, bacon, French toast and Italian-style espresso.

There's one budget room (from $99), which is tiny but attractive; it has a bath outside the room.

HOTEL PARC SUITES
HOTEL **$$**

Map p276 (☑800-949-8630, 514-985-5656; www.parcsuites.com; 3463 Ave du Parc; r/ste from $159/169; P✲🛜; MPlace-des-Arts) Although the building doesn't look promising, this eight-room all-suites guesthouse is a great place to decamp while exploring Montréal. The accommodations range from small studios to only marginally more expensive one-bedroom suites, with a comfy living/dining area and adjoining kitchenette, plus a separate bedroom – all tastefully furnished in a bright, contemporary style.

Staff and owner are friendly and helpful, and deserve kudos for all the freebies thrown in – wi-fi, parking, and long-distance calls to the US and Canada. Mind the steep stairway up to the lobby.

ALACOQUE B&B REVOLUTION
B&B **$$**

Map p276 (☑514-842-0938; www.bbrevolution.com; 2091 Rue St-Urbain; s/d without bath $95/120; P✲🛜; MPlace-des-Arts) This little place offers good rates for its simply furnished rooms. Exposed brick walls and homey touches create a warm ambience, but some beds and furnishings need a refresh. Guests have access to the whole house (kitchen, terrace, garden, dining room and laundry). The included breakfasts are good (croissants, baked goods, homemade jams and eggs cooked to order). There's free parking.

HOTEL 10
BOUTIQUE HOTEL **$$**

Map p276 (☑514-843-6000; www.opushotel.com; 10 Rue Sherbrooke Ouest; d/ste from $169/269; P✲🛜📶; MSt-Laurent) Set in a minimalist art-nouveau building, this designer hotel has contemporary rooms with grays, silvers and creams – giving them an ethereal quality. The baths are sleek and modern (with separate soaking tubs in deluxe rooms), and upper floors have fine views. High marks for the soft, fluffy towels and bathrobes. Avoid the noisy rooms on the lower floors.

CHÂTEAU VERSAILLES
HOTEL **$$**

Map p272 (☑888-933-8111, 514-933-3611; www.chateauversaillesmontreal.com; 1659 Rue Sherbrooke Ouest; r from $175; P🛜; MGuy-Concordia) Spread among three intercon-

nected townhouses, the rooms have a bright color scheme and attractive details (framed art prints and crown moldings), though some rooms are showing their age, the baths need an update and thin walls are a minus. Avoid the street-facing rooms overlooking noisy Rue Sherbrooke.

MANOIR AMBROSE
HOTEL **$$**

Map p276 (☑514-288-6922; www.manoirambrose.com; 3422 Rue Stanley; d $97-150; ✲🛜; MPeel) This hotel consists of two merged Victorian homes in a quiet residential area. Its 22 rooms are comfortably furnished, and the best have nice modern features – iPod docks and large flat-screen TVs – as well as plenty of natural light. On the downside, the hotel feels a bit unpolished and could use an update.

The best rooms are upstairs, so you'll have to hoof it up two or three flights (no lift). Staff are friendly and the location is decent.

AU COEUR URBAIN
B&B **$$**

Map p272 (☑514-439-4003; www.giteaucoeururbain.ca; 3766 Chemin de la Côte des Neiges; s $115-135, d $130-150; P✲🛜; MGuy-Concordia, then bus 165) 🍃 At the foot of Mont-Royal, this striking B&B with a vine-covered courtyard looks like it's been transported straight from Provence. Inside, you'll find a modern style amid small, brightly painted rooms and sun-drenched common areas (dining room, living room and a small gym), where guests are welcome.

The downside: the charm ends at the property line; it's on a busy street across from a hospital. Luckily, street noise is minimal owing to good insulation. Also, it's a long trudge uphill from the metro (but an easy bus ride). Tasty breakfasts showcase products from Québec, while the innkeepers do their best to use sustainable, eco-friendly products such as fair-trade cotton sheets and towels, and mattresses made with natural latex.

LA CITADELLE
HOTEL **$$**

Map p276 (☑514-398-5200; www.mcgill.ca/accommodations/summer; 410 Rue Sherbrooke Ouest; r/ste $119/149; ☉mid-May–mid-Aug; P✲🛜; MPlace-des-Arts) In summer McGill opens its student residence halls to travelers. Lodging is in one of five buildings, each varying in price and features. The pick of the bunch is La Citadelle, a renovated 26-story high-rise with small, handsomely designed rooms with flat-screen TVs, modern bathrooms, plush bedding and superb views (not the dorm rooms we remember). Excellent location.

Other McGill summer options include the nearby hotel-style **Carrefour Sherbrooke** (r $109-$139), the 1960s **New Residence Hall** (r $89) at the foot of Mont-Royal, the budget-oriented **Royal Victoria College** (s/d/tr $45/65/85) and the inviting **Solin Hall** with studios and two-, three- and four-bedroom apartments, near the Atwater market and the Lachine Canal. Check online for details.

ARMOR MANOIR SHERBROOKE   HOTEL $$

Map p276 (☎514-845-0915; www.armormanoir. com; 157 Rue Sherbrooke Est; d incl breakfast $109-149; ☎; Msherbrooke) This engaging conversion of two fine Victorian houses is replete with atmosphere. Its 30 rooms range from small standards to spacious deluxes. The budget rooms are small but cozy with a warm color scheme and attractive furnishings. The best rooms have oversized gilded mirrors, decorative fireplaces and Jacuzzis. Staff are friendly.

HOTEL ZERO 1   HOTEL $$

Map p276 (☎514-871-9696; www.zero1-mtl.com; 1 Blvd René-Lévesque Est; r from $139; ✳☎; MSt-Laurent) This jazzy updated hotel has modern rooms painted in dark, matte-like tones, each with a small kitchenette (minifridge, microwave and sink) and a tiny table and chairs. Rooms in the lower category (Pop) are quite small. There's a lounge-like vibe throughout, and it's steps away from the eateries of Chinatown, or a short stroll uphill to Old Montréal.

Avoid the lower floors due to street noise.

RITZ-CARLTON   LUXURY HOTEL $$$

Map p272 (☎514-842-4212; www.ritzmontreal. com; 1228 Rue Sherbrooke Ouest; r from $480; P✳@☎≋✻; MPeel) This grande dame of Montréal has been impressing guests ever since Liz Taylor and Richard Burton got married here. For its 2012 centenary, it reopened after a four-year, $200 million renovation, with only half as many rooms as before and a new set of luxury residences. Rooms are ultra-opulent, with classic touches and impeccable service.

You can splash out in the Royal Suite, the largest in the city, if you don't mind dropping $10,000 a night.

SOFITEL   LUXURY HOTEL $$$

Map p276 (☎514-285-9000; www.sofitel. com; 1155 Rue Sherbrooke Ouest; d from $251; P✳@☎; MPeel) A solid link in the French luxury chain (and the only Sofitel in Canada), this hotel has stylish, modern rooms and a European feel. Staff hit the right note of sophistication without too much snobbery and the rooms are modern and bright with oversized windows and a subdued color scheme (save for the rich red duvets) with blond-wood details.

LOEW'S HOTEL VOGUE   LUXURY HOTEL $$$

Map p272 (☎514-285-5555; www.loewshotels. com/en/montreal-hotel; 1425 Rue de la Montagne; d from $269; P✳☎; MPeel) This upmarket hotel blends French-empire style with modern luxury. You'll find flat-screen TVs attached to the oversized marble Jacuzzis, an iPod docking station and nicely furnished rooms (though somewhat lacking in individuality). Staff are friendly and efficient, and there's a charming Parisian-style bistro and a small classy bar on-site.

CASTEL DUROCHER   APARTMENT $$$

Map p276 (☎514-282-1697; www.casteldurocher. com; 3488 Rue Durocher; 1-/2-bedroom apt $189/239; P✳@; MMcGill) This family-run establishment occupies a tall, turreted stone house on a peaceful, tree-lined street near McGill University. Those seeking self-sufficiency will find one- or two-bedroom apartments with kitchen units, homey furnishings and artwork covering the walls (the multitalented Belgian owner is an artist, novelist and chocolate-maker extraordinaire). There are discounts for long-term stays.

HOTEL BONAVENTURE   LUXURY HOTEL $$$

Map p276 (☎800-267-2575, 514-878-2332; www.hotelbonaventure.com; 900 Rue de La Gauchetière Ouest; d from $200; P✳@☎≋; MBonaventure) Once part of the Hilton chain, today the Bonaventure is locally owned and has all the deluxe amenities you'd expect in a luxury hotel. All rooms have on-command movies, mahogany furniture, marbled baths and large working areas – and most have panoramic views of downtown. The highlight is the 1-hectare rooftop garden with heated pool, open year-round.

It's connected to the underground city, so you can move around downtown without braving the cold if you visit in winter.

🛏 Quartier Latin & the Village

You'll find a good mix of options in the nightlife-charged areas of the Quartier Latin and the Village. Delightful, superb-quality B&Bs dominate the choices in this part of town. This is also a good place to base yourself, with excellent metro connections and walking access to both downtown and Old Montréal – plus the Plateau is just up the hill.

M MONTREAL   HOSTEL $

Map p278 (☑514-845-9803; www.m-montreal. com; 1245 Rue St-André; dm $18-36, d $80-125; ❄📶; MBerri-UQAM) One of Québec's best hostels, M Montreal makes an excellent base while exploring the city. The rooms are nicely outfitted (though the metal bedframes are a bit institutional), each with a TV and en suite, and some of the rooms have exposed brick walls. The stylish downstairs bar and lounge is the best feature.

There's usually something on: live music, movie nights, karaoke or beer pong. You can also join in on regularly scheduled pub crawls and walking tours.

HOSTEL MONTRÉAL CENTRAL   HOSTEL $

Map p278 (☑514-843-5739; www.hostelmontreal central.com; 1586 Rue St-Hubert; dm/d from $25/85; ❄@📶; MBerri-UQAM) This popular hostel is just steps away from the local bus depot and metro station, and a short stroll from the buzz of Rue St-Denis. Four-, six- and eight-bunk dorms are basic but serviceable, with metal bed frames and tile floors, although in-bed reading lights and in-room fridges are thoughtful features.

Private doubles are clean and simple, but fair value for the price. The usual hostel features are on offer: guest kitchen, laundry and wi-fi throughout. There's also a small terrace and a lobby bar, where you can chat with fellow travelers over a beer.

ALEXANDRIE MONTREAL   HOSTEL $

Map p278 (☑514-525-9420; www.alexandrie-montreal.com; 1750 Rue Amherst; dm $22-30, d with shared bath $70-90; 📶; MBerri-UQAM) Set in a converted multistory brick building, this friendly, welcoming hostel has a good location near the Village and the Quartier Latin. Rooms are clean and nicely maintained with four- to eight-bed bunks and sunny private rooms with shared baths.

The open kitchen and lounge area is a good place to mingle with other travelers.

LE GÎTE DU PARC LAFONTAINE   HOSTEL $

Map p278 (☑514-522-3910, 877-350-4483; www. hostelmontreal.com; 1250 Rue Sherbrooke Est; dm $25, s/tw/d with shared bath from $57/65/70; ☺Jun-Aug; @📶; MSherbrooke) This great summertime option in a converted Victorian house feels more like a guesthouse than a hostel. The rooms are clean, if simply furnished (wood floors and painted wrought-iron beds), and guests can make themselves at home using the kitchen, lounge and laundry. The top-floor terrace, with views over the rooftops, is the best feature.

HÉRITAGE VICTORIEN   B&B $$

Map p278 (☑514-845-7932; www.montrealbed andbreakfast.ca; 305 Rue Ontario Est; r $130-170, ste $150-190; ❄📶; MBerri-UQAM) True to name, this nine-room guesthouse celebrates its Victorian heritage with gorgeous rooms decorated with antiques and boasting period details. You'll find intricately carved wooden headboards, gilt-framed mirrors, clawfoot soaking tubs and portraits from yesteryear, plus modern baths and flat-screen TVs. There's also a garden in back and great buffet breakfasts. Save about $40 per room by staying on weeknights.

Ask the owner about Louise Amelia Monk, who lived with her siblings and parents here in the late 19th century and left behind a diary (on display in the inn).

LA CONCIERGERIE   GUESTHOUSE $$

Map p268 (☑514-289-9297; www.laconciergerie. ca; 1019 Rue St-Hubert; r $130-200; ❄@📶; MBerri-UQAM) Spread across two 1880s greystone buildings, the friendly La Conciergerie offers 17 attractively designed rooms. Each has a queen-sized bed and cheery color schemes, and the best have original details such as crown molding and decorative fireplaces. Only half the rooms have private baths and these tend to be more modern and less characterful than the others.

There's also a lush patio, a Jacuzzi and a small gym.

ALEXANDRE LOGAN   B&B $$

Map p278 (☑514-598-0555, 866-895-0555; www.alexandrelogan.com; 1631 Rue Alexandre-de-Sève; s/d from $110/130, s/d with shared bath from $85/95; ❄@📶; MBeaudry) The friendly host Alain has an eye for details such as original plaster moldings, ornate woodwork and art-deco glass patterns at this award-winning B&B. The splendidly renovated home dates from 1870 and has hardwood floors, high-quality mattresses (two rooms have king-size beds) and big windows, making the rooms bright and cheerful.

Common spaces are also beautifully designed, from the breakfast room to the outdoor terrace complete with flowers and potted plants.

ATMOSPHERE
B&B $$

Map p278 (✆514-510-7976; www.atmospherebb.com; 1933 Rue Panet; d with/without bath from $115/140; ✆; MBeaudry) Set in a beautifully restored 1875 home, Atmosphere lives up to its name. Rooms feature exposed brick, polished wood floors, artful lighting and handsome design flourishes. Rooms and common areas are kept meticulously clean, and Patrick, the friendly host, receives rave reviews for the three-course breakfasts he prepares ($20 extra per person).

The stairs (one steep external, one internal) can be a challenge for those with mobility problems.

AUBERGE LE JARDIN D'ANTOINE
B&B $$

Map p278 (✆514-843-4506; www.aubergelejardindantoine.com; 2024 Rue St-Denis; d/ste from $126/165; ❇@✆; MBerri-UQAM) You'll find a wide range of rooms at this welcoming four-story hotel, handily located in the thick of the Quartier Latin action. Some have carpeting, others have nicely polished wood floors. And while some rooms have classic old-world touches such as exposed brick and wrought-iron bedsteads, others tend toward a modern, cheerful design scheme.

The cheapest rooms are a bit cramped and located on the ground floor. Although it's on busy St-Denis, street noise is rarely an issue owing to double-paned windows.

LA LOGGIA ART & BREAKFAST
B&B $$

Map p278 (✆514-524-2493, 866-520-2493; www.laloggia.ca; 1637 Rue Amherst; s/d $145/170, s/d with shared bath $105/130, studio s/d/tr $165/190/210; P❇✆; MBeaudry) This beautifully maintained B&B has a handful of charming rooms, each with artwork on the walls and attractive furnishings. The best rooms are light and airy with Persian carpets, antique armoires and private baths. Lower-level rooms are a little dark, but still

clean. Good firm mattresses and sound-proof windows ensure a decent night's rest.

For a bit extra, the 'studio' is the pick of the five rooms, with tall ceilings, skylights and colorful artwork. The hosts offer a warm and friendly welcome. Buffet-style breakfasts are simple but adequate.

LE RELAIS LYONNAIS
GUESTHOUSE $$

Map p278 (✆514-448-2999; www.lerelaislyonnais.com; 1595 Rue St-Denis; r/ste $165/275; @✆; MBerri-UQAM) Set in a beautifully restored 19th-century building, Le Relais Lyonnais has seven elegantly furnished rooms. Dark maple floors, exposed brick walls, touches of artwork and wooden blinds give the rooms a classy but masculine look, while white goose-down duvets provide a soft complement. The rooms are a bit small, but high ceilings, oversized windows and rain showers add to the appeal.

Light sleepers beware: front-facing rooms get lots of street noise from lively Rue St-Denis. Suites face the rear and are quieter.

MONTRÉAL ESPACE CONFORT
HOTEL $$

Map p278 (✆514-849-0505; www.montrealespaceconfort.com; 2050 Rue St-Denis; r from $100; ❇@✆; MBerri-UQAM) Back in the '90s this stretch of Rue St-Denis was the stomping ground for the transient and confused, and this address was a notorious flophouse. Things have changed dramatically since then, with this place a shiny example of gentrification in action. Rooms boast trim Ikea-style furnishings, with a desk and a kitchenette, but are quite small.

Street-facing and lower-floor rooms can be noisy (especially on weekends).

AU GÎT'ANN
B&B $$

Map p278 (✆514-523-4494; www.augitann.com; 1806 Rue St-Christophe; r with shared/private bath from $105/150; P❇@✆; MBeaudry) This small red-brick B&B has just a few rooms, all painted in deep, saturated colors (violet, canary yellow, burnt umber), with abstract artwork and comfortable furnishings. The best room (Picasso) has a private bath and tiny balcony. Anne, the doting host, is extremely friendly and happy to share insight about the city. There's a small kitchen for self-catering.

The guesthouse is on a quiet street, a short stroll from the action on Rue St-Denis and just downhill from the Plateau.

GAY STAYS

Any guesthouse in the Village will be gay-friendly – welcoming gay as well as straight travelers. A few perennial favorites include the following:

➡ **La Conciergerie** (p162) Lovely rooms, a terrace and a Jacuzzi.

➡ **Alexandre Logan** (p162) Splendid 19th-century ambience.

➡ **Atmosphere** (p163) Receives rave reviews from readers.

➡ **Turquoise B&B** (p164) Like stepping into a glossy magazine.

➡ **Alacoque B&B Revolution** (p160) Gorgeous antiques in an 1830s setting.

HÔTEL ST-DENIS
HOTEL $$

Map p278 (☎514-849-4526, 800-291-5927; www.hotel-st-denis.com; 1254 Rue St-Denis; d $119-179; P❄☎; MBerri-UQAM) In a good location, this hotel receives positive reviews for its clean, well-maintained rooms with wood floors, trim modern furnishings and comfortable beds. Sizes vary from cramped to rather spacious – avoid the budget rooms if you need space.

For a touch of luxury, opt for the renovated king suites, which have large-screen TVs, iPod docks, a Jacuzzi tub and bath products from Lord & Mayfair.

HÔTEL DE PARIS
HOTEL $$

Map p278 (☎514-522-6861, 800-567-7217; www.hotel-montreal.com; 901 Rue Sherbrooke Est; budget $76-144, d $100-210; P❄☎; MSherbrooke) Inside a turreted Victorian mansion, the Hôtel de Paris doesn't quite live up to its namesake. The most picturesque rooms have balconies overlooking Rue Sherbrooke, though noise should deter light sleepers. Some rooms have been nicely renovated, but the baths are cramped. Budget rooms are small but nicely designed, though some travelers find them a bit expensive.

In the annex across the street are a mix of 'executive rooms,' including several with wood floors, tall ceilings and elegant details (crown molding, decorative fireplaces). It has self-serve continental breakfast.

TURQUOISE B&B
B&B $$

Map p278 (☎514-523-9943, 877-707-1576; www.turquoisebb.com; 1576 Rue Alexandre-de-Sève; s/d with shared bath from $70/90; P❄; MBeaudry) The decor in this plush two-story greystone looks like something out of *Better Homes & Gardens*. Each of the five bedrooms boasts bright colors (yellow, chartreuse or, yes, turquoise) and has a queen-size bed, original moldings and shiny wood floors. Breakfast is served in the large backyard. Baths are shared – there are three for the five rooms.

A LA CARTE B&B
B&B $$

(☎514-593-4005; www.alacartebnb.com; 5477 10th Ave; s/d/apt from $115/130/185; P❄☎; MLaurier, then bus 47) For something completely different, book one of two rooms or a fully equipped two-bedroom apartment at this charming guesthouse in the leafy neighborhood of Rosemont-La Petite Patrie. Rooms are comfortably furnished, and guests can use the dining or living room, and warm up by the wood-burning fireplace on chilly nights.

It's in the eastern part of the city, not far from the Jardin Botanique (2km away). Hosts Petra and Daniel (and their poodle Monsieur Petit) extend a warm welcome. The pair whip up delicious breakfasts and have loads of insight on exploring the neighborhood.

🛏 Plateau Mont-Royal

Staying in the most fashionable district of Montréal means being close to some of the best eateries and nightlife in town. Like the Village, the Plateau is packed with B&Bs; hotels are few and far between.

LE RAYON VERT
B&B $

Map p280 (☎514-524-6774; www.lerayonvert.ca; 4373 Rue St-Hubert; s/d without bath from $67/90; P❄☎; MMont-Royal) This centennial greystone has three comfortable, individual rooms not far from the alternative bustle of Ave du Mont-Royal. Rooms have wood floors and classic wood furnishings (there's even a small chandelier and cornice molding in the Victorian room). The breakfast room recalls a French country inn, but the clincher is the idyllic rear terrace – in summer it's as green as the tropics. Cash only.

LE LIT AU CARRÉ
B&B $$

Map p280 (☑514-524-2506; www.lelitaucarre. com; 3689 Rue Drolet; s/d $135/150, s/d without bath $103/118; ❄@☎; MSherbrooke) On a tree-lined street near leafy Carré St-Louis, this three-room inn rolls out the welcome mat with comfy rooms set in an elegant greystone building. Rooms have hardwood floors, artwork on the walls, a bright color scheme and small balconies (which two rooms share). The cooked breakfasts are excellent.

Unlike many B&Bs, children are welcome, making it a good option for families.

ACCUEIL CHEZ FRANÇOIS
B&B $$

(☑514-239-4638; www.chezfrancois.ca; 4031 Papineau; s/d from $120/145, s/d with shared bath $100/125; P❄☎; MSherbrooke, then bus 24) Overlooking Parc La Fontaine, François indeed gives a warm *accueil* (welcome) to his pleasant and excellent-value five-room guesthouse in the Plateau east. Many guests are repeat visitors, drawn by the spotless and attractive rooms, the delicious breakfasts and the great location (free parking is a bonus).

AUBERGE DE LA FONTAINE
INN $$

Map p280 (☑800-597-0597, 514-597-0166; www. aubergedelafontaine.com; 1301 Rue Rachel Est; r $122-179, ste $159-225; P❄☎; MMont-Royal) A gem of an inn on the edge of Parc La Fontaine, this guesthouse has cheery rooms with comfy beds and touches of artwork. Standard rooms are small, while the best rooms have park views. The spacious suites also have in-room Jacuzzis. The snack refrigerator with free goodies is a nice touch. There's a wheelchair-accessible room available.

GINGERBREAD MANOR
B&B $$

Map p280 (☑514-597-2804; www.gingerbread manor.com; 3445 Ave Laval; r without/with bath from $110/140; P☎; MSherbrooke) The hosts give a warm welcome at this charming B&B near leafy Carré St-Louis. The house itself is a stately three-story townhouse built in 1885 with bay windows, ornamental details and an attached carriage house. The elegant rooms – five in all – are uniquely furnished (only one has a private bath, the others share).

The best rooms have king-size beds and a bay window, but all have decent light. Hot cooked breakfasts (which may include banana walnut pancakes, French toast and fruit salad or croissants) are a bonus.

HÔTEL DE L'INSTITUT
HOTEL $$

Map p280 (☑514-282-5120; www.ithq.qc.ca; 3535 Rue St-Denis; s/d $160/180; P❄☎; MSherbrooke) Set in a sleek glass cube, this modern hotel is run as a training center for the Québec tourism and hotel board. The 42 rooms are well appointed, with oversized flat-screen TVs, iPod docks, a desk and a small couch. They are quite bright, with small balconies – some with decent views. Baths are cramped, but clean and functional.

KUTUMA HOTEL & SUITES
B&B $$

Map p280 (☑514-844-0111; www.kutuma.com; 3708 Rue St-Denis; d/ste from $128/140; P❄☎; MSherbrooke) In an excellent location on lively Rue St-Denis, the Kutuma has the feel of a boutique hotel. Cozy, well-maintained rooms feature safari-theme decor, including animal-print fabrics, potted palms and colorful artwork. Baths are modern and perhaps overly sleek, but the two-person tub in some is a nice feature.

Negatives: some rooms have tiny windows, noise can be an issue on lower floors, and there's no elevator – though staff can help you lug your stuff up the stairs. It's worth dining in the Ethiopian restaurant, Le Nil Bleu, on the 1st floor.

ANNE MA SOEUR ANNE
HOTEL $$

Map p280 (☑514-281-3187; www.annema soeuranne.com; 4119 Rue St-Denis; r $87-220; P❄☎; MMont-Royal) These smart, fully equipped studios fill a valuable niche in the Plateau. They're suitable for short- or long-term stays; each unit has a 'microkitchen' with a microwave and stove, work space and Ikea-style furnishings built into the walls. The cheapest rooms are a little cramped with thin mattresses; others have private terraces, with some overlooking the shady backyard.

Croissants are delivered to your door for breakfast. Noise can be a problem: ask for a room on the garden side, rather than the street side.

SHÉZELLES
B&B $$

Map p280 (☑514-849-8694; www.shezelles. com; 4272 Rue Berri; s/d with shared bath from $80/95, studio s/d $135/150; ☎❄; MMont-Royal) Lyn and Lucie give a warm welcome

THE B&B CONNECTION

For an overview of the many charming B&Bs across Montréal, visit **B&B Canada** (www.bbcanada.com). It currently has more than 40 Montréal B&Bs listed on its network, with photos, room descriptions and reviews.

If you show up in Montréal without a reservation and don't feel like making the rounds, you can always book a place through the city's main tourist office, **Centre Infotouriste** (Map p276; ✆514-844-5400; www.bonjourquebec.com; 1255 Rue Peel; ☺9am-6pm; ☎; ⓂPeel). Keep in mind that it can only book you a room in a guesthouse with which it has an affiliation.

to their cozy four-room guesthouse, which has a warm design of cedar-paneled walls, oak floors and attractive furnishings. The only en suite room has a king-size bed, a kitchenette and a spacious bathroom with a Jacuzzi. The other rooms are smaller but welcoming doubles, each uniquely designed. True to name, the 'skylight room' has a bed directly beneath the skylight, so you might see some stars from your pillow on clear nights.

AU PIANO BLANC
B&B $$

Map p280 (✆514-845-0315; www.aupianoblanc. com; 4440 Rue Berri; s/d from $100/130, without bath from $80/85; ℗☎; ⓂMont-Royal) The 'colors of the sun,' as owner Céline – a former singer, puts it – radiate from this simple five-room B&B a stone's throw from Mont-Royal metro station. Brightly painted rooms, colorful artwork and whimsical bedside lamps add to the good cheer. Some rooms are tiny while others have views of the back terrace.

Some beds are uncomfortable and there's no air-conditioning – only an issue on those torrid August nights.

BIENVENUE B&B
B&B $$

Map p280 (✆514-844-5897, 800-227-5897; www. bienvenuebb.com; 3950 Ave Laval; s/d $110/130, s/d without bath from $85/95; ☎; ⓂSherbrooke) On a peaceful backstreet in the Plateau, Bienvenue is a 12-room Victorian B&B with a range of simple rooms with homey furnishings. The carpeting is a little worn, and some rooms lack air-con and are quite small. Still, all rooms get decent light and some have high ceilings. The hosts are quite friendly and the location is excellent.

There are only three rooms with private baths, though many at least have small sinks.

LE GÎTE
B&B $$

Map p280 (✆514-849-4567; www.legite.ca; 3619 Rue de Bullion; s/d with shared bath from $87/97; ❄☎; ⓂSherbrooke) In a row house just off restaurant-lined Rue Prince Arthur, Le Gîte is a charming B&B. The four rooms have polished wood floors, an attractive minimalist design and striking works of art covering the walls (created by the owner's son). Other nice touches are the small shaded terrace, kitchen use and free laundry.

On the downside, the one shared bath for guests causes a bit of a traffic jam in the mornings, making Le Gîte less than ideal for longer stays.

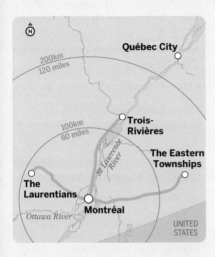

Québec City

OLD UPPER TOWN | OLD LOWER TOWN | ST-JEAN BAPTISTE | MONTCALM |
COLLINE PARLEMENTAIRE | ST-ROCH | STE-FOY-SILLERY

Québec City Top Five

1 Strolling, shopping and admiring the murals, museums and historic buildings in the 17th-century **Quartier Petit-Champlain** (p176).

2 Soaking up spectacular views of **Le Château Frontenac** (p170) from the panoramic riverside boardwalk in summer or the hair-raising toboggan run in winter.

3 Visualizing the legendary rivalry between French and English on a tour of **La Citadelle** (p169).

4 Walking, cycling, cross-country skiing, skating or celebrating **Winter Carnival** (p198) in the city's beautiful and historic Battle-fields Park.

5 Embracing Québec City's festive summer spirit and long day-light hours at street performances along **Terrasse Dufferin** (p171) and open-air concerts in the city's parks.

Explore

The crown jewel of French Canada, Québec City is one of North America's oldest and most magnificent settlements. Its picturesque Old Town is a UNESCO World Heritage Site, a living museum of narrow cobblestone streets, 17th- and 18th-century houses and soaring church spires, with the splendid Château Frontenac towering above it all. There's more than a glimmer of Old Europe in its classic bistros, sidewalk cafes and manicured squares.

You can get a taste of the city in a single day, but linger at least a weekend if you can. The city's compact size makes it ideal for walking, and it shines brightest when you slow down.

The main focus of your visit should be the Old Town, split between the Old Upper Town (Haute Ville), perched above the St Lawrence River on the Cap Diamant cliffs, and the Old Lower Town (Basse Ville), where Samuel de Champlain established the first French foothold in 1608. The Old Town is packed with museums, mansard-roofed houses and cobblestone streets just begging to be explored.

Outside the walls, through the historic town gates of Porte St-Louis and Porte St-Jean, four additional neighborhoods are easily accessible: St-Jean Baptiste, Montcalm, Colline Parlementaire, and St-Roch, each boasting wonderful restaurants, shopping and nightlife. Also noteworthy here are the vast Plains of Abraham, where the British defeated the French in 1759; nowadays enshrined as a national park, this area offers superb recreational opportunities.

Québec City goes to great lengths to entertain visitors. All summer long, musicians, acrobats and actors in period costume take to the streets, while fantastic festivals fill the air with fireworks and song. In the coldest months of January and February, Québec's Winter Carnival (p198) is arguably the biggest and most colorful winter festival around. Fall and spring bring beautiful foliage, dramatically reduced prices and thinner crowds.

Top Tip

Make lunch your main meal. Most restaurants, including some of Québec City's finest, offer midday table d'hôtes (fixed-price menus) for about half the price of a comparable dinner.

The Best...

➡ **Place to Sleep** La Marquise de Bassano (p205)

➡ **Place to Eat** Panache (p190)

➡ **Place to Drink** Le Moine Échanson (p194)

Getting There & Away

➡ **Train** Via Rail (www.viarail.ca) runs four trains daily from Montréal's Gare Centrale to Québec's Gare du Palais (three to 3½ hours, one way/return $87/173).

➡ **Bus** Orléans Express (www.orleansexpress.com) offers frequent bus service from Montréal (three to 3½ hours, one way/return $59/94).

➡ **Car** Driving from Montréal to Québec City takes about three hours, via Hwy 40 (north of the St Lawrence River) or Hwy 20 (south of the river).

➡ **Air** Regular Air Canada flights (45 minutes) run from Montréal to Québec City's Jean Lesage Airport. There are some direct flights from the USA and Europe.

Getting Around

Bus RTC (p240) offers efficient service all around town. To get around the Old Town, your best bet is the nifty Écolobus, which runs on electric power and charges $2 per ride. Single rides on other RTC buses cost $3.25; alternatively, purchase a day pass for $7.50, or a two-day pass for $13.50. The most convenient hub for catching multiple buses is on Pl d'Youville, just outside the Old Town walls. To get here from the Gare du Palais train station or long-distance bus station, take bus 21 or 800.

Need to Know

➡ **Area code** ☏418

➡ **Location** 260km northeast of Montréal

➡ **Tourist Office** Centre Infotouriste (p247)

TOP SIGHT
LA CITADELLE

Towering above the St Lawrence River, this massive, star-shaped fort is a living museum that offers something for all ages. The exhibits on military life from colonial times to today will appeal to anyone interested in Québecois history, while children will be enthralled in summertime by the daily 10am changing of the guard and the beating of the retreat (6pm Saturday).

French forces started building a defensive structure here in the late 1750s, but the Citadelle we know today was built in the early to mid-1800s by the British, who feared two things: an American invasion of the colony and a possible revolt by the French-speaking population (that's why the cannons point not only at the river, but at Québec City itself).

By the time the Citadelle was completed, things were calming down. In 1871, the Treaty of Washington between the United States and the newly minted Dominion of Canada ended the threat of American invasion.

The Citadelle now houses about 200 members of the Royal 22e Régiment. The Vandoos, a nickname taken from the French for 22 *(vingt-deux)*, is the only entirely French-speaking battalion in the Canadian Forces. The second official residence of the governor general (the Queen of England's Canadian representative) has also been located here since 1872.

Hour-long guided tours of the Citadelle are excellent and will give you the lowdown on the spectacular architecture. From late June through October, lantern-lit evening tours are also offered.

DON'T MISS

➡ Summer-only changing of the guard
➡ Beating of the retreat
➡ Panoramas from the northeastern ramparts

PRACTICALITIES

➡ Map p172
➡ ☎418-694-2815
➡ www.lacitadelle.qc.ca
➡ Côte de la Citadelle
➡ adult/child $16/6
➡ ⊙9am-6pm May-Oct, 10am-4pm Nov-Apr

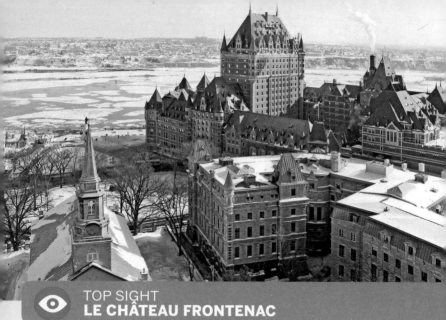

⊙ TOP SIGHT
LE CHÂTEAU FRONTENAC

This audaciously elegant structure is Québec City's most iconic edifice. Its fabulous turrets, winding hallways and imposing wings graciously complement its dramatic location atop Cap Diamant, a cliff that swoops into the St Lawrence River. Over the years, it's lured a never-ending line-up of luminaries, including Alfred Hitchcock, who shot the opening scene of his 1953 mystery *I Confess* here.

It's probably one of the rare hotels where most people in the lobby aren't even guests but rather tourists visiting to get close to the history and architecture (this is the world's most photographed hotel, after all).

Designed by New Yorker Bruce Price (father of manners maven Emily Post), the château was named after the mercurial Count of Frontenac, Louis de Buade, who governed New France in the late 1600s. Completed in 1893, it was one of the Canadian Pacific Railway's series of luxury hotels built across Canada.

During WWII, the Québec Conferences involving British prime minister Winston Churchill, US president Franklin Roosevelt and Canadian prime minister William Lyon Mackenzie King were all held here. Other illustrious guests have included King George VI, Chiang Kai-shek, Princess Grace of Monaco and Paul McCartney.

Sadly, guided tours of the building were discontinued in 2011, but nonguests can still wander through the reception area and stop for a drink or a bite at the hotel's restaurant or bar.

DON'T MISS

➡ A drink in the hotel's panoramic 1608 Bar

➡ Arriving here by *calèche* (horse-drawn carriage)

➡ Views of the château illuminated at night

PRACTICALITIES

➡ Map p172

➡ 1 Rue des Carrières

⊙ SIGHTS

Most of Québec City's sights are found within the compact cluster of Old Town walls, or just outside them, making this a dream destination for pedestrians.

⊙ Old Upper Town

The heart of Québec City, the Old Town is where you will be spending most of your time because it's packed with the city's blockbuster sights and numerous museums on everything from history and the military to religious life in New France. The narrow, winding roads are lined with extraordinary old architecture, with some buildings dating from the 1600s. The grandest military structures, churches and buildings are concentrated in the Old Upper Town.

LA CITADELLE   FORT
See p169.

LE CHÂTEAU FRONTENAC   HISTORIC BUILDING
See p170.

TERRASSE DUFFERIN   PARK
Map p172 Perched on a clifftop 60m above the St Lawrence River, this 425m-long boardwalk is a marvelous setting for a stroll, with spectacular, sweeping views. In summer it's peppered with street performers; in winter it hosts a dramatic toboggan run. Near the statue of Samuel de Champlain, stairways descend to the recent excavations of Champlain's second fort (p175), which stood here from 1620 to 1635. Nearby, you can take the **funicular** (www.funiculaire-quebec.com; one-way $2.25; ⊙7:30am-11pm, to midnight in summer) to the Old Lower Town.

JARDIN DES GOUVERNEURS   PARK
Map p172 (Rue Mont Carmel) Overlooking the St Lawrence River is this leafy gem of a city park, with a monument to legendary generals James Wolfe and Louis-Joseph Montcalm. Even in peak season, it's a peaceful refuge from the holidaying masses.

FORTIFICATIONS OF QUÉBEC
NATIONAL HISTORIC SITE   HISTORIC SITE
Map p172 (✆888-773-8888, 418-648-7016; www.pc.gc.ca/eng/lhn-nhs/qc/fortifications/index.aspx; western entrance 2 Rue d'Auteuil, eastern entrance Frontenac Kiosk, Terrasse Dufferin; ⊙10am-5pm mid-May–mid-Oct, to 6pm Jul & Aug;

🚍3, 11) These largely restored old walls are protected as a Canadian national historic site and a UNESCO World Heritage Site. Walking the complete 4.6km circuit around the walls on your own is free of charge, and you'll enjoy fine vantage points on the city's historical buildings as you trace the perimeter of the Old Town. In summer, 90-minute **guided walks** (adult/child $10/5) are also available, beginning at the Frontenac kiosk (the historic site's information center on Terrasse Dufferin) and ending at Artillery Park. Walks depart at 10:30am and 2:30pm.

ARTILLERY PARK   HISTORIC SITE
Map p172 (www.pc.gc.ca/eng/lhn-nhs/qc/fortifications/natcul/natcul2.aspx; 2 Rue d'Auteuil; adult/child $4/2; ⊙10am-5pm mid-May–mid-Oct, to 6pm Jul & Aug; 🚍3, 7, 11, 28) Open in summer, this park along the Old Town walls was chosen as the site for 18th-century French army barracks, due to its strategic views of the adjacent plateau and the St Charles River, both of which could feed enemy soldiers into Québec City. Visit the **Officers' Quarters** and the **Dauphine Redoubt**, where guides in period dress (ie the garrison's cook) speak in character about barracks life. Don't miss the huge 19th-century model of Québec City in the **Arsenal Foundry**.

After the British conquest of New France, English soldiers moved in and remained here until 1871, when the site was converted into an ammunition factory for the Canadian army. The factory operated until 1964, and thousands of Canadians worked there during the World Wars.

CLIPPETY-CLOPPING THROUGH QUÉBEC'S HISTORIC STREETS

For a scenic journey about town, climb aboard one of Québec City's old-fashioned *calèches* (horse-drawn carriages). While rides are not cheap – $90 for 40 minutes, $170 for 90 minutes, or $250 for two hours (maximum four passengers) – drivers can give you an earful of history as they take you to historic points around the city. Find them by the **Porte St-Louis** (Map p172), in **Parc de l'Esplanade** (Map p172), and at **Place d'Armes** (Map p172) in front of Le Château Frontenac.

Québec City – Old Town

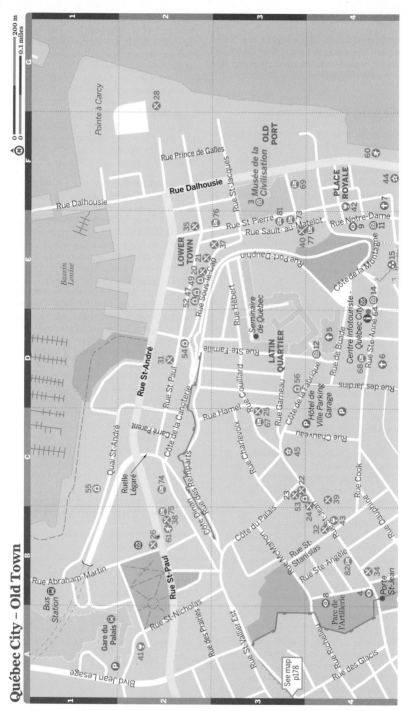

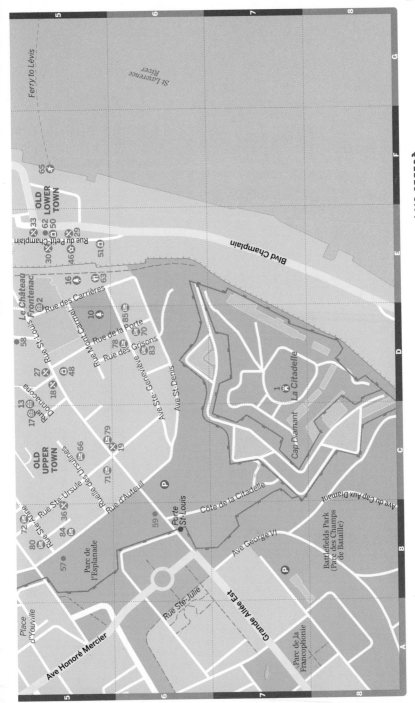

Québec City – Old Town

ST-LOUIS FORTS & CHÂTEAUX NATIONAL HISTORIC SITE   ARCHAEOLOGICAL SITE

Map p172 (www.pc.gc.ca/eng/lhn-nhs/qc/saintlouisforts/index.aspx; adult/child $4/2, incl guided tour $10/5; ⊙10am-6pm mid-May–Aug, to 5pm Sep–mid-Oct) Hidden underneath Terrasse Dufferin are the ruins of four forts and two chateâus constructed by Samuel de Champlain and other early Québec residents between 1620 and 1694. These structures, excavated between 2005 and 2007, served as residences for the French and English governors of Québec for over 200 years before falling victim to bombardment, fire and neglect. In warm weather, Parks Canada offers twice-daily English-language tours of the archaeological site and the artifacts unearthed there.

GOVERNOR GENERAL'S RESIDENCE   HISTORIC BUILDING

Map p172 (☑866-936-4422, 418-648-4322; gg.ca; tours free; ⊙11am-4pm daily Jul & Aug, 10am-4pm daily mid-May–Jun, 10am-4pm Sat & Sun Sep–mid-Oct) FREE Located within Québec's Citadelle, this is one of only two residences in the country where Canada's governor general lives and receives foreign dignitaries. Free 60-minute guided tours are available in warmer weather. It's a small bit of Canadiana right in the heart of Québec.

MUSÉE DE L'AMÉRIQUE FRANCOPHONE   MUSEUM

Map p172 (Museum of French-Speaking America; ☑418-643-2158; www.mcq.org; 2 Côte de la Fabrique; adult/teen/child $8/2/free; ⊙10am-5pm Tue-Sun) On the grounds of the **Séminaire de Québec** (Québec Seminary), this excellent museum is purported to be Canada's oldest. Permanent exhibits exploring seminary life during the colonial era are complemented by temporary exhibitions. The priests here were avid travelers and collectors, and there are some magnificent displays of the scientific objects they brought back with them from Europe, such as old Italian astronomical equipment. There's also a wonderful short film on New World history from a Québecer's perspective.

BASILIQUE-CATHÉDRALE NOTRE-DAME-DE-QUÉBEC   CHURCH

Map p172 (☑418-694-0665; www.nddq.org; 16 Rue de Buade; guided tours $5; ⊙7am-4pm Mon-Sat, 8am-4pm Sun, to 8:30pm daily in summer) Québec's Roman Catholic basilica got its start as a small church in 1647. Despite frequent fires and battle damage over the ensuing years, especially during fighting between British and French armies in 1759, the church was repeatedly repaired and rebuilt, ultimately becoming the much larger cathedral you see today, which was completed in 1925. The interior is appropriately grandiose, though most of its treasures didn't survive the 1922 fire that left behind only the walls and foundations.

Between mid-May and early September, guided tours allow you to visit the basilica's crypt; call ahead or check inside the church for schedules. Everyone from governors of New France to archbishops and cardinals have been laid to rest here.

CATHEDRAL OF THE HOLY TRINITY   CHURCH

Map p172 (☑418-692-2193; www.cathedral.ca; 31 Rue des Jardins; ⊙9am-5pm mid-May–mid-Nov, by arrangement out of season) Built from 1800 to 1804, this elegantly handsome Anglican cathedral was the first ever built outside the British Isles. Designed by two officers from the British army's military engineering corps, it is modeled on London's St Martin-in-the-Fields, with pews built of oak imported from Windsor Castle's Royal Forest. The belltower, an impressive 47m high, competes for attention with the nearby Basilique Notre-Dame. In summer, guides conduct free 10-minute cathedral tours. Out of season, e-mail visit@cathedral.ca to arrange a visit.

Upon its completion, King George III sent the cathedral a treasure trove of objects, including candlesticks, chalices and silver trays. The elaborateness of the gifts heading toward the New World sent London's chattering classes atwitter. The silver

---

ℹ THREE-MUSEUM PASS

Serious museum-goers can save money by purchasing Québec City's three-museum pass, which grants entry into the **Musée de l'Amérique Francophone** (p175), **Musée de la Civilisation** (p179) and **Musée de la Place-Royale** (p179). The cost is $23 for adults, $21 for seniors, $15.50 for students and $7 for children ages 12 to 16; children under 12 are free. Check it out online at www.mcq.org/en/maf/renseignements.html.

CITY OF HISTORICAL SUPERLATIVES

As befits a place that played such a crucial role in the history of the New World, Québec City is awash in historical superlatives. Among other things, the city is home to the continent's first parish church, first Anglican cathedral and first French-speaking university. When you flip through the *Quebec Chronicle-Telegraph* (www.qctonline.com), you're reading North America's oldest newspaper, and if you have to pay a visit to L'Hôtel Dieu de Québec, console yourself with the thought that it's the continent's oldest hospital!

collection is now on permanent display in a new exhibit opened in 2014. The royal box for the reigning monarch or her representative is located in the upper left balcony if you are facing the altar (look for the royal coat of arms).

MUSÉE DES URSULINES MUSEUM

Map p172 (☑418-694-0694; www.ursulines-uc.com/musees.php; 12 Rue Donnacona; adult/youth/child $8/4/free; ☉10am-5pm Tue-Sun May-Sep, 1-5pm Tue-Sun Oct-Apr; ☐3, 7, 11) Housed in a historic convent, this thoughtful, well-laid-out and wheelchair-accessible museum tells the fascinating story of the Ursuline nuns' lives and their influence in the 17th and 18th centuries. The sisters established North America's first school for girls in 1641, educating both Aboriginal and French students. Displays on convent school life are enlivened by a vast array of historic artifacts, including examples of the Ursulines' expert embroidery. The adjoining chapel dates from 1902 but retains some interiors from 1723.

Marie de l'Incarnation, the convent's founder, was one of the most intriguing figures from the order. Leaving a young son in France after she was widowed, she joined the Ursulines and moved to New France, where she lived well into old age. She taught herself Aboriginal languages, and her frequent and eloquent letters to her son back in France are held by historians to be some of the richest and most valuable material available to scholars studying life in the French colony.

MUSÉE DU FORT MUSEUM

Map p172 (☑418-692-2175; www.museedufort.com; 10 Rue Ste-Anne; adult/child $8/6; ☉English shows hourly 10am-5pm Apr-Oct, 11am-4pm Nov-Mar) Completely renovated to celebrate its 50th anniversary in 2015, this mini-museum houses a 30-minute multimedia show that chronicles centuries of attacks on Québec City. It's all played out on a diorama that lights up in the middle of a mini-theater. Even with seven newly installed projectors, it's not exactly high tech, but it does offer a quick, easy-to-grasp audiovisual survey of the battles that shaped Québec City's history. English-language shows are held on the hour, French-language versions on the half-hour.

◉ Old Lower Town

Sandwiched between the Upper Town and the waterfront, this area has the city's most intriguing museums, plus numerous plaques and statues and plenty of outdoor cafes and restaurants along its pedestrian-friendly streets. Street performers in period costume help recapture life in distant centuries.

Teeming Rue du Petit-Champlain is said to be, along with Rue Sous-le-Cap, one of the narrowest streets in North America, and it forms the heart of the **Quartier Petit-Champlain**, the continent's oldest commercial district. Look for the incredible wall paintings that feature on the 17th- and 18th-century buildings.

Place-Royale, the principal square of Québec City's Lower Town, has more than 400 years of history behind it. When Samuel de Champlain founded Québec, it was this bit of shoreline that was first settled. In 1690 cannons placed here held off the attacks of the English naval commander Phipps and his men. Today the name 'Place-Royale' often generally refers to the district.

Built around the old harbor in the Old Lower Town northeast of Place-Royale, the Vieux-Port (Old Port) is being redeveloped as a multipurpose waterfront area.

From the Upper Town, you can reach the Lower Town in several ways. Walk down Côte de la Canoterie from Rue des Remparts to the Vieux-Port or edge down the

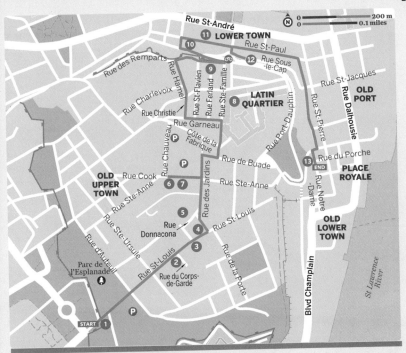

✦ Neighborhood Walk
Historic Stroll Through the Old Town

START PORTE ST-LOUIS
END FRESQUE DES QUÉBÉCOIS
LENGTH 3KM; ONE TO TWO HOURS

This tour encompasses well-known and lesser-known Vieux-Québec attractions. Set off early, before tour buses fill the streets.

Begin at **1 Porte St-Louis**, an impressive gate erected in 1693 (though this version dates from 1878). Follow Rue St-Louis to the corner of Rue du Corps-de-Garde, where a **2 cannonball** sits embedded in a tree (allegedly since 1759). Nearby, **3 47 Rue St-Louis** is where French General Montcalm died, a day after being shot by the British during the destiny-changing Plains of Abraham Battle in September 1759.

At 34 Rue St-Louis, a 1676 home houses the restaurant **4 Aux Anciens Canadiens** (p188). Its steeply slanted roof was typical of 17th-century French architecture. Follow Rue des Jardins to the **5 Ursuline Convent and Museum** (p176), where generations of nuns educated French and Aboriginal girls starting in 1641.

Left down Rue Cook is **6 Edifice Price**, one of Canada's first skyscrapers, built in 1929 for $1 million. Next door, admire the art-deco lobby of Québec City's oldest hotel, the elegant 1870 **7 Hotel Clarendon**.

A short jog along Rue des Jardins and Rue de Buade leads to the Notre-Dame-de-Québec cathedral. To the left is the entrance to the **8 Québec Seminary**; American officers were imprisoned here after their unsuccessful siege of Québec in 1775–76. Detour down Rue Garneau, then descend to **9 Rue des Remparts** for fine views over Québec City's waterfront factory district.

Descend **10 Côte de la Canoterie**, a longtime link between the Lower and Upper Towns. Hope Gate stood atop the *côte* until 1873 to keep the riffraff from entering the Upper Town. Turn right onto **11 Rue St-Paul** (p54), the heart of Québec's antique district, then look at **12 Rue Sous-le-Cap**, a former red-light district. Turn right and follow Rue Sault-au-Matelot to the 420-sq-meter trompe-l'oeil **13 Fresque des Québécois** (p181), where you can pose for requisite photos.

Québec City – Outside the Walls

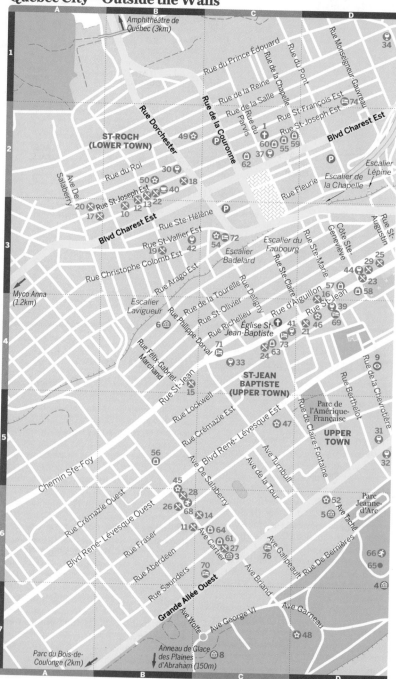

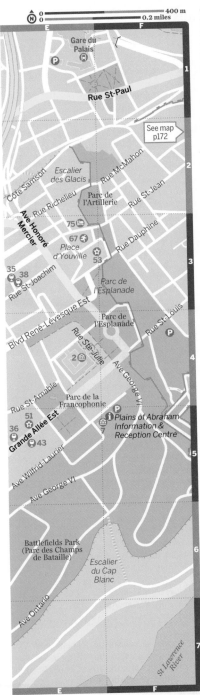

charming and steep Rue Côte de la Montagne. About halfway down on the right there is a shortcut, the Escalier Casse-Cou (Break-Neck Stairs), which leads down to Rue du Petit-Champlain. You can also take the funicular.

★ MUSÉE DE LA CIVILISATION   MUSEUM

Map p172 (Museum of Civilization; ☎418-643-2158; www.mcq.org; 85 Rue Dalhousie; adult/teen/child \$10/3/free, admission free Tue Nov-Mar & 10am-noon Sat Jan & Feb; ☺10am-5pm Tue-Sun) This museum wows you even before you've clapped your eyes on the exhibitions. It is a fascinating mix of modern design that incorporates pre-existing buildings with contemporary architecture. The permanent exhibits, such as the one on the cultures of Québec's Aboriginals and the one titled *People of Québec: Then and Now*, are unique and well worth seeing, and many include clever interactive elements. At any given moment there's an outstanding variety of rotating shows.

This is really the only museum in town that regularly focuses on contemporary issues and culture. Recent special exhibits have focused on topics as diverse as Oceania, ancient Rome, the history of Radio Canada or the work of Québecois writer Michel Tremblay. It's a big place with lots to see, so focus on only one or two exhibitions if you're not planning to make a full day of it.

MUSÉE DE LA PLACE-ROYALE   MUSEUM

Map p172 (☎418-646-3167; www.mqc.org; 27 Rue Notre-Dame; adult/teen/child \$7/2/free; ☺10am-5pm Tue-Sun) This interpretive center touts the Place-Royale neighborhood as the cradle of French history. The exhibits focus on the individual people, houses and challenges of setting up on the shores of the St Lawrence River. It goes a bit heavy on random artifacts, but it still includes some worthwhile displays that help illuminate what local life was like from the 1600s to the 20th century. Children will have lots of fun dressing up in the historical costumes in the basement.

In summer, guides in period garb offer tours of the adjacent Place-Royale.

ÉGLISE NOTRE-DAME-
DES-VICTOIRES   CHURCH

Map p172 (Our Lady of Victories Church; ☎418-692-1650; 32 Rue Sous-le-Fort; ☺9:30am-8:30pm late Jun-Aug, to 4:30pm late May-late Jun) Dating from 1688, and named for French

Québec City – Outside the Walls

victories over the British in 1690 and 1711, this is North America's oldest stone church. It stands on the spot where Champlain set up his 'Habitation,' a small stockade, 80 years prior to the church's arrival. Inside are copies of works by Rubens and Van Dyck. Hanging from the ceiling is a replica of a wooden ship, the *Brézé*, thought to be a good-luck charm for ocean crossings and battles with the Iroquois.

FRESQUE DES QUÉBÉCOIS MURAL

Map p172 (Parc de la Cetière, btwn Rue Notre-Dame & Côte de la Montagne) An obligatory photo stop on any tour of the Old Lower Town, this whimsical multi-story trompe-l'oeil mural was painted in 1998 by a group of artists from Québec and Lyon (France). Samuel de Champlain stands jauntily in the center of the scene, flanked by kids playing hockey and a variety of famous Québecois writers and artists. Step up to the wall and join them!

⊙ St-Jean Baptiste

The heart of this area is Rue St-Jean, which extends from the Old Town west through Porte St-Jean. It's one of Québec's best streets for strolling, with an excellent assortment of colorful shops and restaurants, and hip little cafes and bars. Near the corner of Rue St-Augustin is also where you'll find the epicenter of the city's tiny, unofficial gay 'village.' From Rue St-Jean, take any side street and walk downhill (northwest) to the narrow residential streets like Rue d'Aiguillon, Rue Richelieu or Rue St-Olivier. Note the smattering of outside staircases and row-style houses, some with very nice entrances, typical of Québec City's residential landscape.

⊙ Montcalm & Colline Parlementaire

A stroll west of the Old Town through Porte St-Louis leads to the Montcalm neighborhood, home to several impressive sites, including the historic Battlefields Park, the Québecois parliament building and one of the province's best fine-arts museums. About 10 blocks west of the gate, Ave Cartier is the heart of the upscale Montcalm district, lined with gourmet bistros, cafes, shops and a popular food market (p201).

★ BATTLEFIELDS PARK HISTORIC SITE

Map p178 (Parc des Champs de Bataille) One of Québec City's must-sees, this verdant clifftop park contains the **Plains of Abraham**, site of the infamous 1759 battle between British General James Wolfe and French General Louis-Joseph Montcalm that determined the fate of the North American continent. Packed with old cannons, monuments

and commemorative plaques, it's a favorite local spot for picnicking, running, skating, skiing and snowshoeing, along with Winter Carnival festivities and open-air summer concerts. For information, visit the **Plains of Abraham Information & Reception Centre** (☑418-649-6157, 418-648-4071; www.ccbn-nbc.gc.ca; 835 Ave Wilfrid-Laurier; ⊙9am-5pm Sep-Jun, 8:30am-5:30pm Jul & Aug).

The Plains of Abraham are named for Abraham Martin, a Frenchman who was one of the first farmers to settle in the area. It became an official park in 1908 and has been the site of many modern historical events as well: 'O Canada,' the Canadian national anthem, written by Sir Adolphe Routhier with music by Calixa Lavallée, was sung here for the first time on June 24, 1880.

MUSÉE DES PLAINES D'ABRAHAM MUSEUM

Map p178 (Plains of Abraham Museum; adult/youth/child $12/10/4, incl Abraham's bus tour & Martello Towers $15/11/5; ⊙9:30am-5pm, to 5:30pm Jul & Aug) This museum presents a fine multimedia history show entitled *Battles: 1759–60*. Incorporating maps, scale models, interactive games, period uniforms and clever audiovisual presentations, the exhibit immerses visitors in the pivotal 18th-century battles that shaped Québec's destiny during the Seven Years' War between France and England. The experience is enlivened by firsthand accounts from the French, British, Canadian, and Amerindian protagonists of the period.

In July and August, museum visitors can pay a small extra fee to visit the nearby Martello Towers and take the guided Abraham's Bus Tour (p202).

MARTELLO TOWER 1 HISTORIC BUILDING

Map p178 (☑418-648-4071; adult/youth/child incl Plains of Abraham Museum & Abraham's Bus Tour $15/11/5; ⊙9:30am-5:30pm Jul-early Sep) Despite its small appearance, this early 19th-century defensive tower on the Plains of Abraham – one of four originally built by the British – is jam-packed with fascinating exhibits that explore the towers' engineering history and living conditions for the soldiers based here. History buffs can also seek out the nearby **Martello Tower 2** (Map p178; cnr Ave Taché & Ave Wilfrid-Laurier; ⊙Feb, Jul, Aug & Oct) and **Martello Tower 4** (Map p178; Rue Lavigueur), usually closed to the public but viewable from the outside.

GUIDED WALKING TOURS

Several companies offer guided walking tours of the city; look for them on the left side as you enter the tourist office opposite Le Château Frontenac. Here are a few themed itineraries to get you started:

➡ **Place-Royale from the Present to the Past** (www.mcq.org/place-royale) Visitors can download this free, self-guided podcast tour of the Old Lower Town, produced by the Musée de la Civilisation. The historic walking circuit is divided into five distinct zones surrounding Place-Royale.

➡ **Ghost Tours of Québec** (Map p172; ☑418-692-9770; www.ghosttoursofquebec.com; 34 Blvd Champlain; adult/youth/child under 10 $20/17/free; ⊘English tour 8pm May-Oct) This lantern-lit, 90-minute walking tour of the Old Town, led by a guide in period costume, recounts a series of ghost stories and tales of murders and hauntings, providing a spooky perspective on Québec's historic streets. Tours depart from 94 Rue du Petit Champlain in the Old Lower Town. Tickets may be reserved by phone, online, or at Ghost Tours' office on Blvd Champlain.

➡ **Gourmet Food Tour** (Map p172; ☑866-694-2001, 418-694-2001; www.tours voirquebec.com; 12 Rue Ste-Anne; adult/child $43/25; ⊘tours 2:30pm daily May-Oct, Tue-Sat Nov-Apr) Winding through the St-Jean Baptiste neighborhood, this 2½-hour culinary tour offers tastings of wines, cheeses, crepes, chocolate, maple products and other Québecois specialties at a variety of shops and restaurants. From November through April, a two-person minimum is required to guarantee departure. It's one of several city tours offered by the same company.

(In case you're wondering, Martello Tower 3 was torn down in 1905.)

Inside the park, Martello Tower 2 opens to the public only for special events, which vary from year to year. Recent years have seen it converted into a spooky 'haunted tower' for Halloween; inquire at the Plains of Abraham Information & Reception Centre (p181) for info about current offerings. Martello Tower 4 is in the St-Jean-Baptiste neighborhood between Rue Félix-Gabriel-Marchand and Rue Philippe-Dorion.

MUSÉE NATIONAL DES
BEAUX-ARTS DU QUÉBEC   MUSEUM
Map p178 (☑866-220-2150, 418-643-2150; www.mnbaq.org; Battlefields Park; adult/youth/child $18/5/free; ⊘10am-5pm Tue-Sun Sep-May, 10am-6pm daily Jun-Aug, to 9pm Wed year-round) Carve out at least half a day to visit this excellent art museum. Long one of the province's best, it's slated to expand significantly in 2016 with the opening of the 15,000-sq-meter Pavillion Pierre-Lassonde. Permanent exhibitions range from art in the early French colonies to Québec's abstract artists, with individual halls devoted entirely to 20th-century artistic giants such as Jean-Paul Lemieux and Jean-Paul Riopelle. Another highlight is the Brousseau Inuit Art Collection, a 2639-piece personal collection spanning 50 years.

The museum hosts frequent exhibitions from abroad and elsewhere in Canada. Among its four halls is the Pavilion Charles-Baillairgé, Québec City's former prison. Audioguides are available for the permanent collections and often for temporary exhibitions as well. Other events include film screenings (often documentaries on prominent international artists), drawing and painting classes open to the public, and a concert series.

If all this cultural activity is wearing you out, you can grab a snack or the daily lunch special at the on-site **cafe**, or visit the museum's **restaurant**, which enjoys superb views of Battlefields Park from its bay windows and outdoor terrace.

HÔTEL DU PARLEMENT   HISTORIC BUILDING
Map p178 (Parliament Building; ☑418-643-7239; www.assnat.qc.ca/en/visiteurs; 1045 Rue des Parlementaires; ⊘9am-4:15pm Mon-Fri year-round, plus 10am-4:15pm Sat & Sun late Jun-Aug) **FREE** Home to Québec's Provincial Legislature, the Parliament building is a Second Empire structure completed in 1886. Free 30-minute tours, offered in English and French year-round, get you into the **National Assembly Chamber**, the **Legislative Council Chamber** and the **Speakers' Gallery**. The facade is decorated with 23 bronze statues of significant provin-

cial historical figures, including explorer Samuel de Champlain (1570–1635), early New France governor Louis de Buade Frontenac (1622–98) and the legendary generals James Wolfe (1727–59) and Louis-Joseph Montcalm (1712–59).

On the grounds are more recent figures in Québec's tumultuous history, including Maurice Duplessis (1890–1959), who kept a stranglehold on the province during his 20-year-long premiership. The grounds are also used for staging events during Winter Carnival. Note the flower-trimmed fountain facing the grounds, installed in 2008 to celebrate Québec City's 400th anniversary. It's a fine vantage point for photographing the building.

LA MAISON HENRY-STUART
HISTORIC BUILDING

Map p178 (☑800-494-4347, 418-647-4347; www.maisonhenrystuart.qc.ca; 82 Grande Allée Ouest; adult/child $8/3; ⊙11am-5pm Tue-Sat late Jun–late Aug) This handsomely preserved cottage, built in 1849, once belonged to an upper-middle-class Anglophone family, and contains period furnishings from the early 1900s. Guided tours help elucidate what life was like in those days; tea and lemon cake (included in the tour price) make it all seem that much sweeter. A small but verdant garden surrounds the cottage. Tours are offered hourly; call for the latest schedule.

OBSÉRVATOIRE DE LA CAPITALE
NOTABLE BUILDING

Map p178 (Capital Observatory; ☑888-497-4322, 418-644-9841; www.observatoirecapitale. org; 1037 Rue de la Chevrotière; adult/child $10.25/free; ⊙10am-5pm daily Feb–mid-Oct, closed Mon mid-Oct–Jan) Head 221m up to the 31st floor for great views of the Old Town, the St Lawrence River and (if it's clear enough) even the Laurentians. It all helps to get your bearings, while the information panels along the way will get you up to speed on some of the local history.

◉ St-Roch

Sprinkled with stylish night spots, eclectic eateries, boutiques and vintage shops, St-Roch – 1km west of the Old Town – is one of Québec City's trendiest neighborhoods. Long a working-class district for factory and naval workers, it suffered through three decades of dereliction before experiencing a remarkable rebirth in the 1990s, thanks to an ambitious urban renewal plan that created a public garden, restored a shuttered theater and hired artists to paint frescoes in the neighborhood. Today, the main commercial thoroughfare, Rue St-Joseph, draws a dynamic mix of locals, including many students, immigrants, artists and young professionals.

Thanks to the **Ascenseur du Faubourg**, a free elevator that eliminates much of the climb, pedestrians can get from Rue St-Joseph to Rue St-Jean in 15 minutes or less.

ÉGLISE ST-ROCH
CHURCH

Map p178 (☑418-524-3577; www.saint-roch. qc.ca; 590 Rue St-Joseph Est; ⊙9am-5pm May-Oct, 10am-4pm Nov-Apr) There are giants and then there is this, the biggest church in Québec City. Measuring over 80m long, 34m wide and 46m high including the steeples, it was built between 1914 and 1923. When the original architects died, the neo-Gothic, neo-Roman structure was finished off by Louis-Napoléon Audet, the same man who worked on the monumental Ste-Anne-de-Beaupré Basilica 35km to the east. The marble inside the church is from Saskatchewan. See if you can find faint fossil imprints in it.

In mid-August the church hosts its annual **Bénédiction des Chiens** (Benediction of the Dogs), an event unparalleled elsewhere in Canada. This is followed in September by the **Festival International des Musiques Sacrées de Québec** (Festival of Sacred Music). Both are wonderful times to see the church at its best.

◉ Ste-Foy-Sillery

Ste-Foy and Sillery were actually two separate neighborhoods before municipal mergers joined them together. Both are about 5km west of downtown Québec City, although each still retains its own distinct character. Ste-Foy, roughly north of Blvd Laurier, has a stranglehold on the city's malls but is enlivened by the student population at Université Laval. Sillery, which is roughly south of Blvd Laurier, has leafy streets lined with affluent homes; places like Ave Maguire are lined with charming cafes. Aside from the aquarium, there isn't much here in the way of sights, but if you're in the neighborhood you should make sure to drop by the **Pointe à Puiseaux** down at

QUÉBEC CITY SIGHTS

the foot of Rue d'Église. Here you can take in a gorgeous view of the St Lawrence River.

AQUARIUM DU QUÉBEC
AQUARIUM

(☎866-659-5264, 418-659-5264; www.sepaq.com/ct/paq; 1675 Ave des Hôtels; adult/child $18/9; ⊙9am-5pm Jun-Aug, 10am-4pm Sep-May) Spread across 40 hectares, Québec's aquarium contains some 10,000 aquatic creatures, including freshwater and saltwater fish, amphibians, reptiles, invertebrates and marine mammals. Among its several habitats are a wetlands region and an arctic sector complete with underwater window for observing polar bears. Catch daily events like walrus and polar bear feedings and a trained harbor seal show. Times vary throughout the year; see the website for details. It's 11km west of the city center, near the Pont Pierre Laporte bridge.

There's also a food court with a terrace overlooking the river.

PARC DU BOIS-DE-COULONGE
PARK

(☎418-528-0773, 800-442-0773; 1215 Grande Allée Ouest; ⊙6am-11pm) Not far west of the Plains of Abraham lie the colorful gardens of this park, a paean to the plant world and a welcome respite from downtown. Once the private property of a succession of Québec's and Canada's religious and political elite, this wonderful mix of woodland and extensive horticultural displays has been managed as a public park since 1996.

🍴 EATING

Québec City's restaurant scene has never been better. While the capital has always excelled at classic French food, in recent years a number of new arrivals have put a trendy modern spin on the bistro experience. At the same time, some of the city's most famous chefs have begun embracing the concept of *cuisine boréale*, which emphasizes a return to indigenous northern ingredients such as wild game, seafood, mushrooms, apples, berries and root vegetables. Many of the better places can get a bit pricey, but don't write them off. Do what the locals do; a carefully chosen *table d'hôte* at lunchtime will give you exactly the same food for a more manageable price.

🍴 Old Upper Town

Be choosy about where you spend your money in the Old Town. Though many restaurants have gorgeous settings, and may be fine for coffee, tea or a beer, food can often be disappointing.

★ PAILLARD
CAFÉ-BOULANGERIE
BAKERY, SANDWICHES $

Map p172 (www.paillard.ca; 1097 Rue St-Jean; sandwiches $8-10; ⊙7am-9pm Sun-Thu, to 10pm Fri & Sat) At this bright, buzzy and high-ceilinged space, diners seated at long wooden tables tuck into tasty gourmet sandwiches, satisfying soups and fresh salads. The attached bakery, with its alluring display cases, is downright irresistible – try the *tentation*, a delicious sweet pastry loaded with berries, or indulge in a savory *fougasse* (Provençal-style bread brushed with olive oil and studded with olives and herbs). It's a bit of a madhouse at lunchtime.

CASSE CRÊPE BRETON
CREPERIE $

Map p172 (☎418-692-0438; www.cassecrepebreton.com; 1136 Rue St-Jean; crepes $4.75-9.25; ⊙7am-9:30pm; ⏺) Tiny and unassuming, this perennial favorite specializes in crepes both sweet and savory, along with sandwiches, soups and salads. Some diners like to sit at the counter and watch the chef at work. Seating is first-come, first-served.

CHEZ TEMPOREL
CAFE $

Map p172 (☎418-694-1813; www.facebook.com/cheztemporel; 25 Rue Couillard; mains $11-17; ⊙9am-5pm Sun-Wed, to 9pm Thu-Sat) Hidden away on a side street just off the beaten path, this charming little cafe serves tasty sandwiches, homemade soups and quiches, plus prodigious salads, fresh-baked goods and excellent coffees. It attracts a curious mix of locals and travelers.

CHEZ ASHTON
FAST FOOD $

Map p172 (☎418-692-3055; www.chez-ashton.com; 54 Côte du Palais; mains $4-10; ⊙11am-11:30pm Sun-Wed, to 4am Thu-Sat) For a break from fine dining, head to this Québec City fast-food institution with dozens of restaurants across town. On weekends, revelers flock here in the wee hours of the morning to refuel with the classic Québecois comfort food, poutine (fries smothered in cheese curds and gravy). Ashton also whips up roast-beef sandwiches and decent burgers.

QUÉBEC CITY DINING TIPS

Opening Hours & Meal Times

Most restaurants in Québec City are open for lunch and dinner in the off-season and from about 11am to whenever the last customer leaves in peak summer season or during Winter Carnival. Standard lunch hours are noon to 2:30pm, with dinner from 6pm to 10pm. Places really tend to fill up from 8pm onwards in the francophone tradition. Note that outside of Winter Carnival, many restaurants in winter may be closed Sunday and Monday, or both. Breakfast cafes open around 7am (later on weekends).

How Much?

Midrange places in Québec City will, on average, charge $15 to $30 for a main course. Top-end restaurants run upwards of $30 for a main; a culinary temple of some renown might charge $60 to $100 or more for a four-course gourmet dinner, including wine. Count on $6 to $10 for a glass of drinkable red and $25 to $35 (and up) for a bottle from the house cellar. Taxes amounting to nearly 15% apply at all restaurants. Most do not include taxes in their menu prices, nor do we include them in the price ranges listed here.

Booking Tables

If you're in Québec City between May and October, or during Winter Carnival, definitely book ahead to dine in one of the finer restaurants. During this peak season, popular places can fill up quickly, even at odd times like Monday nights.

Tipping

A tip of 15% of the pretax bill is customary in restaurants. Most credit card machines in Québec will calculate the tip for you based on whatever percentage you specify, or allow you to tip a dollar amount of your own choosing. Some waiters may add a service charge for large parties; in these cases, no tip should be added unless the service was extraordinary. If tipping in cash, leave the tip on the table or hand it directly to staff.

CONTI CAFFE   ITALIAN **$$**

Map p172 (☑418-692-4191; www.conticaffe.com; 32 Rue St-Louis; mains $20-36; ⏰11:30am-11pm) Set on busy Rue St-Louis, this handsome eatery features an enticing mix of Mediterranean flavors. Start off with prosciutto-wrapped shrimp or Cognac-infused lobster bisque, then move on to duck-confit risotto, or grilled lamb chops with fresh rosemary. The dining room is a warmly lit retreat, with exposed brick walls trimmed with art and big windows overlooking the street.

The lunchtime table d'hôte ($13 to $19 for soup or juice, main dish, coffee and dessert) is one of the Old Town's best deals.

BELLO RISTORANTE   ITALIAN **$$**

Map p172 (☑418-694-0030; www.belloristorante.com; 73 Rue St-Louis; mains $16-42; ⏰11:30am-11:30pm) Luc Ste-Croix, former student of French master chef Paul Bocuse, brings his passion for Italian cuisine to this welcoming new eatery near Porte St-Louis. The vast menu ranges from wood-fired pizzas to veal scaloppine to scrumptious risottos. Save room at dessert-time for tiramisu, made the right way with real mascarpone, and finish your evening with a flaming alcohol-infused coffee.

CHEZ BOULAY   BISTRO **$$**

Map p172 (☑418-380-8166; www.chezboulay.com; 1110 Rue St-Jean; lunch menus $17-26, dinner mains $20-34; ⏰11:30am-10pm Mon-Fri, 10am-10pm Sat & Sun) Renowned chef Jean-Luc Boulay's latest venture serves an ever-evolving menu inspired by seasonal Québecois staples such as venison, goose, wild mushrooms and Gaspé peninsula seafood. Lunch specials and charcuterie (cold cuts) platters for two (served 2pm to 5pm) offer an affordable afternoon pick-me-up, while the sleek, low-lit dining area with views of the open kitchen makes a romantic setting for dinner.

.e Château Frontenac (p170) 2. Rue du Petit-Champlain (p176)
lce slide, Carnaval de Québec (p198)

Québec City Top Five

Québec City's historic architecture, dramatic setting and French-Canadian flair make it one of North America's most irresistible destinations. The city's simple charms – strolling atop the Old Town walls or indulging in classic *boulangeries* and bistros – are accessible year-round. Here are five don't-miss attractions:

Quartier Petit-Champlain

Centerpiece of Québec City's 17th-century Old Lower Town, Rue du Petit-Champlain (p176) is most picturesque when seen from the steep heights of Escalier Casse-Cou (Break-Neck Stairs) or from Québec's cliff-hugging funicular. Turn the corner to discover Place-Royale, the city's original square, and the Fresque des Québécois, a whimsical mural featuring Samuel de Champlain and other historical figures.

Le Château Frontenac

The crowning jewel in Québec City's harmonious collection of architectural treasures, this 19th-century **hotel** (p170) is attractive inside and out. Admire it from the boardwalk below, or grab a seat at the hotel bar for sweeping river views.

La Citadelle

Straddling the Plains of Abraham, where France's New World fortunes took a dramatic downhill turn, this star-shaped **fort** (p169) provides stunning Old Town perspectives and a perfect backdrop for understanding Québec's history.

Winter Fun

You haven't really seen Québec City until you've toured the ice sculptures and fur-lined beds of the **Ice Hotel** (p207) or paraded through the streets with Bonhomme de Carnaval, the friendly snowman and official mascot of Québec's **Winter Carnival** (p198).

Summer Festivals

Summertime in Québec City is a never-ending party, with street performers on **Terrasse Dufferin** (p171), spectacular fireworks displays, and open-air concerts in the city's magnificent parks.

AUX ANCIENS CANADIENS   QUÉBECOIS $$

Map p172 (📞418-692-1627; www.auxanciens canadiens.qc.ca; 34 Rue St-Louis; mains $22-92, 3-course menu from $20; ⏱noon-9:30pm) Housed in the historic Jacquet House, which dates from 1676, this place is a well-worn tourist destination, specializing in robust country cooking and typical Québecois specialties served by waitstaff in historic garb. The *menu du jour*, offered from noon to 6pm, is by far the best deal at $20 for three courses, including a glass of wine or beer.

Traditional dishes featured on the menu include bison Bourguignon in cream and blueberry wine sauce, duckling in a maple-syrup reduction, Lac St-Jean meat pie, and wild caribou filet mignon. The restaurant gets its name from the novel *Les Anciens Canadiens* by Philippe-Aubert de Gaspé, who lived in the house from 1815 to 1824. The original rooms have been left intact, resulting in several small, intimate dining areas.

LE PAIN BÉNI   QUÉBECOIS $$

Map p172 (📞418-694-9485; www.painbeni. com; 24 Rue Ste-Anne; mains $23-33; ⏱7:30am-10:30pm daily May-Oct, 7:30-10am daily, 11:30am-2:30pm Tue-Fri & 5:30-10pm Tue-Sat Nov-Apr) A great gourmet outing can be had at this small, unpretentious dining room inside the Auberge Place d'Armes (p207). Le Pain Béni serves an excellent assortment of dishes with Québec highlights. Recent favorites include roasted Québec quail with morel mushrooms, deer tartare with bacon and aged cheddar, and house-made black pudding with star anise. Delectable desserts are the coup de grâce.

LE PETIT COIN LATIN   CAFE $$

Map p172 (📞418-692-0700; 8½ Rue Ste-Ursule; mains $12-30; ⏱7:30am-10pm) For omelets, croissants and bowls of café au lait, this cafe makes a cheerful breakfast stop, especially in summer when the sunny back patio is open. The menu also includes salads, soups and *tourtière* (Québecois elk meat pie). For a cozy wintertime treat, couples can share a *raclette* (a make-your-own Swiss dish of melted cheese, potatoes, grilled meat and pickles).

★LE SAINT-AMOUR   FRENCH, QUÉBECOIS $$$

Map p172 (📞418-694-0667; www.saint-amour. com; 48 Rue Ste-Ursule; mains $40-52, fixed-price menus $68-115; ⏱11:30am-2pm Mon-Fri & 6-10pm daily) One of Québec City's top-end darlings, Le Saint-Amour has earned a loyal following for its beautifully prepared grills and seafood. The soaring greenhouse-style ceiling trimmed with hanging plants creates a warm, inviting setting, and the midday table d'hôte ($25 to $33, available weekdays only) offers that rarest of Upper Town experiences – a world-class meal at an extremely reasonable price.

Perhaps more impressive than the food is the excellent wine selection, with over 10,000 bottles in the cellar.

LE PATRIARCHE   FUSION $$$

Map p172 (📞418-692-5488; www.lepatriarche. com; 17 Rue St-Stanislas; menus $87-107; ⏱5:30-10pm Tue-Sat) The imaginative culinary creations seem almost too lovely to eat at this top-class restaurant, where contemporary artwork hangs on 180-year-old stone walls and ingredients are sourced from an impressive roll call of local suppliers. Choose from three menus nightly, each finished off with a selection of cheeses or Patriarche's trademark *dessert en tryptique*, a trio of stunning desserts.

✕ Old Lower Town

Rue St-Paul, Rue Sault-au-Matelot and Rue du Petit-Champlain are lined with restaurants. In warm weather, they fling their windows open and set up outdoor seating on the streets, creating a terrific atmosphere. In winter the streets outside may be deserted, but the revelry packs indoors, and windows positively glow with the warmth and good cheer inside. Many of the best bistros in town are located here.

BUFFET DE L'ANTIQUAIRE   DINER $

Map p172 (www.buffetdelantiquaire.com; 95 Rue St-Paul; breakfast $5-11, mains $13-19; ⏱6am-9pm) Tucked in among the antique shops and galleries is this convivial old-school diner. Locals and tourists alike crowd in for hearty breakfasts, steaming plates of poutine, savory meat pies and other tasty comfort fare, all served with friendly efficiency by the lone, peripatetic waitress. Grab a booth, a seat at the narrow counter, or a table on the upstairs balcony.

In warm weather, there are also sidewalk tables out front.

SO-CHO
FAST FOOD $

Map p172 (www.so-cho.com; Marché du Vieux-Port, 160 Quai St-André; sandwiches $5.50; ⊙9am-6pm Mon-Fri, to 5pm Sat & Sun) For a snack on the go, locals favor this humble stand inside Marché du Vieux-Port (p199), with its ever-changing array of delectable homemade sausages. Four to 12 flavors are offered each day, from *fines herbes* to lamb with mint and garlic, to be enjoyed on a roll with sauerkraut and mustard.

LE PETIT COCHON DINGUE
CAFE $

Map p172 (☑418-694-0303; www.facebook.com/lepetitcochondingue; 24 Blvd Champlain; mains $7-12; ⊙7:30am-10pm) Near the foot of the funicular, this dapper if touristy cafe and patisserie makes a convenient destination for breakfast, coffee, salads, baguette sandwiches, grilled panini, draft beer and desserts.

★L'ÉCHAUDÉ
FRENCH $$

Map p172 (☑418-692-1299; www.echaude.com; 73 Rue Sault-au-Matelot; lunch menus $15-28, dinner mains $22-36; ⊙11:30am-2:30pm & 5:30pm-11pm Mon-Fri, 10am-2pm & 5:30pm-11pm Sat & Sun) Everything comes beautifully plated and bursting with flavor at this relaxed but classy bistro, one of the rare Old Town eateries where locals regularly outnumber tourists. Classics such as duck confit, *steak frites* and salmon tartare share the menu with daily specials like fish and mussel stew in a lobster-and-wine broth. The terrific wine list favors bottles from France.

LE LAPIN SAUTÉ
FRENCH $$

Map p172 (☑418-692-5325; www.lapinsaute.com; 52 Rue du Petit-Champlain; mains $16-26; ⊙11am-10pm Mon-Fri, 9am-10pm Sat & Sun) Naturally, *lapin* (rabbit) plays a starring role at this cozy, rustic restaurant near the foot of the funicular, in dishes like rabbit cassoulet or rabbit and mushroom puff pastry pie. Other enticements include salads, French onion soup, charcuterie platters and an excellent-value lunch menu (from $15). In good weather, sit on the flowery patio overlooking tiny Félix Leclerc park.

All of the rabbit served here is raised without hormones or antibiotics on a farm in nearby Beauce.

LÉGENDE
QUÉBECOIS $$

Map p172 (☑418-614-2555; www.restaurantlataniere.com; 255 Rue St-Paul; mains $26-32; ⊙5-10pm Sat-Tue, 11:30am-10pm Wed-Fri) Seasonal cuisine and fine wine pairings are the name of the game at this classy newcomer under the direction of renowned restaurateurs Karen Therrien and Frédéric Laplante. Québecois oysters, mackerel, lamb and duck share the menu with artisanal cheeses and specialty ingredients such as birch syrup, chanterelle mushrooms or fiddlehead ferns.

All dishes can be ordered as appetizers or main courses, accompanied by sommelier-selected wines ($6 to $16 per glass).

CAFÉ ST-MALO
BISTRO $$

Map p172 (☑418-692-2004; www.lecafestmalo.com; 75 Rue St-Paul; mains $18-34; ⊙11:30am-2pm & 5:30-10pm) For cozy French bistro atmosphere, you can't beat this cute, traditional hole-in-the-wall down by the Vieux-Port. The menu abounds in bistro classics like homemade cassoulet, *moules marinière* (mussels with garlic, parsley and white wine) and *boudin noir grillé aux pommes* (grilled blood sausage with apples), complemented by Québecois-influenced choices like venison ravioli or grilled salmon with sorrel sauce.

LE MISTRAL GAGNANT
PROVENÇAL $$

Map p172 (☑418-692-4260; www.mistralgagnant.ca; 160 Rue St-Paul; mains $18-34, menus $27-41; ⊙11:30am-2pm & 5:30-9pm Tue-Sat) The sunny flavors of Provence prevail at this eatery down on antiques row near the Vieux-Port. Specialties include bouillabaisse, lamb chops with thyme and basil, and duck breast in peach sauce. Happy yellow tablecloths festooned with olive branches set a festive mood.

LE QUAI 19
QUÉBECOIS $$

Map p172 (☑418-694-4448; www.lequai19.com; 48 Rue St-Paul; mains $25-29; ⊙7:30am-2pm & 5:30-10pm Mon-Fri, 9am-10pm Sat & Sun) Conveniently placed near the meeting of antiques row and the Vieux-Port, this relative newcomer with old stone walls and an open kitchen builds its menu around *cuisine du marché*, market-fresh cuisine that changes with the seasons. Scrumptious breakfasts and brunches, weekday lunch specials (from $15), and full-on three-course dinners ($45) make this an appealing stop any time of day.

LE CAFÉ DU MONDE
BISTRO $$

Map p172 (☑418-692-4455; www.lecafedumonde.com; 84 Rue Dalhousie; 3-course lunch menu $15-20, mains $17-40; ⊙11:30am-11pm

THE QUÉBECOIS TABLE

French food is king in Québec City. The lack of a significant immigrant population means that there is not the kind of massive ethnic smorgasbord that you'll find in Montréal; even so, the quality of restaurants here is outstanding.

Québec City also boasts at least one drink that you won't find in Montréal. Caribou is a potent blend of fortified wine and grain alcohol, sometimes mixed with spices and sweetened with maple syrup. Served hot at outdoor bars and streetside stalls during Québec's Winter Carnival, it's designed to warm body and soul in the coldest depths of winter.

Mon-Fri, 9am-11pm Sat & Sun) This Paris-style bistro is the only restaurant in town directly on the St Lawrence River, although actually getting a table with a view can sometimes be a challenge. Bright, airy and casually elegant, it swears by bistro classics like *steak frites* and duck confit, but there's also a great choice of other dishes, from grilled salmon to deer stew.

Gourmet breakfasts ($14 to $20) are served on weekends, and local Québec produce is featured throughout the menu.

LE COCHON DINGUE
FRENCH $$

Map p172 (☑418-692-2013; www.cochon dingue.com; 46 Blvd Champlain; mains $15-34; ◎7am-10pm Mon-Fri, 8am-11pm Sat & Sun; 🖐) Since 1979, this ever-popular choice has been serving visitors and locals straight-ahead French standbys, from café au lait *en bôl* (in a bowl) to *croque-monsieur,* sandwiches, *steak frites,* salads, mussels or quiche. It's all good day-to-day food and a kid-friendly place to boot. There's outside seating in warm weather that's good for crowd-watching.

★PANACHE
FRENCH, QUÉBECOIS $$$

Map p172 (☑418-692-1022; www.saint-antoine. com/en/dining; 10 Rue St-Antoine; lunch mains $25-35, dinner mains $35-59; ◎7-10:30am, noon-2pm & 6-10pm) Panache, the celebrated restaurant of the Auberge Saint-Antoine (p208), receives top marks for its exquisite, imaginatively prepared Québecois cuisine and top-notch service. Dinners and attractively priced midday table d'hôtes feature locally sourced ingredients like maple-glazed halibut, Appalachian red deer with wild berry sauce or spit-roasted duck. It's set in a stone-walled 19th-century maritime warehouse, with rustic wood beams and a blazing fire in winter.

★TOAST!
BISTRO $$$

Map p172 (☑418-692-1334; www.restaurant toast.com; 17 Rue Sault-au-Matelot; mains $25-38; ◎6-10:30pm Sun-Thu, to 11pm Fri & Sat) Under the direction of Christian Lemelin (voted Québec's best chef in 2014 by a jury of his peers), Toast! is among the city's finest. The house's signature foie gras (see p28) appetizer is followed by a sumptuous array of dishes and a superb wine list, with fiery red decor setting a romantic mood. In summer, dine alfresco in the vine-covered back courtyard.

✖ St-Jean Baptiste

St-Jean outside the walls is Québec City's most popular local thoroughfare, with restaurants for every taste and budget interspersed with some of the town's best groceries and bakeries.

LE BILLIG
CREPERIE $

Map p178 (481 Rue St-Jean; crepes $4-18; ◎11am-10pm Mon-Fri, 10am-10pm Sat & Sun) This Breton-owned creperie excels at crispy *galettes* (buckwheat-flour crepes), from traditional ham-and-cheese to specialty concoctions like merguez sausage, goat cheese and grilled vegetables, or smoked salmon, walnuts and lemon juice, all accompanied by a nice variety of draft beers and ciders. Flaming dessert crepes come with fillings ranging from maple syrup to poached pears, dark chocolate and vanilla ice cream.

ÉPICERIE EUROPÉENNE
DELI $

Map p178 (www.epicerie-europeenne.com; 560 Rue St-Jean; sandwiches $7; ◎9am-6pm Mon-Wed, to 7pm Thu & Fri, to 5pm Sat, 11am-5pm Sun) This gourmet grocery stocks a delectable mix of meats, cheeses, olive oils, vinegars, teas and coffees. It's a good place to buy culinary-themed gifts or picnic supplies; at noon the deli case is well-stocked with delicious pre-made panini such as the Fiorentino (Italian-style roast pork, garlic-marinated spinach and mascarpone) and the Lyonnais (duck pâté, Dijon mustard, cornichons and onion confit).

TUTTO GELATO
ICE CREAM $

Map p178 (☑418-522-0896; www.tuttogelato. ca; 716 Rue St-Jean; cones from $3.75; ⊙9:30am-8pm Mar–mid-Oct, later in summer) People line up at all hours for Tutto Gelato's creamy, rich, homemade ice cream. Over two dozen varieties of the Italian-style gelato and nine different sorbets (plus soy-based varieties for the vegan crowd) vie for attention behind the glass counters. Top picks include blueberry, passion fruit, pistachio, chestnut, green tea, pine nut, mascarpone-nutella, honey-lemon-ginger and chocolate-hazelnut.

CHEZ VICTOR
BURGERS $$

Map p178 (☑418-529-7702; www.chezvictor burger.com; 145 Rue St-Jean; mains $13-18; ⊙11:30am-9pm Sun-Wed, to 10pm Thu-Sat; ☑) One of Québec City's best-loved neighborhood eateries, Chez Victor specializes in juicy burgers, served with a hefty dash of creativity. Choose from deer, salmon, wild boar, straight-up beef or vegetarian, which you can then dress a number of ways (brie, smoked bacon, cream cheese etc). You'll find several other branches around town, including one down by the **Vieux-Port** (Map p172; ☑418-781-2511; 300 Rue St-Paul; mains $13-19; ⊙7:30am-9pm Mon-Fri, 9am-10pm Sat, 9am-9pm Sun).

Side dishes here are also nice, including fresh coleslaw and fries, which you can get with a variety of sauces (including the recommended curry sauce). Dine on the tiny outdoor patio or in the cozy, exposed-brick dining room.

LE HOBBIT
BISTRO $$

Map p178 (☑418-647-2677; www.hobbitbistro. com; 700 Rue St-Jean; mains $16-29; ⊙8am-10pm Mon-Fri, 9am-10pm Sat & Sun) This popular, inviting bistro has outdoor seating, a casual atmosphere and good-value lunch and dinner specials (check out the chalkboard). The classics are all nicely done, including juicy duck confit and *steak frites*. Various fresh pasta dishes and salads round out the menu, and there's a small but fairly priced wine list. Breakfast is served till 2:30pm on weekends.

✖ Montcalm & Colline Parlementaire

Ave Cartier between Grande Allée and Blvd René-Lévesque is packed with upscale delis, bistros and markets. Just around the corner, the nightlife hub of Grande Allée has a sizeable cluster of bars and alfresco restaurants perfect for an evening meal or drink.

PICARDIE
DELI, BAKERY $

Map p178 (www.picardiecartier.com; 1029 Ave Cartier; deli items from $7; ⊙8am-6pm Mon-Wed & Sat, to 7pm Thu & Fri, to 5pm Sun) Featuring a tantalizing array of sweet and savory snacks, this neighborhood *traiteur* (deli) is a browser's delight. The display case up front is devoted to croissants, chocolatines and other baked goodies, while the longer case beyond brims with quiches, salmon pies, gourmet sandwiches, tomato and camembert tarts, and *tartiflette* (an Alpine dish of potatoes, cheese, cream and bacon).

If you've got access to a kitchen, you might even consider the gourmet frozen meals to go, in the freezer opposite the main deli counter.

PÂTISSERIE-CHOCOLATERIE ANNA PIERROT
CHOCOLATE, PASTRIES $

Map p178 (☑418-524-2662; www.annapierrot. com; 1191 Ave Cartier; ⊙7:30am-7pm Sat-Wed, 7am-9pm Thu & Fri) This pastry and chocolate shop in the Halles du Petit Quartier market will prove irresistible to anyone with a sweet tooth. A tempting array of cakes, éclairs, truffles, tarts, petits fours, macarons and more are gorgeously displayed in the wraparound glass case.

★ MORENA
BISTRO $$

Map p178 (☑418-529-3668; www.morena-food. com; 1038 Ave Cartier; mains $15-17; ⊙8am-7pm Mon-Wed, to 8pm Thu & Fri, to 6pm Sat, 9am-6pm Sun) Tucked into a gourmet grocery-deli on tony Ave Cartier, this Italian-themed neighborhood bistro makes a lively but low-key lunch stop. Daily chalkboard specials are beautifully presented, with fresh veggies on the side and a soup or salad appetizer. After 3pm there's an à la carte snack menu. After your meal it's also a fun place to browse for food-related gifts.

Dine solo at the counter or enjoy a tête-à-tête with your traveling companion at one of the little tables for two.

LOCAL KNOWLEDGE

QUÉBEC CITY'S BEST BAKERIES

Like any self-respecting cradle of French culture, Québec is swarming with fabulous bakeries and patisseries – no matter where you are in the city, there's one near you!

Two perennial favorites are **Le Croquembouche** (p192) and **Paillard Café-Boulangerie** (p184). Here are a few others worth trying, if you want to do a little taste-testing as you stroll:

➜ **La Boîte à Pain** (Map p178; www.boiteapain.com; 289 Rue St-Joseph Est; pastries from $2; ⊘6:30am-8pm Mon-Sat, to 5:30pm Sun) Watch through the window as the bakers roll out their dough, then pop in next door and sample the finished product. Among the many treats worth tasting are the gigantic *brioches à la cannelle* (cinnamon rolls). It's down in St-Roch, on the same block as Le Croquembouche.

➜ **Le Paingruel** (Map p178; 375 Rue St-Jean; ⊘7am-6:30pm Tue-Fri, to 5pm Sat) In the heart of St-Jean Baptiste, this place bakes up an ever-changing lineup of hearty breads, from classic baguettes to loaves laced with walnuts, hazelnuts, chocolate and cranberries. Look for the day-by-day schedule of the week's offerings, posted by the front door.

➜ **Le Panetier Baluchon** (Map p178; www.panetier-baluchon.com; 764 Rue St-Jean; ⊘7:30am-7:30pm) In business for over 30 years, this bakery a few blocks west of Porte St-Jean uses organic grains grown on its own farm in Beauce, 55km outside the city.

➜ **Éric Borderon** (Map p178; www.artisanborderon.com; 1191 Ave Cartier; ⊘8am-7pm Mon-Wed, to 9pm Thu & Fri, to 6pm Sat & Sun) Look for this renowned baguette master's stand inside the Halles du Petit Quartier market, in Montcalm.

BISTRO B   BISTRO **$$**

Map p178 (☏418-614-5444; www.bistrob.ca; 1144 Ave Cartier; mains $20-30; ⊘11:30am-2pm Mon-Fri & 6-11pm daily) The brainchild of chef François Blais, formerly of Panache, this place on Ave Cartier draws a well-heeled crowd for business lunches, when reasonably priced specials are chalked up on the giant board above the large open kitchen. New menus are improvised daily based on whatever ingredients are freshest at the Halles du Petit Quartier market down the street.

CAFÉ KRIEGHOFF   CAFE **$$**

Map p178 (☏418-522-3711; www.cafekrieghoff.qc.ca; 1091 Ave Cartier; breakfast mains $7-17, lunch & dinner mains $11-26; ⊘7am-9pm Mon-Fri, 8am-9pm Sat & Sun) Especially appealing in warm weather, this cheerful spot has excellent breakfasts, a pleasant back terrace and a laid-back front porch where you can watch the comings and goings on Ave Cartier. Inside, the dining room is decorated with reproductions from Cornelius Krieghoff (1815–72), one of Québec's master painters of the 19th century, who lived nearby on Grande Allée.

✘ St-Roch

The rejuvenation of St-Roch means everything from shopping to entertainment has become more exciting – and the eating scene is no exception. A youthful population keeps things dynamic, and new places are opening all the time.

★LE CROQUEMBOUCHE   BAKERY **$**

Map p178 (www.lecroquembouche.com; 225 Rue St-Joseph Est; pastries from $2; ⊘7am-6:30pm Tue-Sat, to 5pm Sun) Widely hailed as Québec City's finest bakery, Croquembouche draws devoted locals from dawn to dusk. Among its seductive offerings are fluffy-as-a-cloud croissants, tantalizing cakes and éclairs, brioches brimming with raspberries, and gourmet sandwiches on fresh-baked bread. There's also a stellar array of *danoises* (Danish pastries), including orange and anise, cranberry, pistachio and chocolate, and lemon, ginger and poppy seed.

CAFÉ CRACK GRILL-CHEESE   SANDWICHES **$**

Map p178 (www.crackgrillcheese.com; 199 Rue St-Joseph Est; sandwiches $4.50-10; ⊘10:30am-

8pm) Sharing space with a gourmet cheese shop, this high-ceilinged, brick-walled corner spot raises the humble grilled cheese sandwich to unprecedented heights. The big chalkboard menu lists a dizzying array of choices, from straight-up grilled cheddar 'like Mom used to make' to alternatives that jazz up the concept with fancy cheeses, smoked salmon and trout, mushrooms and dipping sauces.

LA CUISINE DINER $

Map p178 (☑418-523-3387; www.barlautre cuisine.com; 205 Rue St-Vallier Est; mains $10; ☺11am-1am Mon-Wed, 11am-3am Thu & Fri, 2pm-3am Sat, 2pm-1am Sun) Retro decor and comfort food served till the wee hours are the hallmarks of this trendy, low-lit local hangout midway between St-Jean Baptiste and St-Roch. Formica tables, mismatched china and silverware, light fixtures made from colanders, a vintage Wurlitzer jukebox and board games give the place a fun, relaxed feel. On weekend nights, DJs spin everything from electronica to soul.

The menu features five no-nonsense mains each day, from stuffed cabbage to shepherd's pie; if you're still hungry, you can add soup of the day for $3, or coffee and dessert for $4.

BATI BASSAK CAMBODIAN, THAI $

Map p178 (☑418-522-4567; www.bati-bassak. com; 125 Rue St-Joseph Est; mains $12-19; ☺11am-2pm Tue-Fri, 5-9:30pm Tue-Sun) Good Asian food is hard to come by in Québec City, but this bustling Thai-Cambodian eatery is a welcome exception, serving a menu full of tasty meat and fish dishes, along with several veggie offerings. Weekday lunch specials offer especially good value at $10 to $14 including appetizer, tea and dessert. No alcohol is served, but you're welcome to bring your own.

HOSAKA-YA JAPANESE $

Map p178 (☑418-780-1903; www.hosaka-ya. com; 75 Rue St-Joseph Est; mains $11-14; ☺11:30am-2pm Tue-Fri, 5-10pm Tue-Sat) Catering to a young, informal clientele, this straight-ahead noodle house specializes in delicious ramen soups filled with pork, fish, tofu and loads of veggies. Draft beer, wine and a good sake selection make it a cozy place for a sit-down meal, but it's also a great take-out option if you'd rather hunker down in the hotel for a night.

★**CAFÉ DU CLOCHER PENCHÉ** FRENCH $$

Map p178 (☑418-640-0597; www.clocher penche.ca; 203 Rue St-Joseph Est; mains $21-27, brunch & lunch menus from $17; ☺11:30am-2pm & 5-10pm Tue-Fri, 9am-2pm & 5-10pm Sat, 9am-2pm Sun) This splendid, high-ceilinged cafe serves classy bistro fare that proudly shows off local Québecois products. What sets it apart are the delicious – and very rich – weekend brunches, featuring homemade brioches with fresh fruit, crème fraîche and maple syrup, bagels topped with smoked mackerel, or veggie chili served with poached eggs, roasted squash and lime sour cream. Reservations recommended.

L'AFFAIRE EST KETCHUP BISTRO $$

Map p178 (☑418-529-9020; www.facebook. com/laffaireest.ketchup; 46 Rue St-Joseph Est; mains $17-24; ☺6-11pm Tue-Sun) Book ahead for this quirky local favorite with only eight tables. Dressed in T-shirts and baseball caps, bantering relaxedly with one another as they cook on a pair of electric stoves, founders François and Olivier specialize in home cooking with a trendy modern twist. A good selection of wines and mixed drinks is available from the well-stocked bar.

The ever-changing menu ranges from classics like duck breast with lentils, or stewed pork with mashed potatoes, to the unexpected – octopus salad with crunchy vegetables, or lime gelatin with apple, cucumber and mint mousse.

🍷 DRINKING & NIGHTLIFE

Let's be honest. Québec City isn't exactly considered a party town. That said, what the city does offer after dark is quite special, fun and refreshingly attitude-free. What the swankier supper clubs and restaurants may lack in urban edge, they more than make up for in friendly ambience and top-notch service; simply put, you get the feeling that everyone is welcome.

For club, bar and other entertainment listings, pick up the weekly *Voir Québec* (www.voir.ca/quebec; published every Thursday). Other useful free publications include *Scope* (www. quebecscope.com), a glossy monthly that focuses on music and cultural

events, *Fugues* (www.fugues.com), a free monthly gay and lesbian entertainment guide, and *Le Clap* (www.clap.qc.ca), a bimonthly guide to cinema. Have fun!

🍷 Old Upper Town

PUB ST-ALEXANDRE   BAR
Map p172 (📞418-694-0015; www.pubstalexandre.com; 1087 Rue St-Jean; ⏰11am-3am) High ceilings and dark wood house a loyal mix of tourists and locals at this popular English pub. A near encyclopedic range of suds (250 sorts!) and over three dozen types of single malt keep the crowds coming back for more. Live music nightly – Celtic, blues, jazz and more – contributes to the animated atmosphere.

🍷 Old Lower Town

★L'ONCLE ANTOINE   PUB
Map p172 (📞418-694-9176; www.facebook.com/oncleantoine; 29 Rue St-Pierre; ⏰11am-1am) Set clandestinely in the stone cave-cellar of one of the city's oldest surviving houses (dating from 1754), this great tavern pours out excellent Québec microbrews (try the Barberie Noir stout or the strong Belgian-style Fin du Monde), several drafts *(en fût)* and various European beers.

AVIATIC CLUB   WINE BAR
Map p172 (📞418-522-3555; www.aviatic.ca; 450 Ave de la Gare-du-Palais; ⏰11:30am-4pm Mon, 11:30am-10pm Tue-Fri, 5-10pm Sat) This elegant wine bar and restaurant is nestled in the historic Gare du Palais train station and attracts a professional crowd. A rotating list of 50 wines is served by the glass, and a vibrant outdoor terrace opens up in warmer weather.

🍷 St-Jean Baptiste

★LE MOINE ÉCHANSON   WINE BAR
Map p178 (📞418-524-7832; www.lemoineechanson.com; 585 Rue St-Jean; ⏰5pm-1am) A darling of the city's wine connoisseurs, this convivial brick-walled bistro pours an enticing and ever-changing array of wines from all over the Mediterranean, by the glass and by the bottle, accompanied by hearty and homespun snacks ($9 to $16) and main dishes ($18 to $24) such as blood sausage, cheese fondue or lentil soup. Reservations recommended.

Each season brings a new theme, with emphasis placed on a single French region or department (Ardèche, Jura etc) or Mediterranean country. Crowds pour in after work, quickly filling the two rooms to capacity, starting with aperitifs and lingering on through dinner. During business hours it also doubles as a wine merchant, selling hard-to-find bottles to take away.

★LE SACRILÈGE   BAR
Map p178 (www.lesacrilege.com; 447 Rue St-Jean; ⏰noon-3am) With its unmistakable sign of a laughing, dancing monk saucily flaunting his knickers, this bar has long been the watering hole of choice for Québec's night owls, who start or end their weekend revelry here. Even on Monday, it's standing-room only. There's a popular terrace out back; get to it through the bar or the tiny brick alley next door.

LA NINKASI   BAR
Map p178 (📞418-529-8538; www.laninkasi.ca; 811 Rue St-Jean; ⏰11am-3am) Specializing in Québecois microbrews – and nothing but Québecois microbrews – this place has a youthful party vibe, cheap bar snacks and a dozen-plus local beers and ciders on tap at all times, including rotating weekly specials. Occasional live rock bands and other performers keep things hopping on weekend nights.

LE DRAGUE   GAY
Map p178 (www.ledrague.com; 815 Rue St-Augustin; ⏰10am-3am) The star player on Québec City's tiny gay scene, Le Drague comprises a front outdoor terrace, a two-level disco where drag shows are held, a slightly more laid-back tavern, and the men-only Base 3, which…well…let's just say it turns the capital's conservative reputation on its head.

NELLIGAN'S IRISH PUB   PUB
Map p178 (www.pubnelligans.ca; 789 Côte Ste-Geneviève; ⏰4pm-3am) Tucked into a pair of brick-walled upstairs rooms just downhill from Rue St-Jean, this Irish pub makes a cozy spot to sip an Irish whiskey on a cold winter's night or down a few pints on a midsummer's evening. There's also occasional live Irish music and pub grub ranging from Harp-battered fish and chips to rosemary-scented duck poutine.

🍷 Montcalm & Colline Parlementaire

L'INOX
PUB

Map p178 (www.inox.qc.ca; 655 Grande Allée Est; ⊗1pm-3am) At this popular brewpub on the Grande Allée party circuit, the blackboard behind the bar brims with choices, including the citrus- and coriander-scented Trouble-Fête (available year-round), and a rotating lineup of seasonal brews such as Viking, a cranberry-infused concoction inspired by ancient Norse recipes. The outdoor terrace is great for people-watching in summer, or Calvados-spiked hot chocolate during Winter Carnival.

L'ATELIER
COCKTAIL BAR

Map p178 (☑418-522-2225; www.bistro latelier.com; 624 Grande Allée Est; ⊗11:30am-1am Sun-Thu, to 2am Fri & Sat) Bright and buzzy, this new arrival on the Grande Allée drinking scene is a fun spot for late afternoon and evening cocktails. Brick walls, cushioned benches, and a sea of lights and cocktail glasses hanging from the ceiling create a convivial atmosphere for sampling over two dozen creative cocktails with names like 'Absolut Douchebag' and '24 Likes, 9 Comments.'

CHEZ MAURICE
CLUB

Map p178 (www.mauricenightclub.com; 575 Grande Allée Est; ⊗9pm-3am Thu & Fri, 10pm-3am Sat) Sprawling across a gutted, châteaulike mansion and cheekily named after hard-ass former Québec premier Maurice Duplessis, this entertainment complex has three separate partying spaces: the Maurice **nightclub** and disco, whose multiple rooms buzz with youthful energy until the wee hours, the chic **Charlotte Lounge**, and the **Société Cigare**, a refined, chilled-out bar with 200 sorts of cigars to choose from.

CHEZ DAGOBERT
CLUB

Map p178 (☑418-522-0393; http://dagobert. ca; 600 Grande Allée Est; ⊗10pm-3am Wed-Sun) Multifloors, multibars, multiscreens – the capital's classic disco behemoth has everything from live rock to naughty DJs. The music may change, the young, randy crowd stays the same.

🍷 St-Roch

★LA BARBERIE
BREWERY

Map p178 (www.labarberie.com; 310 Rue St-Roch; ⊗noon-1am) This cooperative St-Roch microbrewery is beloved for its spacious tree-shaded deck, its ever-evolving selection of eight home brews, and its unique BYO policy, which allows customers to bring snacks in from the outside. Seasonal offerings range from classic pale ales to quirkier options such as orange stout or hot pepper amber. Undecided? Sample 'em all in the popular eight-beer carousel!

LE NEKTAR
CAFE

Map p178 (www.lenektar.com; 235 St-Joseph Est; ⊗7am-7pm Mon-Wed, 7am-9pm Thu & Fri, 8am-7pm Sat & Sun) Serious coffee lovers should make the pilgrimage down to this splendid little cafe in St-Roch, which serves the best espresso drinks in town. Settling in on the sofa here with a big, velvety latte is one of Québec City's great morning pleasures.

LES SALONS D'EDGAR
BAR

Map p178 (☑418-523-7811; www.lessalonsd edgar.com; 263 Rue St-Vallier Est; ⊗4:30pm-late Wed-Sat, 5:30pm-late Sun) At this unofficial 'official' hangout for the city's theater community, the eavesdropping is as much fun as the drinking – you'll be privy to conversations on roles lost and roles gained.

BRASSERIE LA KORRIGANE
BREWERY

Map p178 (www.korrigane.ca; 380 Rue Dorchester; ⊗2pm-1am Sun-Thu, to 3am Fri & Sat) St-Roch's newest microbrewery features a full rainbow of flavors, including specialty brews such as Emily Carter blueberry beer and the maple-laced Croquemitaine, all served up with pub grub from artisanal producers. You'll also find Sunday improv nights and swing dancing every other Wednesday.

LE BOUDOIR
LOUNGE

Map p178 (☑418-524-2777; www.facebook.com/BoudoirLounge; 441 Rue du Parvis; ⊗4:30pm-3am Wed-Sun) Part restaurant, part nightclub, all scene, this posh but low-key lounge in the hip St-Roch district is pretty much the place for well-heeled locals to party. On weekends two DJs let you choose between downtempo and dancing, while games include billiards, Wii and Pac-Man.

QUÉBEC CITY DRINKING & NIGHTLIFE

☆ ENTERTAINMENT

The performing arts are in fine form in Québec City. The city boasts a symphony orchestra, the Orchestre Symphonique de Québec, and an opera company, Opéra de Québec. Homegrown Québecois bands perform regularly, as do touring bands from across Canada, the US and Europe, especially during the Festival d'Été in July. Live performance venues abound, from concert halls to open-air amphitheaters, to little jazz and rock clubs, to exuberant *boîtes à chanson* (Québec folk-music clubs), where generations of locals dance and sing with uncensored glee. French-language theater is also an interesting scene here, with tons of small companies producing a variety of shows.

☆ Old Upper Town

LES GROS BECS   THEATER
Map p172 (☎418-522-7880; www.lesgrosbecs. qc.ca; 1143 Rue St-Jean; ⊙shows Sep–May; 👪) Devoted to children and young people, this brilliantly creative French-language theater company mounts over a dozen shows annually. Its colorful catalog specifies suggested age ranges – from one to 17 – for every production.

☆ Old Lower Town

THÉÂTRE PETIT-CHAMPLAIN   THEATER
Map p172 (☎418-692-2631; www.theatrepetit champlain.com; 68 Rue du Petit-Champlain) This theater near the base of the funicular is a great place to see Québec's most popular singing stars. It also stages occasional French-language theater productions and comedy gigs.

LE PAPE GEORGES   LIVE MUSIC
Map p172 (☎418-692-1320; www.papegeorges. ca; 8½ Rue de Cul-de-Sac; ⊙4pm-3am Mon-Wed, noon-3am Thu-Sun) With live music at least three nights a week (more in the summer) from 10pm, this charming bar located in a 300-year-old house also serves cheeses, meats and baguettes with a healthy dollop of Québecois culture.

☆ St-Jean Baptiste

PALAIS MONTCALM   LIVE MUSIC
Map p178 (www.palaismontcalm.ca; 995 Pl d'Youville) Just outside the Upper Town's walls, this theater hosts a stellar lineup of concerts year-round, featuring everything from opera and chamber music to jazz and rock. The main performance space, the Salle Raoul-Jobin, is renowned for its superb acoustics.

LE THÉÂTRE CAPITOLE   LIVE MUSIC
Map p178 (☎418-694-4444; www.lecapitole. com; 972 Rue St-Jean) A terrific, historic old theater that now stages everything from musicals to rock concerts. Check out the sumptuous attached hotel (p210). Hitchcock held his *I Confess* premiere here.

FOU-BAR   LIVE MUSIC
Map p178 (☎418-522-1987; www.foubar.ca; 525 Rue St-Jean; ⊙2:30pm-3am) Laid-back and with an eclectic mix of bands, this bar is one of the town's classics for good live music. Fou-Bar is also popular for its reasonably priced food menu and its free *pique-assiettes* (appetizers) on Thursday and Friday evenings.

☆ Montcalm & Colline Parlementaire

GRAND THÉÂTRE
DE QUÉBEC   PERFORMING ARTS
Map p178 (☎877-643-8131, 418-643-8131; www.grandtheatre.qc.ca; 269 Blvd René-Lévesque Est) The Grand Théâtre is the city's main performing arts center with a steady diet of top-quality classical concerts, dance and theater. Major companies that perform regularly here include the **Opéra de Québec** (☎418-529-0688; www.opera dequebec.qc.ca; 1220 Ave Taché), the **Orchestre Symphonique de Québec** (☎418-643-8486, 418-643-8131; www.osq.org) and the **Théâtre du Trident** (☎418-643-5873; www. letrident.com).

KIOSQUE EDWIN-BÉLANGER   LIVE MUSIC
Map p178 (☎418-648-4050; www.ccbn-nbc. gc.ca/en/activities/kiosque-edwin-belanger; Battlefields Park) Each summer dozens of free concerts are staged at this bandstand in the

middle of Battlefields Park (p202). Music covers everything from pop, jazz and world music to blues.

LES VOÛTES DE NAPOLÉON
LIVE MUSIC

Map p178 (☑418-640-9388; www.voutesdena poleon.com; 680A Grande Allée Est; ☺9:30pm-late) At this jubilant *boîte à chanson* (Québecois folk cabaret) it will likely be just you and the locals. There's lively Québecois music nightly, usually of the 'singer-with-guitar' variety, with lesser-known, up-and-coming acts featuring prominently.

CINÉMA CARTIER
CINEMA

Map p178 (☑418-522-1011; www.cinemacartier. com; 1019 Ave Cartier; ☺1pm-late) This beloved neighborhood cinema began as a deliciously old-world little place attached to a video shop, with big comfy chairs and nothing but art-house films. Recently expanded, it still devotes half of its screen space to independent films, but also shows Hollywood blockbusters and family-oriented fare. Most films are alternately shown in their original version and dubbed in French.

☆ St-Roch

★LE CERCLE
LIVE MUSIC

Map p178 (☑418-948-8648; www.le-cercle. ca; 226½ Rue St-Joseph Est; ☺11:30am-1:30am Mon-Wed, 11:30am-3am Thu & Fri, 3pm-3am Sat, 10am-1:30am Sun) This very cool art space and show venue draws a hip crowd for its international DJs and underground bands, ranging from indie rock to electronica, blues to cajun. It hosts numerous other events, including film, fashion and comic strip festivals, book- and album-release parties, wine tastings and more. Affordable tapas, weekend brunches and an atmospheric bar space sweeten the deal.

LA ROTONDE
DANCE

Map p178 (☑418-649-5013; www.larotonde. qc.ca; 336 Rue du Roi) This contemporary dance center presents shows from international touring companies as well as local dancers, including experimental and cutting-edge works. It also offers workshops and classes, and is pivotal in keeping dance alive in Québec. Shows are staged at La Rotonde's main studio on Rue du Roi and at several other venues around town.

SCANNER
LIVE MUSIC

Map p178 (☑418-523-1916; www.scannerbis tro.com; 291 Rue St-Vallier Est; ☺3pm-3am Sat-Thu, 11:30am-3am Fri) Ask any local between the ages of 18 and 35 to suggest a cool place for a drink and this is where they might send you. DJs and live bands serve up a potent musical mix, from heavy metal to hard rock to punk to rockabilly. There's a terrace outside in summer, plus foosball and pool inside year-round.

☆ Elsewhere Outside the Walls

LE CLAP
CINEMA

(☑418-653-2470; www.clap.qc.ca; 2360 Chemin Ste-Foy; ☺11am-midnight) Located in Ste-Foy-Sillery, Le Clap's mandate is to show off the best of what's going on in the film world. On any given afternoon, the eclectic mix here might include the latest indie French film, a Québecois documentary, an American blockbuster, and a live broadcast from the Opéra de Paris. Non-French-language films are sometimes dubbed in French, sometimes subtitled.

> ### GAY & LESBIAN VENUES
>
> The city's gay and lesbian club scene is tiny, with pretty much everything centered around **Le Drague** (p194). Another address of interest is **Galerie DomaHom** (Map p178; www.domahom. com; 221 Rue St-Jean), a cafe-art gallery that features the work of local gay and lesbian artists by day, then morphs after dark into the all-male **Club ForHom** (☑418-522-4918; www. forhom.ca; ☺5pm-1am Tue-Sun), with nightly drink specials, gay film nights and more. Plenty of other bars and clubs are gay-friendly, including Chez Maurice (p195), Chez Dagobert (p195) and Le Sacrilège (p194).
>
> In late August or early September, the city's LGBT community comes out in full force for the annual **Fête Arc-en-Ciel** (p244). For info on parties and other gay events, *Fugues* (www. fugues.com) is the free gay and lesbian entertainment guide with listings for the entire province of Québec.

QUÉBEC WINTER CARNIVAL

Billing itself as the world's largest winter carnival, **Carnaval de Québec** (www.carnaval.qc.ca; ⊙Jan or Feb) is an exuberant celebration of ice, snow and wintry community fun. It begins each year on the third weekend before Ash Wednesday and culminates 17 days later when Bonhomme – the giant smiling snowman and official carnival mascot – bids a wistful adieu to his adoring fans.

In the buildup to Carnaval, the city takes on a new look, as a gargantuan ice palace is built opposite the Parliament Building and the Plains of Abraham get converted into a vast winter playground, with ice slides, snow tubing, dog sledding, sleigh rides, giant rubber duck races for kids, and maple taffy making added to the park's usual repertoire of outdoorsy winter activities.

Special events fill the three weekends of Carnaval, including ice canoe races across the St Lawrence River, magnificent night parades with whimsical floats, and the infamous *bain de neige* (snow bath), in which a few dozen scantily clad – and stark raving mad – people court frostbite by volunteering to dance, roll and cavort in the snow with Bonhomme. Other highlights include action-packed sleigh races and an international ice sculpture competition, with participants from as far away as Morocco.

Carnaval in its current incarnation dates back to 1955 and carries with it several proud traditions. Many carnival-goers emulate Bonhomme's ceremonial attire, sporting the traditional *tuque* (hat) and *ceinture fléchée* (a wide colorful sash worn around the waist). To attend the festivities, you'll need to buy an *effigie* ($15), a miniature representation of Bonhomme that's sold around town and at the entrance to the fairgrounds. Veteran Carnaval-goers proudly wear decades worth of past effigies pinned to their sashes as they wander from event to event.

Revelers stave off the frigid weather by drinking *caribou* – a fortified spiced wine served hot; buy it by the glass, or follow the locals' lead and pick up a *canne*, a hollow plastic cane festooned with Bonhomme's likeness, which can be filled to the brim with *caribou* at stands dotted around town – and used as a walking stick when your gait goes wobbly.

For exact dates and a full schedule of events, see www.carnaval.qc.ca. Bear in mind that the city overflows with tourists during Carnaval, so it's best to book accommodations and restaurants in advance. Oh, and don't forget your warm clothes – you'll need 'em!

Visitors to the Old Town will appreciate Le Clap's Monday and Tuesday afternoon screenings at the Musée de la Civilisation (p179), a new initiative launched in 2014.

AMPHITHÉÂTRE DE QUÉBEC
LIVE MUSIC, SPECTATOR SPORT

(250 Blvd Wilfrid-Hamel) Opened in fall 2015, the city's brand-new $400 million, 18,500-seat Amphithéâtre (also known as the Québecor Arena) hosts rock concerts and is home to the Québec Remparts of the Québec Major Junior Hockey League (p202).

SHOPPING

While it may not have as many big international stores and high-end designer boutiques as some larger cities, Québec is a shopper's paradise in its own special way. Small, unique and authentic little boutiques are this touristy town's claim to retail fame, and the city's small size makes it ideal for strolling around and browsing for surprises. Local clothing, eyewear and jewelry designers, purveyors of specialty foods and homemade chocolate, and the antique dealers down on Rue St-Paul all are representative of the city's small-scale, classy approach to commerce.

You'll find that many stores within the Old Town walls cater primarily (if not exclusively) to tourists, whereas those in the outlying neighborhoods draw a much more local crowd. The best streets for aimless window-shopping include Rue du Petit-Champlain and Rue St-Paul in the Old Lower Town, Ave Cartier in Montcalm, Rue St-Joseph in

St-Roch, and Rue St-Jean (both inside and outside the walls). As a general rule, stores in Québec City keep later hours on Thursday and Friday nights.

🏠 Old Upper Town

SIMONS DEPARTMENT STORE

Map p172 (📞418-692-3630; www.simons.ca; 20 Côte de la Fabrique; ⏰9:30am-5:30pm Mon-Wed, to 9pm Thu & Fri, to 5pm Sat, noon-5pm Sun) One of the city's business success stories, Simons was started as a dry-goods store in the 1800s by the son of a Scottish immigrant. By 1952 his descendants had turned the business into a successful clothing store. It's popular all over Québec for stocking items more cutting-edge than those at competing department stores. There's been a Simons at this location since 1870.

GALERIE D'ART INUIT
BROUSSEAU ET BROUSSEAU ARTS

Map p172 (📞418-694-1828; www.artinuit.ca; 35 Rue St-Louis; ⏰9:30am-5:30pm) Devoted to Inuit carvings from artists all over arctic Canada, this place is gorgeously set up and elaborately lit, with well-trained staff who knowledgeably answer questions. Carvings range from the small to the large and intricate. Expect high quality and steep prices. International shipping is available.

LES 3 TOURS CLOTHING

Map p172 (1124 Rue St-Jean; ⏰9am-5pm Mon-Wed, to 9pm Thu-Sat, 9:30am-5:30pm Sun) Devoted to all things medieval, this Québec company sells clothes, jewelry and accessories, many of them the work of Québecois designers. This is one of many such stores around the province.

🏠 Old Lower Town

MARCHÉ DU VIEUX-PORT FOOD & DRINK

Map p172 (📞418-692-2517; www.marchevieux port.com; 160 Quai St André; ⏰9am-6pm Mon-Fri, to 5pm Sat & Sun) At this heaving local food market, you can buy fresh fruits and vegetables as well as dozens of local specialties, from Île d'Orléans blackcurrant wine to ciders, honeys, cheeses, sausages, chocolates, herbal hand creams and, of course, maple-syrup products. Weekends see huge crowds and more wine tastings than can be considered sensible.

⭐ LA FROMAGÈRE FOOD

Map p172 (Marché du Vieux-Port; ⏰9am-6pm Mon-Fri, to 5pm Sat & Sun) This wonderful little shop just inside the main entrance of the Vieux-Port market sells an awe-inspiring selection of Québecois cheeses. For a notion of the tremendous variety available here, check out the Québec dairy association website, www.ourcheeses.com.

LES BRANCHÉS LUNETTERIE FASHION

Map p172 (www.lesbrancheslunetterie.ca; 155 Rue St-Paul; ⏰10am-6pm Mon-Wed, to 8pm Thu & Fri, to 5pm Sat & Sun) Displaying a fanciful, wildly colorful mix of designer eyewear from Québec, France and Spain, this is a fun place to browse, even if you're not necessarily in the market for new glasses frames. The collection's centerpiece is the room dedicated to frames from **Montures Faniel** (www.monturesfaniel.com), a Québecois business founded by opera-singer-turned-designer Anne-Marie Faniel; her music also graces the store.

CANDEUR BEAUTY

Map p172 (www.candeur.ca; 117 Rue St-Paul; ⏰10am-5pm daily in summer, Sat & Sun only in winter) A great spot for small gifts, this sweet boutique specializes in artisanal Québecois soaps made with goat's milk, herbal oils and other natural ingredients. The beautifully displayed soap selection features a pleasing array of colors and charming French touches, such as the soaps imprinted with fleur-de-lys motifs.

GÉRARD BOURGUET
ANTIQUAIRE ANTIQUES

Map p172 (📞418-694-0896; 97 Rue St-Paul; ⏰10:30am-noon & 1-5pm Mon-Sat) This specialist in Québecois antique furniture has a wide range of lovely pieces, including painted chests, cupboards and tables, as well as a nice selection of ceramics and folk-art wood carvings. The owner makes frequent buying trips, so call ahead to make sure the shop is open.

LE RENDEZ-VOUS
DU COLLECTIONNEUR ANTIQUES

Map p172 (123 Rue St-Paul; ⏰10am-5pm) Antique lamps and silverware from Le Château Frontenac are among the many items crowding the shelves at this well-established shop on the Lower Town's antiques row.

LOCAL KNOWLEDGE

THE INSIDE INFO

➡ **Shopping Streets** Stroll Rue St-Jean outside the walls in St-Jean Baptiste, Rue St-Joseph in St-Roch, Ave Cartier in Montcalm, or Rue Maguire in Sillery.

➡ **Markets** For the freshest cheeses, meats and produce, locals head for the Marché du Vieux-Port (p199) down by the waterfront or Les Halles du Petit Quartier in Montcalm.

➡ **Hangouts** Dance into the wee hours at Le Cercle (p197), or while away a summer evening drinking beer with laid-back locals on the outdoor terrace at La Barberie (p195).

JOAILLERIE JULES PERRIER   JEWELRY

Map p172 (☑418-692-0880; www.jewelryjules perrier.com; 39 Rue du Petit-Champlain; ☺10am-5pm) Passion is the inspiration behind this well-known jeweler's stunning designs, unique earrings, brooches, pendants and more. Still a family business, it's full of precious stones, making browsing in this elegant locale feel like perusing art.

LA PETITE CABANE À SUCRE DU QUÉBEC   FOOD & DRINK

Map p172 (☑418-692-5875; www.petite cabaneasucre.com; 94 Rue du Petit-Champlain; ☺9:30am-5:30pm Sat-Wed, to 9pm Thu & Fri) Maple syrup is a massive industry in Québec, and this touristy little shop sells it in every shape and form: candies, delicacies, ice cream, snacks, syrup-related accessories and, of course, the sweet stuff itself.

🏠 St-Jean Baptiste

★JA MOISAN ÉPICIER   FOOD

Map p178 (☑418-522-0685; www.jamoisan.com; 695 Rue St-Jean; ☺8:30am-9pm Mon-Sat, 10am-7pm Sun) Established in 1871, this charming store bills itself as North America's oldest grocery. It's a browser's dream come true, packed with beautifully displayed edibles and kitchen and household items. Many products fall on the 'You've got to be kidding!' side of expensive, but you'll find items here you've never seen before, along with heaps of local goods and gift ideas.

ÉRICO   FOOD

Map p178 (www.ericochocolatier.com; 634 Rue St-Jean; ☺10:30am-6pm Mon-Wed & Sat, to 9pm Thu & Fri, 11am-6pm Sun, extended hours in summer) The exotic smells and flavors here will send a chocolate lover into conniptions of joy. The main shop brims with truffles, chocolate chip cookies, ice cream and seasonal chocolate treats, while the quirky museum next door has a dress made entirely of chocolate, old-fashioned gumball machines dispensing 25¢ samples, and a window where you can watch the chocolatiers at work.

Don't miss Érico's inspired and ever-changing seasonal offerings: chocolate roses for Valentine's Day, barrel-shaped truffles filled with *caribou* (fortified wine) for Winter Carnival, and chocolate bunnies and chickens at Easter.

ROSE BOUTON   JEWELRY

Map p178 (☑418-614-9507; www.boutique rose.blogspot.com; 387 Rue St-Jean; ☺11am-6pm Tue & Wed, to 7pm Thu & Fri, to 5pm Sat, to 3pm Sun) This colorful shop features a fun mix of earrings, necklaces and pins made on-site, along with an eclectic collection of reasonably priced items created by (mostly) Québecois artists, from notecards to hair accessories.

🏠 Montcalm & Colline Parlementaire

BOUTIQUE KETTÖ   CERAMICS, JEWELRY

Map p178 (☑418-522-3337; www.kettodesign. com; 951 Ave Cartier; ☺10am-5pm Sat, Sun, Tue & Wed, 10am-7pm Thu & Fri) Illustrator Julie St-Onge-Drouin started up Kettö after her illustrative designs kept finding their way onto ceramic surfaces. Now at this big, bright and beautifully set-up boutique, they're on everything from plates and mugs to ceramic jewelry and necklaces. Her designs are sold in small boutiques throughout Québec, but the selection here is better than you'll find elsewhere.

SILLONS   MUSIC

Map p178 (☑418-524-8352; www.sillons.com; 1149 Ave Cartier; ☺10am-9pm Mon-Fri, 10am-5pm

Sat, 11am-5pm Sun) In business for over three decades, this independent music store specializes in jazz, world music and performers from Québec and France. It's a great place to build up your library of Québecois music and learn what's new on the regional scene.

LES HALLES
DU PETIT QUARTIER   FOOD & DRINK

Map p178 (www.hallesdupetitquartier.com; 1191 Ave Cartier; ⏰7:30am-7pm Sat-Wed, 7am-9pm Thu & Fri) Montcalm's very popular indoor food market features individual stalls for bakers, chocolatiers, and fruit, vegetable, cheese, meat and fish vendors, plus a half dozen cafes and restaurants.

St-Roch

MYCO ANNA   FASHION

(☎418-522-2270; www.mycoanna.com; 615 Rue St-Vallier Ouest; ⏰11am-5pm Mon-Wed, to 8pm Thu & Fri, 10am-5pm Sat, noon-5pm Sun) Old meets new at this bright and daring women's fashion line's signature shop. Launched in 1995, Myco Anna is known for bright, patchworky, flirty and sexy dresses – all made from at least some recycled material.

BENJO   TOYS

Map p178 (☎418-640-0001; www.benjo.ca; 543 Rue St-Joseph Est; ⏰10am-5:30pm Mon-Wed, to 9pm Thu & Fri, 9:30am-5pm Sat & Sun) This toy shop gives a glimpse into what the world would be like if kids ran the show. Even the front door is pint-sized (the adult-sized door for grown-ups is off to the side). There's a train that goes around the store on weekends, and arts and crafts for little ones during the week.

JOHN FLUEVOG   SHOES

Map p178 (www.fluevog.com; 539 Rue St-Joseph Est; ⏰10am-6pm Mon-Wed, to 9pm Thu & Fri, to 5pm Sat, noon-5pm Sun) Recently honored as Canada's 'Shoe Person of the Year' (yes, there really is such an award!), Vancouver-based John Fluevog has been designing outlandishly colorful and stylish shoes for over four decades. His Québec City store fits in perfectly with the trendy St-Roch neighborhood.

MOUNTAIN EQUIPMENT
CO-OP   OUTDOOR EQUIPMENT

Map p178 (☎418-522-8884; www.mec.ca; 405 Rue St-Joseph Est; ⏰10am-5pm Sun, to 7pm Mon-Wed, to 9pm Thu & Fri, 9am-5pm Sat) The mountain man (or woman) in all of us needs his fix, especially if you're planning to conquer the great Québec wilderness. Enter this sprawling shop, the largest from the renowned Canadian brand, complete with an outdoor resource center to help you plan your adventure. In winter, it rents out cross-country skis, snowshoes and ice-climbing gear.

JB LALIBERTÉ   CLOTHING

Map p178 (www.lalibertemode.com; 595 Rue St-Joseph Est; ⏰9:30am-5:30pm Mon-Wed, to 9pm Thu & Fri, to 5pm Sat, noon-5pm Sun) Founded in 1867, this furrier has grown into one of Canada's major players. It's not everyone's cup of tea, but you'll find fancy collections of furs, coats, accessories and more, quite reasonably priced.

 # SPORTS & ACTIVITIES

Whether it's summer or deepest, darkest winter, you can expect to find Québec City locals enjoying life outdoors. Aside from strolling the cobblestone streets of the Old Town, there's a whole range of activities on offer in and around town. Inside the city limits there are picturesque parks and paths ideal for an early-morning jog or bike ride, as well as a host of winter sports – skating, cross-country skiing and tobogganing – when the weather turns cold. Just outside of town, you can also go rafting along the Jacques Cartier River or downhill skiing at Mont-Ste-Anne.

There's a large network of bike paths feeding from the Vieux-Port out into the surrounding countryside. Ask for the free bicycle route map at local tourist offices. Île d'Orléans can also be a fantastic setting for a bicycle outing, but because there are no bike paths and heaps of traffic in summer, this route is not recommended for children.

If you prefer a more sedentary approach, take a train ride along the St Lawrence River, or check out the cluster of boat-tour operators moored near Place-Royale; these cross the St Lawrence to Lévis or go downriver towards Montmorency Falls (p209) and Île d'Orléans (p209).

REVIVING QUÉBEC CITY'S LOST HOCKEY IDENTITY

Until 1995, Québec's National Hockey League (NHL) team, the Nordiques, was the sports sensation in town and the city laughed with the team's every success and cried at its every defeat. When rumors began to circulate that the team would be moved, protests were launched and gallons of ink spilled, but the franchise left town anyway. Pretty much any Québecer you talk to will say that the loss of the city's hockey team was their saddest day in sport. But there was also province-wide outrage, as the move put an end to one of the most infamous sports rivalries – between the Nordiques and the Montréal Canadiens. It was especially wrenching as pretty much every hockey fan felt the Nordiques' time had come and that they were on their way to Stanley Cup glory. And win they did. Exactly a year after they moved, the ex-Nordiques, now Colorado Avalanche, took home the 1996 trophy.

In 2015, Québec City took a giant step towards reviving its big-league hockey dreams. The city's brand-new $400 million, 18,500-seat Amphithéâtre (p198), also known as the Québecor Arena, was officially opened in fall 2015, in hopes of luring an NHL franchise back this way (and possibly hosting a future Winter Olympics). For the moment, fans content themselves with supporting the **Québec Remparts** (www.remparts.ca), who play in the Québec Major Junior Hockey League.

★ BATTLEFIELDS PARK   OUTDOORS
Map p178 (Parc des Champs de Bataille; ⊛) Conveniently close to the Old Town and boasting fine views of the St Lawrence River, this vast park is Québec City's prime venue for outdoor activities. You can walk or run along the network of trails, or pound the pavement of a terrific jogging track built atop a former horse-racing course. The park is also ideal for in-line skating and a host of winter activities, including cross-country skiing, skating and snowshoeing.

★ GLISSADE DE LA TERRASSE   SNOW SPORTS
Map p172 (www.au1884.ca; Terrasse Dufferin; per person $3; ⊙11am-5pm Sun-Thu, to 6pm Fri & Sat mid-Dec–mid-Mar; ⊛; ⊟3, 11) Outside Le Château Frontenac, the scenic Terrasse Dufferin on the riverfront stages this invigoratingly fast, triple-chute toboggan run all winter long, weather conditions permitting. Toboggans accommodating up to four people are available for rent at the bottom; buy tickets at the Au 1884 kiosk, then grab your toboggan, walk up to the top and let 'er rip.

★ CORRIDOR DU LITTORAL/
PROMENADE
SAMUEL-DE-CHAMPLAIN   RECREATION PATH
(⊛) Starting southwest of Québec City at Cap-Rouge and extending northeast via the Old Lower Town to Montmorency Falls, the Corridor du Littoral is a 48km multi-purpose recreation path along the St Lawrence River, popular with cyclists, walkers and in-line skaters. The heart of the path is the Promenade Samuel-de-Champlain, an especially beautiful 2.5km section constructed for Québec's 400th anniversary celebrations, lined with sculptures, sports fields and green space, with a cafe and a 25m observation tower at Quai des Cageux.

★ PLACE D'YOUVILLE
SKATING RINK   SKATING
Map p178 (⊋418-641-6256; skating free, skate rentals $8; ⊙noon-10pm Mon-Thu, 10am-10pm Fri-Sun mid-Oct–mid-Mar; ⊛) In the shadow of the Old Town walls, just outside Porte St-Jean, this improvised outdoor rink is one of the most scenic and popular places for ice-skating once winter rolls around. It's a great place to mingle with locals, and you can also rent skates on-site.

ANNEAU DE GLACE DES
PLAINES D'ABRAHAM   SKATING
(⊋418-609-1310; skating free, skate rental per 2hr $8; ⊙10am-10pm Christmas–mid-Mar; ⊛) With a circumference of 400m, this giant open-air skating rink on the Plains of Abraham, west of the Musée des Beaux-Arts, offers free skating all winter, including illuminated night skating, skate rentals, and a snack shack selling hot chocolate to keep you nice and toasty.

ABRAHAM'S BUS TOUR   GUIDED TOUR
Map p178 (adult/youth/child incl Plains of Abraham Museum & Martello Tower 1 $15/11/5; ⊙several departures daily Jul-early Sep) During the summer months, this 40-minute

bus tour makes an entertaining way to get your bearings at Battlefields Park. An actor in period costume points out historical sites of interest and throws in some colorful asides. It departs from the Plains of Abraham Information & Reception Centre (p181), the main gateway to Battlefields Park, which also houses the Musée des Plaines d'Abraham (p181). Admission to the museum and nearby Martello Tower is included with your bus ticket.

CYCLO SERVICES   CYCLING

Map p172 (☏418-692-4052, 877-692-4050; www.cycloservices.net; 289 Rue St-Paul; rental per 2/24hr from $15/35; ☺8:30am-7pm May-Oct, variable hours Nov-Apr; ⚐) This outfit rents a wide variety of bikes (hybrid, city, tandem, road and kids' bikes) and organizes excellent cycling tours of the city and outskirts to places such as Wendake or Parc de la Chute Montmorency. The knowledgeable and fun guides frequently give tours in English. In winter, it rents snowshoes only, and hours are limited; call ahead.

LÉVIS FERRY   FERRY

Map p172 (www.traversiers.gouv.qc.ca; 10 Rue des Traversiers; round-trip adult/child $6.70/4.60) For city views, you can't beat the 10-minute ferry ride to Lévis; boats operate from 6:30am to 2am, departing every 30 to 60 minutes. If you purchase a round-trip ticket, you can remain on the boat for the return journey; there's usually a 20-minute layover in Lévis.

CROISIÈRES AML   CRUISE

Map p172 (☏866-856-6668; www.croisieres aml.com; Quai Chouinard, 10 Rue Dalhousie) Enjoy fantastic city perspectives from AML's small vessels, including the classic sightseeing trip along the St Lawrence River (adult/child $35/20) and a brunch cruise (adult/child $53/31), each 90 minutes in length. Four-hour summer evening cruises (adult/child $49/29) culminate in August with five-course dinner and fireworks cruises during the Grands Feux Loto-Québec festival (adult/child $125/100).

RUNNING ROOM   RUNNING

Map p178 (☏418-522-2345; www.runningroom. com; 1049 Ave Cartier; ☺ 6pm Wed, 8:30am Sun) This Alberta-based athletic shoe chain offers free employee-led group runs on Wednesday afternoons and Sunday mornings. Just meet at the store. Its website also offers downloadable maps of Québec City running routes ranging from 3km to 20km in length.

PARC NATIONAL DE LA
JACQUES-CARTIER   OUTDOORS

(www.sepaq.com/pq/jac; adult/child $7.50/3.25) The mountain and river scenery is picture-perfect at this national park straddling a glacial valley about 40km north of Québec City via Rte 175. There's a range of snow-shoeing and cross-country skiing circuits here, from easy to difficult, and in summer there's excellent hiking, mountain biking and boating.

VÉLOPISTE JACQUES-
CARTIER/PORTNEUF   CYCLING

(www.velopistejcp.com) Formerly a railway line linking St-Gabriel-de-Valcartier and Rivière-à-Pierre, this 68km cycling trail winds its way through verdant country scenery. It's linked to downtown Québec City by another rails-to-trails project, the 22km **Corridor des Cheminots**. (Incidentally, cyclists can also reach this trail by train from Montréal; VIA Rail offers thrice-weekly service from Montréal to Rivière-à-Pierre, the trail's western terminus.)

VILLAGE VACANCES
VALCARTIER   SNOW SPORTS

(☏888-384-5524, 418-844-2200; www.valcartier. com; 1860 Blvd Valcartier, St-Gabriel-de-Valcartier; ⚐) Kids and adults alike love this year-round adventure park 25 minutes north of Québec City. In winter, hurtle down America's largest collection of groomed ice slides in inner tubes and inflatable rafts at speeds approaching 80km/hr. A 1km-long skating path and a kids' play area complete with maze and ice castle offer alternatives for younger or less adrenaline-obsessed visitors. In summer, it converts to an enormous water park. Take Hwy 73 north and exit at St-Émile/La Faune.

EXPEDITIONS NOUVELLE VAGUE   RAFTING

(☏418-520-7238; www.expeditionsnouvelle vague.com; 246 5e Ave, St-Gabriel-de-Valcartier; rafting trips $24-109, 1-/2-day kayaking course from $99/179; ⚐) For close-to-nature excitement less than an hour north of Québec City, head off on a guided rafting trip down the Jacques Cartier River. This outfit offers a broad range of rafting experiences, from the family-friendly two-hour Mini-Rafting (ages three and up) – an ultra-low-key option that offers time for kids to splash in the river – to full-on, adrenaline-packed three- to seven-hour whitewater adventures in Class III, IV and (sometimes) V water. Group and private kayaking lessons are also offered.

LE TRAIN LÉGER
DE CHARLEVOIX   TRAIN TOUR

(☑418-240-4124; www.reseaucharlevoix.com; Montmorency–Baie St-Paul round-trip adult/child $75/38; ⊙Wed-Sun mid-Jun–mid-Oct) Five days a week in summer, this light-rail train travels along a scenic stretch of the St Lawrence River, starting at Parc de la Chute Montmorency (just east of Québec City) and running northeast to the artists' enclave of Baie St-Paul. You can change trains in Baie St-Paul to continue downriver as far as La Malbaie, 140km northeast of Québec City. An extra $5 one-way gets you a guaranteed seat on the river side of the train.

In winter, there's also train service five times daily from Baie St-Paul to the Massif de Charlevoix ski area ($20 round-trip for adults, $10 for children).

ℹ PARKING

Compact Old Québec lends itself better to exploration on foot than by car. If you're driving up here, plan to park your vehicle for as much of your stay as possible.

Parking garages in and around the Old Town typically charge a day rate of $16 to $20 Monday to Friday, and $8 to $12 on weekends. In the Old Upper Town, the most central garage, and one of the cheapest, is underneath the **Hôtel de Ville**, just a couple of blocks from Le Château Frontenac. In the Old Lower Town, there are a couple of convenient lots along Rue Dalhousie. Metered street parking is also widely available, but expensive ($2 per hour). Many guesthouses provide discount vouchers for nearby parking garages.

In winter, nighttime snow removal is scheduled on many streets between 11pm and 6:30am. Don't park during these hours on any street with a '*déneigement*' (snow removal) sign and a flashing red light, or you'll wake up to a towed vehicle and a hefty fine!

LE MASSIF DE CHARLEVOIX   SKIING

(www.lemassif.com; 1350 Rue Principale, Petite-Rivière-St-François; lift ticket adult/youth/child $75/54/37, luge adult/youth $40/36; ⊙mid-Nov–Apr) Serious skiers should consider making the trek 80km northeast of Québec City to this well-regarded ski resort, which has eastern Canada's highest vertical drop and routinely gets more snow than other slopes in the region. In addition to standard skiing and snowboarding, the resort also features a rip-roaring 7.5km groomed luge run, which takes you down the mountain at speeds approaching 50km/h (minimum age 10).

MONT-STE-ANNE   SKIING

(☑418-827-4561, 888-827-4579; www.mont-sainte-anne.com; 2000 Blvd du Beau Pré, Beaupré; ⊙late Nov–Apr) This hugely popular ski resort 45km northeast of Québec City has 71 ski trails, 20 of which are set aside for night skiing (from 4pm to 9pm Wednesday through Saturday). You'll find all sorts of other winter activities here, including cross-country skiing, snowshoeing, skating, ice canyoning and dogsledding. You can rent skis and snowboards too.

STATION TOURISTIQUE
STONEHAM   SKIING

(☑800-463-6888; www.ski-stoneham.com; 600 Chemin du Hibou, Stoneham-et-Tewkesbury; lift ticket adult/youth/child $59/44/28; ⊙Dec–mid-Apr) Smaller than Mont-Ste-Anne but only 30km north of Québec City, Stoneham has 42 slopes for downhill skiing and snowboarding. Its 19 night skiing runs are usually open until around mid-March. Take Hwy 73 north to the Stoneham exit.

🛏 SLEEPING

From old-fashioned B&Bs to stylish boutique hotels, Québec City has some fantastic overnight options. The best choices are the numerous small European-style hotels and Victorian B&Bs scattered around the Old Town. As you'd expect in such a popular city, the top choices are often full, so make reservations well in advance, especially for weekends. It's unwise to show up in the city on a Saturday morning in summer or during holidays and expect to find a room for the same night.

> ℹ **NEED TO KNOW: ACCOMMODATIONS**
>
> Accommodations prices rise in the high-season summer months and during Winter Carnival. At other times, you can usually save 30% or so off the high-season prices.
>
> Budget accommodations also fill up quickly during the high season – with student groups block-booking entire hostels. If you're in a bind, student dorms are available to travelers during the summer at **Université Laval** (☑418-656-5632; www.residences.ulaval.ca/hebergement_hotelier; 2255 Rue de l'Université Laval, Pavillon Alphonse-Marie-Parent, local 1604; s $53-59, d $69-76). Located in the borough of Ste-Foy-Sillery, about a 15- to 20-minute bus ride away from the Old Town, rooms are clean but very plain and have shared baths.
>
> Outlying motels are concentrated primarily in three areas. The first, Beauport, is just a 12-minute drive northeast of the city. To get there, go north along Ave Dufferin, then take Hwy 440 until the exit for Blvd Ste-Anne/Rte 138. The motels are on a stretch between the 500 and 1200 blocks. A second area is located west of the center on Blvd Wilfrid-Hamel (Rte 138) – head west on Hwy 440 to the Henri IV exit. The third area is Blvd Laurier in the borough of Ste-Foy-Sillery. To get there, follow Grande Allée west until it turns into Blvd Laurier.
>
> City buses run to these areas, so whether you have a car or not, they may be the answer if you find everything booked up downtown. The further out you go, the more the prices drop. However, prices are still generally higher than usual for motels, averaging upwards of $100 in high season.
>
> A couple more caveats: first, many guesthouses in the Old Town simply do not have elevators; be sure to inquire on the room location if you're packing a lot of luggage and not keen on walking up a few flights of stairs. Secondly, a minimum stay (usually of two nights) may be required at some places in the height of summer. This is particularly true if arriving on the weekend.

🛏 Old Upper Town

This area has the widest choice of accommodations in town, from hostels and family-run B&Bs to cheap little hotels, intimate, luxurious inns and the granddaddy of them all – Le Château Frontenac.

HI AUBERGE INTERNATIONALE DE QUÉBEC
HOSTEL **$**

Map p172 (☑866-694-0950, 418-694-0755; www.aubergeinternationaledequebec.com; 19 Rue Ste-Ursule; dm $29-34, r without bath $72-84, with bath $100-125, all incl breakfast; ❄@🛜) The frustrating labyrinth of corridors goes on forever, but this lively, well-located place heaves with energy year-round. It attracts a mix of independent travelers, families and groups. Staff are friendly but often harried just trying to keep up with all the comings and goings. It's usually full in summer, despite having almost 300 beds, so book ahead if you can.

AUBERGE DE LA PAIX
HOSTEL **$**

Map p172 (☑418-694-0735; www.auberge delapaix.com; 31 Rue Couillard; dm $29-32, d/tr $80/105, all incl breakfast; @🛜) With welcoming staff, cheerfully painted rooms and a tree-filled garden out back, this funky old-school hostel on a quiet back street feels less institutional than the official HI hostel nearby. Four- to eight-bed dorms are complemented by five coveted private rooms (with shared bath) that must be booked well in advance. Bedding and a continental breakfast are included in the price.

★LA MARQUISE DE BASSANO
B&B **$$**

Map p172 (☑418-692-0316, 877-692-0316; www.marquisedebassano.com; 15 Rue des Grisons; r incl breakfast $110-179; ℗@🛜) The young, gregarious owners have done a beautiful job with this welcoming 19th-century Victorian family home, outfitting its five rooms with thoughtful touches, whether it's a canopy bed or a claw-foot bathtub. It's peacefully placed on a low-traffic street surrounded by period homes, minutes from the important sights. Only two rooms have private baths; the other three share facilities.

Breakfast includes fresh croissants and pastries, meats, hard-boiled eggs, cheese and fruit. Parking nearby, including two spaces just outside the hotel, costs $16 to $22 per night.

CHÂTEAU FLEUR-DE-LYS   HOTEL $$

Map p172 (☑877-691-1884, 418-694-1884; www.lhotel.ca; 15 Ave Ste-Geneviève; d $109-209, q $254; ☏) Delightfully sited opposite the leafy Jardins des Gouverneurs, this rambling old home has rooms of various dimensions outfitted with hand-chosen antiques by new European owners Romuald and Olivier. Top picks include the spacious Governor's Suite overlooking Le Château Frontenac and the St Lawrence River, and the two *chambres d'amis,* snug, budget-priced cuties with interior sink and private bath down the hall.

Rooms on the 2nd floor get more natural light than those on the 1st and 3rd floors or the family rooms in the basement. Optional breakfast costs $10 per person.

★ LES LOFTS 1048   APARTMENT $$

Map p172 (☑418-657-9177; www.condovieux quebec.ca; 1048 Rue St-Jean; apt $170-250; ✳☏) For a welcoming pied-à-terre in the heart of the Old Upper Town, try these gorgeously refurbished, bright, high-ceilinged apartments. Comfortable bedding, full kitchens, ultra-modern baths and laundry facilities make each loft a cozy home away from home. Nearby, the same owner offers the lower-priced **Le Haute Ville** (Map p172; ☑418-657-9177; www.hotelvieuxquebec.ca; 138 Rue Ste-Anne; studio $80-110, apt $110-165; ✳☏) apartments and the spiffy new **Lofts St-Joseph** (Map p178; ☑418-431-9905; www. st-joseph.quebec; 764 Rue St-Joseph; apt $170-250; ✳☏) in St-Roch.

MAISON DU FORT   B&B $$

Map p172 (☑888-203-4375, 418-692-4375; www.hotelmaisondufort.com; 21 Ave Ste-Geneviève; r $139-199; ✳☏) This B&B in a tranquil neighborhood above Le Château Frontenac lacks significant common areas, yet long-time owner Marielle's old-fashioned hospitality makes guests feel instantly at home. Cat lovers will adore friendly house feline Oscar, along with the faux Old Masters cat paintings, wood floors, stone and/or brick walls in many rooms. Spacious corner rooms 6 and 10 are especially inviting.

MANOIR D'AUTEUIL   B&B $$

Map p172 (☑866-662-6647, 418-694-1173; www.manoirdauteuil.com; 49 Rue d'Auteuil; r $99-229, junior ste $289-329; ℗✳@☏) Friendly American expatriate owners Dan and Linda have thoroughly renovated this pair of 19th-century manor houses opposite the Old Town walls, creating a supremely comfortable hotel replete with modern amenities. Rooms range widely in size; the nicest offer high ceilings, stone walls, fireplaces and canopy beds, or, in the case of the Edith Piaf suite, an ultra-spacious blue-tiled bath.

A pair of pretty high-ceilinged breakfast rooms and an outdoor terrace add to the charm.

MANOIR SUR LE CAP   INN $$

Map p172 (☑418-694-1987, 866-694-1987; www.manoir-sur-le-cap.com; 9 Ave Ste-Geneviève; r $85-185, ste $150-240; ℗✳☏) Attractions at this 14-room hotel include the wonderful, quiet location away from the tourist throngs, and the architectural details of the better rooms: attractive stone or brick walls and views of the Jardin des Gouverneurs, the Château or the river. On the downside, some of the smaller rooms have dated furnishings, and the desk staff's attitude is often lackadaisical.

Limited parking is available on-site on weekends; otherwise you can park at nearby garages ($15 to $22).

CHEZ HUBERT   B&B $$

Map p172 (☑418-692-0958; www.chezhubert. com; 66 Rue Ste-Ursule; r without bath incl breakfast $80-155; ℗@☏) This dependable family-run choice is in a Victorian townhouse with chandeliers, fireplace mantels, stained-glass windows, a lovely curved staircase and oriental rugs. The three tasteful, warm-hued rooms, two with a view of the Château, all share a pair of baths and come with a large buffet breakfast and free parking.

AU PETIT HÔTEL   HOTEL $$

Map p172 (☑418-694-0965; www3.sympatico. ca/aupetithotel/home; 3 Ruelle des Ursulines; r $75-150; ✳☏) Sitting on a tranquil dead-end lane, this former rooming house has a range of clean, simply furnished rooms, each with a private bath. Some are small and rather drab, while others are airy and borderline charming. Twelve of the 15 rooms have air-conditioning. Overall, it's good value for the Old Town, and parking right next door costs only $8.

QUÉBEC'S COOLEST HOTEL

Visiting the **Ice Hotel** (Hôtel de Glace; ☑418-875-4522, 877-505-0423; www.hoteldeglace-canada.com; 143 Rte Duchesnay; r from $380) is like stepping into a wintry fairy tale. Nearly everything here is made of ice: the reception desk, the sink in your room, your bed – all ice.

Some 500 tons of ice and 15,000 tons of snow go into the five-week construction of this perishable hotel. First impressions are overwhelming – in the entrance hall, tall, sculpted columns of ice support a ceiling where a crystal chandelier hangs. To either side, carved sculptures, tables and chairs fill the labyrinth of corridors and guest rooms. Children will love the ice slides, while grown-ups gravitate to the ice bar, where stiff drinks are served in cocktail glasses made of ice (there's hot chocolate for the kids too).

The Ice Hotel usually opens from January to March and offers packages starting at $380 per double. Sleeping here is more about the adventure, and less about getting a good night's sleep, although thick sleeping bags laid on plush deer pelts do help keep things cozier than you might expect.

A better option for most people is to buy a **day pass** (adult/youth/child $18/16/9), which allows you to visit the guest rooms and all of the hotel's public spaces, including the ice bar and ice slides. After 8pm, an **evening pass** (adult/youth/child $14/12.50/7) offers access to public spaces only. The hotel is about 15 minutes north of Québec City, via Hwy 175 and Hwy 73. Take exit 154 (Rue de la Faune) off Hwy 73 and follow the signs.

QUÉBEC CITY SLEEPING

FAIRMONT
LE CHÂTEAU FRONTENAC   HOTEL $$$

Map p172 (☑866-540-4460, 418-692-3861; www.fairmont.com/frontenac; 1 Rue des Carrières; r $229-1149, ste $408-2699; P❄🐾) More than a hotel, the iconic Frontenac is one of Québec City's enduring symbols. Fresh off a 2014 makeover, its 611 rooms come in a dozen-plus categories. The coveted river-view rooms range in price from Deluxe units tucked under the 18th-floor eaves to the ultra-spacious Fairmont Gold Signature rooms, with concierge service, curved turret windows and architectural details.

The hotel has over 2000 windows, a variety of elegant salons, bars and restaurants, and 12km of corridors lined with photos of famous guests including Alfred Hitchcock and Paul McCartney. Service is professional and staff are adept at handling the big crowds. While some guests enjoy connecting with a little slice of Québec City history, others feel the grand dame doesn't quite live up to its storied reputation. Check the website for special deals, especially outside the peak summer and Winter Carnival seasons.

AUBERGE PLACE D'ARMES   INN $$$

Map p172 (☑418-694-9485, 866-333-9485; www.aubergeplacedarmes.com; 24 Rue Ste-Anne; r $170-269, ste $260-349; @🐾🔊) Housed in a pair of 17th- and 18th-century buildings in the heart of the Old Upper Town, this cozy inn has some of the most dapper rooms around. Halls and guest rooms are done up in rich crimsons, navy blues and golds, and many rooms have exposed red-brick walls. The funicular to Lower Town is only a few paces away.

This place is also pet-friendly – for $25 extra per night, Fido can sleep beside you!

LE CLOS SAINT-LOUIS   INN $$$

Map p172 (☑418-694-1311, 800-461-1311; www.clossaintlouis.com; 69 Rue St-Louis; r incl breakfast $199-315; ❄🔊) At this four-star boutique hotel between Porte St-Louis and Le Château Frontenac, the owners have retained the building's natural 1844 Victorian charm while adding modern amenities. Most of the 18 spacious, lavishly decorated rooms come with Jacuzzi tubs, beautifully tiled baths, and canopy or four-poster beds. The suites resemble Victorian apartments, apart from the TV in the mini-drawing room.

🛏 Old Lower Town

A cluster of the city's most tantalizing boutique hotels is found in this area, along with a handful of hip, small inns.

HÔTEL BELLEY · HOTEL $$

Map p172 (☑418-692-1694, 888-692-1694; www.hotelbelley.com; 249 Rue St-Paul; r $125-170; ✸🛜) A great place for the young and hip who still like their creature comforts, this personable eight-room hotel offers spacious, uniquely designed rooms with original details including brick walls, wood paneling and beamed ceilings. You might also find French doors, a claw-foot tub – or, on the downside, a very tiny bath. Many rooms include microwave ovens or small refrigerators.

★AUBERGE SAINT-ANTOINE · BOUTIQUE HOTEL $$$

Map p172 (☑888-692-2211, 418-692-2211; $189-549, ste $600-1000; 🅿✸@🛜) Auberge Saint-Antoine is one of Canada's finest hotels, with phenomenal service and endless amenities. The plush, spacious rooms come with high-end mattresses, goose-down duvets, luxury linens and atmospheric lighting, while the halls resemble an art gallery, filled with French colonial relics discovered during excavations to expand the hotel. Panache (p190), the darling of Québec's fine-dining scene, is next door.

HÔTEL LE GERMAIN-DOMINION · BOUTIQUE HOTEL $$$

Map p172 (☑418-692-2224, 888-833-5253; www.germaindominion.com; 126 Rue St-Pierre; r $199-335; 🅿✸@🛜✸) The flagship hotel of a classy Québecois chain, the Dominion combines understated luxury with superb service. It occupies two adjacent historic buildings, one a former bank, one a historic fruit-and-vegetable market. Rooms are quiet, cozy and tastefully designed, with sumptuous mattresses, Egyptian cotton bedding, fluffy towels and bathrobes, good lighting, big windows, attractive woodwork, and glow-in-the-dark bath sinks.

Dogs get first-class treatment too; the $30-per-stay fee gets you a doggie bed, plus food and water bowls.

HÔTEL LE PRIORI · BOUTIQUE HOTEL $$$

Map p172 (☑418-692-3992; www.hotellepriori.com; 15 Rue Sault-au-Matelot; r $135-239, ste $229-399) Housed in the high-ceilinged former workshop of the renowned Baillargé family of architects, the Lower Town's original boutique hotel offers 20 rooms and eight suites with tall windows, exposed brick and stone walls, stylish Italian and Québecois furniture, and other classy amenities. The attached restaurant Toast! (p190) is one of Québec City's finest.

LE SAINT-PIERRE · BOUTIQUE HOTEL $$$

Map p172 (☑888-268-1017, 418-694-7981; www.auberge.qc.ca; 79 Rue St-Pierre; r $145-295, ste $215-365) Fresh off a 2013 makeover, this refined but relaxed boutique hotel has comfy rooms in soothing shades of white, beige and gray, most with hardwood floors and brick or stone walls, plus St Lawrence River views from the 4th floor. Inviting touches include the fireplace and leather chairs in the cozy downstairs lounge, and the ample included breakfast.

HÔTEL DES COUTELLIER · HOTEL $$$

Map p172 (☑418-692-9696, 888-523-9696; www.hoteldescoutellier.com; 253 Rue St-Paul; r $162-253, ste $277-358; ✸@🛜) Convenient to the train station, this handsome small hotel offers style, comfort and friendly service. Refreshingly unpretentious rooms are bright and spacious with modern furnishings (flat-screen TVs, iPod docks and high-end coffeemakers). A tasty continental breakfast is packed in a wicker basket for you every morning and hung outside your door.

HÔTEL 71 · BOUTIQUE HOTEL $$$

Map p172 (☑418-692-1171, 888-692-1171; www.hotel71.ca; 71 Rue St-Pierre; r $179-329, ste $259-409; ✸@🛜) Set in an imposing 19th-century greystone building, Hôtel 71 provides a boutique experience par excellence. Sleek, minimalist rooms offer unstinting comfort, with fantastic mattresses, plush down comforters, 4m-high ceilings, oversized TVs and dramatically lit baths. The penthouse suite, with its wraparound windows, commands some of Quebec City's most astounding perspectives on Place-Royale, the St Lawrence River and Le Château Frontenac.

St-Jean Baptiste

Accommodations here mean you'll be rubbing elbows with locals more than you would in the Old Town.

AU CROISSANT DE LUNE · B&B $

Map p178 (☑418-522-6366; www.aucroissantdelune.com; 594 Rue St-Gabriel; r without bath $85-125, incl breakfast; 🛜) Patricia, Olivier and their two young children offer three comfortable rooms with shared bath at

THE WONDROUS BACKYARD OF QUÉBEC CITY

Québec City is surrounded by stunning countryside with attractions for every interest. The sights below, except for Wendake, can be reached via Rte 138 northeast of town.

Île d'Orléans

This stunning place can be visited on a day trip but is easily worth two days or more. Cut off from the rest of Québec for centuries (the Taschereau Bridge was only built in 1935), its attractions include gorgeous pastoral scenery, riverside villages and 300-year-old stone homes.

Maison Drouin (☎418-829-0330; www.fondationfrancoislamy.org; 4700 Chemin Royal, Ste-Famille; admission $4; ⊙10am-6pm daily mid-Jun–Aug, 10am-4pm Sat & Sun Sep–mid-Oct), a 1730 house, is fascinating as it was never modernized (ie no electricity or running water) even though it was inhabited until 1984. Guides in period dress run tours in summer. At **Parc Maritime de St-Laurent** (☎418-828-9673; www.parcmaritime.ca; 120 Chemin de la Chalouperie, St-Laurent; adult/youth/child $5/3/free; ⊙10am-5pm mid-Jun–mid-Oct) you can learn about the island's ship-building history and enjoy pretty views of the St Lawrence River. There's a **tourist office** (☎418-828-9411, 866-941-9411; www.tourisme.iledorleans.com; 490 Côte du Pont, St-Pierre; ⊙8:30am-6pm early Jun-early Sep, 9am-4:30pm rest of year) just after you cross the bridge onto the island, about a 15-minute drive northeast of Québec City.

Parc de la Chute Montmorency

This 83m-high waterfall is right by the Taschereau Bridge on the way to Île d'Orléans. While it tops Niagara Falls by about 30m, it's not nearly as wide, but what's cool is walking over the falls on the suspension bridge, with the water thundering below. The **park** (☎418-663-3330; www.sepaq.com/montmorencyfalls; 5300 Blvd Ste-Anne) is about 12km northeast of Québec City.

Wendake

The major attraction at this Huron Aboriginal reserve is the **Onhoúa Chetek8e** (☎418-842-4308; www.huron-wendat.qc.ca; 575 Rue Chef Stanislas Koska; 2hr guided tour adult/youth/child $13.50/10.25/8.25; ⊙9am-5pm May-Oct, 10am-4pm Nov-Apr; 🚌), a reconstructed Huron village. Guides explain Huron history, culture and daily life. It's about 20 minutes northwest of Québec City; by car, take Hwy 73 (exit 154).

Ste-Anne-de-Beaupré

About 35km from Québec City, this village is known for its Goliath-sized **Basilique Ste-Anne-de-Beaupré** (www.sanctuairesainteanne.org; 10018 Ave Royale; ⊙8:30am-4:30pm) FREE and its role as a shrine. Try to visit on July 26, Ste-Anne's feast day, when the place goes berserk. The church fills to capacity, the nearby camping grounds are swamped with pilgrims, hotels are booked full and the whole village starts feeling like a kind of religious Woodstock.

this unpretentious family-friendly B&B. Easily the most charming is the two-level Green Room, with its main bedroom under the eaves and a kid-friendly smaller room downstairs. The full included breakfast, featuring homemade yogurt, fresh fruit, waffles and/or French-style crepes, is another plus.

LE CHÂTEAU DU FAUBOURG   B&B $$

Map p178 (☎418-524-2902; www.lechateau dufaubourg.com; 429 Rue St-Jean; r $129-169; P ❋ 🖭) Built by the massively rich Impe-

rial Tobacco family in the 1800s, this is one of the city's most atmospheric B&Bs. The interior is pure British-Lord-of-the-Manor meets French-Marquis style, replete with old oil paintings, antique furnishings and shimmering chandeliers. While some rooms are packed with old-world details, others seem a little cramped (notably the Boudoir du Josephine in the attic).

AUBERGE JA MOISAN   B&B $$

Map p178 (☎418-529-9764; www.jamoisan. com; 695 Rue St-Jean; s $120-150, d $130-160;

(P ❋ 🛜) This lovely top-floor B&B sits above the famous JA Moisan grocery store. Bedrooms are small and tucked under the eaves, while the floor below holds a cluster of common areas, including a parlor, tea room, solarium, terrace and computer room. Gregarious host Clément St-Laurent makes guests feel right at home, and rates include breakfast, afternoon tea and free valet parking.

CHÂTEAU DES TOURELLES
B&B $$

Map p178 (☑418-647-9136, 866-346-9136; www.chateaudestourelles.qc.ca; 212 Rue St-Jean; r incl breakfast $99-179, ste $139-245; 🛜) You'll recognize this B&B by its soaring turret, just west of Rue St-Jean's main cluster of shops and eateries. The new Breton owners have completely refurbished this old house, equipping rooms with pretty wood floors, triple-paned windows, old-fashioned sinks and hi-def TV; other perks include the bright, cozy breakfast area and lounge, and the rooftop terrace with 360-degree city views.

The eight standard rooms in the main building are complemented by a pair of kitchenette-equipped studios and a comfortable suite with its own private terrace and Jacuzzi.

L'HÔTEL DU CAPITOLE
HISTORIC HOTEL $$$

Map p178 (☑418-694-4040, 800-363-4040; www.lecapitole.com; 972 Rue St-Jean; r $155-305; P ❋ 🛜) Directly above the stately Théâtre Capitole (p196), this well-located hotel features rooms of varying size and character; the most attractive units feature exposed brick, floor-to-ceiling windows, balconies overlooking the old city walls and/or velvety red furniture with a touch of old-fashioned theatricality. Staff generally earn high marks for service. There's reasonably priced parking at the public garage across the street.

🛏 Montcalm & Colline Parlementaire

RELAIS CHARLES-ALEXANDRE
HOTEL $$

Map p178 (☑418-523-1220; www.relaischarlesalexandre.com; 91 Grande Allée Est; r $99-144;

(P ❋ 🛜) This small, cozy hotel has a great location near the Musée National des Beaux-Arts and Battlefields Park. Rooms are all different and are best described as low-key and comfortable with modern furnishings. Standard rooms are bright, but with a view onto the parking lot. Some superior rooms have big bay windows and fireplaces. Parking just behind the hotel costs $9 extra.

AUBERGE DU QUARTIER
HOTEL $$

Map p178 (☑418-525-9726, 800-782-9441; www.aubergeduquartier.com; 170 Grande Allée Ouest; r $129-189; P ❋ @ 🛜) Around the corner from restaurant-lined Ave Cartier, this friendly (and gay-friendly) hotel offers sleek modern rooms and professional service. Rooms range in size from small and modestly furnished to spacious numbers with nice extras, such as a fireplace. They're done up in masculine tones with rich burgundies, exposed steel beams or original brickwork adding to the atmosphere.

🛏 St-Roch

Steeply downhill about 1km from the walled city, St-Roch is a less convenient base than other neighborhoods, although the *ascenseur* (a free elevator connecting St-Roch and St-Jean Baptiste) eliminates part of the climb.

HÔTEL LE VINCENT
BOUTIQUE HOTEL $$$

Map p178 (☑418-523-5000; www.hotellevincent.com; 295 Rue St-Vallier Est; r incl breakfast $199-279; P @ 🛜) This hotel's nondescript brick facade may look unpromising, but things improve dramatically inside. The lobby and adjacent stone-walled breakfast area, with their comfy furniture and pleasant fireside reading nook, are instantly inviting, while the rooms upstairs, especially corner suites No 4 and 8, are stylishly comfortable, with brick walls, tall windows, mod couches and sleek bathtubs.

Quintuple-paned windows keep out the street noise. All rooms have plasma TVs with DVD players, ideal for taking advantage of the sizable video library at the front desk.

Understand Montréal & Québec City

Montréal Today

With the approach of its 375th anniversary in 2017, Montréal is preparing to strut its stuff for an international audience. Numerous urban redevelopment projects are underway, including new recreation and performing arts venues, pedestrian-friendly public spaces and revamped infrastructure. There's also a new energy in Montréal politics, as first-term mayor Denis Coderre strives to heal past scars from partisanship and corruption.

Best on Film

The Apprenticeship of Duddy Kravitz (1974) Mordecai Richler's timeless story of a Jewish upbringing.

Jesus of Montreal (1989) A prizewinning take on Montréal and Catholicism.

Incendies (2010) Two siblings confront the mystery of their mother's past.

Funkytown (2011) Bilingual film set against the backdrop of Montréal's 1970s club scene and the burgeoning secession movement.

Best in Print

Two Solitudes (Hugh MacLennan; 1945) One man's struggles with his English- and French-Canadian background.

The Tin Flute (Gabrielle Roy; 1947) A waitress looks for love in the slums of St-Henri.

How to Make Love to a Negro Without Getting Tired (Dany Laferrière; 1985) Provocative debut novel from this Haitian-Québecois author.

Barney's Version (Mordecai Richler; 1997) Richler's acclaimed murder mystery, told by a pair of less-than-reliable narrators.

Gearing Up for a Birthday Bash

Get ready for a big party. Montréal has a triple whammy of anniversary celebrations coming up in 2017: the 375th anniversary of the city's founding, the 150th anniversary of the Canadian Confederation and the 50th anniversary of Expo '67, the World's Fair that focused major international attention on Montréal back in the sixties. Perhaps the biggest promoter of the 2017 festivities is Montréal's new mayor Denis Coderre, whose efforts have included a personal visit to the Vatican to invite Pope Francis to attend!

To mark the occasion, Montréal has unveiled an ambitious series of projects designed to spur economic growth, improve locals' quality of life and attract visitors by showcasing the city's rich history, cultural diversity and artistic creativity.

History takes center stage on the brand-new Promenade Urbaine Fleuve-Montagne, a pedestrian route connecting the St Lawrence River and the slopes of Mont-Royal. Plaques along the route will invite both locals and visitors to contemplate the impact of geography in shaping Montréal's history and culture.

Other initiatives invite visitors to get out and explore the city's outdoor spaces. A brand-new open-air rink at Esplanade Clark will welcome skaters in winter and double as a public square in summer. Across the river, Parc Jean-Drapeau is getting spruced up with a panoramic riverside promenade and a new amphitheatre on Île Ste-Hélène designed to host major shows and festivals year-round. A slew of other new construction is in the works.

As always, Montréal loves any excuse for a good party, so you can expect to see a full lineup of events emerging as the date draws near; see the official 375th anniversary website (www.375mtl.com) for details.

Liveable City

In business and industry, Montréal does well for itself, boasting the highest number of research centers in Canada, an impressive high-tech sector and the third-largest fashion industry in North America (after New York and Los Angeles). While overall the cost of living here is low compared to most Canadian cities, and home prices remain about 40% to 50% cheaper than in Toronto or Vancouver, Montréal has seen a rapid rise in rental prices over the past few years, and gentrification has become a hot topic. The Plateau used to be the affordable bohemian place to live; now those without cash to pay for ever-increasing rents are being pushed out. Consequently, the creative scene is moving up to Little Italy, Mile End and Park Ex. Other pressing issues are the city's aging infrastructure, its high unemployment relative to other Canadian cities, and a city government that many see as cumbersomely complex, inefficient and costly. Montréalers also complain about paying the highest taxes of any province in Canada.

In spite of the city's shortcomings, Montréalers remain proud, citing the city's burgeoning film and music industries, its vibrant multiculturalism and its rich intellectual life. Not surprisingly, Montréal does quite well in quality-of-life surveys (often ranking well ahead of Paris, Barcelona and San Francisco for instance). A 2015 survey by the *Economist* rated Montréal as the world's second most liveable city, while Mercer's annual Quality of Living rankings regularly list Montréal among the top 25 cities globally (the city finished 24th in 2015).

A New Era in Politics

At the local level, Montréal is seeking to regain political equilibrium after a turbulent period in 2012–13 that saw major student protests and three changes of mayor within 12 months. Current mayor Denis Coderre, elected in November 2013, came into office on the heels of corruption scandals that spelled the doom of long-time mayor Gérald Tremblay and his immediate successor, Michael Applebaum. The Liberal-leaning Coderre made ethical integrity a cornerstone of his campaign, pledging to appoint an inspector-general for ethics, limit individual campaign donations to $100, and build a coalition government that would mix political newcomers with seasoned politicians from multiple parties. While Coderre barely squeaked into office with 32% of the vote, his populist, non-partisan style and pragmatic initiatives – such as pledging $50 million a year to fix potholes – have earned him widespread approval during the first half of his four-year term.

Meanwhile, at the provincial level, with the Parti Québecois coming off a 2014 defeat and Québec's newest political party, Coalition Avenir Québec, joining the Liberals in opposing sovereignty, the question of separatism has moved to the back burner.

if Montréal were 100 people

45 would be of Canadian origin
25 would be of French origin
3 would be of North American Aboriginal origin
27 would be of Other origin

language spoken
(% of population)

French   English   Other

population per sq km

MONTRÉAL   QUÉBEC

≈ 105 people

History

Originally the home of Iroquois people, Montréal has a dynamic history as a small French colony, a fur-trading center and a base for industrialists who laid the foundation of Canada. Later eclipsed by Toronto, it has rebranded itself as a powerhouse of French-speaking business and culture.

The Early Settlement

The Island of Montréal was long inhabited by the St Lawrence Iroquois, one of the tribes that formed the Five Nations Confederacy of Iroquois. In 1535, French explorer Jacques Cartier visited the Iroquois village of Hochelaga (Place of the Beaver Dam) on the slopes of Mont-Royal, but by the time Samuel de Champlain founded Québec City in 1608, the settlement had vanished. In 1642, Paul de Chomedey de Maisonneuve founded the first permanent mission, despite fierce resistance by the Iroquois. Intended as a base for converting Aboriginal people to Christianity, this settlement quickly became a major hub of the fur trade. Québec City became the capital of the French colony Nouvelle-France (New France), while Montréal's *voyageurs* (trappers) established a network of trading posts into the hinterland.

As part of the Seven Years' War, Britain clashed with France over its colony in New France. The British victory on the Plains of Abraham outside Québec City heralded the Treaty of Paris (1763), which gave Britain control of New France; it also presaged the creation of Canada itself with Confederation in 1867.

The American army seized Montréal during the American Revolution (1775–83) and set up headquarters at Château Ramezay. But even the formidable negotiating skills of Benjamin Franklin failed to convince French Québecers to join their cause, and seven months later the revolutionaries decided they'd had enough and left empty-handed.

When Jacques Cartier arrived at the St Lawrence River estuary around the time of the feast of St Lawrence in 1535, he gave thanks by naming it after the early Christian saint. It has had many other names – the River That Walks, the Canada River and the Cod River – but St Lawrence eventually stuck.

TIMELINE	1500	1535	1642
	Semi-sedentary Iroquois tribes frequent the island, settling one permanent village, Hochelaga (Place of the Beaver Dam), near present-day McGill University.	French explorer and gold-seeker Jacques Cartier sets foot on the island. He encounters the Iroquis, returning home with 'gold' and 'diamonds' – later revealed to be iron pyrite and quartz.	Maisonneuve and a group of 50 settlers found the colony of 'Ville-Marie.' Frenchwomen Jeanne Mance and Marguerite Bourgeoys establish New France's first hospital and school.

Industry & Immigration

In the early 19th century Montréal's fortunes dimmed as the fur trade shifted north to Hudson Bay. However, a new class of international merchants and financiers soon emerged, founding the Bank of Montréal and investing in shipping as well as a new railway network. Tens of thousands of Irish immigrants came to work on the railways and in the factories, mills and breweries that sprang up along the Canal de Lachine. Canada's industrial revolution was born, with the English clearly in control.

The Canadian Confederation of 1867 gave Québecers a degree of control over their social and economic affairs, and acknowledged French as an official language. French Canadians living in the rural areas flowed into the city to seek work and regained the majority. At this time, Montréal was Canada's premier railway center, financial hub and manufacturing powerhouse. The Canadian Pacific Railway opened its head office there in the 1880s, and Canadian grain bound for Europe was shipped through the port.

In the latter half of the century, a wave of immigrants from Italy, Spain, Germany, Eastern Europe and Russia gave Montréal a cosmopolitan flair that remains unique in the province. By 1914 the metropolitan population exceeded half a million residents, of whom more than 10% were neither British nor French.

In 1940, as Britain struggled against Germany in WWII, Prime Minister Winston Churchill shipped $5 billion in foreign reserves from the Bank of England to Montréal. The fortune was placed in a vault in the Sun Life Building, to fund a British government in exile should the Nazis invade and occupy Britain.

War, Depression & Nationalism

The peace that existed between the French and English citizens ran aground after the outbreak of WWI. When Ottawa introduced the draft in 1917, French-Canadian nationalists condemned it as a plot to reduce the francophone population. The conscription issue resurfaced

THE IRISH IN MONTRÉAL

The Irish have been streaming into Montréal since the founding of New France, but they came in floods between 1815 and 1860, driven from Ireland by the Potato Famine. Catholic like the French settlers, the Irish easily assimilated into Québecois society. Names from this period still encountered today include 'Aubrey' or 'Aubry,' 'O'Brinnan' or 'O'Brennan,' and 'Mainguy' from 'McGee.' In Montréal, most of these immigrants settled in Griffintown, then an industrial hub near the Canal de Lachine. The first St Patrick's Day parade in the city was held in 1824 and has run every year since; it's now one of the city's biggest events. For some terrific reads on the Irish community, check out *The Shamrock and the Shield: An Oral History of the Irish in Montreal* by Patricia Burns and *The Untold Story: The Irish in Canada*, edited by Robert O'Driscoll and Lorna Reynolds.

1721	1760	1763	1832
After years of on-and-off fighting with the Iroquois, the town erects a stone citadel. The colony continues to grow, fueled by the burgeoning riches of the fur trade.	One year after a resounding victory outside of Québec City, the British seize Montréal.	France officially cedes its territories to Britain, bringing an end to French rule in Canada.	Montréal is incorporated as a city following the prosperous 1820s. The Canal de Lachine dramatically improves commerce and transport.

in WWII, with 80% of Francophones rejecting the draft and nearly as many English-speaking Canadians voting for it.

During the Prohibition era Montréal found a new calling as 'Sin City,' as hordes of free-spending, pleasure-seeking Americans flooded over the border in search of booze, brothels and betting houses. But with the advent of the Great Depression, the economic inferiority of French Canadians became clearer than ever.

Québec's nationalists turned inward, developing proposals to create co-operatives, nationalize the anglophone electricity companies and promote French-Canadian goods. Led by the right-wing, ruralist, ultra-conservative Maurice Duplessis, the new Union Nationale party took advantage of the nationalist awakening to win provincial power in the 1936 elections. The party's influence would retard Québec's industrial and social progress until Duplessis died in 1959.

Grand Projects

By the early 1950s, the infrastructure of Montréal, by now with more than a million inhabitants, badly needed an overhaul. Mayor Jean Drapeau drew up a grand blueprint that would radically alter the face of the city, including the metro, a skyscraper-filled downtown and an underground city. The harbor was extended for the opening of the St Lawrence Seaway.

Along the way Drapeau set about ridding Montréal of its 'Sin City' image by cleaning up the shadier districts. His most colorful nemesis was Lili St-Cyr, the Minnesota-born stripper whose affairs with high-ranking politicians, sports stars and thugs were as legendary in the postwar era as her bathtub performances.

The face of Montréal changed dramatically during the 1960s as a forest of skyscrapers shot up. Private developers replaced Victorian-era structures with landmark buildings such as Place Bonaventure, a modern hotel and shopping complex, and the Place des Arts performing arts center. The focus of the city shifted from Old Montréal to Ville-Marie, where commerce flourished.

In 1960, the nationalist Liberal Party won control of the Québec assembly and passed sweeping measures that would shake Canada to its very foundations. In the first stage of this so-called Quiet Revolution, the assembly vastly expanded Québec's public sector and nationalized the provincial hydroelectric companies.

Francophones were able to work in French because more corporate managers supported French-language working conditions. For instance, the nationalization of power companies saw the language of construction blueprints change from English to French.

1833	1840s	1852	1865
Jacques Viger is elected as Montréal's first mayor.	Bad times arrive, with violent protests over colonial reform, and a 1847 typhus epidemic that kills thousands.	The Great Fire burns much of the city to the ground.	Lured by big industry, immigrants arrive by the thousands; Francophones soon outnumber Anglophones. Over the next 40 years, the population quadruples.

THE QUIET REVOLUTION

In the 1960s, the so-called Quiet Revolution began to give French Québecers more sway in industry and politics, and ultimately established the primacy of the French language.

The 'revolution' itself refers to the sweeping economic and social changes initiated by nationalist premier Jean Lesage and others that were intended to make Québecers more in control of their destiny and 'masters at home.' It was an effort to modernize, secularize and Frenchify Québec after years of conservatism under Premier Maurice Duplessis. But this tide of nationalism also had extreme elements.

The Front de Libération du Québec (FLQ), a radical nationalist group committed to overthrowing 'medieval Catholicism and capitalist oppression' through revolution, was founded in 1963. Initially the FLQ attacked military targets and other symbols of federal power, but soon became involved in labor disputes. In the mid-1960s, the FLQ claimed responsibility for a spate of bombings. In October 1970, the FLQ kidnapped Québec's labor minister Pierre Laporte and a British trade official in an attempt to force the independence issue. Prime Minister Pierre Trudeau declared a state of emergency and called in the army to protect government officials. The next day Laporte's body was found in the trunk of a car. By December the crisis had passed, but the murder discredited the FLQ in the eyes of many supporters. In the years that followed, the FLQ effectively ceased to exist as a political movement.

While support for Québec independence still hovers around 30% to 45% in the polls, there's little appetite for another referendum on separation from Canada. Rather, the current generation of voters seems to prefer a path of strong Québecois autonomy within the existing Canadian framework.

Still, progress wasn't swift enough for radical nationalists, and by the mid-1960s they were claiming that Québec independence was the only way to ensure francophone rights.

As the Francophones seized power, some of the old established anglophone networks became spooked and resettled outside the province. By 1965, Montréal had lost its status as Canada's economic capital to Toronto. But new expressways were laid out and the metro was finished in time for Expo '67 (the 1967 World's Fair), a runaway success that attracted 50 million visitors. It was the defining moment of Montréal as a metropolis, and would lay the foundations for its successful bid to host the 1976 Olympics – an event that would land the city in serious debt.

Meanwhile, things continued heating up in the Quiet Revolution. To head off clashes with Québec's increasingly separatist leaders, Prime Minister Pierre Trudeau proposed two key measures in 1969: Canada was to be made fully bilingual to give Francophones equal access to

1867	1867	1917	1959
Railways and an active harbor bring wealth to Montréal.	Tired of colonial rule, representatives of colonies on the Atlantic coast meet and form a Confederation; modern Canada is born.	As war rages in Europe, Québecers feel no loyalty to France or Britain and resent being conscripted to fight. Tensions seethe between Anglos and French Canadians.	St Lawrence Seaway opens, permitting freighters to bypass Montréal. Toronto slowly overtakes Montréal as Canada's commercial engine.

national institutions; and the constitution was to be amended to guarantee francophone rights. Ottawa then pumped cash into French-English projects, which nonetheless failed to convince Francophones that French would become the primary language of work in Québec.

In 1976, this lingering discontent spurred the election of René Lévesque and his Parti Québécois, committed to the goal of independence for the province. The following year the Québec assembly passed Bill 101, which not only made French the sole official language of Québec but also stipulated that all immigrants enroll their children in French-language schools. The trickle of anglophone refugees from the province turned into a flood. Alliance Québec, an English rights group, estimates that between 300,000 and 400,000 Anglos left Québec during this period.

The Not-Quiet Nation of Québec

The Quiet Revolution heightened tensions not only in Québec but across Canada. After their re-election in 1980, federal Liberals, led by Pierre Trudeau, sold most Québecers on the idea of greater rights through constitutional change, helping to defeat a referendum on Québec sovereignty the same year by a comfortable margin. Québec premier Robert Bourassa then agreed to a constitution-led solution – but only if Québec was recognized as a 'distinct society' with special rights.

In 1987 the federal Conservative Party was in power and Prime Minister Brian Mulroney unveiled an accord that met most of Québec's demands. To take effect, the Meech Lake Accord needed ratification by all 10 provinces and both houses of parliament by 1990. Dissenting premiers in three provinces eventually pledged their support, but incredibly the accord collapsed when a single member of Manitoba's legislature refused to sign.

The failure of the Meech Lake Accord triggered a major political crisis in Québec. The separatists blamed English-speaking Canada for its demise, and Mulroney and Bourassa subsequently drafted the Charlottetown Accord, a new, expanded accord. But the separatists picked it apart, and in October 1992, the second version was trounced in Québec and five other provinces. The rejection sealed the fate of Mulroney, who stepped down as prime minister the following year, and of Bourassa, who left political life a broken man.

Referendum & Rebirth

In the early 1990s Montréal was wracked by political uncertainty and economic decline. No one disputed that the city was ailing as the symptoms were everywhere: corporate offices had closed and moved

1959	1967	1970	1976
The strong-arm, anti-labor Duplessis regime ends. Francophone unions and co-operatives are on the rise.	Expo '67 in Montréal marks the centenary of Canadian Confederation, drawing people from across the country and around the world.	The separatist-minded Front de Libération du Québec kidnaps labor minister Pierre Laporte (later killing him). Although the FLQ is discredited, separatism gains support.	The Parti Québécois gains power and passes Bill 101, declaring French the official language. Many businesses leave Montréal, taking 15,000 jobs with them.

their headquarters to other parts of Canada, shuttered shops lined downtown streets, and derelict factories and refineries rusted on the perimeter. Relations between Anglophones and Francophones, meanwhile, plumbed new depths after Québec was denied a special status in Canada.

The victory of the separatist Parti Québécois in the 1994 provincial elections signaled the arrival of another crisis. Support for an independent Québec rekindled, and a referendum on sovereignty was called the following year. While it first appeared the referendum would fail by a significant margin, the outcome was a real cliff-hanger: Québecers decided by 52,000 votes – a razor-thin majority of less than 1% – to stay part of Canada. In Montréal, where the bulk of Québec's Anglophones and immigrants live, more than two-thirds voted against sovereignty, causing Parti Québécois leader Jacques Parizeau to infamously declare that 'money and the ethnic vote' had robbed Québec of its independence.

In the aftermath of the vote, the locomotives of the Quiet Revolution (economic inferiority and linguistic insecurity among Francophones) ran out of steam. Exhausted by decades of separatist wrangling, most Montréalers put aside their differences and went back to work.

Oddly enough, a natural disaster played a key role in bringing the communities together. In 1998 a freak ice storm – some blamed extra-moist El Niño winds, others cited global warming – snapped power masts like matchsticks across the province, leaving over three million people without power and key services in the middle of a Montréal winter. Some people endured weeks without electricity and heat, but regional and political differences were forgotten as money, clothing and offers of personal help poured into the stricken areas. Montréalers recount memories of those dark days with a touch of mutual respect.

As the political climate brightened, Montréal began to emerge from a fundamental reshaping of the local economy. The city experienced a burst of activity as sectors such as software, aerospace, telecommunications and pharmaceuticals replaced rust-belt industries like textiles and refining. Québec's moderate wages became an asset to manufacturers seeking qualified, affordable labor, and foreign investment began to flow more freely. Tax dollars were used to recast Montréal as a new-media hub, encouraging dozens of multimedia firms to settle in the Old Port area.

As Montréal gears up for its 375th anniversary in 2017, the upshot is a city transformed and brimming with self-confidence. The Place des Arts area teems with new restaurants and entertainment venues; Old Montréal buzzes with designer hotels and trendy restaurants; and once-empty warehouses around town have been converted to lofts and offices.

When Mayor Camilien Houde was faced with the proposal of building a road over Mont Royal, he famously retorted, 'A road over the mountain? Over my dead body!' After he died, and was duly buried on the side of the mountain, Mayor Jean Drapeau went ahead with the plan and built the aptly named Voie Camilien-Houde.

1976

Montréal stages the Summer Olympics and goes deeply into debt.

1980

The first referendum on independence ends in a comfortable defeat.

1993

Prime Minister Brian Mulroney steps down after failing to get support for the revised Charlottetown Accord.

1994

Voters go to the polls again, narrowly defeating Québec gaining sovereignty. Over the next decade the separatist movement slowly fizzles.

HISTORY BOOKS

➡ *A Short History of Quebec* (1993, revised 2008; John A Dickinson and Brian Young). Social and economic portrait of Québec from the pre-European period to modern constitutional struggles.

➡ *City Unique: Montreal Days and Nights in the 1940s and '50s* (1996; William Weintraub). Engaging tales of Montréal's twilight period as Sin City and an exploration of its historic districts.

➡ *The Road to Now: A History of Blacks in Montreal* (1997; Dorothy Williams). A terrific and rare look at a little-known aspect of the city's history and the black experience in New France.

➡ *All Our Yesterdays: A Collection of 100 Stories of People, Landmarks and Events From Montreal's Past* (1988; Edgar Andrew Collard). An insightful look at the city's history, streets and squares, with wonderful illustrations.

➡ *Canadiens Legends: Montreal's Hockey Heroes* (2004; Mike Leonetti). Wonderful profiles of some of the key players that made this team an NHL legend and a mythological part of Montréal's 20th-century cultural history.

➡ *The Illustrated History of Canada* (2002; edited by Craig Brown). Several historians contributed to this well-crafted work with fascinating prints, maps and sketches.

Montréal's renewed vigor has lured back some of the Anglophones who left in the 1980s and '90s, and language conflicts have slipped into the background. The impassioned separatists who came of age during the heady days of the Quiet Revolution are older now, and most young Montréalers are at least bilingual. In the 2014 Québec general election, the Parti Québécois earned its smallest share of the popular vote since its inaugural run in 1970. The party's defeat, brought about in part by candidate Pierre Karl Péladeau's strong endorsement of Québecois sovereignty, has led some to speculate that the demographic opportunity for separatism may have ended for good.

The federalist Québec Liberal Party has dominated provincial government for most of the past decade. In 2012, the party suffered its greatest challenge when students staged months of street protests against Premier Jean Charest's plans to end a long freeze on tuition increases. The controversy resulted in hundreds of arrests, passage of a tough new law to curb the protests and a brief return to power in September 2012 for the Parti Québécois, which had promised to do away with Charest's proposed tuition hike. However, the Liberals regained supremacy in Québec's April 2014 elections under new party leader Philippe Couillard.

1998	2005	2011–12	2014
The Great Ice Storm leaves thousands in Montréal and southern Québec without heat or electricity as power lines are severed by ice.	Canada becomes the fourth country in the world to legalize same-sex marriage. Montréaler Michaëlle Jean is installed as 27th governor general of Canada.	Montréal is wracked by months of street protests by students opposed to government plans to increase tuition. Hundreds are arrested.	The Parti Québécois suffers its worst electoral showing in decades, reflecting anemic public support for Québecois sovereignty.

People & Culture

Montréal's social scene is nothing if not passionate. Political apathy can turn into fiery protest overnight, while the potent mix of French, English and many other languages bubbles away in a stew that's sometimes tense. But a love of music, festivals and food somehow makes it all work.

Language

French is the official language of Québec and French Québecers are passionate about it, seeing their language as the last line of defense against Anglo-Saxon culture. What makes Montréal unique in the province is the interface of English and French – a mix responsible for the city's dynamism as well as the root of many of its conflicts.

Until the 1970s it was the English minority (few of whom spoke French) who ran the businesses, held positions of power and accumulated wealth in Québec; more often than not a French Québecer going into a downtown store couldn't get service in his or her own language.

But as Québec's separatist movement arose, the Canadian government passed laws in 1969 that required all federal services and public signs to appear in both languages. The separatists took things further and demanded the primacy of French in Québec, which was affirmed by the Parti Québécois with the passage of Bill 101 in 1977. Though there was much hand-wringing, the fact is that Bill 101 probably saved the French language from dying out in North America. If you're at a party with five Anglophones and one Francophone these days, the chances are everyone will be speaking French, something that would have been rare in decades past.

According to Québec's latest census, native French speakers in the Montréal metropolitan area number 2,395,525, while native English speakers number 439,845. More than 50 per cent of Montréalers from a variety of backgrounds speak both official languages.

Québec settlers were relatively cut off from France once they arrived in the New World, so the French you hear today in the province, known colloquially as Québecois, developed more or less independently from what was going on in France. The result is a rich local vocabulary, with its own idioms and sayings, and words used in everyday speech that haven't been spoken in France since the 1800s. Accents vary widely across the province, but all are characterized by a twang and rhythmic bounce unique to Québec.

To francophone Québecers, the French spoken in France sounds desperately posh. To people from France, the French spoken in Québec sounds terribly old-fashioned and at times unintelligible – an attitude that instantly ruffles feathers in Québec, as it's felt to be condescending.

Québecers learn standard French in school, hear standard French on newscasts and grow up on movies and music from France, so if you speak French from France, locals will have no difficulty understanding you – it's you understanding them that will be the problem. Remember,

The French spoken in Québec has swear words centering on objects used in church services. Where an English speaker might yell 'fuck,' a Quebecer will unleash 'tabarnac' (from tabernacle). Instead of 'oh, shit!,' a Québecer will cry 'sacrament!' (from sacrament). There are also combos like 'hostie de câlisse de tabarnac!' ('host in the chalice in the tabernacle!').

SIGNS OF PRIDE

Québec's French Language Charter, the (in)famous Bill 101, asserts the primacy of French on public signs across the province. Stop signs in Québec read 'ARRÊT,' a word that actually means a stop for buses or trains (even in France, the red hexagonal signs read 'STOP'). Apostrophes had to be removed from storefronts like Ogilvy's in the 1980s to comply with French usage, and English is only allowed on signage provided it's no more than half the size of the French lettering. Perhaps most bewildering of all is the acronym PFK (Poulet Frit Kentucky) for a leading fast-food chain.

The law is enforced by language police who, prompted by complaints from French hardliners, roam the province with tape measures (yes – for real!) and hand out fines to shopkeepers if a door says 'Push' more prominently than 'Poussez.' These days, most Québecers take it all in their stride, and the comical language tussles between businesses and the language police that once featured regularly on evening newscasts and phone-in shows have largely disappeared.

even when French-language Québecois movies are shown in France, they are shown with *French* subtitles.

Young Montréalers today are not particularly concerned about language issues. Most grew up speaking both languages, and people you meet in daily life – store owners, waiters and bus drivers – switch effortlessly between French and English.

Media

Montréal is the seat of Québec's French-language media companies and has four big TV networks. New-media firms such as Autodesk Media and Entertainment are renowned for their animation and special effects, and the Cité du Multimédia center in Old Montréal is an incubator for start-ups.

The *Montreal Gazette* (www.montrealgazette.com) is the major English-language daily, with coverage of national affairs, politics and the arts. The big French dailies are the federalist *La Presse* (www.cyberpresse.ca) and the separatist-leaning *Le Devoir* (www.ledevoir.com).

Le Journal de Montréal (www.journaldemontreal.com) is *the* city's rollicking tabloid, replete with sensational headlines and photos. Though much derided, the *Journal* does the brashest undercover and investigative reporting in town and has the city's biggest daily circulation.

Montréal's last free alternative weekly is the French-language *Voir* (www.voir.ca); it covers film, music, books, restaurants and goings-on about town.

Canada's only truly national papers are the left-leaning Toronto *Globe and Mail* (www.theglobeandmail.com) and the right-leaning *National Post* (www.nationalpost.com). *The Walrus* (www.thewalrus.ca) is a Canadian *New Yorker/Atlantic Monthly*–style magazine, with in-depth articles and musings from the country's intellectual heavyweights. Canada's weekly news magazine *Maclean's* (www.macleans.ca) and the sophisticated general-interest magazine *Maisonneuve* (www.maisonneuve.org) are also full of high-quality writing.

L'Actualité (www.lactualite.com) is Québec's monthly news magazine in French. The Canadian Broadcasting Corporation's site (www.cbc.ca) is an excellent source for current affairs.

English-Language Broadcasters

CJAD 800 AM
(www.cjad.com)
Talk radio

CBC Radio One
88.5 FM (www.cbc.ca/radio)
News and current events

CHOM 97.7 FM
(www.chom.com)
Classic rock

Global Montreal
(www.globalnews.ca/montreal)
Television

CTV Montreal
(www.montreal.ctvnews.ca)
Television

CBC Montreal
(www.cbc.ca/montreal)
Television

Fashion

One of the things visitors first notice here is how well dressed people are – and it's not just the women who stop traffic. Conservative colors prevail in law and banking, but in media, IT and other businesses, local men might sport a chic olive-green suit with a lavender tie, which their counterparts in Vancouver, Toronto or even New York wouldn't dream of donning.

French-language fashion blogs such as Zurbaines (www.zurbaines.com) and Mode Montréal (www.modemontreal.tv) follow the local fashion scene, as do English-language counterparts such as the Montreal Fashion Blog (www. themontrealfashionblog.com) and Vitamin Daily (www. vitamindaily.com/montreal/fashion).

Whether artists, students or entrepreneurs, it seems like everybody knows the look they're going for and pulls it off well. Label watchers put it down to the perfect fusion of European and American fashion – Paris' bold willingness to experiment coupled with an American practicality that makes people choose what's right for them rather than what's necessarily in fashion. In short, Montréalers have fun with clothes and are happy to flaunt it.

Carved in stone on Québec City's Parliament building and emblazoned on every license plate in the province, the simple motto 'Je me souviens' (I remember) eloquently expresses the Québecois sense of pride and identity as North America's largest and oldest French-speaking culture.

Sports

Québecers are active year-round, jogging, cycling and kayaking on warm summer days, with cold wintry days bringing ice-skating, cross-country skiing and pickup hockey games on frozen lakes.

Sporting events – which can essentially be subcategorized as hockey followed by everything else – draw huge numbers of Montréalers. The essential experience is to journey into the great hockey hall of the Bell Centre to catch the Canadiens (www.canadiens.nhl.com) gliding to victory.

Other key spectator moments include watching the mighty Alouettes (www.montrealalouettes.com), a Canadian football team with plenty of muscle (despite being named after a songbird); rooting for the Montréal Impact (www.impactmontreal.com) soccer team; and attending the Formula 1 Grand Prix du Canada (www.circuitgillesvilleneuve.ca).

For those who'd rather join the fray, there are plenty of outdoorsy events. The Tour de l'Île (www.velo.qc.ca), for instance, is one of Montréal's best-loved participatory bike rides, when tens of thousands fill the streets for a fun cycle (28km or 50km) around Montréal. There's a palpable energy in the city that even non-pedalers enjoy.

In winter, green spaces become cross-country ski trails, and ponds and lakes transform into outdoor skating rinks at places like the Old Port and Parc La Fontaine.

Other great ways to enjoy the scenery include white-water rafting down the Lachine Rapids (or surfing them if your life insurance policy is in order), kayaking idly down the Canal de Lachine, or simply heading to 'the Mountain' (Parc du Mont-Royal) for a bit of running, pedal-boating, ice-skating, sledding, snowshoeing, bird-watching or – if it's Sunday – gyrating and/or pounding your drums at the free-spirited tam-tam jam (p115).

Music & the Arts

Montréal is both the undisputed center of the French-language entertainment universe in North America and the cultural mecca of Québec. It is ground zero for everything from Québec's sizable film and music industries to visual and dramatic arts and publishing.

Music

If you come across Rue Rufus Rockhead near Marché Atwater, don't think it's named after a character from *The Flintstones*. Jamaican-born Rufus Rockhead was the owner of Rockhead's Paradise, the hottest downtown jazz club in the 1930s and '40s. It hosted the likes of Billie Holiday, Sarah Vaughan and Sammy Davis Jr.

From Leonard Cohen to Arcade Fire and the Jazz Fest, sometimes it seems Montréal is all about the music. A friend to experimentation of all genres and styles, the city is home to more than 250 active bands, embracing anything and everything from electropop, hip-hop and glam rock to Celtic folk, indie punk and *yéyé* (exuberant 1960s-style French rock) – not to mention roots, ambient, grunge and rockabilly.

Rock & Pop

On the rock scene, Arcade Fire remains one of Montréal's top indie rock bands. Their eclectic folk/rock/indie sound and manic ensemble of instruments have made them critics' darlings since their first album *Funeral* hit the US and UK top 10 lists in 2004. Their 2010 album *The Suburbs* topped charts in several countries and won Album of the Year at the 2011 Grammy Awards, and their 2014 release *Reflektor* was nominated as Best Alternative Music Album at the 2015 Grammy Awards.

In the francophone music industry, the market is crowded with talented artists. Eternal favorites include alternative rocker Louis-Jean Cormier, who won both a Juno and a Félix award for his 2013 release *Le Treizième Étage;* keyboardist Pierre Lapointe; rocker Jean Leloup; and singer-songwriter Ariane Moffatt.

More recent arrivals include singer-songwriter Alex Nevsky, who made a clean sweep of the Félix awards in 2014, taking honors for Best Male Vocalist, Best Pop Album *(Himalaya Mon Amour)* and Best Song ('On Leur A Fait Croire'); indie pop artist Coeur de Pirate, whose first two albums were nominated for Junos; crooner Patrick Watson, known for singing in English and French, as well as playing unusual instruments, such as a bicycle on his song 'Beijing'; and singer-songwriter Marie-Pierre Arthur, whose awards include best new singer-songwriter of 2012 and best album for her 2013 release *Aux Alentours.*

Jazz

In the 1940s and '50s, Montréal was one of North America's most important venues for jazz music. It produced a number of major jazz musicians, such as pianist Oscar Peterson and trumpeter Maynard Ferguson. The scene went into decline in the late 1950s but revived after the premiere of the jazz festival in 1979.

The city's other celebrated jazz pianist, Oliver Jones, was already in his fifties when he was discovered by the music world. Since the 1980s he has established himself as a major mainstream player with impressive technique and a hard-swinging style.

Singer and pianist Diana Krall has enjoyed mass appeal without sacrificing her bop and swing roots. In 1993 she launched her career on Montréal's Justin Time record label, and she remains a perennial local favorite during regular appearances at Montréal's jazz festival.

Originally from New York City, singer Ranee Lee is known for her virtuosity that spans silky ballads, swing standards and raw blues tunes. She has performed with many jazz notables and is a respected teacher on the McGill University music faculty.

Classical

The backbone of Montréal's classical music scene is the Orchestre Symphonique de Montréal. The OSM has won a host of awards including two Grammys and 12 Junos, and it was the first Canadian orchestra to achieve platinum (500,000 records sold), on its 1984 recording of Ravel's *Bolero*.

The smaller Orchestre Métropolitain du Grand Montréal is a showcase of young Québec talent and as such is staffed by graduates from the province's conservatories. The director is Yannick Nézet-Séguin, a Montréaler who became one of Canada's youngest major orchestra directors when he took the baton at age 25 in 2000.

Reflecting the strength and diversity of Québec's film industry, three consecutive Québecois directors earned Oscar nominations in the Best Foreign Film category between 2010 and 2012: Denis Villeneuve for *Incendies*, Philippe Falardeau for *Monsieur Lazhar* and Kim Nguyen for *Rebelle (War Witch)*.

Opera

Over the past 25 years, the Opéra de Montréal has become a giant on the North American landscape. It has staged dozens of operas and hundreds of performances, and collaborated with numerous international companies. Many great names have graced its stages including Québec's own Leila Chalfoun, Lyne Fortin, Suzie LeBlanc and André Turp, alongside a considerable array of Canadian and international talent. The company stages several new operas every season, including classics like *Madame Butterfly* and *The Magic Flute*.

Locally, new operas are not created, but in 1989 the Opéra de Montréal won a Félix award for the most popular production of the season for *Nelligan,* an opera created in Québec about the life of poet Émile Nelligan by André Gagnon; Michel Tremblay wrote the libretto.

SOUNDS OF MONTRÉAL: THE WORLD-RENOWNED JAZZ FESTIVAL

In a city that loves festivals, the **Festival International de Jazz de Montréal** (www.montrealjazzfest.com; ☉late Jun–early Jul) is the mother of them all – erupting in late June each year and turning the city into an enormous stage for 10 days. No longer just about jazz, this is one of the world's biggies, with hundreds of top-name performers bringing reggae, rock, blues, world music, Latin, reggae, Cajun, Dixieland and even pop to audiophiles from across the globe.

It started as the pipe dream of a young local music producer, Alain Simard, who tried to sell his idea to the government and corporate sponsors, with little success. Now it's the single biggest tourist event in Québec, attracting nearly two million visitors to 400 concerts – many say it's the best jazz festival on the planet. Miles Davis, Herbie Hancock, Al Jarreau, Sonny Rollins, Wayne Shorter, Stevie Wonder, Al Dimeola, James Cotton, Booker T Jones, Taj Mahal, John Scofield and Jack DeJohnette are but a few of the giants who have graced the podiums over the years.

Practicalities

The festival website provides all the details; free festival programs are at kiosks around the Place des Arts. Some concerts are held indoors, others on outdoor stages; several downtown blocks are closed to traffic. The music starts around noon and lasts until late evening when the clubs take over.

SUZANNE TAKES YOUR HAND...

Singer-songwriter Leonard Cohen, one of the city's most famous sons, grew up in the wealthy Anglo enclave of Westmount, but was drawn to the streets of downtown and the Old Port. His celebrated 1967 ballad 'Suzanne' was based on his experiences with Suzanne Verdal, then wife of sculptor Armand Vaillancourt. Fans have tried to pinpoint the location of the meeting, and the most likely spot is an old waterfront building along Rue de la Commune in the Old Port. The lyrics refer to 'the lady of the harbor,' which is thought to be the statue atop the Chapelle Notre-Dame-de-Bonsecours at 400 Rue St-Paul Est.

Folk

Best known as an icon of the 1960s, Montréal's native son Leonard Cohen remains one of the world's most eclectic folk artists. Beloved worldwide for his song 'Suzanne,' Cohen experienced a second burst of major creativity in the 1980s and early 1990s that suddenly made him hip again to younger audiences. Now an octogenarian, Cohen has re-emerged with another cycle of albums and embarked on a series of wildly successful world tours to rapturous audiences. He was chosen as Artist of the Year at the 2013 Juno awards, and his most recent release, *Popular Problems*, took Album of the Year at the 2015 Junos.

Other English-language folk singers are few and far between, but it's well worth hearing Montréal-based folk quartet the Barr Brothers if you get a chance.

Chanson

It's hard to understand music in Québec without understanding what they call *chanson*. While France has a long tradition of this type of French folk music, where a focus on lyric and poetry takes precedence over the music itself, in Québec the *chanson* has historically been tied in with politics and identity in a profound way. With the Duplessis-era Québec stifling any real creative production, Québecers were tuned into only what was coming out of France, like Edith Piaf or Charles Aznavour.

The social upheaval of the Quiet Revolution in the 1960s changed all that, when a generation of musicians took up their guitars, started to sing in Québecois and penned deeply personal lyrics about life in Québec and, often, independence.

Longtime favorite Gilles Vigneault is synonymous with the *chanson* 'Gens du pays' (People of the Country), often played on nationalist occasions. Other iconic *chansonniers* include Félix Leclerc, Claude Léveillé, Richard Desjardins and Jean-Pierre Ferland.

These days, younger performers such as Coeur de Pirate or the Soeurs Boulay who embrace the style are usually referred to as *auteurs-compositeurs-interprêtes* (singer-songwriters) rather than *chansonniers*, and their repertoire may include pop and rock as well as *chanson*. To experience this Québecois tradition for yourself, visit a *boîte á chanson* (club where this type of music is played).

William Shatner left his native Montreal for *Star Trek* long ago, but the city still loves him. McGill University, his alma mater, awarded him an honorary doctorate in 2011. 'Don't be afraid of making an ass of yourself,' he told students. 'I do it all the time and look what I got.'

Film & Television

The foundations of Québec cinema were laid in the 1930s when Maurice Proulx, a pioneer documentary filmmaker, charted the colonization of northwestern Québec's gold-rich Abitibi region. In the 1960s, directors were inspired to experiment by the likes of Federico Fellini and Jean-Luc Godard, but rural life remained the subject of most Québecois films. The 1970s were another watershed moment when erotically charged movies such as Claude Jutra's *Mon Oncle Antoine* and Gilles Carle's *La Vraie Nature de Bernadette* sent the province a-twitter.

Montréal finally burst onto the international scene in the 1980s with a new generation of directors such as Denys Arcand, Louis Archambault, Michel Brault and Charles Binamé. That trend has continued into the 21st century with the emergence of acclaimed directors such as Denis Villeneuve, Philippe Falardeau and Kim Nguyen. Films are produced in French but dubbing and subtitling have made them accessible to a wider audience.

Animation, 3D and multimedia technologies have also been a Montréal specialty. Companies such as Softimage and Discreet Logic – now both folded into the much bigger, but still Montréal-based, Autodesk Media and Entertainment – have masterminded the special effects used in countless Hollywood blockbusters, including *Jurassic Park, The Mask, Godzilla, Titanic, Avatar, Harry Potter and the Deathly Hallows* and the *Life of Pi.*

In late August or early September, the Festival du Film de Montréal (www.ffm-montreal.org), one of Canada's largest and most prestigious cinema festivals, brings in filmmakers from all over Québec and around the world.

A hit TV show in French is *Tout le Monde en Parle* (Everybody is Talking About It), a current affairs program hosted by comedian Guy A Lepage. It's controversial, snappy and the first stop for anyone doing anything in Québec's public arena, from politicians and actors to war heroes.

Theater

Founded in 1968, the Centaur Theatre is Québec's premier English-language stage for drama. Initially it featured modern-international playwrights such as Arthur Miller, Bertolt Brecht and Harold Pinter, but the addition of a second stage for experimental theater in the 1970s helped fuel the rise of English-speaking playwrights such as David Fennario, whose award-winning *Balconville*, first performed in 1979, remains a classic. The theater stages its 10-day Wildside Theatre Festival every January.

Québec's fabulously successful Cirque du Soleil set new artistic boundaries by combining dance, theater and circus in a single power-packed show. Now an international phenomenon with $1 billion-plus in annual revenues, the company produces touring shows in places as far flung as Colombia and Australia, and in multiple hotels on the Las Vegas Strip; performances in Québec are not as common as they once were, but if you're lucky, you may still catch a first look at one of their new shows in Montréal's Old Port or elsewhere around the province.

QUÉBEC'S MASTER FILMMAKER

No director portrays modern Québec with a sharper eye than Montréal's own Denys Arcand. His themes are universal enough to strike a chord with international audiences: modern sex in *The Decline of the American Empire* (1986), religion in *Jésus of Montréal* (1989) and death in the brilliant tragicomedy *The Barbarian Invasions*, which won the 2003 Academy Award for Best Foreign Film (the first, and so far the only, Canadian film to ever win an Oscar in that category).

Born in 1941 near Québec City, Arcand studied history in Montréal and landed a job at the National Film Board making movies for Expo '67. The young director was a keen supporter of francophone rights and the Quiet Revolution, but became deeply disillusioned with Québec politics in the 1970s. His most recent works include *L'Âge des Ténèbres*, which was the closing film of the Cannes Film Festival in 2007, and *Le Règne de la Beauté* (2014).

One of Québec's most famous playwrights is Michel Tremblay, whose plays about people speaking in their own dialects changed the way Québecers felt about their language.

Dance

Montréal's dance scene crackles with innovation. Virtually every year a new miniseries, dance festival or performing arts troupe emerges to wow audiences in wild and unpredictable ways. Hundreds of performers and dozens of companies are based in the city and there's an excellent choice of venues for interpreters to strut their stuff; Agora de la Danse and Circuit-Est Chorégraphique are two of the best.

Several major companies have established the city's reputation as an international dance mecca. Les Grands Ballets Canadiens attracts the biggest audiences, while Les Ballets Jazz de Montréal, La La La Human Steps, Compagnie Marie Chouinard, Cas Public, O Vertigo, Daniel Léveillé Danse and Par B.L.eux are troupes of international standing.

Montréal boasts two great contemporary dance festivals. The Festival TransAmériques (www.fta.qc.ca) in late May/early June focuses on new creations by Canadian and international performers. The Quartiers Danses festival (www.quartiersdanses.com) in September stages performances at venues ranging from the Atwater Market to the Montréal Museum of Fine Arts and Parc du Mont-Royal.

Montréal resident Margie Gillis is a modern dancer of international renown who combines performing, teaching and choreography all over the world. She has choreographed solo shows for Cirque du Soleil and in 2013 was named an Officer of the Order of Canada for her lifelong artistic achievement.

Literature

Montréal proudly calls itself the world's second cradle of French-language writers – after Paris, of course. But the city also boasts intimate links to many English-language writers of repute.

Caustic, quick-witted and prolific, Mordecai Richler was the 'grumpy old man' of Montréal literature in the latter part of the 20th century. Richler grew up in a working-class Jewish district in Mile End and, for better or worse, remained the most distinctive voice in anglophone Montréal until his passing in 2001. Most of his novels focus on Montréal and its wild and wonderful characters. For another engaging English-language perspective on the province, check out the award-winning mystery novels of Louise Penny, whose protagonist Chief Inspector Armand Gamache unravels murders set in both small-town and urban Québec.

On the French side, Québec writers who are widely read in English include Anne Hébert, Marie-Claire Blais, Hubert Aquin, Christian Mistral and Dany Laferrière. For stories about everyday life on the Plateau, try Michel Tremblay's short stories.

Roch Carrier's short story 'Le Chandail de Hockey' (The Hockey Sweater), is well known by hockey fans. Due to a mail-order mix-up, a child is forced to wear a Toronto Maple Leafs jersey in a small Québec town teeming with Montréal Canadiens fans. It's a parable of the friction between French and English populations.

Painting & Visual Arts

Québec's lush forests and icy winter landscapes have been inspiring landscape artists since the 19th century. Horatio Walker was known for his sentimental interpretations of Québec farm life such as *Oxen Drinking* (1899). Marc-Aurèle Fortin (1880–1970) is famed for his watercolors of the Québec countryside. His portraits of majestic elms along Montréal avenues can be viewed in the Musée des Beaux-Arts. Québec's surrealist-influenced Automatistes movement of the 1940s produced a number of artists, including Jean-Paul Riopelle (1923–2002), whose works are on permanent display at Montréal's Musée d'Art Contemporain and Québec City's Musée National des Beaux-Arts.

Architecture

Montréal's split personality is nowhere more obvious than in its architecture, a beguiling mix of European traditionalism and North American modernism. Lovingly preserved Victorian mansions and stately beaux-arts monuments rub shoulders with the sleek lines of modern skyscrapers, lending Montréal's urban landscape a creative, eclectic sophistication all of its own.

Old-World Icons

Architectural Montréal is perhaps most easily understood by its neighborhoods and its icons. In Old Montréal, a plethora of 19th-century and some 18th-century buildings crowd in cobblestone streets, where horse-drawn carriages impart a flavor of Europe some 100 years ago; no wonder it's the setting for so many films. The representative structure here is the stunning Basilique Notre-Dame (p48) from the mid-19th century. Indeed, for most of its modern history, the city's architecture has been characterized by churches, reflecting the Catholic and Protestant churches' influence on its development. Their innumerable metallic roofs earned Montréal its nickname – La Ville aux Cent Clochers (City of 100 Steeples). When Mark Twain visited in 1881, he famously remarked, 'This is the first time I was ever in a city where you couldn't throw a brick without breaking a church window.'

Today, however, Old Montréal is also home to modern eyesores that clash with the heritage structures: the 500 Place d'Armes building and the Palais de Justice building, relics of the 1960s and 1970s, make no attempt to fit in. Still, Old Montréal is one of the most homogenous neighborhoods of the city. Today's strict building codes require extensive vetting before new construction can begin.

For many visitors, the weathered greystones, such as the old stone buildings along Rue St-Paul, offer the strongest images of Old Montréal. The style emerged under the French regime in Québec (1608–1763), based on Norman and Breton houses with wide, shallow fronts, stuccoed stone and a steep roof with dormer windows. Locals soon adapted the blueprint to Montréal's harsh winters, making the roof less steep, adding basements and extending the eaves over the walls for extra snow protection.

From the 19th century, architects tapped any number of retro styles: classical (Bank of Montréal), Gothic (Basilique Notre-Dame) and Italian renaissance (Royal Bank), to name a few. As Montréal boomed in the 1920s, a handful of famous architects such as Edward Maxwell, George Ross and Robert MacDonald left their mark on handsome towers in Old Montréal and downtown. French Second Empire style continued to be favored for comfortable francophone homes and some public buildings, such as the Hôtel de Ville (City Hall; p51).

Downtown is a multifaceted jumble of buildings where run-down 20th-century brick buildings abut shiny new multipurpose complexes. Sometimes one building straddles the historical divide: the Centre Canadien d'Architecture (p79) integrates a graceful historical greystone right into its contemporary façade. Other important buildings

VICTORIAN BEAUTIES

Montréal boasts the largest collection of Victorian row houses in North America. Numerous examples can be viewed in the Plateau, along Rue St-Denis north of Rue Cherrier or Ave Laval north of Carré St-Louis. Visitors are inevitably charmed by their brightly painted wrought-iron staircases, which wind up the outside of duplexes and triplexes. They evolved for three important reasons: taxes (a staircase outside allowed each floor to count as a separate dwelling, so the city could hike property taxes), fuel costs (an internal staircase wastes heat as warm air rises through the stairwell) and space (the first and second floors were roomier without an internal staircase).

were meant to break with the past. Place Ville-Marie (p76), a multi-towered complex built in the late 1950s, revolutionized urban architecture in Montréal and was the starting point for the underground city.

Transforming Downtown

Must-Sees in Montréal

Basilique Notre-Dame (p48)

Hôtel de Ville (City Hall, p51)

Biosphère (p68)

Oratoire St-Joseph (p131)

Olympic Stadium (p230)

Since the 1960s, the government has spent billions developing tourist attractions and infrastructure in Montréal, and the resultant architectural boom has greatly transformed the city. Expo '67 spurred the construction of experimental edifices such as Habitat 67 (p69), a controversial apartment building designed by Montréal architect Moshe Safdie when he was only 23; located on a promontory off the Old Port, it resembles a child's scattered building blocks. Other structures with 1960s roots include Buckminster Fuller's Biosphère (p68), which once wore a skin made of spherical mesh, and the Casino de Montréal (p69), which cleverly merges two of the most far-out pavilions of Expo '67. The 1976 Olympics saw an explosion of large-scale projects, the most notorious of which, the Olympic Stadium (p135), serves as a reminder of the pitfalls of constructing costly white elephants. Despite its reputation, many admire the stadium's dramatic tower, which leans at 45 degrees and is home to an observation deck.

One of the largest redevelopment projects in Canada was Montréal's $200 million Palais des Congrès (p55) convention center, inaugurated in 1983 and expanded between 1999 and 2002. The Palais and its adjacent squares form a mini-district known as the Quartier International that unites downtown and Old Montréal by concealing an ugly sunken expressway. Nearby, in the Quartier Latin, the 33,000-sq-meter Bibliothèque et Archives Nationale du Québec (p92) opened to huge success in 2005, with crowds of Montréalers visiting the building each day.

The government has also invested millions of dollars in Montréal's public thoroughfares. 'The Main' (Blvd St-Laurent) has been spruced up with the widening of sidewalks, the planting of trees and the addition of street lights in certain stretches. A similar facelift for Rue Ste-Catherine, completed in 2012, involved the installation of new sidewalks and paving stones. Rue Notre-Dame, long a two-laned nightmare pocked with potholes (but nonetheless an important artery into Old Montréal), is also slated for a major overhaul that will convert it into a landscaped boulevard with four lanes in each direction, flanked by multi-purpose recreation paths.

Into the Future

Never a city to rest on its laurels, Montréal continues to jazz up its urban landscape with new architectural ventures.

Montréal's most ambitious urban renewal project in recent years has been the Quartier des Spectacles, on the edge of the Quartier Latin and downtown. Since 2007, the $150 million project has completely

Above: Buildings on Blvd René-Lévesque, Montréal
Right: Habitat 67 (p69), Montréal

CANADA'S STAR ARCHITECT: MOSHE SAFDIE

Born in Haifa, Israel, in 1938, Moshe Safdie graduated from McGill University's architecture program in 1961 and became almost an instant star. He was only 23 when asked to design Habitat 67 (p69), which was actually based on his university thesis. Now based in Boston, Safdie has crafted a stellar career gravitating toward high-profile projects where he can unleash innovative buildings with just the right dash of controversy to get people talking about them.

Most notably, Safdie designed the $56 million, 4000-sq-meter Holocaust Memorial in Jerusalem, Israel, which opened in 2005. He also designed Ottawa's National Gallery of Canada, which opened in 1988 with its trademark soaring glass front, and the Vancouver Library Square, which evokes the Roman Colosseum.

More recently, Safdie's design for the Kauffman Center for the Performing Arts in Kansas City, Missouri, which opened in 2011, features dramatic swooping curves and resembles a giant paper lantern or beehive.

Safdie was made a companion of the Order of Canada in 2005, Canada's highest civilian honor.

revitalized a 1-sq-km area bordered roughly by Rue Berri, Rue Sherbrooke, Blvd René-Lévesque and Rue City Councillors. The result is a culturally rich district that currently houses 80 arts venues, including 30 concert halls and numerous galleries and exhibition spaces. The Quartier is now home to 12,000 residents and hosts several big-ticket festivals, including the Montréal Jazz Festival. Its success has inspired arts and urban planning professionals from around the world, who have come from as far away as New Zealand to study it as a model for integrating the arts with urban living and work spaces.

Major milestones in the Quartier des Spectacles' development include the 2009 opening of the Place des Festivals, a vast open-air entertainment venue with a colorfully lit 235-jet fountain, and the 2011 inauguration of the Maison Symphonique de Montréal – the new home of Montréal's symphony orchestra. In 2017 the National Film Board of Canada is scheduled to open its own newly constructed headquarters here.

Montréal is transforming itself yet again with the construction of several new public spaces for its 375th anniversary celebration in 2017. In addition to recreation and entertainment venues, plans call for construction of a new square near the heart of the city at Champ-de-Mars, which will improve pedestrian access between Old Montréal (Vieux-Montréal) and downtown while simultaneously offering the aesthetic benefit of covering over part of the Ville-Marie Expressway. Nearby Pl Jacques-Cartier in Old Montréal will also get a major facelift.

Meanwhile, the city is pushing ahead with the multi-billion-dollar construction of two super-hospitals. The McGill University Health Centre (MUHC), billed as North America's most advanced medical research center, opened its sparkling new 500-room Glen facility in Westmount in April 2015. Downtown, the Centre Hospitalier de l'Université de Montréal (CHUM) is incorporating two vestiges of 19th-century Montréal into its own ultra-modern hospital: the Maison Garth, an 1871 home demolished to make room for the hospital, will have its facade reconstructed stone by stone, while the Église de St-Sauveur, a church dating to 1865, will be crowned with a reproduction of its original 200-foot steeple. Both are to be fully integrated into the new hospital facility when it opens in spring 2016.

Looking further ahead, the federal government has announced that it will replace the aging Champlain Bridge with a modern new span across the St Lawrence River, scheduled for completion in 2018.

Québec City History & Culture

While Montréal reigns supreme as Québec's largest and most cosmopolitan city, Québec City's cultural identity rests on its dual role as the seat of provincial government and the cradle of French civilization in the Americas. The capital of Nouvelle France still exudes the spirit of days past, revealing deep French roots in everything from its atmospheric 17th- and 18th-century architecture to the overwhelming prevalence of French language and cuisine. Despite its strong historic ties, the city also has a vibrant modern side, with a flourishing arts scene and a jam-packed cultural calendar.

History

The first significant settlement on the site of today's Québec City was a 500-strong Iroquois village called Stadacona. The Iroquois were semi-nomadic, building longhouses, hunting, fishing and cultivating crops until the land got tired, when they moved on.

French explorer Jacques Cartier traveled to the New World in 1534, making it as far as the Gaspé Peninsula before returning to France. His second trans-Atlantic voyage in 1535 brought him further up the St Lawrence River, where he spent a long and difficult winter encamped at the foot of the cliffs of present-day Québec City. Cartier lost 30 of his men to scurvy (the rest survived in large part thanks to traditional remedies provided by the Iroquois) before beating a retreat back to France in May 1536. Cartier returned in 1541 hoping to start a post upstream in the New World, but again faced a winter of scurvy and disastrous relations with the indigenous population; this last failed attempt set back France's colonial ambitions for more than half a century.

Explorer Samuel de Champlain is credited with founding the city in 1608, calling it Kebec, from the Algonquian word meaning 'the river narrows here.' Champlain established forts and dwellings around present-day Place-Royale, laying the groundwork for the thriving capital of Nouvelle-France (New France). The English successfully attacked in 1629, but Québec was returned to the French under a treaty in 1632. As the 17th century progressed, Ursuline and Jesuit missionaries arrived, bolstering Québec City's status as the most important French settlement in the New World.

Great Britain continued to keep its eye on Québec, launching unsuccessful campaigns to take the city in 1690 and 1711. In 1759, General Wolfe finally led the British to victory over Montcalm on the Plains of Abraham. One of North America's most famous battles, it virtually ended the long-running conflict between Britain and France. The Treaty of Paris gave Canada to Britain in 1763. And in 1775, the American revolutionaries tried to capture Québec but were promptly pushed back. In 1864, meetings were held in the city that led to the formation of Canada in 1867. Québec City became the provincial capital.

Hands-on History Hot Spots

Parc des Champs de Bataille (p181), Montcalm

Musée de la Place-Royale (p179), Old Lower Town

La Citadelle (p169), Old Upper Town

Musée de la Civilisation (p179), Old Lower Town

THE QUÉBECOIS ETHOS

Québec City has a reputation for being square and conservative (that is, at least from the Montréal perspective) and locals often refer to Québec City as a 'village' with equal parts affection and derision. Though it has all the big-city trappings, the core downtown population numbers under 200,000.

Although Québec City locals are very proud, there's a time in many people's lives, usually after high school or university, when they decide whether they are going to 'try' Montréal or stay put. As the 'everything' capital of French Canada, from arts and business to science, technology and media, Montréal exerts a considerable pull on ambitious Québec City natives. However, that means that those creative, dynamic people who ultimately choose to stay in Québec City do so because they really love the city and strongly identify with its unique culture.

Québec City is notorious in Montréal and the rest of Canada as a challenging place for outsiders to establish themselves in the long-term. With a near-homogenous French-Catholic population, community ties go *way* back. In fact, professional and social networks are often established by the end of high school. Even French-speaking Québecers from elsewhere in the province say these networks are extremely difficult to penetrate.

Québec City Architectural Gems

Le Château Frontenac (p170), Old Upper Town

Cathedral of the Holy Trinity (p175), Old Upper Town

Hôtel du Parlement (p182), Colline Parlementaire

Église Notre-Dame-des-Victoires (p179), Old Lower Town

La Maison Henry-Stuart (p183), Montcalm

In the 19th century, the city lost its status and importance to Montréal, but when the Great Depression burst Montréal's bubble in 1929, Québec City regained some stature as a government center. Then, in the 1950s, a group of business-savvy locals launched the now-famous Winter Carnival (p198) to incite a tourism boom.

Poor urban planning led to an exodus to the suburbs, leaving downtown depopulated and prone to crime. Things started to turn round in the 1990s, with the rejuvenation of the St-Roch neighborhood and diversification of the economy. Université Laval also moved some of its apartments downtown, bringing an influx of young students.

In 2008, Québec City threw a monumental bash in honor of its 400th anniversary, an expression of local pride that drew in tens of thousands of visitors and added several features to the city's landscape, including new public green spaces along the St Lawrence River. The city's cultural scene continues to thrive with the opening of the Amphithéâtre du Québec in 2015 and the expansion of the Musée National des Beaux-Arts in 2016.

Arts

Visual Arts

Many artists have been bewitched by the beauty of Québec City and its surrounding countryside.

Jean-Paul Lemieux (1904–90) is one of Canada's most accomplished painters. Born in Québec City, he studied at L'École des Beaux-Arts de Montréal and later in Paris. He is famous for his paintings of Québec's vacant and endless landscapes. Many of his paintings are influenced by the simple lines of folk art. There's a hall devoted to his art at the Musée National des Beaux-Arts du Québec (p182).

Alfred Pellan (1906–88) was another renowned artist who studied at the local École des Beaux-Arts before moving to Paris. He later became famous for his portraits, still lifes, figures and landscapes, before turning to surrealism in the 1940s.

Amsterdam-born Cornelius Krieghoff (1815–72) was acclaimed for chronicling the customs and clothes of Québecers in his paintings. He is known especially for the portraits of the Wendats, who lived around Québec City.

Francesco Iacurto (1908–2001) was born in Montréal but moved to Québec City in 1938. His acclaimed works are dominated by the town's streetscapes, landscapes and portrayals of Île d'Orléans.

Music

Québec City has plenty to offer music lovers. The respected Orchestre Symphonique de Québec and the terrific Opéra de Québec both perform at Le Grand Théâtre de Québec between September and May. Some of the province's biggest rock and pop music stars, such as Jean Leloup and Bruno Pelletier, also started out here, as did the politically charged hip-hop trio Loco Locass. There's a brash and independent spirit among the eclectic mix of active bands here, but because the scene is so small, most musicians eventually relocate to Montréal for its thriving club scene and music industry ties. For the latest developments in local music, ask around at music stores like Sillons (p200) and clubs such as Le Cercle (p197) or Scanner (p197), or check out entertainment listings at *Voir Québec* (www.voir.ca/quebec) and *Québec Scope* (www. quebecscope.com).

Films

Following are some films in which Québec City gets center stage:

I Confess (Alfred Hitchcock; 1953) Québec City has never looked better than when Hitchcock's lens caressed the city's atmospheric old-world edges in this film-noirish suspense thriller based on a French play.

Les Plouffe (Gilles Carle; 1981) Based on a novel by Roger Lemelin, this film depicts a family's struggles in Depression-era Québec City.

Les Yeux Rouges (The Red Eyes; Yves Simoneau; 1982) A Québec City–set thriller with two cops on the trail of a deranged strangler.

Le Confessionnal (The Confessional; Robert Lepage; 1995) Sometimes retracing Hitchcock's steps, Lepage builds a beautiful portrait of Québec City through a man's quest to uncover a family secret.

Ma Vie en Cinémascope (Bittersweet Memories; Denise Filiatrault; 2004) Recounts the life story of singer Alys Robi, Québec's first international superstar, brilliantly portrayed by Pascale Bussières.

Literary Looks at Québec City

Shadows on the Rock
(Willa Cather)

To Quebec and the Stars
(HP Lovecraft)

Where the River Narrows
(Aimee Laberge)

Bury Your Dead
(Louise Penny)

Theater

Canada's French-language TV and film industries are firmly based in Montréal, but Québec City's active theater scene holds its own – though its tight-knit nature cuts both ways. An actor here with a creative or original idea can write a script and have it produced – something that might take years, if it happened at all, in Montréal. On the other hand, plays produced here can't always draw an audience in Montréal; to cite one famous example, the brilliant one-woman show *Gros et Détail* by Québec City actor Anne-Marie Olivier, about people in the St-Roch neighborhood, was a hit in Québec City, France and several countries in francophone Africa, yet when Olivier tried to get it produced in Montréal, she was rejected on the basis that it focused too much on Québec City.

In the performing arts realm, Québec City's most famous native son is award-winning playwright and director Robert Lepage. While his best-known works feature Québec City, he has also achieved major international success, becoming the first North American to direct a Shakespeare play at London's Royal National Theatre (1992's *A Midsummer Night's Dream*); directing Richard Wagner's Ring Cycle for New York's Metropolitan Opera in 2010–12; and creating two major touring shows for Cirque du Soleil (*Kà* and *Totem*). Recent projects closer to home include the 2013 film *Triptyque* (Lepage's first movie in 10 years); the *Image Mill*, a gigantic sound-and-light show exploring Québec City's history, which was projected against oversized grain silos in the Vieux-Port (Old Port) between 2008 and 2013; and an ambitious project to build a $60 million, 625-seat new theater, Théâtre Le Diamant, just outside Québec City's old town walls.

Cultural Events

Québec City loves a good festival. Warm weather here lasts only a few short months, so locals make the most of it. In midsummer you'll find residents celebrating in city parks and streets, especially on June 24, Québec's 'national' holiday, and during the fabulous 11-day Festival d'Été (p25) in July, when Québecois musicians share the stage with performing artists from around the globe.

Winter, the longest season, holds an equally special place in the hearts of Québec City residents. The annual 17-day Winter Carnival (p198) is perhaps Québec's most beloved cultural event, presided over by Bonhomme de Neige, a giant snowman clad in a traditional Québecois hat and sash who has become one of the city's most beloved symbols. Local residents join Bonhomme in droves to celebrate the joys of the northern winter – staging ice canoe races across the St Lawrence River, horse-drawn sleigh competitions, colorful night parades, and rides for all ages on dog sleds, snow tubes and ice slides.

Language

Montréalers and Québec City locals can easily recognize each other at parties just by their accents. Linguists consider Québec City's accent to be purer and closer to international French, while Montréal's accent is thicker and more prone to Anglicisms. Although Québec City has far fewer native English speakers than Montréal, children study English from primary school onwards. Even so, if you venture very far outside Québec City's walls or into the surrounding countryside, you'll find people who are not used to speaking or hearing much English.

Québec City Media

Quebec Chronicle-Telegraph
(www.qctonline.com)
English news weekly

Le Soleil
(www.lapresse.ca/le-soleil)
French daily

Le Journal de Québec
(www.journaldequebec.com)
French daily

Voir Québec
(www.voir.ca/quebec)
French entertainment weekly

Survival Guide

Transportation

ARRIVING IN MONTRÉAL

Most travelers arrive in Montréal by air. Located west of downtown, Pierre Elliott Trudeau International Airport has frequent connections to cities in the US, Europe, the Caribbean, Latin America, Africa and the rest of Canada. It's easy to drive to Montréal from elsewhere in Canada or the US if you have the time, or take the train or intercity coach from cities such as Toronto or New York.

Flights, cars and tours can be booked online at lonely planet.com/bookings.

Air

Montréal is served by **Pierre Elliott Trudeau International Airport** (www.admtl. com), known in French as Aéroport Montréal-Trudeau. It's about 21km west of downtown and is the hub of most domestic, US and overseas flights. Trudeau airport (still sometimes known by its old name, Dorval airport) has decent connections to the city by car and shuttle bus.

To/From the Airport
BUS
Bus 747, the cheapest way to get into town, takes 45 to 60 minutes. Buses run round the clock, leaving from just outside the arrivals hall and dropping passengers downtown at the Gare d'Autocars and the Berri-UQAM metro station, in the Quartier Latin. The $10 fare can be paid by Visa, MasterCard or cash at vending machines in the international arrivals area, or tickets may be bought on board (coins only, exact change). Your ticket gives you unlimited travel on Montréal's bus and metro network for 24 hours.

CAR
Driving to or from downtown takes 20 to 30 minutes (allow an hour during peak times). As you exit the airport, follow signs for Autoroute 20 Est, which will take you into the heart of downtown along the main Autoroute Ville Marie (the 720).

SHUTTLE
Several hotels run shuttles from the airport to Downtown or further afield. **Autocars Skyport** (www. skyportinternational.com; one-way/return $90/157) runs express shuttles to the Mont-Tremblant ski resort in winter and summer.

TAXI
It takes at least 20 minutes to get downtown from the airport and the fixed fare is $40. Limousine services ($55 to $60) are also available.

Bus

Most long-distance buses arrive at Montréal's **Gare d'Autocars** (895 Rue de la Gauchetière Ouest; Ⓜ Berri-UQAM).

If buying tickets here for other destinations in the province, allow about 45 minutes before departure; most advance tickets don't guarantee a seat, so arrive early to line up at the counter.

Train

Canada's trains are arguably the most enjoyable and romantic way to travel the country. Long-distance trips are quite a bit more expensive than those by bus, however, and reservations are crucial for weekend and holiday travel. A few days' notice can cut fares a lot.

Gare Centrale (Central Train Station; 895 Rue de la Gauchetière Ouest) is the local hub of **VIA Rail** (www. viarail.ca), Canada's vast rail network, which links Montréal with cities all across the country.

Amtrak (www.amtrak.com) provides service between New York City and Montréal on its Adirondack line. The trip, though slow (11 hours), passes through lovely scenery along Lake Champlain and the Hudson River.

ARRIVING IN QUÉBEC CITY

Québec City is a great weekend trip from Montréal, and many travelers arrive by car, bus or rail. The drive is about three hours. VIA Rail's trains take only slightly longer (3¼ hours).

Highway networks connect Québec's capital with the rest of the province. Québec City has frequent air connections to Canadian and US destinations, as well as less-frequent flights to Mexico and the Caribbean.

Air

Québec City's petite **Aéroport International Jean-Lesage de Québec** (☑418-640-2700; www.aeroportdequebec.com; 505 Rue Principal) lies about 15km west of the center. It mostly has connections to Montréal, but there are also flights to Toronto, Ottawa, Chicago, Newark, New York City (JFK) and Caribbean resorts such as Cancún and Varadero. Check the website for additional destinations.

To/From the Airport

CAR

It takes about 25 minutes to drive from Québec City's airport to the Old Town. The most straightforward route is to take Rte 540 S/ Autoroute Duplessis, merge onto Rte 175 N, then follow this northeast as it changes names from Blvd Laurier to Rue Grand Alleé, crosses through the Old Town gate, and finally becomes Rue St-Louis.

TAXI

A taxi is your best option for travel between the airport and downtown Québec City, as there is no convenient public transportation along this route.

A taxi costs a flat fee of $34.25 to go into the city, or $15 if you're only going to the boroughs surrounding the airport. Returning to the airport, you'll pay the metered fare, which should be less than $30. **Transport Accessible du Québec** (☑418-641-8294; www.taq.qc.ca) offers a transit service for people with disabilities.

Bus

Orléans Express (www.orleansexpress.com) runs daily services between Montréal's main bus station, Gare d'Autocars, and Québec City's **Gare du Palais bus station** (Map p172; ☑418-525-3000; 320 Rue Abraham-Martin). Prices for the journey (three to 3½ hours) start at $59/94 for a one-way/return ticket.

If you're coming from Montréal, your bus may first stop 10km west of the center at **Ste-Foy-Sillery Station** (3001 Chemin des Quatre Bourgeois), so ask before you get off.

Car

Québec City lies about 260km northeast of Montréal (three hours by car). The most common routes are Autoroute 40 along the north shore of the St Lawrence River, and Autoroute 20, on the south shore.

Train

VIA Rail (www.viarail.ca) has several trains daily between Montréal's Gare Centrale and Québec City's **Gare du Palais** (450 Rue de la Gare du Palais). Prices for the 3½-hour journey start at $87/173 for a one-way/return ticket.

Service is also good along the so-called Québec City–Windsor corridor that connects Québec City with Montréal, Ottawa, Kingston, Toronto and Niagara Falls.

GETTING AROUND MONTRÉAL & QUÉBEC CITY

Bus & Metro

Montréal

STM (Société de Transport de Montréal; www.stm.info) is the city's bus and metro (subway) operator. Schedules vary depending on the line, but trains generally run from 5:30am to midnight from

---

CLIMATE CHANGE & TRAVEL

Every form of transport that relies on carbon-based fuel generates CO_2, the main cause of human-induced climate change. Modern travel is dependent on aeroplanes, which might use less fuel per kilometer per person than most cars but travel much greater distances. The altitude at which aircraft emit gases (including CO_2) and particles also contributes to their climate change impact. Many websites offer 'carbon calculators' that allow people to estimate the carbon emissions generated by their journey and, for those who wish to do so, to offset the impact of the greenhouse gases emitted with contributions to portfolios of climate-friendly initiatives throughout the world. Lonely Planet offsets the carbon footprint of all staff and author travel.

LONG-DISTANCE BUS LINES

Galland Laurentides (☎877-806-8666, 450-687-8666; www.galland-bus.com; 1717 Rue Berri) Provides bus service from Montréal to Mont-Tremblant and other destinations in the Laurentians.

Greyhound (www.greyhound.ca) Operates long-distance routes to Ottawa, Toronto, Vancouver, Boston, New York City and other points throughout Canada and the United States.

Limocar (www.limocar.ca) Offers bus service from Montréal to the Eastern Townships.

Moose Travel Network (www.moosenetwork.com) Popular with backpackers, this network operates several circuits around Canada, allowing travelers to jump on and jump off along the way. Pickup points are in Montréal, Québec City, Ottawa and Toronto, among other places. Destinations within Québec include Mont-Tremblant and the Gaspé Peninsula.

Orléans Express (www.orleansexpress.com) Makes the three-hour run between Montréal and Québec City.

Sunday to Friday, slightly later on Saturday night (to 1:30am at the latest).

A single bus or metro ticket costs $3.25. Two-ride tickets ($6) are also available in metro stations. If you're sticking around Montréal for longer, you'll save money by buying a rechargeable **Opus card**; the card costs $6 up front, but can be recharged at a discounted rate for 10 rides ($26.50), one day of unlimited rides ($10), three days ($18), a week ($25.50, Monday to Sunday) or a calendar month ($82).

Buses take tickets or cash but drivers won't give change. If transferring from the metro to a bus, use your original metro ticket as a free bus transfer. If you're switching between buses, or between bus and the metro, ask the driver for a free transfer slip (*correspondance* in French).

Québec City

White-and-blue city buses operated by **RTC** (Réseau de Transport de la Capitale; ☎418-627-2511; www.rtcquebec.ca) cost $3.25 with transfer privileges, or $7.50 for the day. Many buses serving the Old Town area stop at

Pl d'Youville just outside the wall on Rue St-Jean. Buses 21 and 800 go to the Gare du Palais, the central long-distance bus and train station.

Bicycle
Montréal

Montréal's bicycle paths are extensive, running more than 500km around the city. Useful bike maps are available from the tourist offices and bicycle rental shops.

Top bike paths follow the Canal de Lachine and then up along Lac St-Louis; another popular route goes southwest along the edge of the St Lawrence River, passing the Lachine Rapids, then meeting up with the Canal de Lachine path.

BIXI

One of the best ways to see the city is by the public bike-rental service **Bixi** (http://montreal.bixi.com; basic fees per 24/72hr $5/12, usage fees per 45/60/90min free/$1.75/3.50; ⏱24hr mid-Apr–Oct). Short-term subscription fees allowing you to use the system for 24 or 72 hours are very reasonably priced, and the 400 rental

stations are almost ubiquitous, spaced only a few blocks apart throughout the downtown area.

In Montréal, bicycles can be taken on the metro from 10am to 3pm and after 7pm Monday to Friday, as well as throughout the weekend. Officially cyclists are supposed to board only the first carriage of the train. In addition, eight of Montréal's city bus lines are equipped with bike racks, which may be used any time of day. See the STM website (www.stm.info) for details.

There are also bike paths around the islands of Parc Jean-Drapeau, the Île de Soeurs and Parc du Mont-Royal.

BICYCLE RENTAL
Ça Roule Montréal (p64)
Le Grand Cycle (p115)
My Bicyclette (p88)

Québec City

Québec City has an extensive network of bike paths (some 70km in all), including a route along the St Lawrence which connects to paths along the Rivière St-Charles. Pick up a free map at the tourist office or at local bike shops.

Just across from Québec City's train station is **Cyclo Services** (p203).

Boat

Cruise vessels ply the St Lawrence River for day trips and longer cruises.

Croisières AML (p203)

St Lawrence Cruise Lines (☎800-267-7868; www.stlawrencerivercruise.com) Offers the three- to six-day Canadian Connection Cruise between Kingston, Ontario and Québec City.

CTMA Group (☎888-986-3278; www.ctma.ca) Runs week-long cruises from Montréal to the picturesque Îles de la Madeleine in the Gulf of St Lawrence, with intermediate

Calèche

Montréal

The picturesque horse-drawn *calèches* (carriages) seen meandering around Old Montréal and Mont-Royal charge about $53/85 for a 30-/60-minute tour. They line up at the Old Port and at Pl d'Armes. Drivers usually provide running commentary, which can serve as a pretty good historical tour.

Québec City

In Québec City, *calèches* cost $90 for a 40-minute tour for up to four passengers. You'll find them just inside the Porte St-Louis, in the Parc de l'Esplanade and near Le Château Frontenac.

Car & Motorcycle

Border Crossings

Continental US highways link with their Canadian counterparts along the border at numerous points. The main US highways leading directly into Québec include the I-87 in New York, I-89 and I-91 in Vermont, and US-201 in Maine. During summer and on holiday weekends, waits of several hours are not uncommon at major USA–Canada border crossings such as Detroit, Michigan; Windsor, Ontario; Fort Erie, Ontario; Buffalo, New York; Niagara Falls; and Rouse's Point, New York. Smaller crossings are generally much quieter.

If you have difficulty with the French-only signs in Québec, pick up a decent provincial highway map, sold at service stations and usually free at tourist offices.

Visitors with US or British passports are allowed to bring their vehicles into Canada for up to six months.

Car Rental

Trudeau airport has many international car-rental firms, and there's a host of smaller operators in Montréal. Whether you're here or in Québec City, rates will swing with demand so it's worth phoning around to see what's on offer. Advance bookings via online sites often offer the best rates, and airport rates are normally better than those in town.

To rent a car in the province of Québec you must be at least 21 years old and have had a driver's license for at least a year.

Major companies usually have locations in both Montréal and Québec City.

Avis (☎514-866-2847; www.avis.ca; 1225 Rue Metcalfe)

Budget (www.budget.ca) Multiple locations, including Montréal's Gare Centrale.

Discount Car (☎514-286-1929; www.discountcar.com; 607 Blvd de Maisonneuve Ouest) Good, competitive rates. Canadian owned.

Hertz (☎514-938-1717; www.hertz.ca; 1073 Rue Drummond)

Rent-a-Wreck (☎514-484-3871; www.rentawreck.ca; 6340 Rue St-Jacques) Often the best rates. In Montréal only.

Road Rules

➡ Fines for traffic violations, from speeding to not wearing a seat belt, are stiff in Québec. You may see few police cars on the roads, but radar traps are common. Motorcyclists are required to wear helmets and to ride with their lights on.

➡ Traffic in both directions must stop when school buses stop to let children get off and on. At the white-striped pedestrian crosswalks, cars must stop to allow pedestrians to cross the road.

➡ Turning right on red lights is illegal in Montréal. However, it is legal everywhere else in Québec, including Québec City, as long as there is no sign posted specifically prohibiting such turns.

➡ In both Montréal and Québec City, a flashing green light means that you are allowed to turn left (similar to a green left-turn arrow in the United States).

➡ Québec's blood-alcohol limit while driving is 0.08%, as opposed to the 0.05% limit in most other Canadian provinces. Driving motorized vehicles (including boats and snowmobiles) under the influence is a serious offense in Canada. You could land in jail with a court date, heavy fine and suspended license. The minimum drinking age is 18 – the same age as for obtaining a driver's license.

TRAVEL & DISABILITY

Nonprofit organization **Kéroul** (www.keroul.qc.ca) is dedicated to making travel more accessible to people with limited mobility. Its excellent guide **The Accessible Road** (www.larouteaccessible.com) covers Montréal, Québec City and 15 other tourism areas in Québec, highlighting access facilities in each.

Watch for the **Tourist & Leisure Companion Sticker**, which indicates free access to facilities for those traveling with people with a disability or mental illness. The website www.vatl.org has a full list of participating sites throughout Québec.

→ In winter, parking on city streets is periodically prohibited to facilitate snow removal in both Montréal and Québec City. In Montréal, yellow and black signs marked 'Déneigement' (snow removal) or 'Opération Neige' indicate the hours when parking is prohibited (usually 7am to 7pm, or 7pm to 7am). In Québec City, snow removal is typically scheduled between 11pm and 6:30am on any street with a 'déneigement' sign accompanied by a flashing red light. Heed the signs, or you'll wake up to a towed vehicle and a hefty fine.

→ Québec mandates that cars have snow tires on during winter.

Taxi

Flag fall is a standard $3.45, plus another $1.70 per kilometer and 63¢ per minute spent waiting in traffic. Prices are posted on the windows inside taxis. In Montréal try **Taxi Champlain** (☑514-273-2435; www.taxichamplain.qc.ca) or **Taxi Co-Op** (☑514-725-9885; www.taxi-coop.com). In Québec City, try **Taxis Coop** (☑418-525-5191; www.taxiscoopquebec.com).

TOURS

Montréal

Fitz & Follwell (☑514-840-0739; www.fitzandfollwell.co; 115 Ave du Mont-Royal Ouest) Ranging from family-friendly city explorations to cycling tours of Montréal's brewpubs, this acclaimed bike shop's tours take in Plateau Mont-Royal, the Old Port, the Canal de Lachine and other city highlights. It also offers walking tours and winter tours that incorporate skating, sledding and snowshoeing.

Amphi Tours (☑514-849-5181; www.montreal-amphibus-tour.com; 1hr tour adult/youth/child $35/25/18; ☺May-Oct) This brightly painted 'amphibus' tootles around Old Montréal before plunging into the St Lawrence River for a cruise along the waterfront.

Guidatour (☑514-844-4021; www.guidatour.qc.ca; ☺Sat & Sun mid-May–mid-Jun, daily late Jun–mid-Oct, Sat only Dec) In business for more than three decades, the experienced bilingual guides of Guidatour paint a picture of Old Montréal's eventful history with anecdotes and legends. They also offer culinary tours, plus a 'Christmas Secrets of Old Montréal' tour in December.

Héritage Montréal (☑514-286-2662; www.heritagemontreal.org; tours $15; ☺Sat & Sun Aug & Sep) In August and September, this independent, nonprofit organization conducts ArchitecTours, a series of architecture-based tours that focus on a different neighborhood every week. The departure point varies; check the schedule online and show up early, as tickets are sold on a first-come, first-served basis.

Les Fantômes du Vieux-Montréal (☑514-844-4021; www.fantommontreal.com; 360 Rue St-François-Xavier; adult/youth $22/14.50) Gives 90-minute evening tours tracing historic crimes and legends, led by guides in period costume. You'll hear talk of hangings, sorcery, torture and other light bedtime tales on this good-time evening outing.

Québec City

Ghost Tours of Québec (p182)

Les Tours Voir Québec (Map p172; ☑418-694-2001, 866-694-2001; www.toursvoirquebec.com; 12 Rue Ste-Anne; tours from $23) This group offers excellent tours on the history, architecture and food of Québec City. The popular two-hour 'grand tour' takes in the Old City's highlights, while the food tour includes tastings of wines, cheeses, crepes, chocolate, maple products and other Québecois specialties at a variety of shops and restaurants. Reserve ahead.

Old Québec Tours (Map p172; ☑418-664-0460, 800-267-8687; www.tours vieuxquebec.com) This tour operator offers a variety of tours: walking tours of the Old City, double-decker bus tours, or out-of-town excursions to Montmorency Falls, Ste-Anne-de-Beaupré and Île d'Orléans. It also offers whale-watching expeditions in summer.

Directory A–Z

Courses

Cooking

Académie Culinaire du Québec (Map p268; ☑514-393-8111, 877-393-8111; www.academieculinaire.com; 360 Rue du Champ de Mars, Montréal; Ⓜ Champ-de-Mars) This esteemed cooking academy conducts regular cooking workshops and short courses encompassing classic French themes such as Parisian bistro cooking, sauces and artisanal baking, along with more international fare. Some classes at the main Montréal branch are offered in English. The branch in Québec City (☑418-780-2211; 2740 Blvd Laurier) has fewer courses, all in French.

Mezza Luna Cooking School (p128)

Language

MONTRÉAL

Concordia University Centre for Continuing Education (Map p272; ☑514-848-8600; www.concordia.ca; 1600 Rue Ste-Catherine Ouest; Ⓜ Guy-Concordia) Offers 40-hour conversational and written French courses from $320.

McGill University School of Continuing Studies (Map p276; ☑514-398-6200; www.mcgill.ca; 11th fl, 688 Rue Sherbrooke Ouest; Ⓜ McGill) Year-round, accredited intensive and part-time courses in French.

Montréal International Language Centre (Map p272; ☑800-363-3541, 514-939-4463; www.cilm.qc.ca; 2000 Rue Ste-Catherine Ouest; Ⓜ Atwater) Tailor-made language courses at this offshoot of LaSalle University.

YMCA (Map p276; ☑514-849-8393; www.ymcalanguages.ca; 5th fl, 1440 Rue Stanley; Ⓜ Peel) Offers day and evening French courses as well as an intensive summer camp. The four- to seven-week sessions cost between $171 and $764.

QUÉBEC CITY

École de Langues de L'Université Laval (☑418-656-2321; www.elul.ulaval.ca; 1030 Ave des Sciences-Humaines, Bureau 2301 2nd fl, Pavillon Charles-De Koninck) Université Laval's Language School offers 15-week fall and winter courses or five-week spring and summer courses. You can be set up in accommodations with a Québecois family or stay in a campus residence.

Customs Regulations

For the latest customs information, contact the Canadian embassy or consulate at home, or go to the 'Visit as a Tourist' section of the Canadian government website (www.cic.gc.ca).

➡ All fruit, vegetables and plants must be declared when crossing into Canada. For current restrictions, visit www.inspection.gc.ca.

➡ Visitors to Québec aged 18 and older can bring up to 8.5L of beer or ale, 1.5L of wine or 1.14L (40oz) of other liquor without paying duty or taxes. In addition, the following quantities of tobacco products may be brought into the country duty-free: 50 cigars, 200 cigarettes, 200g of tobacco and 200 tobacco sticks. Individual gifts valued at $60 or less are also duty-free.

➡ US residents may bring back $800 worth of goods duty-free, plus 1L of alcohol (but you must be aged 21 or over), as well as 200 cigarettes and 100 non-Cuban cigars.

Discount Cards

The **Montréal Museums Pass** allows free access to 39 museums for three days of your choice within a 21-day period ($75). For an extra $5, the pass comes with three consecutive days of free access to bus and metro. It's available from the city's tourist offices, or you can buy it online (www.museesmontreal.org).

Electricity

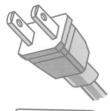

120V/60Hz

120V/60Hz

Emergencies

Police, Ambulance, Fire
(☎911) Use the all-purpose emergency number to call an ambulance, report a fire, or request immediate police assistance.

Québec Poison Control Centre (Centre Antipoison du Québec; ☎1800-463-5060)

Gay & Lesbian Travelers

Fugues (www.fugues.com) is the free, French-language, authoritative monthly guide to the gay and lesbian scene for the province of Québec. It's an excellent place to find out about the latest clubs and gay-friendly accommodations.

Montréal is a popular getaway for lesbian, gay and bisexual travelers. The gay community is centered in the Village, and it's huge business. The weeklong **Montréal Pride** (www.fierte montrealpride.com) attracts hundreds of thousands every August, while the **Black & Blue Festival** (www.bbcm. org) in early October features major dance parties along with cultural and arts events.

Québec City's gay community, while smaller, is also well established, with its own pride festival, the **Fête Arc-en-Ciel** (www. arcencielquebec.ca), in early September and a handful of popular nightspots along Rue St-Jean.

Gays and lesbians are generally well integrated into Montréal life. In neighborhoods such as the Plateau, for example, two men holding hands in public will scarcely raise an eyebrow. By contrast, Québec City tends to be a bit more conservative, and open displays of affection between same-sex couples may attract more attention.

Montreal Gay & Lesbian Community Centre & Library (☎514-528-8424; www.ccglm.org; 2075 Rue Plessis; ◷1-6pm Mon-Fri, to 8pm Wed; ⓜBeaudry) has been around since 1988 and provides an extensive library and loads of info on the city's gay and lesbian scene.

Internet Access

Wi-fi is widely available throughout Montréal and Québec City, at tourist offices, hotels, cafes and many restaurants. Except in a few high-end hotels, it's generally free of charge.

For a map of hundreds of places where you can get online for free in Montréal, see **Île Sans Fil** (www.ilesans fil.org). For info on free wi-fi hot spots elsewhere in the province of Québec, including Québec City, visit **Zap Québec** (www.zapquebec.org).

If you're not traveling with a computer, many hotels have one available for guests.

Legal Matters

If you're charged with an offense, you have the right to public counsel if you can't afford a lawyer.

Generally speaking, it's an offense to consume alcohol anywhere other than at a residence or licensed premises, which technically puts parks, beaches and the rest of the great outdoors off-limits. Montréal has sidestepped this restriction with a city ordinance that allows for alcohol to be 'consumed in a park with a meal'; even so, it's best to be discreet, and bear in mind that disturbance of the peace or loitering in any park between 11pm and sunrise remains a criminal offense.

Maps

If you're going to explore Montréal or Québec City in detail – and prefer to use something other than smartphone maps or guidebook maps – you can get detailed maps online from **Mapart** (www.mapartmaps.com) and at **Aux Quatre Points Cardinaux** (Map p278; www.aqpc.com; 551 Rue Ontario Est; ◷10am-6pm Mon-Wed, to 9pm Thu & Fri, to 5pm Sat; M Berri-UQAM) in Montréal.

Medical Services

Canadian health care is excellent but it's not free to visitors, so be sure to get travel insurance before you leave home.

Canada has no reciprocal health care with other countries and nonresidents will have to pay up front for treatment (often in cash) and wait for the insurance payback.

Medical treatment is pricey (less so by US comparison), and long waits – particularly in the emergency room – are common. Avoid going to the hospital if possible.

Clinics

If you're sick and need some advice, call Québec's provincial **Health Hotline** (📞811), which is staffed by nurses 24 hours a day.

For minor ailments in Montréal, visit the **CLSC** (Centre Local de Services Communautaires; 📞514-934-0354; www.santemontreal.qc.ca; 1801 Blvd de Maisonneuve Ouest; ☺8am-8pm Mon-Fri; M Guy-Concordia) clinic downtown. In Québec City, visit the **CLSC de la Haute-Ville** (📞418-641-2572; www.csssvc. qc.ca; 55 Chemin Sainte-Foy; ☺8am-8:30pm Mon-Fri, to 4pm Sat & Sun).

Emergency Rooms

MONTRÉAL

Montréal General Hospital (📞514-934-1934; www.muhc.ca/mgh; 1650 Ave Cedar; M Guy-Concordia)

MUHC Glen Hospital (📞514-934-1934; www. muhc.ca; 1001 Blvd Décarie; M Vendôme) Montréal's brand-new, state-of-the-art emergency hospital, affiliated with McGill University Health Centre, opened in April 2015.

This is the best option for English-speaking patients.

QUÉBEC CITY

Hôpital Laval (📞418-654-2114; www.chuq.qc.ca; 2705 Blvd Laurier, Ste-Foy) Affiliated with Université Laval, this emergency facility is 9km southwest of the center.

L'Hôtel-Dieu de Québec (📞418-691-5042, 418-525-4444; www.chuq.qc.ca; 11 Côte du Palais) Québec City's oldest and most centrally located hospital.

Pharmacies

The big pharmacy chains are **Pharmaprix** (www.pharma prix.ca) and **Jean Coutu** (www.jeancoutu.com). Some branches stay open late.

Money

ATMs

Montréal and Québec City have droves of ATMs linked to the international Cirrus, Plus and Maestro networks, not only in banks but also in pubs, convenience stores and hotels. Many charge a small fee per use, and your own bank may levy an extra fee – it's best to check before leaving home.

Changing Money

The main shopping streets in Montréal, including Rue Ste-Catherine, Blvd St-Laurent and Rue St-Denis, have plenty of banks. There are also foreign-exchange desks at the main tourist office, the airport and the casino.

Opening Hours

Banks Most open 10am to 3pm Monday to Friday (later on Thursday).

Bars & Pubs Many open from 11:30am until midnight or longer; those that don't serve food may not open until 5pm or later.

Government Offices Generally open 9am to 5pm weekdays.

Museums Most open 10am or 11am and close by 6pm. Most close Monday but stay open late one day a week (typically Wednesday or Thursday).

Post Offices Open 8am to 5pm Monday to Friday.

Restaurants Generally open 11:30am to 2:30pm and 5:30pm to 11pm; cafes serving breakfast open between 7am and 9am.

Tourist Attractions In Québec City and outside Montréal most attractions shut down or operate sporadic hours outside busy summer months.

Post

Standard 1st-class airmail letters or postcards up to 30g cost 85¢ within Canada, $1.20 to the US and $2.50 to all other destinations. For general information, contact **Canada Post** (Postes Canada; 📞416-979-3033, 866-607-6301; www.canadapost.ca).

Montréal's **main post office** (Map p276; 677 Rue Ste-Catherine Ouest; ☺7am-7pm Mon-Fri, 10am-5pm Sat, 11am-5pm Sun; M McGill) is the largest but there are many convenient locations around town. In Québec City, the **post office** (Map p172; 5 Rue du Fort; ☺8am-5:30pm Mon-Fri) in the Upper Town is conveniently located near the main tourist sites and offers the biggest selection of postal services, including a philatelic counter.

Stamps are also available at newspaper shops, convenience stores and some hotels.

Public Holidays

Banks, schools and government offices close on Canadian public holidays, while museums and other services go on a restricted schedule. This is also a busy time to travel.

PRACTICALITIES

→ Smoking is prohibited in all enclosed spaces such as restaurants, bars and clubs. Many people light up on outdoor patios.

→ Local currency is Canadian dollars ($). Canadian coins come in 1¢ (penny), 5¢ (nickel), 10¢ (dime), 25¢ (quarter), $1 (loonie) and $2 (toonie) pieces. Paper currency comes in $5 (blue), $10 (purple), $20 (green) and $50 (red) denominations.

→ A tip of 15% of the pretax bill is customary in restaurants. Most credit-card machines in Québec will calculate the tip based on the percentage you specify, or allow you to tip an amount of your choice. If tipping cash, leave the tip on the table or hand it directly to staff.

→ Canada uses the metric system. Distances are stated in kilometers, and measurements such as height and weight are usually expressed in kilograms, meters and centimeters.

Residential leases in Montréal traditionally end on June 30, so the roads are always clogged on July 1 (semiofficially known as Moving Day) as tenants move to their new homes.

School students break for summer holidays in late June and return to school in early September. University students get even more time off, breaking from May to early or mid-September. Most people take their big annual vacation during this summer period. Schools also break in late February or early March for the *semaine de relâche* (winter break); ski areas near Montréal and Québec City may get more crowded during this period.

The main public holidays:

New Year's Day January 1

Good Friday & Easter Monday Late March to mid-April

Victoria Day May 24 or nearest Monday

National Aboriginal Day June 21 (unofficial)

St-Jean-Baptiste Day June 24

Canada Day July 1

Labour Day First Monday in September

Canadian Thanksgiving Second Monday in October

Remembrance Day November 11

Christmas Day December 25

Boxing Day December 26

Safe Travel

→ Violent crime is rare (especially involving foreigners). Even so, as in all big cities, it's best to stay alert for petty theft and use hotel safes where available.

→ Cars with foreign registration are occasionally targeted for smash-and-grab theft. As in any big city, don't leave valuables in the car.

→ Take special care at pedestrian crosswalks in Montréal: unless there's an *arrêt* (stop) sign, drivers largely ignore these crosswalks.

→ It is illegal in Canada to carry pepper spray or mace. Instead, some women recommend carrying a whistle to deal with attackers or potential dangers. If you are sexually assaulted, call ☑911 or the local **Sexual Assault Center** (☑in Montréal 514-398-8500, in Québec City 418-522-2120) for referrals to hospitals that have sexual-assault care centers.

Telephone

The area code for the entire island of Montréal is ☑514; Québec City is ☑418. When you dial, even local numbers, you will need to punch in the area code as well.

Toll-free numbers begin with ☑800, ☑866, ☑877 or ☑888 and must be preceded with 1. Some numbers are good throughout North America, others only within Canada or one particular province.

Dialing the operator (☑0) or the emergency number (☑911) is free of charge from both public and private phones. For directory assistance, dial ☑411. Fees apply.

With the advent of cell phones, public phones have become a rarity. When you do find them they will either be coin-operated (local calls cost 50¢) or accept phone cards and credit cards.

Cell Phones

The only foreign cell phones that will work in North America are triband models operating on GSM 1900. If you don't have one of these, your best bet is to buy an inexpensive phone with prepaid minutes and a rechargeable SIM card at a consumer electronics store such as **Best Buy** (www.bestbuy.ca).

US residents traveling with their phone may have service (though they'll pay roaming fees). Get in touch with your cell-phone provider for details.

Phonecards

Bell Canada's prepaid cards, in denominations of $5, $10 and $20, work from public and private phones. There are also plenty of local phonecards offering better rates than Bell's, sold at convenience stores, newsstands and websites such as www.thephonecardstore.ca.

Time

Montréal is on Eastern Time (EST/EDT), as is New York City and Toronto – five hours behind Greenwich Mean Time.

Canada switches to daylight-saving time (one hour later than Standard Time) from the second Sunday in March to the first Sunday in November.

Train schedules, film screenings and schedules in French use the 24-hour clock (eg 6:30pm becomes 18:30) while English schedules use the 12-hour clock.

Tourist Information

Québec's province-wide tourist bureau, **Tourisme Québec** (☑877-266-5687; www.tourisme.gouv.qc.ca), operates tourist offices (known as Centres Infotouristes) in both Montréal and Québec City. Offices in both cities share a central phone number and website.

Both cities' airports also have information kiosks that open year-round.

Centre Infotouriste – Montréal (Map p276; ☑877-266-5687, 514-873-2015; www.tourisme-montreal.org; 1255 Rue Peel; ☺8:30am-7pm; ⓜPeel) Information about Montréal and all of Québec. Free hotel, tour and car reservations, plus currency exchange.

Tourist Welcome Office – Old Montréal (Map p268; www.tourism-montreal.org; 174 Rue Notre-Dame Est; ☺9am-7pm Jun-Sep, 10am-6pm May & Oct; ⓜChamp-de-Mars) Just off bustling Pl Jacques-Cartier, this helpful little office is always humming.

Centre Infotouriste – Québec City (Map p172; ☑418-649-2608, 877-266-5687; www.bonjourquebec. com; 12 Rue Ste-Anne; ☺9am-5pm Nov-Jun, to 7pm Jul & Aug, to 6pm Sep & Oct) Québec City's main tourist office, in the heart of the Old Town, opposite Château Frontenac.

Travelers with Disabilities

In Montréal, most public buildings – including tourist offices, major museums and attractions – are wheelchair accessible, and many restaurants and hotels also have facilities for the mobility-impaired. Almost all major bus routes are serviced by NOVA LFS buses adapted for wheelchairs, and eight metro stations on the Orange Line have elevators, making them accessible to manual and motorized wheelchairs with a maximum length of 46" and a maximum width of 26". Visit www.stm.info/en/access for information about boarding procedures on both the metro and the adapted buses.

In Québec City, bus lines 21, 800, 801, 802 and 803 are wheelchair accessible. The 'Accessibility' section of the www.rtcquebec.ca website has more details.

The following are also useful:

Access to Travel (www.accesstotravel.gc.ca) provides details of accessible transportation across Canada.

Kéroul (☑514-252-3104; www.keroul.qc.ca) Has detailed information about accessible travel on its website, offers packages for disabled travelers going to Québec and Ontario, and publishes *Québec Accessible,* listing hotels, restaurants and attractions throughout the province.

VIA Rail (www.viarail.ca) Accommodates people in wheelchairs with 48 hours' notice. Services on board the train include wheelchair tie-downs, grab bars in washrooms and narrow wheelchairs for boarding, detraining and accessing the washrooms. Details are available at Montréal's Gare Centrale and Québec City's Gare du Palais, or on the Accessibility page of the VIA Rail website.

Transport Accessible du Québec (☑418-641-8294; www.taq.qc.ca) Wheelchair-adapted vans available. Make reservations at least 24 hours in advance.

Transport Adapté du Québec Métro Inc (☑418-687-2641) Has 20 wheelchair-adapted minibuses that carry passengers to sections of Québec City not served by the public RTC buses. You must make reservations at least eight hours in advance of your trip.

Visas

Citizens of dozens of countries – including the USA, most Western European countries, Australia, Japan and New Zealand – don't need visas to enter Canada for stays of up to 180 days. US permanent residents are also exempt.

Nationals of around 150 other countries, including South Africa and China, must apply to the Canadian visa office in their home country for a temporary resident visa (TRV). See www.cic.gc.ca for full details.

Single-entry visitor visas are valid for six months, while multiple-entry visas can be used for up to 10 years, provided that no single stay exceeds six months. Either type of visa costs $100. Extensions cost the same price as the original and must be applied for at a Canadian Immigration Center one month before the current visa expires. A separate visa is required if you intend to work in Canada.

Language

Canada is officially a bilingual country with the majority of the population speaking English as their first language. In Québec, however, the dominant language is French. The local tongue is essentially the same as what you'd hear in France, and you'll have no problems being understood if you use standard French phrases (provided in this chapter).

Of course, there are some differences between European French and the Québec version (known as 'Québécois' or *joual*). For example, while standard French for 'What time is it?' is *Quelle heure est-il?*, in Québec you're likely to hear *Y'est quelle heure?* instead. Other differences worth remembering are the terms for breakfast, lunch and dinner: rather than *petit déjeuner*, *déjeuner* and *dîner* you're likely to see and hear *déjeuner*, *dîner* and *souper*. Québec French also employs a lot of English words; eg English terms are generally used for car parts – even the word *char* (pronounced 'shar') for car may be heard.

The sounds used in spoken French can almost all be found in English. If you read our pronunciation guides as if they were English, you'll be understood. There are a couple of exceptions: nasal vowels (represented in our guides by o or u followed by an almost inaudible nasal consonant sound m, n or ng), the 'funny' *u* (ew in our guides) and the deep-in-the-throat *r*. Syllables in French words are, for the most part, equally stressed. As English speakers tend to stress the first syllable, try adding a light stress on the final syllable of French words to compensate.

WANT MORE?

For in-depth language information and handy phrases, check out Lonely Planet's *French phrasebook*. You'll find it at **shop. lonelyplanet.com**, or you can buy Lonely Planet's iPhone phrasebooks at the Apple App Store.

BASICS

Hello.	*Bonjour.*	bon·zhoor
Goodbye.	*Au revoir.*	o·rer·vwa
Excuse me.	*Excusez-moi.*	ek·skew·zay·mwa
Sorry.	*Pardon.*	par·don
Yes./No.	*Oui./Non.*	wee/non
Please.	*S'il vous plaît.*	seel voo play
Thank you.	*Merci.*	mair·see

How are you?
Comment allez-vous?   ko·mon ta·lay·voo

Fine, and you?
Bien, merci. Et vous?   byun mair·see ay voo

What's your name?
Comment vous   ko·mon voo·
appelez-vous?   za·play voo

My name is ...
Je m'appelle ...   zher ma·pel ...

Do you speak English?
Parlez-vous anglais?   par·lay·voo ong·glay

I don't understand.
Je ne comprends pas.   zher ner kom·pron pa

ACCOMMODATIONS

Do you have any rooms available?
Est-ce que vous avez   es·ker voo za·vay
des chambres libres?   day shom·brer lee·brer

How much is it per night/person?
Quel est le prix   kel ay ler pree
par nuit/personne?   par nwee/per·son

Is breakfast included?
Est-ce que le petit   es·ker ler per·tee
déjeuner est inclus?   day·zher·nay ayt en·klew

dorm	*dortoir*	dor·twar
guesthouse	*pension*	pon·syon
hotel	*hôtel*	o·tel
youth hostel	*auberge de jeunesse*	o·berzh der zher·nes

Signs	
Entrée	Entrance
Femmes	Women
Fermé	Closed
Hommes	Men
Interdit	Prohibited
Ouvert	Open
Renseignements	Information
Sortie	Exit
Toilettes/WC	Toilets

a ... room	*une chambre ...*	ewn shom·brer ...
single	*à un lit*	a un lee
double	*avec un grand lit*	a·vek un gron lee
with (a) ...	*avec ...*	a·vek ...
air-con	*climatiseur*	klee·ma·tee·zer
bathroom	*une salle de bains*	ewn sal der bun
window	*fenêtre*	fer·nay·trer

DIRECTIONS

Where's ...?
Où est ...? oo ay ...

What's the address?
Quelle est l'adresse? kel ay la·dres

Can you write down the address, please?
Est-ce que vous pourriez es·ker voo poo·ryay
écrire l'adresse, ay·kreer la·dres
s'il vous plaît? seel voo play

Can you show me (on the map)?
Pouvez-vous m'indiquer poo·vay·voo mun·dee·kay
(sur la carte)? (sewr la kart)

EATING & DRINKING

What would you recommend?
Qu'est-ce que vous kes·ker voo
conseillez? kon·say·yay

What's in that dish?
Quels sont les ingrédients? kel son lay zun·gray·dyon

I'm a vegetarian.
Je suis zher swee
végétarien/ vay·zhay·ta·ryun/
végétarienne. vay·zhay·ta·ryen (m/f)

Cheers!
Santé! son·tay

That was delicious.
C'était délicieux! say·tay day·lee·syer

Please bring the bill.
Apportez-moi a·por·tay·mwa
l'addition, la·dee·syon
s'il vous plaît. seel voo play

I'd like to reserve a table for ...	*Je voudrais réserver une table pour ...*	zher voo·dray ray·zair·vay ewn ta·bler poor ...
(eight) o'clock	*(vingt) heures*	(vungt) er
(two) people	*(deux) personnes*	(der) pair·son

Key Words

appetizer	*entrée*	on·tray
bottle	*bouteille*	boo·tay
breakfast	*déjeuner*	day·zher·nay
cold	*froid*	frwa
delicatessen	*traiteur*	tray·ter
dinner	*souper*	soo·pay
fork	*fourchette*	foor·shet
glass	*verre*	vair
grocery store	*épicerie*	ay·pees·ree
hot	*chaud*	sho
knife	*couteau*	koo·to
lunch	*dîner*	dee·nay
market	*marché*	mar·shay
menu	*carte*	kart
plate	*assiette*	a·syet
spoon	*cuillère*	kwee·yair
wine list	*carte des vins*	kart day vun
with/without	*avec/sans*	a·vek/son

Meat & Fish

beef	*bœuf*	berf
chicken	*poulet*	poo·lay
crab	*crabe*	krab
lamb	*agneau*	a·nyo
oyster	*huître*	wee·trer
pork	*porc*	por
snail	*escargot*	es·kar·go
squid	*calmar*	kal·mar
turkey	*dinde*	dund
veal	*veau*	vo

Fruit & Vegetables

apple	*pomme*	pom
apricot	*abricot*	ab·ree·ko
asparagus	*asperge*	a·spairzh
beans	*haricots*	a·ree·ko
beetroot	*betterave*	be·trav
cabbage	*chou*	shoo

celery	céleri	sel·ree
cherry	cerise	ser·reez
corn	maïs	ma·ees
cucumber	concombre	kong·kom·brer
gherkin (pickle)	cornichon	kor·nee·shon
grape	raisin	ray·zun
leek	poireau	pwa·ro
lemon	citron	see·tron
lettuce	laitue	lay·tew
mushroom	champignon	shom·pee·nyon
peach	pêche	pesh
peas	petit pois	per·tee pwa
(red/green) pepper	poivron (rouge/vert)	pwa·vron (roozh/vair)
pineapple	ananas	a·na·nas
plum	prune	prewn
potato	pomme de terre	pom der tair
prune	pruneau	prew·no
pumpkin	citrouille	see·troo·yer
shallot	échalote	eh·sha·lot
spinach	épinards	eh·pee·nar
strawberry	fraise	frez
tomato	tomate	to·mat
turnip	navet	na·vay
vegetable	légume	lay·gewm

Other

bread	pain	pun
butter	beurre	ber
cheese	fromage	fro·mazh
egg	œuf	erf
honey	miel	myel
jam	confiture	kon·fee·tewr
oil	huile	weel
pepper	poivre	pwa·vrer
rice	riz	ree
salt	sel	sel
sugar	sucre	sew·krer
vinegar	vinaigre	vee·nay·grer

Drinks

beer	bière	bee·yair
coffee	café	ka·fay
(orange) juice	jus (d'orange)	zhew (do·ronzh)
milk	lait	lay
red wine	vin rouge	vun roozh

tea	thé	tay
(mineral) water	eau (minérale)	o (mee·nay·ral)
white wine	vin blanc	vun blong

EMERGENCIES

Help!
Au secours! — o skoor

Leave me alone!
Fichez-moi la paix! — fee·shay·mwa la pay

I'm lost.
Je suis perdu/perdue. — zhe swee·pair·dew (m/f)

Call a doctor.
Appelez un médecin. — a·play un mayd·sun

Call the police.
Appelez la police. — a·play la po·lees

I'm ill.
Je suis malade. — zher swee ma·lad

It hurts here.
J'ai une douleur ici. — zhay ewn doo·ler ee·see

I'm allergic (to ...).
Je suis allergique (à ...). — zher swee za·lair·zheek (a...)

SHOPPING & SERVICES

I'd like to buy ...
Je voudrais acheter ... — zher voo·dray ash·tay ...

Can I look at it?
Est-ce que je peux le voir? — es·ker zher per ler vwar

I'm just looking.
Je regarde. — zher rer·gard

I don't like it.
Cela ne me plaît pas. — ser·la ner mer play pa

How much is it?
C'est combien? — say kom·byun

It's too expensive.
C'est trop cher. — say tro shair

There's a mistake in the bill.
Il y a une erreur dans la note. — eel ya ewn ay·rer don la not

bank	banque	bonk
internet cafe	cybercafé	see·bair·ka·fay
tourist office	office de tourisme	o·fees der too·rees·mer

Question Words		
What?	Quoi?	kwa
When?	Quand?	kon
Where?	Où?	oo
Who?	Qui?	kee
Why?	Pourquoi?	poor·kwa

Numbers

1	*un*	un
2	*deux*	der
3	*trois*	trwa
4	*quatre*	ka·trer
5	*cinq*	sungk
6	*six*	sees
7	*sept*	set
8	*huit*	weet
9	*neuf*	nerf
10	*dix*	dees
20	*vingt*	vung
30	*trente*	tront
40	*quarante*	ka·ront
50	*cinquante*	sung·kont
60	*soixante*	swa·sont
70	*soixante-dix*	swa·son·dees
80	*quatre-vingts*	ka·trer·vung
90	*quatre-vingt-dix*	ka·trer·vung·dees
100	*cent*	son
1000	*mille*	meel

TIME & DATES

What time is it?
Y'est quelle heure? — il ay kel er

It's (eight) o'clock.
Il est (huit) heures. — il ay (weet) er

Half past (10).
(Dix) heures et demie. — (deez) er ay day·mee

morning	*matin*	ma·tun
afternoon	*après-midi*	a·pray·mee·dee
evening	*soir*	swar
yesterday	*hier*	yair
today	*aujourd'hui*	o·zhoor·dwee
tomorrow	*demain*	der·mun

Monday	*lundi*	lun·dee
Tuesday	*mardi*	mar·dee
Wednesday	*mercredi*	mair·krer·dee
Thursday	*jeudi*	zher·dee
Friday	*vendredi*	von·drer·dee
Saturday	*samedi*	sam·dee
Sunday	*dimanche*	dee·monsh

TRANSPORTATION

I want to go to ...
Je voudrais aller à ... — zher voo·dray a·lay a ...

At what time does it leave/arrive?
À quelle heure est-ce qu'il part/arrive? — a kel er es kil par/a·reev

Does it stop at ...?
Est-ce qu'il s'arrête à ...? — es·kil sa·ret a ...

I want to get off here.
Je veux descendre ici. — zher ver day·son·drer ee·see

a ... ticket	*un billet ...*	un bee·yay ...
1st-class	*de première classe*	der prem·yair klas
2nd-class	*de deuxième classe*	der der·zyem las
one-way	*simple*	sum·pler
return	*aller et retour*	a·lay ay rer·toor

aisle seat	*côté couloir*	ko·tay kool·war
boat	*bateau*	ba·to
bus	*bus*	bews
cancelled	*annulé*	a·new·lay
delayed	*en retard*	on rer·tar
first	*premier*	prer·myay
last	*dernier*	dair·nyay
plane	*avion*	a·vyon
platform	*quai*	kay
ticket office	*guichet*	gee·shay
timetable	*horaire*	o·rair
train	*train*	trun
window seat	*côté fenêtre*	ko·tay fe·ne·trer

I'd like to hire a ...	*Je voudrais louer ...*	zher voo·dray loo·way ...
car	*une voiture*	ewn vwa·tewr
bicycle	*un vélo*	un vay·lo
motorcycle	*une moto*	ewn mo·to

child seat	*siège-enfant*	syezh·on·fon
helmet	*casque*	kask
mechanic	*mécanicien*	may·ka·nee·syun
petrol/gas	*essence*	ay·sons
service station	*station-service*	sta·syon·ser·vees

Can I park here?
Est-ce que je peux stationner ici? — es·ker zher per sta·syo·nay ee·see

I have a flat tyre.
Mon pneu est à plat. — mom pner ay ta pla

I've run out of petrol.
Je suis en panne d'essence. — zher swee zon pan day·sons

GLOSSARY

allophone – a person whose mother tongue is neither French nor English

Anglophone – a person whose mother tongue is English

beaux arts – architectural style popular in France and Québec in the late 19th century, incorporating elements that are massive, elaborate and often ostentatious

Bill 101 – law that asserts the primacy of the French language in Québec, notably on signage

boîte à chanson – club devoted to *chanson française* (folk music from Québec or France)

brochette – kebab

cabane à sucre – place where the collected maple sap is distilled in large kettles and boiled as part of the production of maple syrup

calèche – horse-drawn carriage that can be taken around parts of Montréal and Québec City

Cantons de l'Est – Eastern Townships, a former Loyalist region southeast of Montréal toward the US border

cinq à sept – literally means five-to-seven, but refers to happy hours

correspondance – a transfer slip like those used between the métro and bus networks in Montréal

côte – a hill, as in Côte du Beaver Hall

dépanneur – called 'dep' for short, this is a Québec term for a convenience store

Estrie – a more recent term for *Cantons de l'Est*

First Nations – a term used to denote Canada's indigenous peoples, sometime used instead of Native Indians or Amerindians

Francophone – a person whose mother tongue is French

Front de Libération du Québec (FLQ) – a radical, violent political group active in the 1970s that advocated Québec's separation from Canada

gîte (du passant) – French term for B&B or similar lodging

Hochelaga – name of early Iroquois settlement on the site of present-day Montréal

Je me souviens – this Québec motto with a nationalist ring ('I remember') appears on license plates across the province

loonie – Canada's $1 coin, named for the loon stamped on one side

Mounties – Royal Canadian Mounted Police (RCMP)

Québecois – the French spoken in Québec; someone from the province of Québec; someone from Québec City

Refus Global – the radical manifest of a group of Québec artists and intellectuals during the Duplessis era (1944–59)

SAQ – Société des Alcools du Québec, a state-run agency that sells wines, spirits, beer etc

téléroman – a type of Québec TV program that's a cross between soap opera and prime-time drama, in French

toonie – also spelled 'twonie,' the Canadian $2 coin introduced after the *loonie*

MENU DECODER

ailes wings

allongé watered-down espresso

apportez votre vin or AVV bring your own bottle

boire drink

bouteille bottle

brochette kebab

casse-croûte a snack bar

cretons pork spread with onions and spices

entrée appetizer

escalopes tenderized, boneless meat

foie de veau calf liver

le déjeuner breakfast

le dîner lunch

le souper dinner

maison homemade, by the chef

manger to eat

menu dégustation a multi-course tasting menu

pâté pâté, as in pâté de foie gras

pâtes pasta

plat dish

plat du jour daily special

plat principal main dish

poutine French fries served with gravy and cheese curds

rillettes pastelike preparation of meat

ris de veau veal sweetbreads

service compris service included

stimés hotdog with a steamed bun

table d'hôte fixed-price meal (of the day)

taxes incluses taxes included

toastés hotdog with a toasted bun

tourtière Québec meat pie usually made of pork and beef or veal, sometimes with game meat

verre glass

Behind the Scenes

SEND US YOUR FEEDBACK

We love to hear from travelers – your comments keep us on our toes and help make our books better. Our well-traveled team reads every word on what you loved or loathed about this book. Although we cannot reply individually to your submissions, we always guarantee that your feedback goes straight to the appropriate authors, in time for the next edition. Each person who sends us information is thanked in the next edition – and the most useful submissions are rewarded with a selection of digital PDF chapters.

Visit **lonelyplanet.com/contact** to submit your updates and suggestions or to ask for help. Our award-winning website also features inspirational travel stories, news and discussions.

Note: We may edit, reproduce and incorporate your comments in Lonely Planet products such as guidebooks, websites and digital products, so let us know if you don't want your comments reproduced or your name acknowledged. For a copy of our privacy policy visit lonelyplanet.com/privacy.

OUR READERS

Many thanks to the travelers who used the last edition and wrote to us with helpful hints, useful advice and interesting anecdotes: Adrian Toutoungi, Denise Crawford, Elizabeth Johnson, Henry Luiker, Jean-Marc East, Jeff Jones, Jim Floyd, Marc Bartschat, Michael Graupner, Noam Schimmel, Sabrina Olender.

AUTHOR THANKS

Regis St Louis

Although I researched my sections during the coldest days of the year, the warmth and kindness of locals and friends made up for the polar temperatures. Special thanks to Catherine Binette and Patricia Maunder for extensive city insight, and the many Quebecers who shared tips: Jaaron, Roberto, Sarah, Emily, Saman, Isabelle and Jeremy. Thanks also to Thibault and Marine for their kind hospitality, and Gregor for a fun meet-up on the road. Big thanks to Cassandra, Magda and Genevieve, who make homecomings the best part of travel.

Gregor Clark

Un grand merci to the many people who shared their love and knowledge of Québec with me, especially Lucien and Daniel Beaumont and Catherine Binette. Back home, big hugs to Gaen, Meigan and Chloe, who helped me immeasurably in exploring Québec City's wintry streets and honing my skills on the ice slides at Winter Carnival.

ACKNOWLEDGMENTS

Cover photograph: Basilique Notre-Dame, Montréal, Walter Bibikow/AWL.

Montréal Metro map: Société de transport de Montréal (STM). © STM 2015

THIS BOOK

This 4th edition of Lonely Planet's *Montréal & Québec City* guidebook was researched and written by Regis St Louis and Gregor Clark. The previous two editions were written by Timothy N Hornyak, Gregor Clark, Regis St Louis and Simona Rabinovitch. This guidebook was produced by the following:

Destination Editor Alexander Howard

Product Editors Elizabeth Jones, Luna Soo

Senior Cartographer Corey Hutchison

Book Designer Katherine Marsh

Assisting Editors Sarah Billington, Melanie Dankel, Carly Hall, Kellie Langdon, Gabrielle Stefanos

Cover Researcher Campbell McKenzie

Thanks to Sasha Baskett, Ryan Evans, Anne Mason, Wayne Murphy, Martine Power, Diana Saengkham, Angela Tinson, Amanda Williamson

See also separate subindexes for:

EATING P259

DRINKING & NIGHTLIFE P260

ENTERTAINMENT P261

SHOPPING P262

SPORTS & ACTIVITIES P262

SLEEPING P263

Index

🍷 DRINKING & NIGHTLIFE

INDEX ENTERTAINMENT

🔒 SHOPPING

⚽ SPORTS & ACTIVITIES

SLEEPING

Montréal Maps

Sights
- Beach
- Bird Sanctuary
- Buddhist
- Castle/Palace
- Christian
- Confucian
- Hindu
- Islamic
- Jain
- Jewish
- Monument
- Museum/Gallery/Historic Building
- Ruin
- Shinto
- Sikh
- Taoist
- Winery/Vineyard
- Zoo/Wildlife Sanctuary
- Other Sight

Activities, Courses & Tours
- Bodysurfing
- Diving
- Canoeing/Kayaking
- Course/Tour
- Sento Hot Baths/Onsen
- Skiing
- Snorkeling
- Surfing
- Swimming/Pool
- Walking
- Windsurfing
- Other Activity

Sleeping
- Sleeping
- Camping

Eating
- Eating

Drinking & Nightlife
- Drinking & Nightlife
- Cafe

Entertainment
- Entertainment

Shopping
- Shopping

Information
- Bank
- Embassy/Consulate
- Hospital/Medical
- Internet
- Police
- Post Office
- Telephone
- Toilet
- Tourist Information
- Other Information

Geographic
- Beach
- Gate
- Hut/Shelter
- Lighthouse
- Lookout
- Mountain/Volcano
- Oasis
- Park
- Pass
- Picnic Area
- Waterfall

Population
- Capital (National)
- Capital (State/Province)
- City/Large Town
- Town/Village

Transport
- Airport
- BART station
- Border crossing
- Boston T station
- Bus
- Cable car/Funicular
- Cycling
- Ferry
- Metro/Muni station
- Monorail
- Parking
- Petrol station
- Subway/SkyTrain station
- Taxi
- Train station/Railway
- Tram
- Underground station
- Other Transport

Note: Not all symbols displayed above appear on the maps in this book

Routes
- Tollway
- Freeway
- Primary
- Secondary
- Tertiary
- Lane
- Unsealed road
- Road under construction
- Plaza/Mall
- Steps
- Tunnel
- Pedestrian overpass
- Walking Tour
- Walking Tour detour
- Path/Walking Trail

Boundaries
- International
- State/Province
- Disputed
- Regional/Suburb
- Marine Park
- Cliff
- Wall

Hydrography
- River, Creek
- Intermittent River
- Canal
- Water
- Dry/Salt/Intermittent Lake
- Reef

Areas
- Airport/Runway
- Beach/Desert
- Cemetery (Christian)
- Cemetery (Other)
- Glacier
- Mudflat
- Park/Forest
- Sight (Building)
- Sportsground
- Swamp/Mangrove

LITTLE ITALY

LITTLE ITALY

OUTREMONT

MILE END

WESTMOUNT

VERDUN

PLATEAU MONT-ROYAL

QUARTIER LATIN

THE VILLAGE

DOWNTOWN

CHINATOWN

OLD MONTRÉAL

LONGUEUIL

ST-LAMBERT

Parc Maisonneuve

Parc Olympique

Parc Sir Wilfred Laurier

Parc La Fontaine

Parc du Mont-Royal

Cimetière Notre-Dame-des-Neiges

Parc Summit

Parc Westmount

Île Ste-Hélène

Parc Jean-Drapeau

Île Notre-Dame

Parc de la Voie Maritime

Lac des Régates

St Lawrence River

0   2 km
0   1 mile

OLD MONTRÉAL

Rue Ste-Catherine Ouest

Sq Phillips

Rue St-Edward

Pl Phillips

Rue St-Alexandre

Côte du Beaver Hall

Blvd St-Laurent

Rue St-Dominique

Blvd René-Lévesque Ouest

Rue de Bleury

Rue Anderson

Rue Jeanne-Mance

Rue St-Urbain

Rue Clark

70

Rue Carmichael

49

55

Rue Dowd

72

48

84

Rue Belmont

58 56

37 53

Place Sun-Yat-Sen

Rue de la Gauchetière Ouest

59

42

Ave Viger Ouest

CHINATOWN

Place-d'Armes

See map p277

Square-Victoria

20

Autoroute Ville-Marie

76

25

65

Rue St-Antoine Ouest

109

Rlle des Fortifications

2

114

Sq Victoria

32 106

Rue St-Jacques

68

Pl d'Armes

18

29

15 110 10

23

8

85

Caleche Rides

35

Rue Notre-Dame Ouest

66

54

Rue de l'Hôpital

92

43

63

Rue Ste-Hélène

64

31

Basilique Notre-Dame

Rue de Brésoles

7

105

80

77

100

40

OLD MONTRÉAL

73

83

69

Rue Le Moyne

46 104

33 107

Rue St-Maurice

60

87

67

96

86

19

90

Rue St-Henri

Rue de Longueuil

Rue McGill

57

22

39

45

62

113

14

26

Pl Royale

108

81

99

4 36

95

16

Rue William

52

47

Pl d'Youville

3

78

Rue Ottawa

9

50

Conveyor Pier

61

Rue des Soeurs-Grises

Rue Marguerite d'Youville

Rue Normand

Rue St-Pierre

Rue de la Commune Ouest

27

Quai Alexandra

Rue Wellington

17

Promenade du vieux-Port

71

Rue Prince

Rue Queen

Rue King

Bassin Alexandra

Parc des Écluses

44

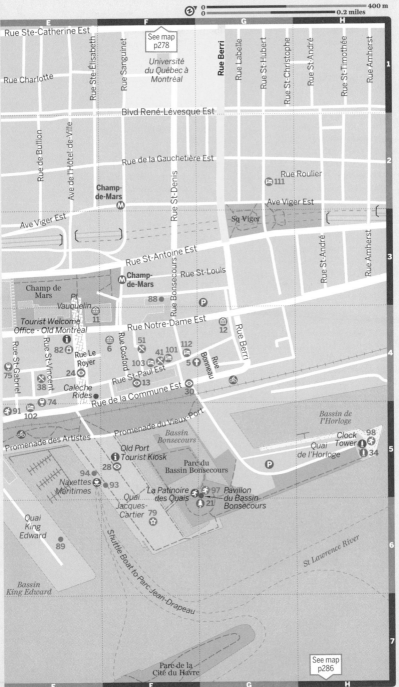

0   400 m
0   0.2 miles

Rue Ste-Catherine Est

See map
p278

Rue Berri

Rue Ste-Élisabeth
Rue Sanguinet
Université
du Québec à
Montréal
Rue Labelle
Rue St-Hubert
Rue St-Christophe
Rue St-André
Rue St-Timothée
Rue Amherst

Rue Charlotte

Blvd René-Lévesque Est

Rue de Bullion
Ave de l'Hôtel-de-Ville
Rue de la Gauchetière Est
Rue St-Denis

Rue Roulier
111

Champ-
de-Mars
M

Ave Viger Est
Sq Viger

Ave Viger Est

Rue St-Antoine Est

Rue St-André
Rue Amherst

Rue Bonsecours
Rue St-Louis

M Champ-
de-Mars

Champ de
Mars
Pl
Vauquelin
11

88

P

Tourist Welcome
Office - Old Montréal
82
6
Rue Le
Royer
Rue Gosford
51
41 101 112
Rue Notre-Dame Est
12
Rue Berri

103
5
Rue Bonneau

75
24
Rue St-Paul Est
13
Rue St-Gabriel
Rue St-Vincent
38
Calèche
Rides
30

74
91
102
Rue de la Commune Est

Promenade du Vieux-Port
Bassin
Bonsecours
Bassin de
l'Horloge

Promenade des Artistes
Clock
Tower
98
Quai
de l'Horloge
34

Old Port
Tourist Kiosk
28

94
Navettes
Maritimes
93
Quai
Jacques-
Cartier
79
La Patinoire
des Quais
97
21
Parc du
Bassin Bonsecours
P
Pavillon
du Bassin
Bonsecours

Quai
King
Edward
89

St Lawrence River

Bassin
King Edward

Shuttle Boat to Parc Jean-Drapeau

Parc de la
Cité du Havre

See map
p286

OLD MONTRÉAL *Map on p268*

OLD MONTRÉAL

DOWNTOWN (WEST)

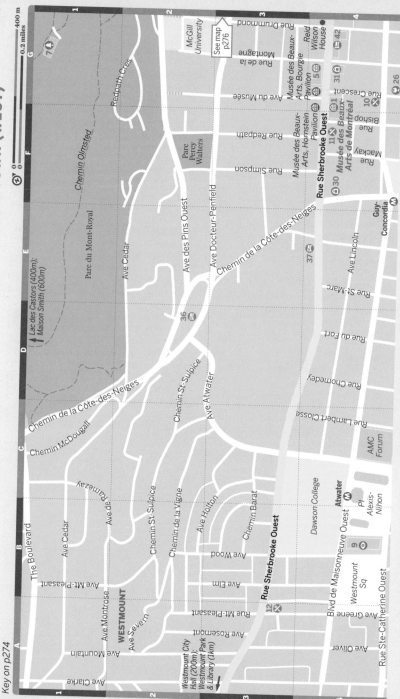

Key on p274

0 0.2 miles
0 400 m

McGill University

See map p276

Lac des Castors (400m);
Maison Smith (600m)

Westmount City
Hall (200m);
Westmount Park
& Library (1km)

DOWNTOWN (WEST)

DOWNTOWN (WEST)

DOWNTOWN (WEST) *Map on p272*

DOWNTOWN (EAST) *Map on p276*

◎ Sights (p74)

1 Cathédrale Christ Church	C5
2 Cathédrale Marie-Reine-du-Monde	B6
3 Galeries d'Art Contemporain du Belgo	D5
4 Illuminated Crowd	B4
5 Maison Alcan	A4
6 Maison du Festival Rio Tinto Alcan	E5
7 McGill University	B3
8 Musée d'Art Contemporain	E5
9 Musée McCord	C4
10 Musée Redpath	B3
11 Place des Arts	E4
12 Place du Canada	B6
13 Place Ville-Marie	C5
14 Rue Sherbrooke Ouest	A4
15 Rue Ste-Catherine Ouest	B5
16 Square Dorchester	B5
17 Square Victoria	D7
18 St James United Church	D5
19 St Patrick's Basilica	D6

✕ Eating (p79)

20 Bistro Isakaya	E3
21 Café Parvis	D4
22 Ferreira Café	A4
23 Foodlab	F5
24 Furusato	E3
25 Jatoba	C5
26 Le Balsam Inn	B5
27 Le Taj	A4
28 Lola Rosa	D2
29 Pikolo Espresso Bar	E3
30 Reuben's	A5

◎ Drinking & Nightlife (p82)

31 Benelux	E3
32 Biru	D5
33 Bleury Bar à Vinyle	E4
34 Club Soda	F5
35 Dominion Square Tavern	B5
36 Furco	D4
37 House of Jazz	D4
38 Le Vieux Dublin Pub & Restaurant	C5
39 NYKS	D5
40 Pub Ste-Élisabeth	G5
41 Pullman	E3

◎ Entertainment (p83)

42 Cinéma Banque Scotia Montréal	B5
43 Cinéma du Parc	E2
44 Foufounes Électriques	G5
45 I Musici de Montréal	G3
L'Astral	(see 6)
Les Grands Ballets Canadiens de Montréal	(see 11)
46 Metropolis	G5
47 Monument National	F5
Opéra de Montréal	(see 11)
Orchestre Métropolitain	(see 48)
48 Orchestre Symphonique de Montréal	F4
Place des Arts	(see 11)
49 Pollack Concert Hall	C3
50 Salsathèque	A5
51 SAT	F5

◎ Shopping (p87)

52 Eva B	F4
53 Henri Henri	G5
54 Hudson Bay Co	C5
55 Les Cours Mont-Royal	B4
56 Place Montréal Trust	B4
57 Roots	B5

◎ Sports & Activities (p88)

Ashtanga Yoga Studio	(see 3)

◎ Sleeping (p159)

58 Atrium	B7
59 Héritage Montréal	G3
60 McGill University School of Continuing Studies	C4
61 Montréal Alouettes	D1
62 YMCA	A4
63 Alacoque B&B Revolution	F3
64 Armor Manoir Sherbrooke	G3
65 Castel Durocher	D3
66 Hotel 10	F3
67 Hotel Bonaventure	B7
68 Hotel Parc Suites	E3
69 Hotel Zero 1	F6
70 La Citadelle	D3
71 L'Abri du Voyageur	F5
72 Le Gîte du Plateau Mont-Royal	G2
73 Manoir Ambrose	A3
74 Sofitel	A3
75 Trylon Apartments	E3
76 University Bed & Breakfast Apartments	C2

DOWNTOWN (EAST)

DOWNTOWN (EAST)

Key on p275

0 400 m
0 0.2 miles

See map p281

See map p278

Parc du Mont-Royal

Molson Stadium 61

McGill University

QUARTIERS DES SPECTACLES

Place-des-Arts

Ave des Pins Est

Ave des Pins Ouest

Rue Guilbault

Rue des Pins Ouest

Rue Peel

Ave Docteur-Penfield

Rue Drummond

Rue Stanley

Rue McTavish

Rue University

Ave Lorne

Rue Aylmer

Rue Milton

Rue Durocher

Rue Hutchison

Ave du Parc

Rue Prince-Arthur Ouest

Rue Jeanne-Mance

Rue Ste-Famille

Rue St-Urbain

Rue Clark

Blvd St-Laurent

Rue St-Dominique

Ave Coloniale

Rue de Bullion

Ave de l'Hôtel-de-Ville

Rue Sherbrooke Est

Rue Sherbrooke Ouest

Rue Metcalfe

Rue Mansfield

Ave McGill College

Rue Victoria

Ave Union

Rue City Councillors

Ave du Président Kennedy

Rue Milton

Blvd de Maisonneuve Ouest

Rue Ontario Ouest

Rue Evans

Rue Ontario Est

Rue St-Norbert

Blvd de Maisonneuve Est

Rue de Montigny

Rue Mayor

Rue Aylmer

Blvd de Maisonneuve Ouest

St-Laurent

McGill

Peel

Louis-Joseph Forget House

73
74
14
27
5
22
62
55
56
60
4
6
10
7
76
28
49
65
37
21
36
70
41
29
24
33
31
20
68
43
75
63
66
52
72
64
59
45
11
48

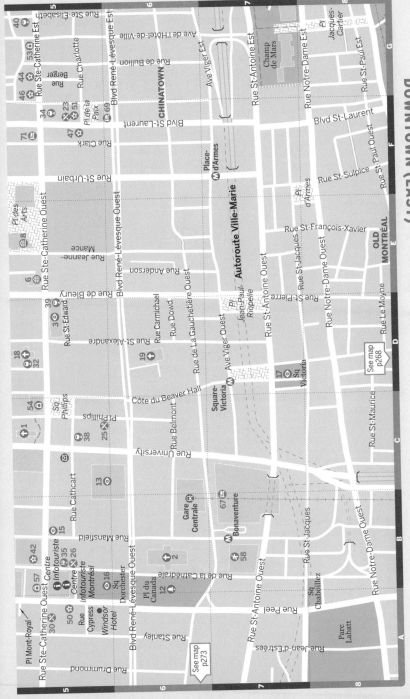

278

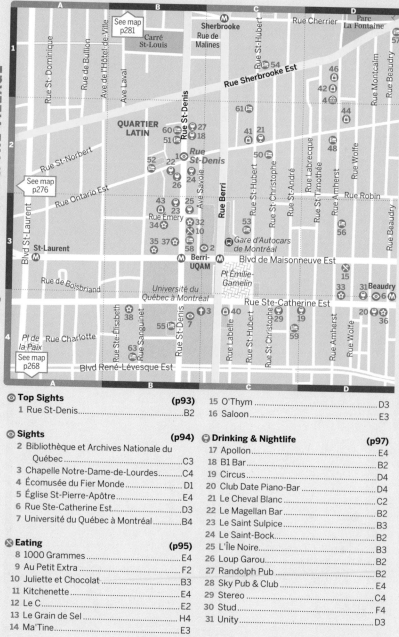

QUARTIER LATIN & THE VILLAGE

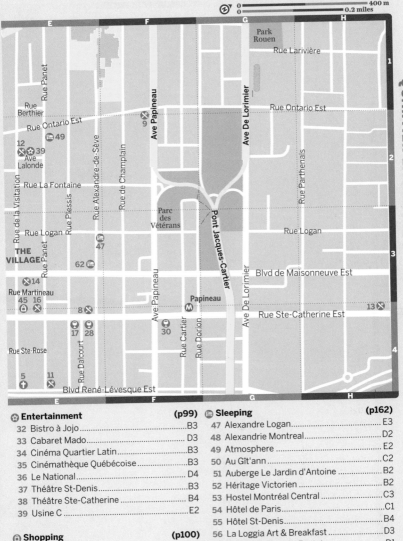

PLATEAU MONT-ROYAL

Key on p282

0   0.2 miles
0   400 m

Tri Express (350m)

Blvd St-Joseph Est

Rue de Lanaudière

Rue Chambord

Rue de Brébeuf

Rue de la Roche

Ave du Mont-Royal Est

Ave Christophe Colomb

Rue Généreux

Rue Boyer

Rue de Mentana

Rue St-Hubert

Rue Gilford

Rue Resther

Rue Pontiac

Rue de Bienville

Rue Rivard

Laurier

Mont-Royal

Rue St-Denis

See map p285

Rue Villeneuve Est

Rue Gilford

Rue Drolet

Blvd St-Joseph Est

Rue Elmire

Rue de Bullion

Ave Coloniale

Rue St-Dominique

Blvd St-Laurent

Ave du Mont-Royal Est

Ave l'Hotel-de-Ville

Ave Henri-Julien

Ave Laval

Ave Marie-Anne Est

Ave l'Hotel-de-Ville

Ave Coloniale

Rue de Bullion

Rue Rachel Est

Parc du Portugal

Blvd St-Joseph Ouest

Rue Villeneuve Ouest

Rue Villeneuve Ouest

Ave de l'Esplanade

Ave du Mont-Royal Ouest

Rue St-Urbain

Rue Marie-Anne Ouest

Rue Clark

Rue Rachel Ouest

Ave de L'Esplanade

Rue Jeanne-Mance

Parc Jeanne-Mance

Ave du Parc

Parc du Mont-Royal

La Tulipe (250m);
La Porte Rouge (350m);
La Distillerie (550m)

Rue Marie-Anne Est

PLATEAU MONT-ROYAL

Rue St-Christophe

Rue St-André

Rue St-Hubert

Rue Berri

Ave Bureau

Rue Rachel Est

Accueil Chez François (450m)

Rue Rachel Est

PLATEAU MONT-ROYAL

PLATEAU MONT-ROYAL *Map on p280*

LITTLE ITALY, MILE END & OUTREMONT Map on p284

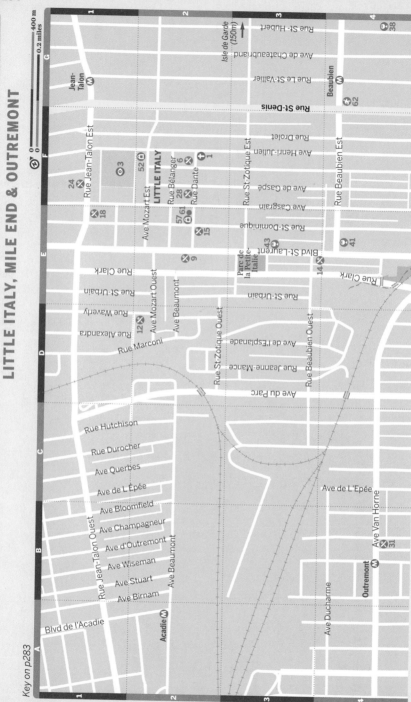

LITTLE ITALY, MILE END & OUTREMONT

400 m
0.2 miles

Rue Jean-Talon Est

Jean-Talon Ⓜ

Rue St-Denis

Isle de Garde
(150m) →

Ave de Chateaubriand

Rue Le St-Vallier

Beaubien Ⓜ

Rue St-Hubert

38

62

24

3

52

6

1

28

LITTLE ITALY

Rue Bélanger

Rue Dante

Rue Drolet

Ave Henri-Julien

Rue St-Zotique Est

Rue Beaubien Est

18

57 61

15

Ave Mozart Est

Ave de Gaspé

Ave Casgrain

Rue St-Dominique

9

Rue Clark

Rue St-Urbain

Ave Mozart Ouest

Ave Beaumont

43

41

14

Blvd St-Laurent

Parc de
la Petite-
Italie

Rue St-Urbain

Rue St-Zotique Ouest

Rue Clark

12

Rue Alexandra

Rue Waverly

Rue Marconi

Ave Beaumont

Rue Jeanne-Mance

Ave de l'Esplanade

Rue Beaubien Ouest

Ave du Parc

Rue Hutchison

Rue Durocher

Ave Querbes

Ave de L'Épée

Ave de L'Epée

Ave Van Horne

Ave Bloomfield

Ave Champagneur

Ave d'Outremont

31

Ave Wiseman

Ave Beaumont

Outremont Ⓜ

Ave Stuart

Ave Birnam

Rue Jean-Talon Ouest

Blvd de l'Acadie

Acadie Ⓜ

Ave Ducharme

PARC JEAN-DRAPEAU

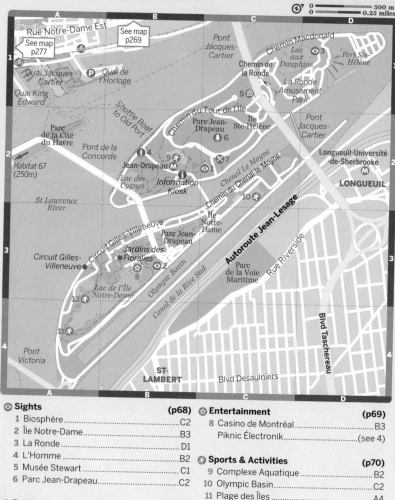